THE TRIGGER MEN

MARTIN DILLON

MAINSTREAM
PUBLISHING

EDINBURGH AND LONDON

Reprinted, 2008

First published in Great Britain in 2003 by
MAINSTREAM PUBLISHING COMPANY (EDINBURGH) LTD
7 Albany Street
Edinburgh EH1 3UG

ISBN 9781840189025

This edition, 2004

Reprinted 2003 (twice), 2004

A catalogue record for this book is available from the British Library

Printed in Great Britain by
Clays Ltd, St Ives plc

CONTENTS

ACKNOWLEDGEMENTS

To interviewees and secondary sources I would like to express a debt of gratitude, without them my task would have been much more difficult. Many had been questioned before but felt that because a decent time interval had elapsed, they could provide me with additional information with the benefit of honest recall. Some still work in the security forces and, like others who have retired from intelligence work, they wanted their identities protected.

I also owe a great deal to my publisher, Bill Campbell, for his persuasiveness and support and to Graeme Blaikie, the Mainstream editorial coordinator. My wife, Violeta, slaved over the manuscript as it progressed and kept me focused while she constantly checked facts and syntax.

It would not be possible to write books about the Ireland conflict without an important intellectual input from friends. They include my parents, Gerard and Maureen, and two superb retired detectives – Jimmy Nesbitt and Johnston 'Jonty' Brown; the journalist and writer, Hugh Jordan and his editor at *Sunday World*, Jim McDowell; and Trevor Hanna, who has been a stalwart of journalism in Ireland.

Jim Campbell is mentioned in this book because his courageous reporting and his friendship have always been important to me. He was one of the few journalists shot and injured because of his writings. The attempt on his life did not deter him from pursuing the truth even though a bullet remains lodged in his spine. Ed Curran, editor of the *Belfast Telegraph*, and Martin Lindsay, editor of *Sunday Life*, supported my work from the outset. Ed helped bring my story of the Shankill Butchers to a wide audience.

Others who contributed by their presence in my life include my brother Dr Patrick Dillon and his wife, Lorraine; Damien Dillon, my twin; my sisters, Imelda Feinberg and Ursula and her husband Brian McLoughlin; Eamann McMenamin; Ian Kennedy of Straight Forward Productions and his wife, Cecilia; Moore and Sandra Sinnerton; the journalist Henry McDonald; Colin Lewis; John Nicholson; Dudi and Michael Appleton; Dessie O'Hagan; John Bach; and A.T.Q. Stewart, one of Ireland's finest historians. My thanks and admiration go to the writer Tim Pat Coogan and to Gordon Thomas, my co-author on *The Assassination of Robert Maxwell: Israel's Super Spy*.

Thanks also to friends in Bulgaria, Germany, France, Britain and the United States. Some resist categorisation but they all provided an intellectual impetus to my life: Larry and Iris Gardner of New York City; Vanya and Belin Tsvetkova of Bourgas; Chris and Val Ludlow of St Romain; Charente, who provided a bolthole at a time when I needed one; Alan and Brebner Anderson of London; Crispin Avon, also of London; Jane Fulthorpe, author, and her husband, Colin, of London and St Romain; Kenny McCoy and his sons, Kenny jnr and Conor, of New York; Natatalia Mount, my stepdaughter, and her husband, Andrew Mount, founders of Flux Art Space, also of New York; Climent Atanassov, one of Bulgaria's finest artists, of Sofia; Frank Schulte, FBI Special Agent (retired), of San Diego; Eugene Devlin, of New York; Dimiter Kumurdjiev, the outstanding lawyer and EU expert, and his journalist wife, Antonia, of Sofia; Nickolai Berof and Valery Borisov, attorneys, also of Sofia; Russell Smith and Eamon Dornan, lawyers with Smith, Dornan, Shea in Montauk and New York City; Michael Tauck, the eminent film lawyer, of Hamburg; Poli Anatachkova of Sofia; Nickolai Petrov, journalist, also of Sofia; Nadia Katherine Dillon, my daughter, of St Astier, Dordogne; Crawford Anderson Dillon, my stepson, of London; Lucien Mount, my grandson, of New York; Ed Harris, the consummate film actor, of Malibu; Dr Svetlin Ivanov and his wife, Dr Valeria Ivanova, of New York; Plame and Norah Danchev of New York; Hubert and Fess Winstead of North Carolina; David and Monique Alyward of Fonteau, Dordogne; Alain and Patricia Pillaud, also of Fonteau; Francois Bouan, poet-philosopher, and his partner, Agnes – the 'fifty-fifty' couple, of Brantome, Dordogne.

Special thanks are due to Angela Wright, and her husband, Kieran, in New York, and to Yvonne Murphy and her staff running the Political Collection of the Linenhall Library, Belfast; as well as to the staff of the Irish News library.

PREFACE

In August 1969, following an invasion of Catholic districts in Belfast by Protestant mobs, British troops arrived in the city as saviours of the Catholic community. Initially, the troops were welcomed like long-lost cousins from across the Irish Sea but that was not to last. Perhaps there was an inevitable naiveté on both sides. The British Army knew little about the variables in the Ireland historical mix and Catholic nationalists and republicans were still imbued with an inherited anti-Britishness.

More significant, Northern Ireland's Protestant Unionist Government did not have the capacity to reform itself. Despite its record of bigotry and political repression, it was allowed to remain in place. That was the beginning of major political blunders. Leaving the Stormont Government in place permitted Unionists to continue to rule and influence British policy-making in 10 Downing Street. That decision served a narrow Unionist agenda which defined the problem in Northern Ireland as a 'truculent and subversive Catholic minority'. It reflected the unchanging Unionist thesis from the setting up of the State half a century earlier.

For some political observers in London, it was the Old Irish problem emanating from a Protestant majority's siege mentality and Catholic resentment of the partition of Ireland. The analysis ignored the origins of the ongoing conflict – the abdication of responsibility by successive British Governments in London. For decades, British political leaders viewed Northern Ireland as a seemingly intractable problem and preferred a hands-off policy. The most dangerous consequence of Britain's failure to accept responsibility for an integral part of the United Kingdom was that sovereign British Governments allowed subordinate Unionist administrations to act as though they were sovereign institutions. British political leaders cared little that Protestant majority rule was maintained through repressive legislation, resulting in the denial of British civil rights to Catholics. Therefore no one in Westminster saw the writing on the wall when Catholic civil rights marchers took to the streets in the mid 1960s. There was no recognition that all those historical variables in both communities were the sparks that would ignite a bonfire and a long war.

In 1968 and in the early months of 1969, as civil rights protests led to conflict between the two communities, politicians in London looked on in disbelief. There was a distinct lack of political intelligence within the British Labour Government led by Harold Wilson. In a bitterly ironic twist of history, the Labour Home Secretary, Jim Callaghan, decided to brief himself on the situation. To his astonishment, he found Northern Ireland listed in a single, dusty file in an office cabinet. Other files in that cabinet dealt with the issuing of dog licensing laws and rules governing London taxis. Clearly, from a British perspective, Northern Ireland had really been a place apart where other rules had applied. That arrangement had been fine as long as the Unionists across the Irish Sea kept the historical enmity between the two communities under wraps. Some might reasonably argue that London's ignorance was bliss until reality set in. But that all changed in August 1969 when the Unionist Government could not hold the line against increasing violence, especially from within its right-wing supporters on the ground and the B Specials, its anti-Catholic paramilitary police force. The invasion of Catholic areas in West Belfast by Protestant mobs assisted by the B Specials led to the burning of hundreds of Catholic homes and the displacement of thousands of Catholic families. Old hatreds were reactivated, forcing the British Government to end its hands-off policy and send in troops.

For a British Army that had only previously been involved in colonial emergencies in Kenya, Oman, Aden and Cyprus, its generals and soldiers on the ground in Northern Ireland seemed, at the outset, to enjoy peacekeeping duties. Soldiers positioned themselves between the warring Protestant and Catholic factions and were welcomed, particularly by the Catholics. But that was merely the calm before the storm. Had the Unionist Government been immediately abolished when the British Army moved in and a meaningful dialogue instituted to create a fair political framework to accommodate the loyalties and cultural traditions of both communities, a long war might never have begun.

Instead, in June 1970, the Labour Government in London was replaced by a Conservative administration led by Edward Heath whose Home Secretary, Reginald Maudling, unlike his predecessor, Jim Callaghan, had no desire to find a political solution. Maudling, Heath and Unionist leaders in Northern Ireland felt it was up to the British Army to solve the problem and there was a precedent for such a view. The Army had been the means by which Britain had extracted itself from other colonial situations. However, the British Government had no wish to abolish Stormont even though it had a structure which replicated former colonial outposts like Aden and Cyprus. There was a Governor, Lord Grey, and a Police Chief. They, and the British Commander of Land Forces, could have formed a troika to run Northern Ireland in the absence of the Stormont Government. It had been the tried and tested method elsewhere and it had worked.

By telling the Army to find a solution, the British Government failed to recognise that there were several dangerous ingredients inherent in that policy. The Army would instinctively rely on its colonial experience to shape its strategy and, like any army, it would need to define its enemy just as successive British generals had done in Kenya, Aden and Cyprus. By the time the Army was asked to find a solution, some of the historical variables within Catholic nationalist politics had begun to coalesce to shift the focus from civil rights to traditional anti-Britishness.

Throughout the 1960s, the IRA had moved to the political left, experimenting with Marxist–Leninist principles. It had placed its traditional Irish republicanism, with a goal of a united Ireland at its core, on the back burner. As a result, when Catholics were under siege in August '69, the IRA found itself militarily unprepared. There were few weapons in its arsenal in Belfast and the IRA leadership in Dublin was reluctant to provide weapons which might lead to a bloodbath in the north of the island. The Catholic community turned against the IRA and a new IRA was formed – the Provisionals. They immediately assumed the mantle of romantic nationalism with its blood sacrifice tradition and trigger man ethos.

In the early months of the birth of the Provisionals, the majority of recruits were not motivated by any deep philosophical commitment to republican ideals. However, a massive influx of recruits was the dynamic to energise a republican movement which had been in decline throughout Ireland for two decades. Overnight it was propelled towards the traditional republican thesis of uniting Ireland through armed struggle.

The arrival of the Provisional IRA on the military/political stage in January 1970 was not of itself the determining factor in an inexorable path to all-out war. The British Army provided the impetus for the Provisionals' recruitment drive by alienating the Catholic population. The one event that characterised the beginning of a failed British military and political policy happened on 3 July 1970, one week after Home Secretary Reginald Maudling paid his first fleeting visit to Belfast.

An arms raid by troops on the Lower Falls, where the Official IRA – not a potent threat to the Army – had its headquarters, led to confrontation and developed into a full-scale riot followed by a gun-battle. The British Army, in a massive show of strength, sealed off the Lower Falls, fired at least 1,600 canisters of CS gas, imposed a curfew and the following day ransacked houses in the neighbourhood. The military operation, with its excessive use of 3,000 soldiers, terrorised children and elderly people. It further alienated Catholics and appalled moderate Catholic opinion throughout Ireland. For journalists like me who observed it, there was sufficient evidence to conclude that the Army had been given free rein to act out its colonial experience.

The use of Scottish soldiers, who had an historical attachment to the politico-religious ideals of Northern Ireland Protestants, resulted in the destruction and defacing of many religious statues in Catholic homes. The imposition of a curfew was later successfully challenged in the courts and charges dropped against many people, including journalists arrested when the curfew took effect. The overwhelming use of heavy military vehicles, the blanketing of the area with CS gas, the staggering number of rounds fired by soldiers as opposed to those fired by the Official IRA, demonstrated not only considerable military planning but implied that the initial arms raid which led to the curfew had been a deliberate ploy to create the kind of confrontation whereby the British Army could show who was boss. Four civilians were shot dead, an armoured vehicle killed another and there were 67 injured. The Army judged the operation a success because soldiers seized over 100 weapons, ranging from shotguns to pistols, rifles, machine guns and several hundred pounds of gelignite.

It was a classic example of the way the Army had operated in colonial emergencies and, as Field Marshal Lord Michael Carver later told me, 'It was a crude operation.' It indicated that the Army had the political authority to 'take off the gloves' and its enemy had been clearly defined. For many observers, the enemy was not the IRA but the Catholic population.

Within GEN 42, a secret Cabinet committee in 10 Downing Street, Prime Minister Edward Heath and his Home Secretary, Reginald Maudling, applauded the troops for what republicans called 'The Rape of the Falls', and what others referred to as the 'Lower Falls Curfew'.

It was the beginning of a military policy that had the backing of the Governments in London and Belfast. To further compound matters, the Lower Falls Curfew was followed by another major political-military blunder – the introduction of internment without trial on 9 August 1971. Internment was solely directed at the Catholic population and many young and elderly men were unceremoniously dragged from their homes and brutalised in the early hours of 9 August. Some turned out to be student activists and trade union representatives. The Army mistakenly relied on outdated police Special Branch files and, during the initial arrest operation, soldiers discovered that many of those listed in the police files were dead. The Provisional IRA, still in its infancy, lost few of its leaders to the internment swoops whereas the Official IRA, with a longer history of subversive activity, found its senior ranks seriously depleted.

Unknown to British Army generals such as Michael Carver, 12 men in the first batch of detainees were subjected to in-depth interrogation techniques perfected by British Military Intelligence. Prime Minister Edward Heath later denied knowledge of 'special treatment' meted out to the 12 but his Intelligence Coordinator, Sir Dick White, who was also a member of the secret Cabinet committee, GEN 42, had full knowledge of the affair. The 'special treatment' involved the use of 'hooding' and 'white noise', techniques later condemned by the Court of Human Rights in Strasbourg.

If the Lower Falls Curfew was a serious political-military blunder, internment without trial provided the genesis for the Provisional IRA's ability to sustain a long war. It created the dynamic for the Provisionals to depict themselves as freedom fighters and the British Army as an army of occupation bent on repressing the Catholic community.

By the end of 1971, internment was perceived in London as a positive solution and within GEN 42, Prime Minister Heath, Home Secretary Reginald Maudling and Lord Chancellor Quintin Hogg (later to be known as Lord Hailsham) tried to persuade British generals to take a harder line with the IRA and Catholic rioters. The mindset within that Cabinet committee, whose members included the hard-line Unionist Prime Minister Brian Faulkner, was that Catholics were 'enemies of the British Crown'.

In the spring of 1972, Lord Chancellor Hogg recklessly told Heath that rioters were indeed 'enemies of the Crown' and that soldiers were legally entitled to shoot them. Heath conveyed the advice to General Carver.

To his credit, Carver responded that such a policy was illegal and he would not enforce it. He reminded Heath that, as Prime Minister, he would not be in the dock if soldiers were subsequently charged with murder.

Months before the exchanges between Carver and Heath, British paratroopers and generals subliminally anticipated the thinking of their political leaders and shot 13 civilian protesters on the streets of Derry. The event would become known as Bloody Sunday. While the Catholic community battled with the British Army, Protestants were frightened and felt politically isolated. They had witnessed major changes to their way of life and their own historical demons came into play. For decades, they were content to let the State, its special powers legislation and the paramilitary B Specials protect them and their rights from the enemy within – republicans, often defined as the minority population. They were unable to understand that Catholic demands for basic British rights were not unreasonable. They saw the civil rights protests as yet another example of the dangers emanating from the other community. Unfortunately, they were served by politicians who maintained power by exacerbating, rather than calming, Protestant fears. They were also victims of British policy-making, which ignored the inadequacies of the Unionist political machine. When the British Army defined its enemy in the summer of 1970, that was exactly what Unionists wanted to see. Those most committed to such a policy were loyalists – the right-wing fringe of Unionism. Their instinct was not to sit back and allow the IRA to undermine the Union with Great Britain and attack the forces of the Crown. Their duty was to be part of the battle. That quickly emerging thesis led to the formation of a range of loyalist paramilitary organisations, including the largest, the Ulster Defence Association. For the British Army, reflex violence by loyalists was not a threat to them. Some army commanders, and others within the military intelligence apparatus, believed the arrival of the UDA was a positive development to be exploited.

In the period from July 1970 to June '72, all the ingredients were in place for a long, as well as dirty, war in which trigger men and terror bosses soon became heroes and the number of victims steadily multiplied. The dirty war was a direct consequence of the policies of the Heath Government, which allowed the intelligence apparatus of the State to operate without judicial oversight. As this book will show, the origins of British political and military policies led to some of the darkest episodes of the conflict. From that early period of the '70s, the intelligence community pursued strategies which frequently contravened the rule of law. Counter-gangs were created and terrorist agents recruited who undertook assassinations on behalf of the State.

This book deals with some of the prominent trigger men and terror bosses of the Ireland conflict. They were snipers, bombers, cut-throat killers, agents and double agents, bizarre clergymen, paedophiles and ideologues. The book examines their social and family backgrounds, as well as historical factors which helped shape them into cold-blooded killers. It analyses their politico-religious fanaticism, the unparalleled narcissism which characterised many of their actions, and their modus operandi. It provides answers as to why they were imbued with inherited prejudice and blind hate. The majority of the trigger men were in paramilitary ranks but others were in uniform and in the State's intelligence apparatus. Criminality, perverse sex, betrayal, torture, sectarianism and competing ideologies are all elements in this hideous catalogue of brutality. In writing this book, I sought to make no distinction between the crimes of the assassins in both communities, nor have I tried to minimise the killings committed by members of the British Army and parts of the State intelligence apparatus. The majority of the personalities featured in the pages to follow were heroes in their own communities and organisations. Many remain icons of terror, while others, who were unmasked as paedophiles, Mafia-type godfathers and informers, no longer have the status they once enjoyed.

This book is not intended to be a history of the Troubles. It aims to provide insights into the motivations and the crimes of killers and terror bosses who thrived on tribal hatreds, ignorance and inherited prejudices.

1

'KING RAT'

PART 1: FORMATIVE YEARS OF A KILLER

Billy Wright strutted across the Protestant paramilitary stage with a Bible in one hand and a gun in the other. He confided to me that he sometimes 'walked with God' and at other times with 'the Devil'. When he pulled a trigger, he claimed it was for 'God and Ulster' but retrospectively he would say he had been walking with the Devil. One may ask if he ever knew which influence was greater on his life as a trigger man – God or the Devil?

His detractors will say it was the Devil. His supporters believe he was a bible-loving Christian defending his homeland from godless subversives. There is no dispute that he was a lethal trigger man and terror boss. His entry into the world of paramilitarism, his flirtation with religious fundamentalism and his influence on the peace process in Northern Ireland in the 1990s set him apart as a unique loyalist in the conflict.

The use of the term 'loyalist' to define an extreme position within the Protestant-Unionist majority has its roots in the early days of the Troubles. At the start of the 1960s, the term defined not simply loyalty to the Union with Great Britain but ultra elements within a Protestant working-class political dynamic. Loyalists were opposed to any reform of the State, especially accommodation of Catholic demands for social and political change.

The singular voice of loyalism was the Reverend Ian Kyle Paisley, the son of a Baptist minister. His firebrand preaching was imbued with fundamentalist oratory and dire warnings about Catholic agitation. In essence, his doctrine, embodied in the slogan 'No Surrender', linked him to Unionist orthodoxy. He warned that any concessions to Catholics constituted a betrayal of the Church of Rome and presented a threat to the Union with Britain, which Protestants were duty-bound to defend. Within its narrow, bigoted confines, Paisleyism spoke to a Protestant siege mentality dating back to the seventeenth century. It activated deep-seated fears within the Protestant community that any semblance of change in the status quo, namely Unionist political domination, could lead to a resurgence of Catholic nationalism and republicanism. The ultimate effect would be a weakening of the Union and Protestants being swallowed up in a Catholic-dominated United Ireland.

Paisley's thesis was not new in the short history of the Northern Ireland State or, for that matter, in the overall history of Ireland. But, coming at a time when Catholics were demanding what amounted to basic British civil rights such as 'One Man–One Vote', it had a malign impact on the political environment. Some Unionist leaders dismissed Paisley as a nonentity while others, among them Cabinet ministers like Bill Craig and Brian Faulkner, flirted with the Paisley thesis. It suited Faulkner's political ambitions to one day become Prime Minister because it reached down to the very core of Unionism. It touched the bedrock of Protestant working-class support and the unquestioning loyalty the working class had historically given to its leaders, based always on a similar agenda. The Unionist monolith, from the beginning of the twentieth century, had survived on an exploitation of Protestant working-class fears. Whenever loyalty was in doubt, Unionist politicians reminded supporters their security depended on containing the threat from within. The enemy was depicted as the other population – Catholics, with the IRA in their midst, plotting to usurp power. As part of the fiction to enable those fears to find fertile ground, extreme legislation in the form of the Special Powers Act was enacted to curtail cultural and political expressions by Catholics.

The character of the State was inherently structured to minimise employment opportunities, housing equity and electoral freedom for Catholics. One of the unfortunate consequences of Unionist majority rule was its unique control over the destiny of the Protestant population. It deprived Protestant working-class politicians from recognising their constituents could also benefit from social and political reform. As a consequence, Protestant voters never questioned their leaders. Loyalty was given and based on a Unionist principle that only through political cohesiveness could the Union with Britain remain intact. It meant that anyone, especially Catholic agitators who threatened that cohesiveness, symbolised an enemy within.

A close study of the genesis of the Troubles illustrates that Paisley's influence was seminal in the gradual disintegration of public order. His large presence on the political scene, mixing fundamentalist oratory and sectarian ranting, struck fear and suspicion into the minds of less politically aware Protestants. He focused on loyalty to 'God and Ulster', depicting the other community as a real threat to Protestant heritage and culture. In his agenda, anyone 'pandering' to Catholic demands for civil rights was guilty of treason. Underpinning his philosophy was a principle that when your leader – namely the Unionist Prime Minister of the time, Captain Terence O'Neill – opens the door to the enemy by talking about reform, he should be unseated.

In 1966, the shooting of Catholics in Malvern Street in the Shankill by members of the Ulster Volunteer Force demonstrated that some people had decided to heed Paisley's warnings. His thesis was taking root within a core of Unionists most frightened by his dire predictions. Investigative writers agree that the UVF activists of the mid 1960s were highly influenced by Paisleyism.

In Malvern Street the gun returned to the politics of Ireland with a vengeance. During the '60s, Paisley succeeded in cutting a swathe through Unionism, detaching those he defined as most loyal to the core principles of the 'God and Ulster' thesis – loyalists within the Protestant working class. His contribution to the overall political dynamics of his own community cannot be underestimated. He, more than any other political leader, contributed to the fracturing and dismantling of the Unionist monolith. His efforts led to a weakening of the Unionist Party and the creation of a loyalist rump defined by paramilitarism and fundamentalism.

When I spoke to Billy Wright in his Portadown home in 1996, it was clear he was one of those paramilitaries who had embraced the Paisley 'gospel' of fusing politics and religion. I was conducting research for my book *God and the Gun* and my focus was on whether violence in Wright's life had been determined by his religious convictions. I did not question him about his childhood when Paisley was stomping round Mid-Ulster preaching his message of hate and damnation. Wright was reluctant to discuss his childhood, preferring to briefly depict his early years as a rosy period. He told me he had lived with a foster family and interacted well with Catholics. In the course of my investigations for this book, I uncovered a disturbing account of his childhood, details of a dysfunctional family life and astounding disclosures about his life as a terrorist and how he acquired the moniker 'King Rat'.

Billy Wright was born William Stephen Wright in 1960 in Wolverhampton in the English Midlands. His parents, David Wright and Sarah, née

McKinley, were natives of Portadown. At the time of Billy Wright's birth they had two other children – Elizabeth, aged four, and Jackie, three. In 1961, another child, Angela, was born and she would remain close to her brother, Billy, for the next three decades. In 1964, the Wright family moved back to Portadown where David Wright began working in his uncle's shoe repair shop in the centre of the town. Life for young Billy Wright and his sisters was no utopia, especially when they steadily became aware of the precarious nature of their parents' marriage. The instability in the family found expression in Billy's behaviour. He was a troubled child who exhibited wayward traits. His sister Angela remembers him taking her to steal apples from an orchard at Batchelor's Way and how they were chased by the owner and almost caught. It was a minor offence but, in his case, it was symptomatic of a developing unruliness. Angela recalls a Christmas Eve when he took her to Woolworths. 'He had decided we would get presents for the poor people. We filled bags with stuff and were caught. The police arrived and took us to our parents.'

On the face of it, those episodes could be interpreted as childish pranks if they had not been part of a wider pattern of a child out of control. There were also disturbing things happening in the lives of one of his siblings. According to Angela Wright, her mother worked in a hotel in the town and when she had time for shopping she left her young daughters in the care of a 'man friend'. Elizabeth was sexually abused by her mother's friend but did not tell her parents. Now aged five, Billy Wright began to spend a significant amount of time with his maternal uncle, Cecil McKinley, and Angela believes he was the defining influence on her brother's subsequent political development. 'Uncle Cecil was a very kind man. Billy adored him but he was a big man in the Orange Order and very anti-Catholic. I think he was the one who had the greatest influence on our Billy in his youth.'

An insight into Billy Wright's thinking can be seen in an event which occurred in 1966 at the time of the Malvern Street shootings. Paisley was stomping through Northern Ireland and Angela Wright remembers being at a Guy Fawkes celebration when Paisley spoke to the crowd. 'We were all at a Guy Fawkes rally when Paisley was present and spoke to the crowd who were burning an effigy of Guy Fawkes. Billy turned to me, pointed to the effigy, and said, "That's the man who tried to blow up Parliament and he deserved what he got." Then I saw Paisley and the sight of him terrified me, but Billy said, "Angela that man is gonna change things for us."'

Things were certainly about to change within the Wright family but not in a positive way. In 1966, Sarah Wright gave birth to her fifth child, Connie, but the arrival of an addition to the family did not signal celebration. The social welfare authorities were sufficiently concerned about the children that the girls, one of them a baby in a cot, were placed in care at Guildford. Billy remained with his father and grandparents. After a time, the children returned to the family home but not to a happy one. Within a year, Sarah Wright packed her bags and took a boat from Belfast to Liverpool. It was the last time her children would ever see her.

The welfare authorities placed all four girls in a care home run by the Church of Ireland. It catered for a complement of forty children, boys and girls, ranging in ages from one to eighteen. Older children, often young men, were given the responsibility for supervising the younger children. Billy Wright remained for a short period with his father and was then transferred to a foster care establishment in South Armagh, close to the border with the Irish Republic. In that foster setting, there was a smaller complement of children in the care of a family who had knocked together three houses to create space. The facility handled approximately 20 children, boys and girls, in ages ranging from childhood to 18 years. Separating Billy Wright from his siblings caused great distress and who made the decision remains a mystery for his sister, Angela. 'Elizabeth, Jackie and I were really upset that Billy wasn't allowed to join us. We asked why because there was space but nobody could give us an answer. I used to sit at a window looking out, crying and wondering where my brother was. Elizabeth, the eldest, took it really badly.'

Life for Angela and her sisters in care was far from idyllic. Angela believes she was dyslexic but no one cared. Her lasting memory is of 'appalling' social conditions in the institution. 'I remember standing naked while they painted us with a solution to get rid of scabies. We all had lice in our hair. Elizabeth just couldn't cope. She also missed Billy. She had psoriasis and, as a result, she became aggressive. I remember stealing chocolate from a room to give to my baby sister, Connie, and was caught. They treated me like a common criminal. The whole atmosphere was difficult. We all had to do chores – especially the youngest – washing baths, floors, toilets etc. Once, with some of the younger boys, I was caught stealing apples from the orchard of the church next to the care home. The punishment was terrible. I was made to lie naked beside the boys in a room. One of the boys, Robert, committed suicide later in life.'

Angela was ten when she was made to lie with boys as a punishment but other events took place that were to leave searing mental scars on her and her sister, Elizabeth. 'I was ten when I was first raped in the home. Several of the older boys were abusing the girls. I was taken to a tent in a field and raped. A hand was placed over my mouth and I was told not to scream or tell anyone or I would get a beating,' Angela explained.

For her, it was the beginning of a cycle of abuse which would last almost three years until the abusers were old enough to be sent out into society. She still remembers the names of all of them. She also became aware that her sister, Elizabeth, had suffered an even worse fate of abuse from the time she arrived in foster care. Perhaps for that reason, Elizabeth, according to Angela, became so 'troublesome' she was sent to South Armagh where Billy was fostered. The only insight into Billy Wright's life at that time comes from conversations Angela had with her sister in response to questions from me. In the following account of a telephone conversation, Angela refers to her sister by her pet name, Libby.

'Libby told me that Billy was cold and quiet. She felt he didn't love her but he later told me that wasn't so. She felt that he had seen too much stuff in the home and didn't want to talk about it.'

When I asked Angela if her brother had ever been sexually abused, she responded with a frankness which characterised her answers to all my queries. 'I have to say I think he was. I feel that something happened. Libby has always felt the same way. It's just my closeness to him over the years that makes me think that.'

Her belief he was sexually abused has to be considered in the context of the fact that he confided in her and she was the sibling closest to him throughout his life. He even telephoned her at the care home where she lived. There can be little doubt that, knowing his sisters were being sexually abused, he became a 'cold and quiet child'. Angela subscribes to the theory that his personality traits of coldness and timidity in his youth were directly related to him knowing two of his sisters were being abused. 'Billy knew what happened to us. He probably knew there was nothing he could do about it. No one can understand what it would have felt like for a kid like our Billy who loved us.'

If there was anger welling up in him, it had to find expression and it did, but not towards the abusers. Aged 12, he painted an 'Up the UVF' sign on a Catholic school in Markethill and, when apprehended, refused to remove it. As punishment, he was transferred to Rathgael, an institution for young offenders. He was there a short time when he escaped and telephoned Angela, who was still in care. He was subsequently re-arrested and returned to Rathgael. Some of the borstal inmates he befriended were young, hardened criminals with paramilitary connections. By that stage, he was already acutely aware of the conflict in Northern Ireland and his heroes were UVF gunmen. When he was released into his father's custody, aged 13, he was an ideal candidate for the Young Citizens Volunteers, the junior ranks of the UVF.

Looking back, Angela, with some justification, believes her brother always wanted a family 'to cling to' and the YCV provided it for him. There was a camaraderie and a sense of security in being a paramilitary. However, there were multiple factors shaping his life. The pro-Paisley sentiments he expressed at the formative age of six years had become his doctrine of politico-religious fundamentalism. There were also the anti-Catholic rantings of his uncle, Cecil McKinley, and his anger about the treatment of his sisters in care. There is the possibility that he too was sexually abused. Combined with his natural waywardness, those were powerful elements in propelling him towards a violent career.

In 1996, when I spoke to him about his early years, he waxed lyrical about his time in South Armagh, never at any stage admitting he and his sisters had been in foster care. He told me he played Gaelic games with Catholics from Whitecross and met them at dances in the local Orange Hall. Looking back, it is clear to me he had blotted out, or consciously revised, aspects of his early years. In contrast, Angela has never sought to hide the past, believing it has helped explain many aspects of her brother's life of terror and his underlying motivations for killing people.

By the time she was 14, she and her sisters were living with their father at Jervais Street in Portadown. She believes, contrary to what has previously been written about her brother, that he joined the YCV when he was 14. It was 1974 and Northern Ireland was in the grip of the Ulster Workers Council Strike. On every street corner, members of the UDA and UVF manned barricades and brought the society to a virtual standstill.

I was a BBC journalist at the time and the Corporation's management in Belfast asked me to use my contacts within the UDA to acquire UDA passes to enable executives to travel through loyalist barricades and buy petrol without the risk of having their cars hijacked. Pressure on the BBC was such that journalists were told by management figures not to précis UDA statements for broadcast but to carry them on air in a verbatim format. Essentially, the BBC became a propaganda vehicle for the loyalist paramilitaries, a claim that BBC executives later denied. Second time round, when Paisley attempted to replicate the UWC Strike, the Corporation held meetings with British Government representatives at Stormont Castle on the outskirts of Belfast to plan a joint information strategy to negate Paisley's efforts to cripple the society. Part of that strategy, explained by the BBC Controller, Dick Francis, at an editorial meeting I attended, was that news producers and editors should only rely on constant updates from Stormont Castle and not from a Strike Committee.

At the time of the 1974 Strike, Billy Wright and others in the YCV were involved in sectarian attacks on Catholic students and Catholic homes. A year later, a policeman told a court that the YCV had been established 'with the sole purpose of killing Catholics and attacking Catholics' houses'. In Billy Wright's own words, he 'offered [himself] up to the YCV', because he was 'impressed by ordinary working men who were heroes'.

'We had training sessions from UVF volunteers in Mid-Ulster where I lived. We were taken away and trained in the use of weapons and explosives. We were taught that the emotional fear within the human being emanates from the stomach and one can actually control that fear. If one says, "I'm frightened", and then tackles that consciously, quite rapidly you can overcome your fear . . . the fear of death or whatever. I firmly believe I'm immune . . . it doesn't affect me.'

His heroes and the men who trained him were hardcore members of the UVF. Among them were Robin Jackson, known as 'The Jackal', Horace Boyle, Wesley Sommerville and Thomas Crozier. Sommerville, aged 25, and Crozier were also members of the Ulster Defence Regiment. One of the disturbing aspects of this period in Wright's life is that membership of the UDA and the UDR was not legally incompatible. The UDA, despite its history of grisly murders dating back to 1972, remained a legal organisation. The UDR Commander, Denis Ormerod, told journalists it was a 'perfectly acceptable arrangement'. Unlike the UDA, the UVF from 1966 onwards was an illegal body yet it also had links to the UDR through membership and the sharing of UDR intelligence files through its ties to the UDA. The UDR also provided weapons training and, in Wright's case, it was obvious from his connection to Sommerville and Crozier.

His commitment to the YCV, through acts of vandalism, intimidation and terror, impressed senior figures in the UVF. The 'cold' blond boy Elizabeth observed at Mountnorris had been transformed into a tall, secretive teenager operating in a shadowy world. He had a new 'family' – an organisation with a ruthless history of sectarian murders and bombings.

He quickly learned about the level of collusion between members of the UDA/UVF and the security forces in Mid-Ulster. Some of those who presented the loyalist paramilitaries with files on Catholics and suspected republicans were members of the RUC Reserve. Understanding the value of collusion later enabled him to clinically target members of the republican movement. One has only to look at his heroes to understand the pervasive influence they had on his life while he was in his teens.

In the early hours of a July morning in 1975, Horace Boyle, a major in the UVF, and Wesley Sommerville led a UVF unit out of Portadown. Within the unit were some members of the UDR in service uniforms.

They travelled to the main Belfast–Dublin Road at a point between the towns of Banbridge and Newry where they set up what appeared to be a bona fide security forces' roadblock. The aim was to stop a van carrying members of the Miami Showband on their way to Dublin after a gig in the predominantly Protestant town of Banbridge. Once stopped, a bomb would be secreted on the bus and the band permitted to make its way to Dublin where the bomb was timed to explode. The explosion would have the effect of killing the Catholic members of the band and illustrating that more border security was needed because even Catholic musicians from the Republic were involved in terror. The operation did not work out as planned. The bomb exploded as it was being loaded on the bus, killing Boyle and Sommerville. One of the musicians, Des McAlea, later testified that before the explosion Boyle, who was the terrorist leader, had been angry with his men when two of them joked with the musicians about the success of that night's gig.

The musicians were told to place their hands over their heads and face a ditch when first taken from the vehicle. Stephen Travers, a guitarist who had joined the band six weeks earlier, heard the explosion, felt a searing heat and was flung into a ditch. There was sub-machine gun fire and someone said, 'C'mon, those bastards are dead. I got them with dumdums.' Travers had been hit by a dumdum bullet that exploded in his body but he and McAlea survived. With Boyle and Sommerville dead, the other UVF operatives shot and killed three of the musicians. The band's leader, Francis 'Fran' O'Toole was hit with 23 rounds and forensic evidence confirmed he was shot as he lay face upwards on the ground.

One of the most disturbing aspects of the Miami Showband murders was that prior to the crime, Sommerville had been listed on Special Branch files as a terrorist suspect yet no effort had been made to remove him from the Ulster Defence Regiment. A Special Branch file contained information linking him to an attempt to blow up a section of a Catholic housing estate in Coalisland in 1974. As for Horace Boyle, four days before the Miami Showband murders, he and Robin 'The Jackal' Jackson executed 45-year-old Billy Hanna, a part-time UDR captain and member of the UVF. Hanna was singled out as an informer and Jackson was the shooter in his murder. Jackson shot Hanna at point-blank range in the head and again as he lay dying on the ground.

Billy Wright later told me the deaths of Boyle and Sommerville were the impetus for him moving up the ranks of the YCV and joining the UVF. Chris Anderson, in his book *The Billy Boy*, claimed that on the night the two UVF men died, Wright joined the senior wing of the UVF. Angela Wright does not agree. She says her brother was already a member of the UVF before the 'Miami Massacre'. If she is correct, his assertion he joined because of the deaths of Sommerville and Boyle was a deliberate lie. Perhaps, in revising his history he preferred to be linked to the two killers he so much admired. Therefore, it had not mattered much to him that they had planned to kill five innocent musicians. He joined the UVF some time between spring and summer of 1975 when he attended an initiation ceremony and swore an oath on a Bible while standing under an Ulster Constitution flag. Before taking the oath, he was asked by senior UVF men present at the ceremony if he wished to reverse his decision to join. 'I took the oath. I was not pressurised,' he told me.

While Billy was leading a life of terror, Angela was working in a garment factory outside Portadown to save enough money to make a life outside Northern Ireland. Unlike her brother, she had no attachment to tribal politics and had her own 'demons'. She was haunted by her past in foster care and believed the awful memories would not dissipate until she lived abroad. 'I wanted out of Northern Ireland – away from it all. I had been brutalised and constantly relived those terrible days. As for our Billy, he was always going to be in trouble. He was very secretive and quiet though he could be humorous in certain company – even articulate if it was about politics. He remained very close to me even then.'

Within the Wright family, life had dramatically changed. David Wright was living with Kathleen McVeigh, a Catholic from Garvagh. According to Angela, she and Elizabeth did not relate well to their stepmother. Meanwhile, Elizabeth was training as a nurse but was still suffering emotionally from the effects of her traumatic past. As for her brother, Billy, he had suddenly decided to leave the UVF and join either the British Army or the Israeli Defence Force.

To those unfamiliar with the peculiar politics of Northern Ireland, his desire to join the Israeli Defence Force related to one of those bizarre characteristics of loyalism. The UVF, as I will explain in depth later in this book, was highly influenced by Tara, a shadowy organisation run by a notorious paedophile evangelist, William McGrath, a member of Paisley's Free Presbyterian Church. McGrath propounded the absurd theory that Ulster Protestants were descended from the Lost Tribes of Israel. A British Intelligence agent from the 1950s, McGrath promoted joint membership of the UVF and his own group, Tara. He fed UVF personnel a nonsensical diet of Biblical references fused with wild political theories. His influence filtered down through loyalist paramilitary ranks and led to young thugs like Billy Wright claiming an affiliation with Israel and wearing a Star of David.

In the 1980s, I met a Protestant who had served in the Israeli Defence Force. On his return to Northern Ireland, the Israeli Intelligence Service, Mossad, encouraged him to join the UDR and supply them with British military files on the IRA. He passed British Intelligence files to a Mossad *Katsa* – intelligence officer – at the Israeli Embassy in London. At the time, Margaret Thatcher had banned Mossad from operating in Britain and their files on the IRA were slowly becoming outdated. Their need to know about IRA operatives related to their global war against terrorism. They were especially keen to track the IRA's arms dealings with the Libyan regime, the Basque separatist group, ETA, and Yasser Arafat's PLO.

According to Angela Wright, her father was not keen to sign papers for his son to join the British Army. Perhaps he thought his son was too young to make such a decision and should get a job or pursue his education. Billy Wright's wish to join a regular army was fleeting and he soon returned to his terrorist career, which took him deeper into the world of murder. His career choice was self-evident when he was arrested and taken to Castlereagh Holding Centre in Belfast where suspected terrorists were subjected to lengthy interrogations, supervised by members of Special Branch. Sometimes suspects were brutalised but the major part of the interrogation process was to seek information, acquire confessions and attempt to recruit suspects as informers or terrorist agents. British Intelligence agencies also had an input to the interrogation process through their links to Special Branch. The distinction between an informer and a terrorist agent is significant and I make the following observations since the issue recurs in later stories.

An informer was often a criminal on the fringes of paramilitary life who would pass information to the authorities in return for the police overlooking his activities. A terrorist agent was someone recruited as a constant source – a person who was an important cog in the terrorist machine. As an agent, a terrorist was encouraged to act as a terrorist in order to maintain his cover, or to carry out killings on behalf of his intelligence handlers. During interrogations, if a suspect was known to be a terrorist, greater efforts were made to turn him into a terrorist agent. Various techniques were used, including blackmail and threats that the suspect would be exposed to his fellow terrorists as an informer. Blackmail took the form of threats to reveal details of a person's sexual proclivities, extramarital affairs or crimes committed without the knowledge of terrorist leaders. There were also blandishments in the form of money and, in the case of loyalist terrorists, appeals were made to their inherited loyalty to Britain.

When Billy Wright entered the interrogation centre he was 16 years old and, irrespective of the anti-interrogation techniques he was taught by the UVF, he was no match for skilled personnel who had days to question and observe him. He later described his interrogation experience to his sister, Angela. 'Billy said he was abused and humiliated in Castlereagh. What really angered him was that Jim Wright, whom he knew, was present when they told him to bend over and shoved a pencil up his rectum. One of the interrogators said, "So, you think you're a big lad." Billy knew Jim Wright was from Portadown and expected him to intervene but he didn't.'

Jim Wright was no relation to Billy Wright. He was a 43-year-old policeman from Portadown. He was also a gospel singer, prominent in the Salvation Army. Married with four children, he died four years later when the INLA planted a bomb under his car. His 21-year-old daughter was injured in the explosion.

The outcome of Billy Wright's interrogation was a confession admitting membership of the UVF and involvement in terrorism in Mid-Ulster. He was charged with possessing weapons, found guilty and sentenced to six years in the Maze prison. Due to his age, he was confined to H Block 2 for young terrorist offenders. Within the Maze, terrorism took on a different character, no less significant than the killings and bombings on the outside. Prisoners received political education classes and advanced terror lessons to prepare them for the time when they would be released. Wright's unswerving commitment to the UVF soon raised his profile in H Block 2 and he was appointed commander of his wing of the block. While in the Maze he had his first face-to-face encounter with members of the Provisional IRA. He later boasted about it to Angela. 'Billy told me he met Bobby Sands who later became the famous IRA hunger striker. He said Sands used to joke, "I'm gonna get you", and Billy replied, "Not if I get you first".'

Angela, the only sibling who constantly visited him in the Maze, had plans for his future, which did not include terrorism. In three years she had saved enough money to fulfil her ambition of making a new life. Despite what she calls, 'opposition from my father', she moved to Edinburgh when she was 17. As soon as her brother was released from the Maze in the spring of 1980, she contacted him. By then, she was an established and respected member of the staff at the Peebles Hydro Hotel. 'I wanted Billy to join me to get him away from the life he had been living. I knew the hotel chef and he promised to give him a job washing dishes in the kitchen.'

On his release from prison, he formed a relationship with Thelma Corrigan whom he would later marry. The relationship seemed to be another turning point in his life. He closely related to his girlfriend's family history, which mirrored the troubled times in Northern Ireland. Her father and brother had been ambushed and killed by the IRA. Angela says acquiring a girlfriend did not deter him from accepting her offer to work in Scotland and that he indicated his desire to escape the clutches of the UVF. 'Looking back, I think he really wanted to put it all behind him. I genuinely believe that,' she told me.

Shortly after he began working in the hotel kitchens, Angela left Scotland for a better job in the Isle of Man, promising that when she settled there she would send for him. Several weeks later she received a disturbing telephone call. 'I was told Billy had been arrested but was back in Portadown. He had only been in the Scotland job six weeks. He was arrested by officers from Scotland Yard's Anti-Terrorist Squad.'

He was held for questioning and returned to Northern Ireland under an anti-terrorism exclusion order banning him from further entry into Britain. While researching that turn of events in his life, I spoke to a retired British Intelligence officer who had been a source for me when I worked on previous books. I asked him to find out why Wright was arrested in Scotland and whether his association with Scottish members of the UVF sparked the arrest. My source remarked: 'You're entering dangerous waters, my friend. Let's just say there was a request to apprehend him and it came from Special Branch in Northern Ireland and people linked to them whom I am not going to specify. The request was routed through the Special Branch department, which dealt with what you may call informers or terrorist agents. There were people with a special interest in him. Whatever that was, I am not in a position to investigate on your behalf. To put no finer a point on it, if that lad had obligations, I would not be shocked. It would not be far-fetched to conclude that he was held for questioning and excluded to maintain his cover with fellow travellers in the UVF. That is conjecture, of course.'

During conversations with Angela Wright in New York, where she lives with her husband, Kieran, who hails from Tipperary in the Irish Republic, I made no mention of what my intelligence source said. I simply asked her for her understanding of why her brother was suddenly arrested in Scotland as he tried to make a life away from terrorism. Her initial response confirmed he was as surprised at the drastic change in his fortunes. 'I spoke to Billy shortly after his return to Portadown. He assured me, and I believed him, that he had wanted out of the terrorist thing. He was shocked at his arrest.'

I pressed her further and she dropped the following bombshell about a subsequent conversation she had with him about the Scotland Yard intervention. 'To this day, I remember him telling me that he had wanted out. I can still remember what he said. He said, "The Government isn't gonna let me out. I'm in for life." I knew then and from later things he said to me that he did shit things for the British. I know it . . . believe me, I just know it.'

If her memory of the conversation with her brother is accurate – so much else she told me contained no embellishment – then who was controlling the terrorist destiny of Billy Wright? Had he been recruited during his formative years when he was interrogated in Castlereagh? If so, it would have been important for his intelligence handlers to find a way to return him to paramilitary ranks. From previous research for other books, I learned that many senior UVF/UDA operatives were recruited as terrorist agents and permitted to continue their targeting of Catholics and suspected members of the IRA. For some readers, Angela Wright's belief that her brother had a dual terrorist role may seem fanciful in light of the fact that shortly after his return from Scotland he was implicated in terrorism on the evidence of a UVF supergrass, Clifford McKeown.

He was sent to Crumlin Road prison to await trial on charges of attempted murder and carrying out explosions. However, within a year the case against him collapsed and he was back on the streets. There may well be an explanation for that. In my book *The Dirty War* I revealed how British Intelligence and Special Branch placed two terrorist agents in prison on trumped up charges to enable them to feed bogus information to IRA leaders in the prison in order to destabilise the IRA's prison leadership. The fact that McKeown named Wright to investigating detectives could have forced his handlers to incarcerate him to protect his cover, knowing the case against him would not hold up.

Clifford McKeown provided information about 25 men from the Mid-Ulster area but in July 1982 he had a change of heart and withdrew his allegations about Wright; 18 of the others were subsequently convicted of minor offences. If, indeed, Wright was a terrorist agent, then after the supergrass trial he had implacable credentials in the UVF. Angela visited him while he was on remand in prison and again he told her, 'I'm in for life. There is no way out.' She confronted him about Clifford McKeown's claim that he was a murderer. 'Billy denied it. I was angry but I knew our Billy. I knew he had pulled a trigger. Years later when I asked him if he had killed a particular Catholic, he said he hadn't, so I asked him if he had ordered others to kill the man and he said he couldn't answer that. He just knew I disapproved of the killing of another human being.'

Shortly after his release from prison, he returned to terrorism and quickly ran into trouble. The story goes that, while removing weapons from a UVF arms dump with three other operatives, a covert SAS team ambushed him. His companions were caught but he ran off on foot and scores of bullets were fired at him as he escaped.

In his book *The Billy Boy*, Chris Anderson said he spoke to the three operatives who were captured and they told him if Wright had not escaped, the four of them would have been executed by the SAS. The authorities were unable to prove Wright was the fourth UVF operative. He was questioned by police and released.

When I examined details of this episode, I felt that there could well be an alternative explanation for Wright's miraculous escape on foot from a unit of the world's most elite special forces. I spoke to a former senior Provisional IRA operative and another from the UVF who had left their respective organisations in the late 1980s. I related to them Wright's claim that the SAS unit fired 400 rounds at him, and that some of the bullets were aimed at hedges and ditches where they believed he was hiding. I pointed out to the former terrorists that I had been told the SAS team had been acting on a tip-off. Both men expressed the view that the SAS rarely missed their targets and shooting off 400 rounds could have been a ploy to convince Wright's companions the SAS were intent on killing him. The Provisional IRA operative put it this way.

'It sounds to me like Wright was the man who tipped off the Brits or Special Branch and orders were given to let him escape. The SAS don't miss people at that kind of range. They're expert marksmen with night-sight capability. The 400 rounds sounds to me like a deliberate ploy to create the impression that Wright was on their target list and could not be an informer. You have to remember that when somebody escapes with that kind of ease, he is always debriefed by people up the line because there is the possibility he deliberately compromised his fellow operatives. Firing 400 rounds at him would have put paid to any suspicion in the UVF that Wright was dirty. One of our people, Francis Hughes, shot and killed an SAS man in a covert operation. Another SAS man was shot but still fired off a lot of rounds and shot Francie. That's how Francie was captured before he eventually died on hunger strike. What you're telling me about Billy Wright stinks of a set-up. But that's just my opinion and people will say that where I'm coming from I would say that anyway. But, believe me, I know about these things and I'm not spinning one for you because it was Billy Wright. Had he been one of ours, I would have had him hauled in no matter his rank. I'd have had our people interrogate him about every detail of what happened. The loyalists weren't as tight as us, or as shrewd as our internal security guys. Maybe in the UVF his rank would have got him out of any trouble in that regard.'

From the moment Wright seemingly escaped the clutches of the SAS, he made it known to anyone who was prepared to listen that he was on an SAS and anti-terrorist units' hit list. If that was so, they had ample opportunity to kill or compromise him and they did neither. There was an almost paradoxical flavour to his rhetoric after the episode. On the one hand, he said the British were out to get him while, at the same time, he applauded the security forces. When friends visited him, he often removed a bullet-ridden leather jacket from a cupboard, saying it was his most important treasure – the jacket of a UVF operative shot by the SAS in the 1970s. Occasionally, he would even become emotional as he ran his hands across the jacket.

Angela kept in touch with him in the early 1980s after she moved to Limerick in the Irish Republic. She was intrigued to discover he had renewed an interest in Biblical studies, which he had developed while in prison.

Evangelical conversion was a phenomenon closely linked to loyalist prisoners, ranging from members of the infamous Shankill Butchers gang to Kenny McClinton, a ruthless UDA gunman who later became a born-again preacher. In my book *God and the Gun*, I attributed the phenomenon to the fact that when men involved in reflex sectarian murders ended up in prison serving life sentences, they felt detached from the support mechanisms of their respective terrorist organisations. They had time to ponder the reasons for grisly crimes, which had no clear political agenda. The solitariness of a prison cell, without the expectation of an early release, encouraged many of them to read the Bible.

None of the converts was from the IRA, an organisation with a long history of incarceration, prison agitation and a defined ideology. IRA personnel understood from the history of republicanism that prison was a reality and serving time in prison was an accepted part of being involved in armed struggle. Historically, the IRA used the prison system as an extra-curricular dimension to its war. Prisoners were politically educated and further trained in the use of weapons. The prison regime created by the IRA enabled men to deal with incarceration without feeling isolated from the campaign on the outside.

In contrast, many loyalists involved in sectarian killings had difficulty dealing with the solitariness and loneliness of prison life. They found it difficult to understand that the State they thought belonged to them had imprisoned them for attacking the perceived enemies of the State. Lonely and confused, many of them temporarily turned to the Bible for comfort. Others, with a devious agenda, took the born-again road in order to convince judges they had reformed and were entitled to reduced sentences or early release. In the majority of cases, the conversion experience was not lasting.

During his time in Crumlin Road prison, Wright established friendships with UVF men from the heartland of the Shankill, regarded as the birthplace of the modern UVF. Among those with whom he came into contact and admired were members of the Shankill Butchers, including their leader, Lenny Murphy, and the UDA trigger man, Kenny

McClinton. Angela remembers how her brother frequently expressed a fascination with the Shankill. 'Billy had this thing about the Shankill. He was always visiting that area. He made a lot of friends with people he really admired.'

One of those friends was a notorious UVF killer, Johnny 'Mad Dog' Adair, a former skinhead. But, for all the discussions Wright had in the Shankill with killers and bombers, the God virus had infected him and in 1983 he did a 'lot of soul searching'. Like so many other phases in his life, God and the Bible would play only an intermittent role while he honed his skills as a trigger man and terrorist leader.

PART 2: BIBLE AND GUN

If Billy Wright's religious conversion had been real, it would have been truly remarkable, though I tend to believe that it was just another facet of a troubled and complex personality. At the outset, however, it seemed that he had genuinely swapped a pistol for a Bible. For two years, he became a travelling evangelist, visiting towns in the Irish Republic he studiously avoided during his time as a terrorist. He also went on several occasions to Scotland, using his new-found role to enable him to bypass the previous anti-terrorism order excluding him from entering Britain. Those trips took place not long before he decided to put aside his Bible. I asked his sister, Angela, why he made numerous trips to cities like Glasgow. 'Billy always had strange and secretive contacts in Scotland. I often wondered what it was all about. He never talked about the guys he met there or what he discussed with them. That was a part of his life that was a mystery.'

Between 1983 and 1985 his journeys across the Irish Sea were ostensibly to spread the gospel. In 1996, I asked him if he had been drawn to religion as a means of connecting him to his childhood when he had been a churchgoer. 'In my cell I started to read the Bible more out of boredom. I always had a deep respect for God and Christ. I studied it but had no real commitment to it.'

So why did he, in his words, suddenly choose to 'live quietly with Christ' and forsake terrorism? Apparently, he was seeking answers to the nature of his life and the course he had taken. He told me he had been apprehensive about committing himself to Christian ideals, knowing such a metamorphosis would require a rigorous adherence to principles alien to his role as a terrorist. 'Such was the depth of my belief in my country and the people that I found it difficult to disassociate myself from Northern Ireland and its people. That was later to be my downfall in walking with Christ.'

Angela kept in contact with him while he pursued the evangelical path and she was living in Limerick in the Irish Republic when she became pregnant. With no family support, she telephoned her brother. 'I told Billy I was pregnant. He didn't want me to have the baby in the Irish Republic. I was in labour and returned to Portadown. Billy took me to Craigavon Hospital and, on 21 July 1983, I gave birth to my son, Stephen. Billy was very kind when it came to helping his family. His family always meant a great deal to him and he was very caring to kids.'

She saw his kind side reflected in his short-lived fundamentalist preaching but, in order to understand the character of his professed religious conversion, it is important to examine the role of Kenny McClinton who remained a constant influence on his life into the 1990s. McClinton was a member of the UFF, the UDA's military wing. He was jailed in 1977 for murdering a Catholic father taking his son to school and a Protestant bus driver who had refused to support the UDA. Thirteen years older than Wright, he was the product of a dysfunctional childhood with an alcoholic, abusive father. As a terrorist, he recommended to his UFF bosses in the Shankill area that they should cut off the heads of Catholics and impale them on railings in West Belfast.

When McClinton was apprehended by police, he showed no remorse, lied to them, refused to divulge the names of his accomplices and ensured his terrorist crimes between 1972 until his first murder in 1975 would always remain a mystery. Yet, in discussions with me in 1996 after he had become a born-again preacher, he insisted that he had been glad the police took him off the streets. That was part of the fiction he created to hide the true character of his earlier life. He tried to tell me that by 1977 he had become 'tired of creating Catholic widows and orphans' and was spiritually relieved. His arrest, he declared, meant a 'terrible threat to society' was removed from the streets. I asked him how that equated with his failure to deliver up his accomplices. 'I was not going to be a Judas Iscariot because he is the most reviled man in the Scriptures. I still had a high moral code that I would not be an informer.'

McClinton's response was hardly worthy of a con man. He admitted to me that he had committed 'heinous crimes' but not the 'grossest'. Again, he was not going to be a Judas and provide police with details of those acts of terrorism. In prison, he was known as 'the maniac' because of his violent behaviour but after he immersed himself in the Bible, he transformed himself into a crusading evangelist. He and Wright met in prison and their relationship became more intense after McClinton was guaranteed early release in 1993.

Despite McClinton's claim to be a man of God, his doctrine was of a politico-religious nature with sectarian overtones – fundamentalism acquired through contact with a Texas-based ministry run by a former Watergate burglar, and of course Paisleyism. While Wright gave himself to a similar conversion diet, he was unable to curb his basic instincts and the need to be involved in terrorism. In 1985, he returned to the fold of his 'family' – the UVF. According to him, events beyond his control detached him from the path of 'walking with Christ'.

He claimed the Anglo-Irish Agreement of 1985 forced him to restart his paramilitary career. It was Prime Minister Margaret Thatcher's policy to initiate closer links between the Dublin and London Governments as a means of finding an agreed solution in Northern Ireland. One of its radical components was a joint ministerial body based at Maryfield on the outskirts of Belfast. Its role was to monitor the core complaints and aspirations of both communities. Unionists saw the Agreement as a betrayal likely to lead ultimately to a United Ireland. There were massive demonstrations and serious threats to public order from the UDA/UVF. If Wright was a terrorist agent, there was no better time for his handlers to have forced him back into service to provide surveillance and information on the strategy of loyalist paramilitaries. That would explain why he suddenly abandoned the 'religious life'. However, he offered me a very different explanation.

'I was emotionally torn in two. The British Government betrayed our people. It created bitterness in my heart and I knew that was a contradiction in relation to living with Christianity . . . It's about a defence of the faith, the culture and the politics. We have a right to fight, to defend and to die for what we believe is the truth. Should that truth disappear, then in our opinion, it will lead to the losing of the souls of our people.'

In his words, the 'defining moment' when he returned to violence related to an event he observed in 1986 on the streets of Portadown during clashes between the police and rioters after an Apprentice Boys' parade was banned from marching through a Catholic area. 'I watched young Keith White being killed. I was just feet from him. The RUC killed him with a plastic bullet. In one estate, a hundred people were injured with plastic bullets. I stood on the streets of Portadown and watched the Law of the land, which claimed to be above the people, killing, beating, sexually molesting and urinating on churches. At the same time, the IRA had taken out six leading loyalists I had known in Belfast. The bitterness that was going on inside me told me I could not walk with God.'

If one is to place any credence on his justification for resuming violence, one has to look at certain aspects of it. His allegation that police officers sexually molested people in Portadown was without foundation. Even republicans, who constantly condemned the RUC for excessive force, never accused policemen of such a crime. But in his mind it happened, and he had personally observed the rape of his sister earlier in his life. Angela Wright, in conversations with her sibling, Elizabeth, was provided with a horrific account of how she was raped in the presence of their brother.

'Billy saw it happen and tried to stop it but the rapist who was almost 18 put his hands over Billy's mouth and threatened him. As Billy stood outside the door of a room, Libby was raped inside the room. I later heard the rapist was in the UDR.'

Another fact Billy Wright neglected to acknowledge when he spoke to me about the 'defining moment' was that Keith White was not an innocent bystander. He was a member of the YCV, the UVF's youth wing, and was a key player in the rioting. Wright's subsequent justification for re-joining the UVF seemed, much in keeping with McClinton rhetoric, to represent a conveniently revised piece of history. The UVF was happy to see him back in its ranks and told him to make the Mid-Ulster Brigade a more effective force. Within two years, he achieved that goal and became a ruthless, efficient operator.

Angela had moved to New York but, like so much else in her troubled life, she appeared to have little luck. In desperation, she turned for help to her brother. 'I found myself with my son, Stephen, in a homeless shelter with no money. I telephoned Billy and asked him to take my son and he agreed. He was like that. There was a loving side to him when it came to children.'

Stephen was sent to Northern Ireland to live with his uncle Billy, his wife and their two children. Family life did not prevent the trigger man from making Mid-Ulster units more effective or from personally participating in operations. When there were no obvious republican targets he encouraged his men to randomly kill Catholics. An example of their gruesome handiwork was the murder of 19-year-old Denis Carville. He was sitting in a car with his girlfriend when a gunman approached, asked his religion and the name of his parish priest. Carville replied truthfully and was shot through the head at point-blank range. Wright later insisted that he had never been sectarian and told his sister, Angela, that he liked Catholics. 'Billy was not anti-Catholic. He was anti-republican and anti-IRA. He met all my Catholic friends and when I married Kieran, who is from Tipperary in the Irish Republic, he got on well with him.'

He did establish a rapport with Angela's husband, a Catholic, but I contend it related to self-image since few loyalist paramilitaries who killed innocent Catholics ever admitted to me they were sectarian. He wanted people to see him as a soldier but it was just another part of the fiction which he further articulated in later life when he began to speak openly about his paramilitary status. Nonetheless, aside from the sectarian killings, which he authorised and participated in, he proved effective in targeting republicans in Mid-Ulster. He had help from the security forces in the form of intelligence files, much in the same way as the UVF and UFF in Belfast were provided with documents by agents of the State. Some of his operations were privately applauded within the security-intelligence apparatus. One was the murder of Gervais Lynch who was shot multiple times in his home near Lurgan. In Belfast UVF circles, the trigger man was reputed to be Wright, though he always denied personal involvement in killings. He was astutely aware of the law, of the presence of informers in the UVF and the danger that an admission to murder might later be used against him by a police informer. In essence, he had no intention of leaving his fingerprints on terror as long as he had others he could order to commit crimes. He also had an eye for propaganda and occasionally, when an innocent bystander was killed in operations, he issued statements claiming the killing on behalf of a bogus loyalist organisation. He used such a ploy after the slaughter of three teenagers, employing the name Protestant Action Force.

By 1991, his notoriety placed him at the top of IRA and INLA assassination lists. At the same time, detectives regularly visited his home, or arrested him for questioning as to his whereabouts at the time of particular killings. Other visits by detectives were to warn him about his personal security after Special Branch learned republicans were planning to kill him.

Wright's strategy in Mid-Ulster was to create a reign of terror. If he could not kill members of the IRA, he would target their families, their relatives or associates. Two brothers were gunned down in their home in front of their 11-year-old sister and RUC detectives were convinced that Wright was present at that double murder. Kathleen O'Hagan was shot dead in her home even though she was pregnant. Wright's units, despite heavy security in Mid-Ulster, operated with impunity.

His public profile as a ruthless terrorist was highlighted by the *Sunday World* newspaper and one of its energetic and courageous journalists, Martin O'Hagan. Marty lived in Mid-Ulster and knew every UVF and UDA leader in the region. He had developed his talent for writing controversial stories under the leadership of *Sunday World* editor, Jim Campbell. Throughout the Troubles, Campbell never shied away from reporting the truth about loyalist killers. He angered Robin Jackson, Wright's UVF associate, by referring to him as 'The Jackal'. Jackson responded by asking the UVF in the Shankill to kill the newspaper editor. Campbell was shot in the hallway of his home in North Belfast but survived. To this day he has a bullet lodged in his spine. Marty O'Hagan set his sights on exposing Wright and gave him the moniker 'King Rat'. It quickly became apparent to people outside the paramilitary world that 'King Rat' was Billy Wright. It was not long before Marty received death threats and went to live in Cork and later in Dublin.

The early '90s were a violent time and, in the shadows, the British Government conducted a secret dialogue with the IRA and made overtures to the UVF. The UVF, in what may have been its first foray into discussions about a peaceful solution to the conflict, allowed one of its senior figures to attend a meeting in Dublin with a motley assortment of political activists. In retrospect, it provided the seeds of a dialogue but it did not have Wright's approval. In Mid-Ulster, he was a law unto himself. However, the UVF's unwillingness to curb his power would soon prove problematic. His personal life was also changing dramatically, much to the dismay of his sister, Angela. He left his wife, Thelma Corrigan, and set up home with a girlfriend, Eleanor Reilly.

Another development, which signalled a major shift in his life, though he did not anticipate its potential impact, was the setting up of the Combined Loyalist Military Command. It brought together the leaders of the UVF/UDA/Red Hand Commandos as a mechanism for papering over rifts which had frequently led to feuding between the three groups. Within the UVF itself, there was a developing political debate about a way forward and what Wright heard did not please him. He was told elements of the Shankill leadership were flirting with the kind of Marxist principles which had long been promoted by the Official IRA and its Workers Party. Wright was ultra conservative and any talk of socialism or Marxism smacked of 'godless communism'.

The UVF tendency to tinker with socialist ideas had its roots in the early '70s when Gusty Spence, the 'hero' of the 1966 Malvern Street shootings, began a prison dialogue with members of the Official IRA. As a consequence, Spence began to articulate a political philosophy alien to the Protestant working class and ultra elements within loyalism. He argued that, for too long, the Protestant working class had pledged unquestioning loyalty to 'their masters' – land-owning Unionist politicians educated in English public schools like Eton. He believed Protestants had, like their Catholic counterparts, suffered social deprivation but not articulated their grievances. His views were regarded as dangerous by the right-wing in his own community but found fertile ground among young UVF volunteers who met him in prison. Through them, Spence's doctrine filtered down through the ranks but was quickly stamped out because it too closely equated to republican ideology, even if that related to the Official IRA which was non-sectarian and had maintained a cease-fire from 1972.

When the CLMC declared a cease-fire in 1994, it angered Wright but he understood UVF unity required his public support for the move. Within Mid-Ulster UVF ranks, however, he made no attempt to hide his disillusionment with the suspension of hostilities. He described the cease-fire as 'a capitulation' to Dublin and warned it was only a matter of time before the Irish Government had a direct say in the affairs of Northern Ireland. It was familiar Paisley rhetoric with its origins in the 1960s. He had, he told his units, 'the IRA on the run' and it was the time to increase, not end hostilities.

UVF leaders in the Shankill heard the rumblings of discontent from Mid-Ulster and rumours that Wright was describing them as 'a bunch of Marxists'. If Wright had wanted to choose a time to demonstrate to his leaders he was not the only dissident, and that peace was the wrong choice, the summer of 1995 provided him with an ideal opportunity.

In the context of the peace process, Catholics had strongly articulated a need for reform in terms of the yearly assertion by Orangemen that they had an historic right to march through Catholic districts. One of those historic symbols of the territorial imperative of Orangeism, and by Catholic definition, triumphalism, was the annual Portadown march through the Garvaghy Road estate, after a service at Drumcree churchyard. The British Government took the unprecedented step of banning the march from entering the Catholic district, setting off a chain of events which threatened the peace process and ultimately changed the course of Wright's life.

In the wake of the ban, Wright organised a stand-off at Drumcree with Orangemen and other loyalist elements demanding capitulation to their historic marching rights. Television news coverage had Wright centre stage, dressed in jeans like a neighbourhood thug, his head shaven. Only his sister, Angela, knew that he was going prematurely bald and believed a shaven head made him youthful.

The stand-off, during which members of the UVF and YCV planned an assault on police and Army lines, continued for several days. Behind the scenes, Wright used intermediaries, some of them politicians, to warn the authorities that if the ban on the march was not lifted, there would be chaos. The British Government capitulated. The next day, in a scene which hardly spoke of humility or respect for the other community, a jubilant Ian Paisley, walking hand-in-hand with the Unionist leader, David Trimble, led a march through the Catholic area. For Trimble, it was a classic error of judgment at a time when Northern Ireland needed cooler heads and not triumphalist displays.

Wright made it clear publicly he had been vindicated and, in so doing, acquired the status of the most important loyalist leader in Northern

Ireland. When an Orange parade through a Catholic district in Belfast was banned, Wright went there hoping to repeat his success in Portadown, using confrontation and dire threats. He expected the UVF in the Shankill to support him and place its Belfast units on standby. He argued that, through a combination of street confrontation and the potential for widespread violence, the British Government would again back down. The UVF leadership refused to support him. The British Government remained steadfast and the ban held, partly due to secret assurances from the UVF leadership it would not back Wright. On his return to Portadown, speaking to Mid-Ulster units, he scolded the UVF leaders in the Shankill. They had 'surrendered', he ranted. What he really meant was they did not share his fundamentalism and his admiration for Paisley. The following is a transcript of his answers to my questions about that issue.

Q. What were the underlying factors that propelled you back to a life of violence?

A. The Protestants of County Armagh, the Protestants of Portadown have overcome so much . . . There's so much depth to their suffering that they'll never give up. You can go back to 1641. Of all the issues which typify us, of all the issues with the northern Irish sphere, the parades issue is the most important. It is the faith combined with the culture . . . The leadership of the loyalists was so out of step because they'd left the faith.

Q. Are you saying that the leadership of the UVF, the political leadership, was not willing to take on the Drumcree issue?

A. That's correct. They had set aside the faith because of their socialist philosophy . . .

In the summer of 1996, the Drumcree March issue resurfaced and it was clear the British Government had decided Wright would not have his way. An informer in the UVF leadership in Belfast told police Wright was considering acting independently of the organisation's leadership, with the aim of causing widespread violence if the parade was not permitted to proceed down the Garvaghy Road. Privately, the UVF again let it be known to British Government sources Wright would not have their support. The RUC and Army sealed off the route from Drumcree to the Catholic area and initiated a massive security operation throughout Portadown and other towns and cities in Northern Ireland. During several days of a stand-off in Drumcree churchyard, Wright considered various options including violence. Some of his operatives decided to cheer him up and give him a birthday present. They kidnapped a 37-year-old Catholic taxi-driver, Michael McGoldrick, shot him four times in the head and then fired another round into his face to 'finish him off'. Wright denied involvement. However, there was credible evidence that he had planned to abduct several priests. The British Government, on advice from the RUC, again capitulated and the march was forced down the Garvaghy Road.

In the Shankill, the UVF leadership was angry Wright had broken the CLMC cease-fire by permitting the murder of Michael McGoldrick. They accused him of planning operations without consulting them. For Wright, the UVF had, in his familiar parlance, 'surrendered' and only through his threats had Protestants won the day at Drumcree for two years running. By now, there was a real sense in the Shankill that he thought he was bigger than the UVF. His frequent public appearances appeared to show he revelled in his loyalist 'superstar' status. The UVF gave its answer to his open displays of insubordination by announcing, on 2 August, it was disbanding its Portadown unit while it investigated its activities. The UVF action was to reassure fellow members of the CLMC it could control its own personnel.

A former member of the UVF provided me with the following explanation of Wright's confrontation with his bosses: 'Behind the scenes the British Government was putting pressure on us to deal with Wright because they felt things could get out of control and wreck the peace process. To some of us who knew Billy and respected him, it seemed as if he had pushed the wrong button. He was driving a wedge through our ranks, splitting the organisation. The UDA also felt it. Some suggested that he had lost it – that fame had gone to his head. We needed unity and he was putting that in jeopardy. It was giving our enemies an opportunity to say we should be the target because we were the obstacle to peace. There were people in British and Irish circles who were happy with what he was doing and the IRA loved it.'

Some leading members of the UVF in Mid-Ulster began to distance themselves from Wright, but figures like Robin 'The Jackal' Jackson with long standing connections to British Intelligence agencies supported him. Wright told friends there were other senior UVF officers in Mid-Ulster who agreed with him but they had given their allegiance to the bosses in Belfast for monetary reasons. He was referring to the fact that, while he had tried years earlier to stamp out criminal elements in the Mid-Ulster Brigade, he had been forced to turn a blind eye to the activities of some of his associates who had criminal ties to leading UVF figures in Belfast.

The war of words between Wright and UVF leaders in the Shankill was deliberately leaked to the media. Sources I talked to confirmed that the UVF began a disinformation campaign against him, telling journalists he was a drug dealer and an informer. Those accusations were followed by a CLMC threat that he would be executed if he did not leave Northern Ireland by midnight of 1 September.

From his early days in foster care, he had never backed away from threats, irrespective of their source. When he was young, he had been unable to prevent his sister being raped but, after his teenage years, he feared no one. The CLMC decree came as no surprise to him because he had been toying with the idea of setting up his own loyalist paramilitary organisation which he hoped would promote his personal brand of fundamentalism. His appeal to grass roots loyalists shocked the CLMC when a massive rally in support of him took place in Portadown. Those present were angered by the CLMC death threat and made clear their opposition to it.

Prominent at the rally was the Reverend William McCrea, a singer-preacher and one of Paisley's most loyal followers. Wright saw his support as an imprimatur from on high – possibly from Paisley. McCrea stood on a platform with Wright to address a crowd and packed ranks of the media. To add to the solemnity of the occasion, the shaven-headed Wright forsook his jeans and customary denim shirt which hid his numerous tattoos, and appeared for the television cameras in a suit. It was an attempt at respectability but he resembled an undertaker rather than a stockbroker.

Within days of the rally, he announced the formation of the Loyalist Volunteer Force. It comprised UVF and UDA dissidents who shared his view that a cease-fire was a declaration of failure and that there were not enough fundamentalist Christians in paramilitary ranks. The UVF and UDA, he told recruits, were full of 'criminals and communists'. His public announcement indicated his disdain for the UVF's Shankill leadership and its inability to enforce its threat to execute him. The creation of the LVF led to an increasingly bitter war of words in the media. The UVF depicted him as a 'dupe of Paisley' and denied that it was Marxist. The organisation was genuinely concerned that he had publicly flouted its authority and, more significantly, that he was a magnet for young, hard-line men in its ranks. The UDA was also worried about losing recruits and tried to persuade the UVF to fulfil its threat to kill him. But for the UVF, Wright was too big a fish to fry. He was popular, perhaps more popular than many of those opposed to him.

He was not long in charge of the LVF when he was arrested and accused of intimidating a Protestant housewife, Gwen Reid, a mother of four. Despite the seriousness of the offence and his terrorist history, he was released on bail. When he appeared in court in January 1997, the Prosecution alleged he had threatened to shoot Mrs Reid to prevent her giving evidence against associates over an assault in Portadown. He was found guilty but refused to appear before the judge to receive an eight-year prison term. The authorities incarcerated him in Maghaberry prison but it did not prevent him communicating with the LVF and devising a terror strategy. Under his leadership, the LVF expanded and acquired rifles, handguns and explosives. Some of the guns were provided by his contacts in Scotland.

Within a month of his arrival in Maghaberry, he requested a transfer to the Maze prison where he could be reunited with LVF personnel. He was attracted to the more relaxed atmosphere of the Maze where he could do his daily workout routine. It was also reassuring for him that competing paramilitary groups in the Maze had a policy of not targeting each other. It was a safer place for him to be imprisoned and that became evident to him when Christopher 'Crip' McWilliams and John Kennaway, INLA prisoners in Maghaberry, were involved in what was described as a botched attempt to kill a disaffected member of their organisation. They later claimed their target had been Billy Wright. McWilliams and Kennaway were transferred to the Maze, the most heavily fortified prison in Europe, where they joined other colleagues on Wings C & D of H Block 6, which housed INLA prisoners.

Wright's request for a transfer was granted and he arrived in the Maze on 26 April. For the next six months, he wrote letters to friends and associates, had his daily workout and sent secret communications to his units in the field. All the time, he was not far from the INLA wings where McWilliams and Kennaway were spending their time devising a means to assassinate him. In New York at around 6 a.m. on 27 December, Angela Wright found she could not sleep. Her husband had not long returned from work in their bar-restaurant and he was snoring loudly. 'The dog was also barking and I just got out of bed. I thought, since it was five hours behind in New York, I would telephone my sister Connie and her husband, Jim. I wanted to ask them if they enjoyed Christmas. They're a nice couple. He is originally a Catholic and is involved in missionary work. I was talking on the telephone to Jim when he stunned me with news that Billy had just been shot dead. It had just been announced on the midday television news.'

McWilliams and Kennaway, with the assistance of another INLA operative, had succeeded in their mission to kill 'King Rat'. They waited until he was in a prison van ready to be taken to another part of the prison to meet his girlfriend, then shot him seven times. His death mirrored his life but had, according to Angela, not been unexpected. 'Billy said he would never see the new millennium. I could understand if those guys had killed him on the outside, but not in prison. There was something else behind his murder.'

The LVF reacted to his demise by killing innocent Catholics. When more than 30,000 people attended his funeral, theories surfaced, which had the support of his father, David Wright, that the INLA had acted in collusion with British Intelligence personnel. It was an unusual claim coming from within loyalism, which had always denied collusion of any kind between the loyalist paramilitaries and agencies of the State intelligence apparatus. Nonetheless, the INLA throughout its turbulent history was one of the most intelligence-penetrated terror groups. Chris Anderson in his book *The Billy Boy* argued there was a conspiracy surrounding the murder and that there were many unanswered questions about how the INLA managed to smuggle weapons into the Maze and kill such a high-profile prisoner, given the security of the establishment. Anderson's analysis of events connected with events in the Maze prior to the murder provided a compelling case that the INLA trigger men could not have acted alone.

Personally, when I learned of Wright's death, I was inclined to believe his killers, possibly without knowing it, had been assisted by someone within the intelligence community. At the time of his death, Wright, even from within prison, was the biggest threat to the peace process. He had succeeded in fracturing loyalism but, most significantly, his new terror organisation was not built for dialogue with the other community. I have no evidence to conclude other influences were at work in his murder, but the Provisional IRA privately supported the conspiracy theorists. One could argue that, in so doing, the Provisionals were merely articulating their oft-repeated allegation, denied by loyalists, that Special Branch and others were intricately involved in a dirty war going back to the beginning of the Troubles. What most troubled me about his murder were comments made to me by his sister, Angela, regarding her visit to Maghaberry prison, weeks before he was transferred to the Maze.

'I will always remember what he said to me when I challenged him about what was going to happen to my son, Stephen, while he spent eight years in prison. He turned to me, his finger pointed at me. You always knew when our Billy pointed his finger at you that he was serious. He said: "I'll be outta here in two months and I'll be going to England. Stephen will know where I am." I shook my head but he insisted he'd be out and in England within two months. He said: "Then, it'll be over."'

I pressed Angela several times about her recollection of the Maghaberry meeting and she never wavered from what she first told me. I put it to her he could have been trying to tell her he was, for his own security, being transferred to an English prison. She dismissed that explanation. 'No, absolutely not. That's not the case. Billy was telling me that he would be outta prison in two months and would then go to

England. He had looked after my Stephen all those years and he knew that I was worried about him. It's not something Billy would have said unless he was sure of what he meant.'

She believed her brother had struck a deal with 'the British' for 'the shit' he had done for them. 'I still remember him saying there was no way out. I still remember when he was sent back from Scotland him saying they would never let him go and he wasn't talking about the UVF.'

I never doubted her sincerity and respected the fact she allowed me glimpses into the personal life of her family. I had to ask myself if it was possible she had misinterpreted what he said or whether there was an alternative explanation for his comments. I reached the conclusion, in the light of the many hours I spent talking to her, that her account of conversations with him had never changed in detail or emphasis. I had my own questions.

Was it likely that he could have been offered a deal which would have been condemned by Catholics and the Irish Government? Was it possible the British Government privately told him he could serve out his sentence in England? If so, was that done to defuse his influence among LVF prisoners in the Maze who were, even from within the prison, orchestrating murders on the outside which damaged the peace process?

If, as I suspect, he was a terrorist agent, did his handlers convince him he would be freed in order to silence him at that juncture, knowing plans were afoot to assassinate him when he was transferred to the Maze? Those questions are in the realm of conjecture. However, in the light of other stories in this book, the case for British Intelligence collusion in his murder would not be outside the realms of probability. Perhaps Wright was a difficult agent to control and those running him feared that, at some time in the future, he would divulge his dealings with them. He was angry he was sent to prison for eight years and blamed his enemies in the RUC for setting him up. I am convinced he was offered a deal when he arrived in Maghaberry. What it was I do not know but I place a lot of reliance on what he told his sister. In many meetings with me in New York, she often returned to her belief, it was 'the Government' that would not 'let him out' and he was 'in for life'.

In the overall story, she is also a victim. When fellow bar staff and customers in New York learned that she was 'King Rat's' sister she was humiliated as well as verbally and physically abused. Despite New York's massive population, parts of it can resemble a village. Gossip among the Irish, not Irish Americans, tends to be rife. When Billy Wright rose to prominence, it did not take long for word to spread that his sister worked in Manhattan.

'Guys, mostly from Northern Ireland, hurled abuse at me. I was spat on. My hair was pulled. Drinks were poured over me – even plates thrown at me. I would move from bar to bar but it didn't matter – somebody found out and word spread that I was there. I was labelled just because of my brother yet I had been a good person living for over 20 years in New York.'

To add to her woes, in 1998, her son was taken off a New York-bound plane at Shannon Airport and returned to Belfast. Her experiences were classic examples of what would have happened if she had worked in a bar in downtown Belfast. She expected New York to be different. She was unaware immigrants often bring their worst national traits with them when they settle or work in other countries. Slim, blonde and vivacious, with the hint of an American accent, she has always tried to hide her own personal pain. Yet the constant threat of being recognised is something unlikely to dissipate while she resides in New York. While tribalism and its oral history tradition continue to dominate the politics and history of Ireland, she will continue to be a victim even 3,000 miles from the seat of the conflict.

She contends that much of the unhappiness of their respective childhood years helped shape her brother's life. In particular, she talked to me about a disturbing set of experiences she and her brother shared and which I am not at liberty to reveal for legal reasons. Those experiences were clearly of a character which would have adversely impacted upon young minds. There may be truth in her assertion, though I believe there were numerous variables in the mix that helped shape a ruthless killer. The fundamentalist dimension to his religious ethos is one of those variables. I raised it in discussions with her, and she responded by telling me about several 'strange' conversations with him.

'Years before the bombing of the World Trade Center, Billy told me I was living in "the city of sin". He said the Trade Center towers would be destroyed and it would happen from the air. It scared me the way he said it and I told a friend I was working with in *The Irish Punt* in Manhattan. I knew she would think I was crazy but she remembered what I told her when the Towers collapsed on 9/11.'

His use of 'city of sin' and his prediction about the towers were evocative of biblical imagery – of thunderbolts – the Tower of Babel. He also told Angela before his death in 1997 that he would not see a Third World War which would happen between 2003 and 2006. 'I said to him, "Oh, you mean the Middle East – somewhere like Iraq", and he replied that it would be North Korea.'

North Korea would seem an unlikely reply because it was not a news item in the mid '90s, or even immediately prior to his death in 1997. I wondered how he had settled on that country and then realised, through the terrorist turned preacher, Kenny McClinton, he would have learned about that last communist bastion. After his release from prison in 1993, McClinton maintained a close relationship with Wright and, according to Angela, arranged for one of his associates from a Texas-based evangelical ministry to talk to her brother. A close study of similar groupings in the United States shows they are heavily influenced by ultra-right Republican politics and see the fight against communism as the final battle. It is likely that McClinton's Texas associate convinced Wright North Korea would be the next major battleground. In 2003, when tensions mounted between the US and North Korea, Angela interpreted her brother's comments as 'strange' predictions rather than the more likely explanation they were symptomatic of a long-term evangelical view of the world, in place from the Korean War and the Cold War.

After Wright's death, a gable wall mural in his honour was unveiled on the Shankill Road. It read: 'Loyalist Martyr King Rat'. It was the moniker given to him by Martin O'Hagan, the *Sunday World* journalist. Marty mistakenly believed he was safe to return to Northern Ireland and the Lurgan area where he had his roots. Little did he realise Wright's violent legacy was alive and lethal. In the autumn of 2001, Marty was shot dead while returning with his wife from a late-night drink at a local bar.

2

UNDERCOVER TRIGGER MEN

The undercover war in Northern Ireland had its origins in the early 1970s when the British Military/Intelligence apparatus set in place a policy that remained unchanged for over two decades. It is difficult to ascertain how high up the political ladder information was passed about the genesis of that shadowy war, but it is not inconceivable that knowledge of it reached the secret Cabinet committee, GEN 42, under the leadership of Prime Minister Edward Heath. The committee's Coordinator of Intelligence, Sir Dick White, knew about it through his links to Military Intelligence outfits and the two intelligence services, MI5 and MI6. As for British Army generals, they had been made aware of a counter-insurgency plan as early as the autumn of 1970 and approved it. The plan envisaged the use of tactics developed during colonial 'emergencies' and involved the creation of special teams interspersed with enemy 'irregulars'. In Army speak, they were known as 'counter gangs'. Heath and other members of his Cabinet may not have wished to know the minutiae of what transpired in the British Army's undercover war, but they received briefings about its successes and controversial tactics. They also knew the credentials of Brigadier Frank Kitson, the man who spearheaded the plan and whose ideas shaped it.

The concept of counter-insurgency had its roots in British colonial warfare in Malaya, Kenya, Oman and Aden. It was, perhaps, inevitable that an army with such a past would seek to apply what it had learned to Northern Ireland. In 1969, the British Army arrived in force in Northern Ireland, with no experience of dealing with strife within the United Kingdom. Therefore, generals relied on their colonial past. That was self-evident with the arrival in power of the Heath Government in

June 1970 and Heath's belief that it was up to the Army to find a solution. A month later, during the Lower Falls Curfew, the Army behaved as though it were operating in Cyprus. It was not simply, in the words of General Carver, 'a crude operation' but one that was lifted directly from a colonial military handbook. One year later, the introduction of internment, the use of hooding suspects, special interrogation methods and an overall abuse of power showed that Army strategy was part of a continuum of an earlier military mindset. It would be much too easy to attribute the failure of the Army during that period to its generals. The real failure lay with the Conservative Government in London and two men in particular – Prime Minister Edward Heath and his Home Secretary, Reginald Maudling. They abdicated responsibility for finding a political solution and told the Army to sort out the situation. The British Army had successfully done just that in previous 'emergencies' but those campaigns were not within the 'gates of Rome' – the streets of the United Kingdom. As a consequence, the Army could only do what it had been trained to do and counter-insurgency was one of its preferred tactics.

An early indication of Heath's failure to monitor the activities of the Army and its intelligence wing occurred at the time of internment without trial in August 1971. Prior to the arrest of suspects, the intelligence wing devised a plan to use 'special' interrogation techniques against 12 of the first batch of suspects as a precursor to a much wider policy. The 'special' techniques were the use of hooding and white noise. According to General Carver, he was not informed about it. Heath later denied knowing about it, yet his Intelligence Coordinator, Sir Dick White, was kept informed about it from the outset of its planning.

When the British generals decided to use more unorthodox methods to deal with the conflict, they turned to Brigadier Frank Kitson, one of their most secretive and revered figures. He arrived in Northern Ireland in 1970 in command of 39 Brigade and, given that it was the early stages of the conflict, his appointment was indicative of a belief within the higher echelons of the military that his special expertise was the required panacea. That leads one to conclude that the Army had clearly defined its enemy and its role was no longer one of containment or restoring civil order by keeping the communities from killing each other.

The Army top brass regarded Kitson as a precise, experienced military thinker. He had distinguished himself in Kenya, Cyprus and Oman. In those areas of conflict he was credited with developing the counter-gang aspect of counter-insurgency warfare. That involved the creation of special units of terrorist agent irregulars. In colonial 'emergencies', they were recruited from enemy ranks after they had been identified as suitable fodder during lengthy, intense interrogations. Regular British Army personnel supervised the 'gangs'. They often committed crimes, which were blamed on insurgents as a means of criminalising them. Another important facet of the Kitson strategy was to generate terror in order to detach the local population from the rebels in its midst.

Before his arrival in Northern Ireland, Kitson had been at Oxford University writing a book, *Low Intensity Operations – Subversion, Insurgency and Peacekeeping*, one of the central themes of which was the need for the British Army to create a specialist force to combat insurgency. He even envisaged a situation in which the Army's conventional role would prove inadequate in dealing with internal strife within the United Kingdom. That illustration of his foresight, combined with his military record, convinced his superiors that he was the person equipped to devise a policy for dealing with subversives in Northern Ireland.

A striking aspect of his posting was that he was not a general but that did not matter. As Commander of 39 Brigade, he had the flexibility afforded to a general. Generals and officers of lower ranks I have spoken to over the years speak with awe when his name is mentioned, yet he has studiously avoided the media and has never publicly sought to vindicate his past. His counter-insurgency theories were widely circulated in the upper ranks of the Army before 1970 and parts of his book were read at secret Military Intelligence seminars. The book offers a valuable insight into the specialist force he had in mind and how his 'formula' for success could be applied to Northern Ireland:

> An effective way of dealing with the problem would be to establish a unit which would carry out the two separate functions of setting up or reinforcing the intelligence organisation and of providing men trained in operations designed to develop information by special means. If a unit of this kind were formed the element designed to set up or reinforce the intelligence organisation would consist of a number of officers available to move at short notice when needed. These men would be majors or captains and they would be backed by a number of other ranks to act as drivers and clerks. The unit would be a relatively large one in which case there might be three or four groups each consisting of a major and several captains, the major being intended for deployment to a provincial or county intelligence headquarters,

and the captains to districts; a unit of this size would be commanded by a lieutenant-colonel or senior major who could deploy to the intelligence headquarters of the country concerned.

In his book, Kitson ruminated about the teams, which would be built by the men he described above. They would be comprised of mostly younger men and be divided into cells.

> The actual organisation of the cadre must be geared to the fact that, once deployed, the men in it will be used to direct indigenous teams rather than to operate themselves. On this assumption, it should be in a position to provide a number of cells, each consisting of an officer and one or two training sergeants.

His vision was for a small number of SAS specialists, whom he had recently served with in Oman, to form the nucleus of a counter-insurgency psychological unit. These specialists would set up the cells, or smaller units, with one officer and two sergeants. He provided a diagram of the command structure of such a unit. It would, he said, operate independently of the regular army on the scene. The purpose of special units would be shaped by the overall situation, but the smaller units – officer, two sergeants and a driver – would be deployed for undercover intelligence tasks. In particular, he emphasised that independence was a central function of his plan and as Commander of 39 Brigade he had all the independence he needed.

On his arrival, he began setting up the MRF. It is worth noting that the initials, MRF, have come to mean different things over the years. A court in 1973 was told that it stood for Military Reconnaissance Force yet it was also known as the Mobile Reconnaissance Force. The IRA preferred to call it the Military Reaction Force. Within the Army's inner sanctum, it was sometimes jokingly called the 'Bomb Squad'. Years later, it became 14th Intelligence Company, sometimes listed as 14 Int. As with many military/intelligence undercover organisations during the Troubles, name changes were often deliberate attempts at deception by intelligence agencies and British Governments to disguise the origins and dubious activities of various groupings.

On the moment journalists discovered the existence of an undercover organisation, the official response was that 'it had been disbanded'. A striking example was the story of an MRF-type unit, 4 Field Survey Troop. It had a seemingly innocuous and non-lethal name for a unit involved in highly dubious shootings in South Armagh. The unit's headquarters were located at Castledillon and some of its personnel operated across the Irish border in contravention of the Irish Republic's territorial integrity.

When questions were later asked in the Westminster Parliament about the activities of the unit, the response from Roger Freeman, Parliamentary Under-Secretary for the Armed Forces, was typical of the deception to which I have referred. He insisted that the unit existed from 1973 and was disbanded in 1975. He claimed that all documentation relating to it had been shredded in accordance with 'normal procedures'. Asked to elaborate on the work of the unit, he replied that it had been part of the Royal Engineers regiment, involved in map-reading and aerial photography. It was an explanation unworthy of a parliamentarian. To add to the mystery, no such Troop Survey Unit was listed as part of the Royal Engineers at that time.

Two killings by Kitson's MRF personnel in 1972 raised the spectre that his specialist unit was not simply designed for reconnaissance and intelligence gathering. Before those killings happened, an episode not deemed at that time to reflect a new military strategy illustrated the cowboy nature of MRF soldiers and the orders under which they were operating.

On the morning of 15 April, two Catholic brothers, Gerry and John Conway, were walking citywards on the Whiterock Road in the Ballymurphy area. They had made the trip each Monday to Friday on their way to catch a bus to Belfast city centre where they had a stall for selling fruit and vegetables. As they casually strolled and chatted, they were unaware that they were being observed from a car travelling slowly in their direction. When they reached the junction of Whiterock Road and Ballymurphy Road, they turned to see the car speeding towards them and slamming to a halt. The brothers, fearing loyalists were about to kill them, began running as three men jumped out of the car. Almost immediately, bullets whizzed past the brothers as they tried to seek the shelter of an alley between houses. Both of them were hit but not seriously wounded. One of the gunmen in pursuit continued firing. Residents of the neighbourhood rushed into the street to the aid of the Conway brothers and the gunmen backed off towards their car.

Within minutes, as the gunmen stood beside their car, two Saracens — armoured personnel carriers — arrived on the scene with an ambulance, which transferred the two injured men to hospital. Locals later described the gunmen as dressed in grey trousers and ribbed, brown pullovers. The gunman who pursued the Conway brothers was said to be fair-haired. After the shooting, he was seen standing beside his car talking into a microphone. Once regular soldiers were on the scene, a uniformed officer told one of the gunmen, 'You've got the wrong bloody men.' Their targets had not been the Conways but Provisional IRA gunmen Jim Bryson and Tommy 'Todler' Tolan, who had escaped two months earlier from the Maidstone prison ship. One of the Conways was said to have resembled Jim Bryson.

Within 30 minutes of the incident, the Army 'Press Desk' at Lisburn headquarters issued a damage-limitation statement in accordance with policy instituted by Kitson in respect of any shootings by MRF personnel. The statement claimed that a 'mobile patrol' had encountered men on the Whiterock Road and one of the men was on the Army's wanted list. The patrol had come under fire and returned fire, wounding one man who dropped his pistol and escaped. It was a tissue of lies and a major feature of military accounts of many undercover shootings then and in subsequent years.

The gunmen in the car that day were MRF personnel in a structure Kitson had outlined in his book. There was a driver, a junior officer and two sergeants. Their 'back up', in the form of personnel ready to control media reporting of the episode, was an integral part of the psychological operations unit envisaged by Kitson. In the reflex news environment of Northern Ireland, it was British Army policy to shape the public's understanding of events in a fashion that suited strategy. It was considered essential to distort the truth when necessary, even if future events might conflict with the real-time accounts. Put simply, it was about telling a big lie, knowing that the truth would later be swamped in a plethora of reports about other incidents.

In this particular shooting, as in others, it was cleverly claimed that a third person – a gunman who had fired on the MRF unit – had escaped. No attempt was made to find the gun allegedly dropped by the third person or to interview the Conway brothers. In fact, no forensic tests were carried out on the clothing of the Conways because the Army knew they had shot the wrong men. The targets for assassination were Bryson and Tolan. There were other questionable shootings at that time when no Army statement was issued and people were deliberately encouraged to believe that the perpetrators were loyalists. In this incident, the MRF unit remained on the scene because they thought they had successfully taken down two of the most important IRA men in Belfast. They wanted to ensure that, even though they were injured, they did not escape with the help of locals.

One month later, on the night of 12 May, vigilantes from the Catholic ex-Servicemen's Association were manning a barricade on Finaghy Road North in West Belfast. They were chatting and smoking when a fellow member of CESA, 44-year-old Patrick McVeigh joined them. None of the group was armed. Their role was to alert people in the event of a loyalist attack on the area, though rumour had been circulating for some time that strange cars, possibly with military personnel on board, had been seen cruising streets in the district. The naiveté of the men at that barricade symbolised the period. In reality, they were not capable of thwarting an attack by gunmen or bombers. The presence of CESA personnel at barricades was merely an attempt by the organisation to demonstrate to loyalists that its former British soldiers, all of them Catholic, were experienced at defence. It was bravado rather than a serious belief that men like McVeigh, a father of six children, could stop a bullet.

On the night of 12 May, it was too late for McVeigh and his companions to take cover when a car approached and automatic fire was directed from it. The car sped off, did a U-turn and passed the scene of the shooting. It then travelled at speed along Riverdale Park South towards the Lisburn Road, leaving McVeigh dying in a pool of blood. Four of his companions were injured. Within minutes, as in the Conway brothers shooting, regular troops were at the barricade. An hour later, the Army's 'Press Desk' issued a statement to the media that five men had been shot after a one-hour gun-battle between troops and the IRA. The following morning, a second statement alleged that when soldiers reached the barricade, McVeigh had already been removed from the scene and the other injured transferred to Musgrave Park Hospital.

By the time that second statement was released, Kitson's MRF personnel, headquartered at Lisburn to handle media coverage of their operations, knew that regular soldiers had not found weapons beside the bodies of McVeigh and the other injured. That was not to be the end of the fabrication of a story. A third statement was released, attributing the attack on the CESA personnel to 'persons unknown', a military euphemism for loyalist paramilitaries. A high-ranking police officer, disgruntled with the Army's version of events, leaked details about the four wounded and identified the shooters as British Army operatives.

The readiness of the Army and Kitson's MRF to lie and cover up their complicity in murder and attempted murder was only matched by the way they manipulated the judicial process. They displayed little regard for the truth and that travesty was designed to protect the MRF, at all costs, from scrutiny and accountability.

In December 1972, the Army accepted responsibility for the killing of

McVeigh and the wounding of the others, an admission which was totally at variance with previously published statements from the 'Press Desk'. If the admission appeared to reflect a contrite position, it was not genuine. Statements alleged to have been taken from soldiers involved in the drive-by shooting were read to an inquest but the soldiers in question were not made available for cross-examination by lawyers representing Mrs McVeigh and the other families. The soldiers, in their statements, claimed that one of the vigilantes had fired at them but did not name a suspect or imply that it was McVeigh or any of the four who were wounded. Like so much of the military fiction of the time, and reflected in the statements issued after the shooting of the Conway brothers, there was left open the suggestion that a gunman, not identified, had fired and fled the scene.

The inquest heard from Detective Chief Superintendent Drew of the RUC that forensic tests were carried out on the clothing of the vigilantes and no lead residue was discovered to indicate that McVeigh and the four wounded had discharged a firearm. Drew also confirmed that he learned of the Army's role in the incident 12 hours after it happened. In total contrast, an Army officer gave evidence that, even though he arrived at the barricade minutes after the shooting, he had only learned of military involvement on the day of the inquest. Considering the fact that he would have been briefed by the Army's legal team before the inquest hearing, it seems unlikely he would not have known it was an Army operation until the moment he appeared in court. There is, however, another explanation if one is to believe his story. Kitson insisted that independence should be a core ingredient in his 'formula'. That would, as a consequence, have ensured that regular Army officers, and this one in particular, were kept in the dark about the MRF. It is also possible to reach that conclusion in light of the fact that no mention of the existence of the MRF was made to the inquest court. The impression was left, with all present, that the shooters were regular soldiers. An Army witness told the coroner that no action had been taken against them.

In this instance, as in others, it was clear that legal advisers to the MRF had spent some time constructing an apparent admission of guilt wrapped in a tissue of deceit. After the fact, as statements in the wake of the shooting demonstrated, the Army, especially those tasked to provide cover stories for the MRF, was adept at constructing plausible accounts of events.

One has to see the willingness of MRF teams to kill without fear of legal retribution as a serious misuse of the judicial process and a clear policy that reached very high into the politico-military apparatus. MRF soldiers in both the incidents I have described would not have been able to operate with apparent impunity unless men like Brigadier Frank Kitson had been accorded a carte blanche freedom of action. It was also feasible for the MRF in the sectarian lawlessness of 1971–73 to allow for some of their operations to be attributed to 'persons unknown'. That is not to argue that elements of the British Army, including the MRF, were responsible for many sectarian killings but it leaves open more than just a possibility that some of the assassinations they carried out were wrongly deemed to be the work of the UDA and UVF.

Events in the early hours of Wednesday, 27 September 1972 further spoke of the presence of trigger men in the ranks of the British Army. At 15 minutes past midnight, two Catholics, Daniel Rooney, 19, and his friend, Brendan Brennan, 18, were shot from a passing car in the Falls area. They were standing at St James Crescent and St Katherine's Road when two cars approached. A burst of gunfire from the second car cut down both men. Rooney died later in hospital and, though seriously wounded, Brennan survived. In time to capture the morning headlines, the Army's 'Press Desk' issued a statement about the shooting. Like previous statements, it was alleged that shots were fired at a 'surveillance patrol and two hits were claimed' by soldiers in the patrol.

Within 12 hours of the shooting, Lieutenant Colonel Robin Eveleigh of the Royal Green Jackets, stationed in the area where the shooting had taken place, confidently announced to journalists that Daniel Rooney had been an IRA gunman. That was easy to allege, given that Rooney was dead. Eveleigh also explained that 'plain-clothes soldiers' operated in the area for purposes of 'reconnaissance'. They were, he added, in place to 'see what the IRA were doing'. He then went on to claim, with some confidence, that Brennan had, in the past, been seen by one of his soldiers in possession of a gun. It was alleged he had even boasted to soldiers from previous regiments that he had shot soldiers. Eveleigh, for the benefit of the media, produced a bullet-riddled car and said it was the one fired on by Rooney and Brennan. It later transpired that these allegations against Brennan and Rooney had no foundation in fact.

Either Lieutenant Colonel Eveleigh had been badly briefed or his mouth worked faster than his brain. He had not figured on the fact that there was credible eyewitness testimony which provided an entirely different account of events. Rooney's 22-year-old sister, Mary, was crossing the street to her brother when she saw a burst of gunfire from a car that drove past him. There were other witnesses who observed cars cruising the neighbourhood days prior to the shooting. The body of evidence to contradict Eveleigh was so compelling that it was submitted to the Human Rights Court at Strasbourg by the Attorney General of the Irish Republic.

One is obliged to ask if Kitson, in his grand design of a specialist unit, mistakenly recruited soldiers who proved unpredictable and whether the lack of a legalistic oversight of the MRF led to the shootings I have outlined. In other words, were MRF teams given a loose set of guidelines easily interpreted as a policy to assassinate at will suspects on the Army's wanted lists? Was there an assassination policy in place?

On the latter point, I found no evidence, but there was a strategy that permitted assassinations. Kitson's colonial experience and his choice of men to lead his mobile teams may well have hampered his judgment and allowed for a cowboy mentality to develop within MRF squads. Some of those he chose were selected from a 'trawling mission' within the ranks of soldiers who had operated in the insurgency campaign in Oman. Others were discovered in a search for Ulster-born soldiers in regular regiments.

Northern Ireland was not the jungles of Kenya, the streets of Cyprus and Aden or the desert of Oman, it was an integral part of the United Kingdom with media scrutinising the conflict. Later, rather than sooner, that would open a window into the world of Kitson and the MRF. I am inclined to the view that Kitson's MRF experiment was, from the outset, open to abuse. While he may have thought he was establishing a specialist counter-insurgency combat unit, he was placing gung-ho trigger men on the streets. Their independence from the regular British Army gave them an imprimatur to operate wildly. They were clearly confident that a higher structure was in place to fabricate accounts of their operations and protect them from the normal rule of law.

Some journalists, long after the MRF became 14th Intelligence Company, described MRF operations as a 'series of cock-ups'. That view originated in attempts by the British Military to retrospectively deflect from the truth of MRF operations. The three shootings I have outlined were not 'cock-ups' and such a term unreasonably diminishes the culpability of the Army Command and the British Government.

The existence of the MRF was revealed in Belfast's High Court in June 1973 as a result of an incident on the Glen Road in West Belfast in June of the previous year. It involved, once again, shots fired from a passing car at a group of Catholic taxi-drivers at a bus stop. A bullet entered the bedroom of a nearby house, wounding a man lying in bed. News coverage of the shooting attributed it to loyalists and then to a feud between the two wings of the IRA.

The most intriguing aspect of this shooting on 22 June 1972 is that it occurred two days after Prime Minister Edward Heath's Northern Ireland Secretary, William Whitelaw, sent two of his aides to meet IRA leaders, David O'Connell and Gerry Adams. Whitelaw's intention was to hammer out details for an IRA cease-fire to precede formal talks between the IRA and the British Government. As I pointed out in an earlier chapter, there were people within the military apparatus opposed to an IRA cease-fire. The shooting by the MRF could have been aimed at scuppering talks by initiating a feud between the Provisionals and the Officials, or encouraging the Provisionals to engage in a tit-for-tat war with loyalists. None of those potential consequences happened at that stage.

The Provisionals confronted Whitelaw's aides about the shooting. They pointed out it was Army-inspired and demanded action. Whitelaw ordered that those responsible be brought to justice. Some RUC detectives, who for some time had felt that Army undercover patrols were operating without any normal controls, shared his concern. They had witnessed the shootings described and were powerless to properly investigate them. Their inability to penetrate the MRF to interview the shooters was compounded by the fact that RUC Special Branch worked closely with Kitson's teams, especially ones devoted to even more secret operations. When detectives asked to speak to soldiers, the requests were regularly denied. When they were given access, it often proved futile because the soldiers in question had been debriefed with the assistance of the Army's legal advisers. Pressure not to prosecute was also applied to the Prosecution Service at a very high political level. Nonetheless, Whitelaw believed elements of the Army were deliberately sabotaging his efforts in Northern Ireland. On a Sunday morning, he stormed into the sleeping quarters of a general and lambasted him for leaking disinformation to the media to compromise the political process.

In July 1973, I was one of several journalists covering the Belfast Magistrates' Court when two members of the MRF were escorted into the dock. They were Captain James Allister McGregor, 29, and Sergeant Clive Graham Williams, 25. McGregor was charged with possessing a Thompson sub-machine gun and ammunition. Williams faced the same charge but more serious charges were included in his indictment – the attempted murder of three men and the wounding of a fourth.

Several months later, in the same court, charges of possessing a Thompson sub-machine gun and ammunition were dropped against the MRF officers. McGregor was freed and Williams was left to face the more serious charges. Little attention was given to the fact that both men had been in possession of a Thompson, the favoured weapon of the IRA. It was a cumbersome .45 calibre weapon compared with the Army's regular-issue Sterling.

When Williams entered the dock alone at Belfast High Court, he claimed that he was a former military policeman and, in June 1972, was commander of a unit of the Army's Military Reconnaissance Force attached to 39 Brigade. He did not refer to it as the Mobile Reconnaissance Force and specified that its role was surveillance in areas difficult for regular troops to operate.

His evidence was tailored to reveal as little as possible about the MRF. That was achieved in the months prior to the hearing while he was on bail and was coached by the Army's legal advisers. He told the court that there were 40 men in the MRF in June 1972. They had 'civilian powers' to move about areas and possessed their own armoury. There were 15 men in his unit, divided into squads of two or four. They operated in civilian-type vehicles.

He went on to explain that at the time of the shooting on the Glen Road he had received a fresh intake of 'members'. He briefed them that morning before taking them to a firing range for weapons training. The weapons he chose for the exercise were standard Army-issue guns and ones used by terrorists, in particular the Thompson sub-machine gun.

In telling the story about the weapons training and the use of a Thompson, he cleverly inserted a significant element of his defence. However, one must wonder how, during a brief training spell with many guns, he was able to train new recruits in the use of a Thompson. The fact is that the inclusion of the Thompson accounted for his use of it at the shooting of 22 June.

He conveniently told the court that, when the weapons training session at Kinnegar Firing Range ended, he asked technicians to fix a radio in his car. That implied that he was engaged in so many tasks that morning that he was not planning an operation. Instead, he gave orders for two MRF squads to patrol the city centre and Andersonstown. When he began the journey back from Lisburn to his base at Palace Barracks with some of the new recruits, the Thompson was concealed in a bag under the rear seat. He knew about it and intended returning it to the MRF's personal armoury at Palace Barracks. If that was so, why not all the other weapons on the firing range? Why just the Thompson? Those questions were not put to him.

In order to explain why he took a detour through the heavily populated Andersonstown on his way back to base, he said that it was to familiarise the new recruits with enemy territory. Normally he would not, he said, have made such a detour.

Asked by Counsel why the Thompson had been wrapped and hidden under the rear seat of his car, he responded that regular soldiers 'are our biggest enemy because if a gun is seen in a vehicle, they will open fire and we will be dead'. He added that MRF squads were normally issued with automatic pistols and, or, Sterling sub-machine guns. On that day, he made two 'passes' through the Andersonstown and Suffolk districts and ordered another squad to drive down the Glen Road. That squad radioed him that they had seen a man with a pistol at the Bunbeg bus terminus on the Glen Road. He told the other squad to make another 'pass' and they radioed back with the same observation. Williams decided to investigate and, as he approached the bus terminus, he came under fire from what he judged to be the gunman.

The trial judge in the case, Ambrose MacGonigal, bears mention because he was a former member of the elite British Special Boat Squadron. His brother, Eoin, had died in the first Long Range Desert Group operation in North Africa during the Second World War. The LRD had been the forerunner of the Special Air Service (SAS). Judge MacGonigal, as I discovered in covering trials over which he presided, had a reputation for favouring the evidence of British Army witnesses. I learned that during a trial intermission he was so angry with a soldier who wilted under defence cross-examination that he took off his wig and flung it across his Chambers. Williams did not need much help from MacGonigal. It was enough for him to tell the court that his reason for opening fire that day was that a gunman had fired at him.

Some of what he told the court about the MRF was accurate, especially the structure of its mobile squads and the figure of 40 men attached to his unit. However, it is what he kept secret that really matters in a complete evaluation of the organisation. He walked from court a free man but it is not known if he returned to the MRF.

The main base of MRF operations was in the centre of Palace Barracks at Holywood on the outskirts of Belfast and was supported by psychological operations personnel located at Army HQ in Lisburn. The Psychops specialists liaised with Special Branch and other elements of Military Intelligence and compiled data on suspects. They also fed disinformation to the media in the form of cover stories in the wake of MRF operations. The MRF's reach extended well beyond Belfast into cities like Derry but its major operations were in Greater Belfast.

Names like OP Whiterock were given to MRF teams who concentrated solely on the Ballymurphy area and that included mobile squads of the type involved in the shooting of the Conway brothers. There were also teams devoted to running operations with the MRF's 'irregulars' – informers and terrorist agents. The 'irregulars', most of whom were trained by MRF operatives, provided targeting information in the areas from which they originated and also took part in limited operations. Sometimes they would be hidden in armoured personnel carriers and driven through areas to spot and identify suspects. From time to time, they were taken to interrogations and, from concealment, were asked to provide information on suspects being questioned by Special Branch officers.

In a village near Strabane, the MRF ran a small transport and plant company as a front for maintaining cross-border surveillance on the IRA and to identify republicans who were known to be involved in smuggling. A former intelligence operative told me it was 'an ideal front because we could not trust Customs and Excise. It allowed our people to move around unhindered.'

The history of the MRF and its shadowy world of sex, terrorist agents and dubious operations is the stuff of fiction. It was only opened up to scrutiny because of the intelligence war between the Provisional IRA's internal security apparatus and Kitson's squads. According to IRA Intelligence, their insights into the MRF resulted from events in the Lower Falls in Belfast in the summer of 1972. It was then that the Intelligence Officer, D Company, 2nd Battalion of the Provisional IRA, expressed reservations about Seamus Wright, a married man in his 20s from a well-known republican family. Wright was regarded as a committed and experienced active service volunteer in an IRA Company which had gained a reputation for killing soldiers. In the months leading up to the summer, D Company units were also involved in the massive bombing of commercial targets in the city centre and were constantly the target for MRF surveillance. The threat posed by D Company units had not escaped Kitson and regular arrest swoops were ordered to disrupt their activities and identify leading operatives. Sometimes, those detained were screened along the lines used by Kitson's operatives in Kenya and Oman and MRF 'irregulars' were used to help build dossiers on men believed to be vulnerable to recruitment.

The Provisional IRA's Belfast Brigade was familiar with the Army's technique of recruiting informers and handed the task of rooting them out to its Internal Security personnel. The IRA mole-hunters maintained contact with the Intelligence officers of companies and battalions in the Belfast area and were ready at any time to interrogate and execute suspected spies. In the violent atmosphere of 1972, rumour was rife and there was incipient paranoia about the numbers of informers in the ranks of the IRA. A scintilla of evidence was often enough for the mole-hunters to execute anyone suspected of working for the Army or Special Branch. In many respects, the members of the Internal Security department were similar to Mafia-type enforcers.

Kitson's interrogation experts concentrated on recruiting 'irregulars' in their early 20s. It was believed that older members of the IRA with experience of previous conflict and incarceration would not break easily under intense interrogation, threats of blackmail or blandishments in the form of cash or a promise of a new life outside the country. In 1972, the IRA had not developed anti-interrogation techniques or a sophisticated internal security apparatus but that would change when it learned about the secret world of the MRF.

Seamus Wright's absences from his stomping ground in the Lower Falls were the catalyst for bringing him to the attention of the D Company Intelligence Officer. In accordance with IRA rules, the IO mentioned the matter to his Officer Commanding who suggested that a 'casual watch' be kept on Wright. The IO interpreted that to mean constant surveillance. After Wright was arrested by the Army, held for questioning and released, the IO, as a normal procedure, decided to question him. Wright complained that the Army had given him a rough time and asked him to name leading members of D Company but he had refused. It sounded like a reasonable explanation and nothing in his demeanour suggested he was lying. However, the IO intuitively felt it wise to maintain a watch on his fellow volunteer.

A short time later, Wright was again reported absent when other volunteers went looking for him to take part in an operation. The IO paid a visit to his wife who said her husband was in England looking for work and produced a letter from him, stamped with an English postmark. At that time, there was no mandate preventing members of the IRA from leaving the country to seek employment but the IO expected that, even as a courtesy, Wright should have informed him he was not going to be available for action. That is where the matter rested for several weeks until the IO once more spoke to Mrs Wright. She explained her husband was still on a job search and she hoped to join him in England when he found work. More time passed, with no sightings of Wright, and the IO spoke to one of Wright's neighbours. The neighbour revealed that Mrs Wright had been 'away on a trip but was now home'. She had told neighbours that she had visited her husband in England but had no desire to settle there. Within weeks, Seamus Wright returned home and resurfaced in his old haunts in the Lower Falls. The IO had become deeply suspicious, due in part to the fact that, during the period he had Wright in his sights, there had been a series of damaging arrests of D Company operatives, weapons seizures and missions compromised. The only volunteer he could identify with erratic behaviour was Wright. The IO took his concerns to his OC who ordered Wright's arrest. Several armed volunteers seized Wright and took him to a house off Leeson Street in the Lower Falls. He was familiar with the drill, which often meant a brutal interrogation and a swift execution. Suspected informers were generally stripped to their underpants to humiliate them and to make them feel vulnerable under questioning. Frequently, more brutal methods were used.

A young woman whose father faced such an ordeal told me about interrogation techniques during my stay in a Belfast hotel in the mid 1990s. She said her father was submerged in water and a large quantity of alcohol forced down his throat before he was killed. Known in IRA circles as 'The Monkey', he ferried bombs into the city centre. His fate was sealed when Brendan Davison, a member of the IRA's Internal Security apparatus, fingered him as an informer. Davison was a terrorist agent and deliberately sacrificed 'The Monkey' to take the heat off himself. In a bitter twist of irony, loyalists later killed Davison, unaware that he was working for British Military Intelligence and Special Branch. The IRA, unaware of his treachery, gave him a massive send-off and buried him in its revered Republican Plot in Milltown Cemetery. When I revealed his double life in my book *The Dirty War*, I received death threats. A leading Provisional had his girlfriend pass a message to me that it would not be safe for me to be seen near the Markets area where Davison's supporters lived. Unfortunately, I worked at the BBC, a five-minute walk from that area.

The prospect of a brutal interrogation and a bullet to the back of the head did not frighten Seamus Wright. He shrewdly saw a way out of his predicament. As an MRF agent, he had learned that he had value, so why should that not apply to the IRA? It was a gamble and the only card in an otherwise stacked deck, so he decided to play it. A member of the IRA team involved in interrogating him disclosed to me: 'When we catch a guy who has been turned by the Brits, we know he knows he has a value to us. He has learned that by the very fact that the Brits have convinced him that he has a value. When you look at the two poles of the argument, he is expendable as far as both sides are concerned. When it comes to the sting, winning matters and not the survival of the double agent.'

Special Branch recruited Wright while he was being interrogated at Castlereagh holding facility. It was put to him that he had been involved in an explosion that killed a soldier. The evidence presented to him was enough to convince him that someone in the IRA had 'grassed'. He was offered immunity from prosecution in return for working for the authorities and agreed rather than face a prison term. Special Branch did not tell him who his new bosses would be but they had someone in mind. Special Branch officers at Castlereagh were constantly on the lookout for potential recruits for the MRF, illustrating the close links between the two groupings. I contend that of all the intelligence groupings in the shadowy undercover war of the Troubles, the most influential was

Special Branch. It was powerful because it controlled information. Like the Foreign Office that remains in place no matter which party finds itself in Government in the United Kingdom, Special Branch was intact irrespective of the changing personalities and structures of other intelligence bodies. It forged and maintained links to Military Intelligence units, as well as MI5 and MI6. It secretly ran its own agents and provided agents for the MRF, 14th Intelligence Company and others.

Wright was such an agent. After his interrogation, Special Branch officers transported him to a special MRF compound in the centre of Palace Barracks. There, he met young men like himself who were housed in military accommodation on the base. He was told that he was recruited to play a role in the 'defeat of all terrorism'. I assume the phrase 'all terrorism' was used to convince him that he was not going to be used in a war only directed at republicans. The phrase, I believe, was also designed to divest him of any feeling he may have had that his role was that of informer and traitor. Within 24 hours, he was flown to an Army base in England and trained in man-to-man surveillance techniques and how to shake off IRA scrutiny of his movements.

On his return to Belfast, he began his role as an agent, making frequent trips to the MRF compound to provide his handlers with information on D Company and other IRA units and operations in West Belfast. His trips to Palace Barracks were the 'absences' listed by the IO of D Company.

There was an amateurish aspect to the MRF's handling of agents like Wright. For example, his Special Branch handlers, working in conjunction with the MRF, encouraged him to write letters to his wife during extended stays at Palace Barracks. These were then posted from England and stamped with an English postmark. It was arranged for his wife to visit him at an accommodation address in London in the hope he could persuade her to live there. His MRF and Special Branch handlers felt that the presence of his wife in Belfast distracted him from his 'work' because he was constantly concerned about her safety. His extended stays at the MRF compound were necessitated by the work he was doing. Often, he was taken out in military vehicles, under concealment with a photographer, and asked to identify people he suspected or knew to be in the IRA.

In MRF parlance, he was a 'Fred'. There have been numerous explanations for the use of the term, including the fact that a Colonel Fred Allen, nicknamed 'Bald Eagle', was involved in intelligence work which overlapped with the MRF. Ian Rycroft, an officer familiar with the workings of the MRF, provided me with another explanation: 'The "Freds" referred to Fred Flintstone, a popular cartoon character.

Anyway, some of the touts looked like the Fred Flintstone family.'

Rycroft also told me that some of the MRF's Whiterock OP activities were 'hilarious in retrospect'. On the contrary, there was nothing laughable about Seamus Wright's dilemma. He was caught between both sides and was an expendable pawn in a dirty war. The MRF had never told him he would be executed if he did not work for them, but the IRA did. The Provisionals left him in no doubt that, if he did not become an IRA double agent, his wife could also be killed. He agreed and was encouraged to make regular trips to Palace Barracks. The IO primed him with information to pass to his handlers, such as the locations of small ammunition dumps. Wright was told the ploy would convince his Special Branch handlers of his loyalty to them.

Through Wright, the IRA learned a great deal about the modus operandi of Kitson's mobile teams and the use of 'Freds'. He told the IO about other 'Freds', some of them loyalists, adding that they did not associate freely and 'tended to avoid each other'. After several weeks as a double agent, Wright asked for a meeting with the IO, warning that he had important information. It turned out that he had heard MRF specialists talking in code about a secret operation which they said was very successful. Then, he provided a devastating piece of detail: 'There is a guy I have seen in the MRF compound and he is one of us. He comes and goes freely and even wears a pistol in a shoulder holster.'

Before the IO could ask the identity of the person, Wright blurted out the name, Kevin McKee. There was shock on the faces of the IO and his fellow interrogators. McKee was an IRA volunteer in his early 20s, based in the Ballymurphy area. More significantly, he was the nephew of Billy McKee, one of the revered founders of the Provisional IRA. The moment Kevin McKee became part of the equation, the IO, with approval from his OC, restricted knowledge of his operation to a tight grouping of IRA intelligence personnel. McKee was seized and his personal weapon removed. He told his captors he had bought it from friends of a dead IRA man. It was a pearl-handled pistol of a type not normally carried by IRA gunmen.

McKee broke under interrogation within 24 hours because he realised the IRA knew too much about his role in the MRF. He turned out to be a mine of information. His importance within the MRF was in part due to the enthusiasm he applied to the role of agent. Wright confirmed that McKee strutted around the MRF compound like one of the specialists. The MRF leadership probably treated him differently because he was the nephew of Billy McKee and had access to high-grade intelligence.

He revealed to his IRA interrogators that the MRF was running the Four Square Laundry service in West Belfast. It was a bogus operation that allowed them to collect clothing and forensically test it for lead residue and explosives traces before cleaning it and returning it to residents in a republican stronghold like Andersonstown. The Four Square was popular in Catholic areas because it provided an excellent service with prices that undercut competitors. He also talked about a massage parlour on the Antrim Road in the north of the city. A husband and wife team ran it. He was an ex-republican internee and she was Protestant. While she masturbated clients, or had sexual intercourse with them, she plied them with questions supplied by Special Branch officers. MRF electronic specialists recorded their replies in an upstairs room of the building.

McKee's revelations forced the D Company IO to refer the matter to his seniors on the IRA's Belfast Brigade. From that moment, the IRA moved swiftly to confirm McKee's information while an IRA squad moved Wright and McKee out of Belfast. McKee was placed in a cottage in a remote area of South Armagh.

Within five days, IRA surveillance of the Four Square Laundry and the massage parlour confirmed the accuracy of McKee's information. On 2 October, after a plan was approved by senior officers from the Belfast Brigade's three battalions, squads of IRA gunmen were dispatched to attack and kill operatives in a laundry van, personnel in the massage parlour and anyone at offices in College Square in the centre of the city.

The attack on the laundry van claimed the life of its driver, Sapper Ted Stuart, but his companion, Lance Corporal Sarah Warke, who had the task of knocking doors and collecting laundry, escaped. At 397 Antrim Road, the location of the massage parlour, the IRA operation was bungled when a gunman with a Thompson sub-machine gun slipped on a staircase, loosing off rounds from his weapon. A client in a waiting-room was shot and wounded as the IRA gunmen fled the scene. At College Square, gunmen found the MRF premises abandoned.

The IRA informed the McKee family that Kevin McKee's fate was sealed but his execution would not be made public because of the prominent role of his uncle in the IRA. Orders were sent to the location where he was held that he should be afforded Catholic last rites and secretly buried. A week later, a communication reached the IRA's Belfast Brigade that the family holding McKee had formed a close relationship with him and could not kill him. The IRA turned to Jim Bryson, the Ballymurphy OC, and he had no such qualms. Accompanied by his friend, Tommy 'Todler' Tolan, he went straight to the location. In accordance with the IRA's *Green Book* rules, Bryson informed McKee why he was about to be shot. A priest was summoned and, under cover of darkness beside a freshly dug grave, he read the last rites. McKee was forced to kneel, his hands tied behind his back and a hood covering his head. When the priest had heard McKee's last confession, Bryson and Tolan each fired a shot into the back of McKee's head.

One of the IRA men who was closely involved in the interrogation of McKee later told a senior Provisional that he could never fully understand some aspects of McKee's character. One was that McKee was clearly thrilled by the status afforded him within the MRF and the fact that he was permitted to carry a personal pistol. There was also his bravado until the very end of his life when he accepted his execution without protest. I was told by a senior IRA operative involved in the interrogations of Wright and McKee: 'McKee was naive, he was brash, and you knew he enjoyed his notoriety, his immunity, but what I will never understand is that he accepted death as if it was a fact of life.'

Wright was not the same personality. From all accounts, he was a married, family man unwittingly caught up in a web of intrigue. The demise of both young men was quickly described by the IRA as 'disappearances'. The Wright family was informed that Seamus vanished, the implication being that the Army removed him from the scene. I learned that, like McKee, he was also executed. Some years after Kevin McKee's death, his family got its wish and was told by the IRA where he was buried. His corpse was secretly dug up and removed to Milltown Cemetery in Belfast for a private burial. As for the Wright family, I am not in a position to state what happened to his remains though it is possible the same arrangement was made, since he was also from a prominent republican family. When I revealed in *The Dirty War* that Bryson executed McKee, I unknowingly created friction between family factions in Ballymurphy and was quietly warned by the IRA that it would be unwise for me to visit that district. The warning was not a threat and was conveyed as advice that some people in Ballymurphy might independently kill me if I was foolish enough to fall into their hands.

The IRA had temporarily dealt a serious blow to MRF operations. Through their interrogations of Wright and McKee, the organisation learned a great deal about the recruitment of terrorist agents from within IRA ranks. In order to further damage Kitson's 'formula' they passed the identities of loyalist 'Freds' to the UDA. However, the MRF continued to operate and went through a name change to 14th Intelligence Company in late spring of 1973. Kitson, the bête noir of the IRA, was moved out of Northern Ireland in April 1973, probably because his name had become too closely associated with counter-insurgency and provided the IRA with 'ammunition' in its ongoing propaganda war.

By then, the IRA was attributing every dirty trick to Kitson — incorrectly, I contend. For example they accused him of being the architect of internment without trial. That was untrue. He opposed the introduction of internment in August 1971 because he felt there was insufficient intelligence to make it successful. In that assertion, he was right because the Provisionals were unscathed by the policy through late '71 and into the summer of 1972. He would certainly have advocated its introduction in 1972 when men like Wright and McKee were providing much more critical information about the Provisional IRA.

In retrospect, Kitson instituted a strategy that was adopted and continued throughout the Troubles. During his time, the MRF liaised with 12 Intelligence Security Company based in Army HQ at Lisburn. It had upwards of 200 staff, maintained files on suspects as well as agents and provided legal advice and cover for operations. It also handled the campaign of disinformation and misinformation in the wake of shootings by the military. It was through 12 Intelligence Company that links were established with the Special Military Intelligence Unit comprised of a leadership of 70 officers and non-commissioned personnel. The SMIU was a mechanism intended to bring together Special Branch and other intelligence groupings in a sharing of information. Ironically, its men on the ground often worked independently and were rarely in place long enough to hone their skills or ensure the long-term safety of agents. Their independence, like that of the MRF, allowed for dubious operations. Included in the mix were the two major intelligence services, MI5 and MI6, further complicating the overall sharing, distribution and effectiveness of intelligence.

The MRF, under Kitson, established close links with MI5 and not MI6, whose 'meddling' in Northern Ireland was outside its remit as a foreign intelligence body. Its area of responsibility was the Irish Republic but it had, from the end of the Second World War, run Cold War agents in Northern Ireland. It was especially concerned about the Marxist leanings of the Official IRA in the '60s. At that time, MI5 paid little attention to Northern Ireland, depending on information from RUC Special Branch. It was only with the outbreak of the Troubles that MI5 chose to assert its legislative right to claim Northern Ireland as its turf.

The lack of political and judicial oversight of the activities of the intelligence community from the early 1970s onwards led to serious abuses and the running of terrorist agents in a counter-gang strategy. Kitson was not only the architect of a counter-insurgency 'formula', he was the man who set in place a mindset and modus operandi which did not dissolve with his departure. In fact, it became even more sophisticated. We may never know how many illegal operations were conducted but an examination of the trigger men in the ranks in the early '70s allows for reasonable deductions that there were many more than I have outlined. With the exposure of the terrorist agent Brian Nelson in the late 1980s, there was clearly a direct link to a strategy which began 20 years earlier under the leadership of Frank Kitson.

3

ASSASSIN IN THE RANKS

Some years ago, a former member of the SAS Regiment who had served in Oman in the late 1960s and early '70s contacted me. He had been part of what was called the 'British Army Training Team' (Batt). In the late '60s it was under the command of Major General Timothy Creasey. Team (Batt) was involved in training enemy 'irregulars' to fight in support of Britain's close friend in the Middle East, the Sultan of Oman. US Special Forces from Fort Bragg in North Carolina were also there for joint counter-insurgency exercises with their British counterparts. At that time, the British Army had a longer history of running counter-terror operations than any other Western country. This SAS source told me: 'We were in Oman to train our own people and enemy insurgents – recruited as "irregulars". Soldiers from regular regiments were sent to learn from specialists like me and US Special Forces got training from us.'

He further explained that, after he retired, he read two of my books – *Political Murder* and *The Dirty War* – and was intrigued to see references to a soldier he had known in Oman. That soldier was Albert Walker Baker who had served under him. Walker Baker later claimed he had gone AWOL from his regiment before he resurfaced in the ranks of the UDA in East Belfast in 1972. My SAS source, a native of Belfast, was intrigued by that claim. 'When I read what you wrote about him, I could not believe my eyes. I remembered him as a young guy who hailed from my hometown. I saw him as a committed soldier and not the type to go AWOL or get involved in that kind of terrorist stuff back home. He was tough and had good training in Oman but he didn't have to use it against his own people.'

Albert Walker Baker was 22 when he returned to his native Belfast during a period of considerable turmoil. He had acquired an English accent but that was the only feature which seemed to distinguish him from his Belfast roots. His arrival in the Province coincided with a search for Ulster-born soldiers in Oman and regular British regiments. Ian Rycroft who served in Team (Batt) was aware of the search. 'Quite a number of guys who served in Ulster in the early '70s were in Oman before and after their tours. There was quite a trawl round British regiments for Ulstermen.'

The exact date Walker Baker returned home remains a mystery but evidence suggests it was some time between January and April 1972. He quickly adapted to the streets of East Belfast where criminality and paramilitary activity strangled the political climate. Throughout the city, assassins on both sides were venting their anger and exacting revenge. A major campaign of sectarian assassinations was in its infancy and the major culprits were the UDA/UVF and Red Hand Commando. It was the period of post-internment violence, Bloody Sunday and the collapse of the Unionist-dominated Stormont Government. The UDA was steadily becoming the largest paramilitary body, boasting a membership of 50,000 men. It was also an organisation run by thugs and criminals. There was no vetting of recruits and young men, many of them with criminal records for assault, burglary and theft, flocked to the UDA's headquarters on the Newtownards Road in East Belfast to join up.

There was, at that time, a genuine fear within the Protestant community that its political world was collapsing and, with it, everything Protestants had striven to defend, including their religious and cultural heritage. They had watched the increasing level of Provisional IRA violence and felt it was time to strike back.

Walker Baker's military training made him an ideal UDA recruit. He had no difficulty being accepted because he had a personal military weapon and the ability to train young men in the UDA ranks. However, it was his swagger, self-confidence and willingness to delve into the seamier side of life on the streets which quickly endeared him to UDA leaders.

The episode that cemented his reputation as a tough guy was a robbery at the Vulcan Bar on the Newtownards Road, not far from UDA HQ. He walked into the bar with three UDA thugs, slammed his .45 pistol on the counter and demanded the takings. The bartender handed over £821. The robbery was symptomatic of the character of the UDA, which promoted racketeering and extortion. The funds from criminal enterprises never found their way into the coffers of the organisation to purchase arms but into the pockets of many of the leaders. Collections for loyalist prisoners were also regarded as spoils.

The confident way Walker Baker carried out the robbery, without a disguise, enhanced his status and also demonstrated that bar and business owners lived under a reign of terror. Tommy Herron, the UDA leader in East Belfast, was impressed by Walker Baker's brazenness. He was even more impressed by his military training and his boasts of how he had learned to kill while in the Army and during a tour of duty overseas. Within a short time, the soldier who told Herron he had taken time out from his regiment to help the loyalist cause, became a constant feature in the UDA leader's life. Recognising his propensity for violence, his knowledge of weapons and killing skills, Herron made him his personal bodyguard.

That role took Walker Baker into the higher echelons of the UDA, especially its oversight committee, the Inner Council. It was made up of Herron and senior UDA figures from across Northern Ireland who had carved out their own turf. Some even gave themselves grandiose ranks such as Lieutenant Colonel and Brigadier as if they were running a disciplined army, but that was far from the reality.

Walker Baker loved the role of bodyguard and the freedom it gave him to strut around bars and UDA HQ with his personal weapon on view. He was especially pleased to be able to provide security when the Inner Council met in the Girton Lodge and Park Avenue hotels in East Belfast. Their meetings were to discuss strategy, sort out turf wars, discuss past and future killings and, above all, carve up the spoils of war. Walker Baker later spoke about his bodyguard position, with reference to the Girton Lodge hotel.

'I was bodyguard for the Inner Circle. I knew Tommy Herron, Andy Tyrie and Ned McCleary, the whole lot of them. I was their bodyguard. I used to do security on the whole territory and there was me, —, —, — and a few others who were also doing security at the hotel. We'd move into the hotel and fake the waiters' coats and things. We'd be armed and we'd be walking through the hotel and down the lobbies and corridors underneath.'

While their bodyguards patrolled at the Girton Lodge, members of the Inner Council consumed large quantities of alcohol, served by bona fide hotel waiters. In April, during an Inner Council meeting, one of the waiters, Philip Anthony Fay, came to the attention of Herron. Walker Baker later remembered the episode. 'The Inner Council was in this room and ordered drinks and Fay came with the drinks, and Tommy Herron – I don't know where he got the information – but he found out the geezer was a Catholic. He ordered his assassination in case he heard anything.'

Nineteen-year-old Philip Fay was indeed a Catholic and it was not the first time he had been summoned to carry large trays of drinks to the Inner Council 'suite'. Fay was one of those naive young victims of the early days of the Troubles who was oblivious to the dangers lurking in the workplace, or for that matter in the area where he lived. His ignorance of the sectarian complexities of Belfast was evident in the fact that he lived with Andrew Baxter, a Protestant friend, in East Belfast. Their house at 83 Island Street was in the UDA's heartland. He was not the first, and would not be the last, Catholic barman, to mistakenly believe that it was safe to work in bars in loyalist neighbourhoods. Those who knew him said that he was friendly, inoffensive and industrious. He never discussed politics or religion.

On 12 August 1972, he received a letter from the more upscale Stormont hotel, also in East Belfast, stating that he could start work there in a week's time. Unfortunately, he would never take up that job offer because his fate was sealed. Five days later, Herron told his bodyguard: 'Go to 83 Island Street. There are two blokes living there. You'll know Fay because he is the one with the curly hair and moustache. Make sure you do him right. Shoot him in the back of the head so that if he is still living, his brain will be damaged and he will not be able to identify you.'

The casual way Herron ordered the killing was indicative of his cruelty and sense of power. It also was amateurish in its detail, especially the reference to leaving Fay brain dead. It may have been an attempt by the UDA leader to impress the soldier and, if it was, it did not work. It was clear, however, that Herron had made inquiries about Fay and did not want his friend, Baxter, shot.

Walker Baker did not question Herron's order. He went to a UDA weapons dump and removed a .32 pistol and ammunition. In the early hours of 18 August, he made his way to Fay's home and hammered on the door with his fist. It was some time before Fay got out of bed and answered the door. When he did so, the UDA assassin held him at gunpoint.

For reasons that Walker Baker never explained, he asked Fay if he was a Catholic. Maybe he doubted Herron's judgment or he was keen to ensure he did not mistakenly shoot Fay's Protestant friend, Andrew Baxter. When Fay admitted his religion, he was told to turn round with his back to his assassin. He was shot though the back of the head and fell to the ground. In a manner that would become a familiar trait in subsequent murders, Walker Baker bent over Fay and, in an execution style, fired three bullets into Fay's head, behind his left ear. The coup de grâce was not what Herron had ordered but it symbolised the clinical ruthlessness of Walker Baker. It implied that he was not unfamiliar with firearms and assassination methods. Most terrorists would have fled the scene after the first shot but not this assassin. He kicked Fay's body into the hallway, closed the door and strolled down the street to a rendezvous with Herron. When they met up, Herron asked if Fay was dead and Baker replied that he was, to which Herron retorted: 'He'd better be.'

Walker Baker, in the killing of Fay, exhibited total control and a lack of fear of being apprehended. The method of killing was evocative of the murders by 'irregulars' in the Kenya campaign as well as Aden, Cyprus and Oman. Fay's friend, Andrew Baxter, was in the house that night but did not find his friend's body until 7.30 a.m. He told detectives he was a 'deep sleeper' and had not heard the four gunshots.

Herron and other members of the Inner Council were provided with graphic descriptions of the murder and that further enhanced Walker Baker's reputation as a trigger man. He was now part of what Herron referred to as his Number One Assassination Team. One month later, another Catholic barman walked into the assassin's sights. This time it was Paul McCartan, a middle-aged man who, like Fay, lived in a Protestant section of East Belfast.

As night fell on East Belfast, McCartan was stopped by a mobile RUC patrol as he walked unsteadily along the Newtownards Road. A police sergeant later said that he saw McCartan fall and assisted him to his feet. According to the sergeant, he was able to stand 'fairly steady'. From later forensic evidence, it was estimated that his blood alcohol level at the time exceeded 290mg/100ml. The sergeant said that he asked McCartan if he wanted a lift home but McCartan declined, saying he would rather walk. Walker Baker later offered an entirely different account of McCartan's journey in 'enemy' territory. 'This man McCartan was picked up at the corner of Finmore Street. He was let out of the police Land-Rover 50 yards from where we picked him up and we were standing waiting for him. They knew we were there.'

He added that police knew who was responsible for murders in East Belfast and, by allowing McCartan to walk through that part of East Belfast, they signed his death warrant. The allegation was based on supposition and not fact. Nonetheless, it was irresponsible of the police to fail to ensure that McCartan was protected. Police spoke to him and must have known by his name that he was a Catholic. While drunk, he was especially vulnerable. It was an area where hard men gathered on corners, suspicious of any stranger who passed by and ready to abduct anyone who turned out to be from the other community. The police patrol should have taken McCartan home, even if that meant acting against his wishes.

Walker Baker later claimed that he targeted McCartan because it was UDA policy to 'keep the pot boiling' and to frighten the IRA and the Catholic community. I believe that was revisionist justification for his actions. Yes, there was a UDA/UVF policy to terrorise the Catholic community but, in many instances, it was blood lust and opportunity that led to sectarian killings. McCartan was in the wrong place at the wrong time.

There has never been a detailed description of the moment McCartan was abducted and transported to the upstairs room of a house near UDA HQ. But we know for certain that in the house he was subjected to brutal questioning by members of the Number One Assassination Team, with Walker Baker playing a prominent role. The victim admitted that he was a Catholic and was given a severe beating by everyone present. He was then bundled into a car and taken to a nearby stretch of waste ground and made to kneel. Walker Baker then shot him three times through the back of the head. The murder, like many others in loyalist areas of East and West Belfast, confirmed a lack of serious RUC and Army scrutiny of the UDA and UVF. That was a reality that had not escaped Walker Baker. It was one of the primary reasons he so confidently committed murders without being concerned that the police or military were watching him, or might interrupt his killing spree. From then onwards, he was at the core of the UDA's East Belfast leadership and frequently drank with members of the Inner Council. He was privy to the organisation's strategy, especially its campaign of murders, and was always on hand to kill when someone was abducted.

There was a sharing of intelligence between the UDA and loyalist sympathisers about Catholics who traditionally drank in bars in East Belfast or visited Protestant friends. Sometimes, a barman informed the UDA that a Catholic frequented the premises where he worked. Walker Baker's next target, 21-year-old James McCartan, illustrated that phenomenon. No relation of Paul McCartan, he was a native of the predominantly Protestant town of Holywood, outside Belfast. He had no connections to republican groupings and, like Fay, had Protestant friends. For the latter reason, he may have chosen to avoid discussing topics which related to politics and the religious divide.

On 3 October, he joined a group of Protestant friends who were having a pre-wedding celebration in East Belfast. They had drinks in the Toby Jug bar before going to a disco at the Park Avenue hotel. During the disco, McCartan was stopped and questioned by several young men in the toilets. They asked if he was called McCartan and he replied in the negative. He was also asked if he was called Rice to which he replied 'No'. Both questions revealed that someone on the premises knew his identity. The second question was particularly intriguing because he had an uncle named Rice who also lived in Holywood. The bouncer at the disco told those questioning McCartan not to cause any trouble but McCartan's friend, John Jamison, saw the writing on the wall. He decided it was time to leave and escorted McCartan from the hotel. Once outside, Walker Baker and six of his associates confronted them. Jamison thought it best if he spoke to them. 'These fellows stopped me and Jimmy. One of them said Jimmy was called McCartan but I replied it was not so. This fellow said: "I don't care. He's going for a ride with us."'

'This fellow' was Albert Walker Baker. Jamison protested as Walker Baker's associates grabbed his friend, but his efforts failed and he was punched and kicked to the ground. His girlfriend, Geraldine, rushed forward to prevent McCartan being dragged into a car. Walker Baker, who was subduing McCartan, punched her in the face. As a parting comment, before he left with McCartan, Walker Baker shouted at Jamison: 'He's a Fenian bastard.'

Within minutes, McCartan was driven to the home of a UDA leader and dragged by the hair to an upstairs room. Other men were there waiting for his arrival and clearly had prior notice of his abduction. He was ordered to stand with his face to a wall while Walker Baker went to another room to discuss with fellow members of the Number One Assassination Team whether they should deal with McCartan right away or take him to another location. Baker returned to McCartan and held a .32 pistol to his head while the other members of his cabal tried to reach a decision. Finally, it was unanimously agreed, as recommended by Walker Baker, that they take their victim to Jones Club at Clermont Street, a short distance away. The reasoning behind that decision would soon become clear as McCartan was placed in a car and driven to the club.

The aim of the assassins was to have a 'rompering' and that required space and a bar for dispensing alcohol. The term 'rompering' derived from a popular children's television programme which relied on catchphrases such as 'romper, bomper, stomper do'. 'Romper Rooms' were illegal loyalist paramilitary drinking clubs where revellers often watched innocent Catholics being tortured. A detective, who investigated several grisly murders of that period in the Shankill area, told me that on one occasion he went to a club to gather evidence and was appalled at what he found. 'It was like a butcher's shop. There was blood on the walls, on the floor and on tables. The problem was that no one legally owned the club and therefore there was nobody to prosecute. The fact that so many people witnessed the brutality meant that all of them were guilty and no one, after seeing such a thing, was likely to come forward with evidence. I could not, in my life, understand how so many people could sit drinking and watching another human being treated so cruelly.'

James McCartan was about to be 'rompered', but not before those present poured themselves drinks. What happened next is one of many killings which have haunted me from the moment I first learned about them. In many respects, even in 2003, I can find few words to adequately convey the depths of depravity in that club on that night, or the sheer cruelty of Walker Baker. It is impossible for me to imagine what McCartan must have felt as the 'rompering' began.

All the men present punched him and kicked him when he failed to answer questions to their satisfaction. He truthfully admitted he was not a member of the IRA but that was not what they wanted to hear, so the beating became more severe. The lead interrogator was the soldier, Walker Baker. He took a pickshaft handle and, with considerable force, struck McCartan's spine several times until the young man collapsed. He then ordered his companions to lift McCartan into a Christ-like pose, his arms outstretched and the palms of his hands open. As McCartan was held tight by at least four men, Walker Baker produced a dagger and twice plunged it through McCartan's left palm. He then stabbed him in the right palm.

There is no exact record of how long this part of the torture lasted but it was certainly not over. The assassins toasted each other with drinks and Walker Baker ordered that the belt of McCartan's trousers be loosened. His trousers were dragged to his ankles and Walker Baker threatened 'to cut off his balls'. Instead, he ran the sharp dagger up McCartan's left buttock, opening up a long, shallow incision. Someone produced two lengths of rope. One rope was tied to McCartan's right hand and another round his ankles. Some of those present began to swing him in a seesaw motion and then dropped him on his head on the concrete floor.

The mindless assassin, Walker Baker, later said McCartan at that stage was 'in a bad way'. What he really meant was that it was time to end the grisly 'entertainment'. Accompanied by some of those present, he drove his victim to Connswater Bridge off the Newtownards Road and then frog-marched him to a stretch of waste ground. A green hood was placed over his head and he was made to kneel. The use of the hood was merely part of the ritual and not a deliberate attempt by Walker Baker to avoid looking at his victim. As the others watched, he shot McCartan through the back of the head and, in a fashion now familiar with his style of execution, he bent down and fired two rounds into McCartan's right ear. In a subsequent conversation with an English policeman, Walker Baker attempted to justify the killing. 'He was a wanted IRA man who was pointed out to us at a dance. I slit him up the right side. I must have broken his spine with a pickshaft.'

It was a false justification and did not fully illustrate his role in the awful torture of McCartan.

Between November '72 and the beginning of February '73, Walker Baker's life remains a mystery. At the beginning of January, as if in a script from a bizarre drama, Herron announced that he was calling an end to sectarian killings. In a statement circulated among UDA members across Belfast, the Inner Council ordered an end to killings and warned that if it was not heeded the killers themselves would be 'eliminated'. Herron, in a unique piece of double-speak, claimed that the UDA had compiled a dossier on the 'motives behind sectarian killings'. He did not have specific information about those responsible but was certain a 'small number of extremists' were involved. When asked if he really meant that UDA men who ignored his warning would be eliminated, he said: 'What the UDA meant to convey was that the assassins will be eliminated by way of educating those responsible for the futility of their course. The UDA believes it has a very big influence and can drastically reduce, if not completely stop, the killings, will tackle the questions of why murders should stop and, also from the angle why, through ill-advised Government action, the situation should never have arisen.'

That would explain why, for several weeks, Walker Baker was not murdering people. However, mystery surrounds what he had been doing in November and December of '72. The UDA's promise of an end to sectarian assassinations proved bogus. In the first week of February, Walker Baker took part in a grenade attack on Catholic workers in East Belfast. Herron and other members of the Inner Council hatched the plan which was intended to cause multiple deaths. Walker Baker and operatives chosen by him were told to attack a bus carrying Catholic workers through the Cherryvalley areas of East Belfast. What transpired is that 44-year-old Eugene Patrick Heenan was killed and several of his workmates injured.

In the spring of '73 there were two major confrontations in East Belfast between the UDA and the British Army. Herron expected Walker Baker with his military experience to teach members of the Parachute Regiment a lesson. The UDA chief was sorely disappointed because his bodyguard remained in the background during the clashes with troops. Perhaps Walker Baker realised that going up against paratroopers was potentially a deadly enterprise. Others have suggested that his loyalty to the British Army was his reason for not firing on fellow soldiers. His inactivity during those street confrontations, in which the much-vaunted UDA proved no match for the paratroopers, aroused suspicion that he was working for Military Intelligence. There was the added fact that the Provisionals had informed the UDA of the existence of loyalist 'Freds' without specifying, at that time, names provided by Wright and McKee. That generated paranoia in UDA circles, especially in East and West Belfast where there was a developing antagonism towards the Army.

Once again, like so many of the episodes surrounding the soldier-assassin's life, there is no way to determine what he was up to between the time of the grenade attack in February and 31 May of that year. At 1.13 p.m. on that May day, in a startling departure from his life as a trigger man, he walked into Warminster County police station in England to spill the beans on his life in the UDA. Why he chose that police station is another mystery. The only conclusion one could draw is that it was near the regimental headquarters of the Royal Irish Rangers. He later claimed, without specifying a date, that he had left Belfast, returned to his regiment and was court-martialled for being absent without leave.

He told the Warminster police station duty sergeant, Anthony Godley, that he wished to confess to four murders and eleven robberies. He explained that he had begun to read the Bible and he could no longer 'bear the thoughts' of what he had done. It was a curious, if not false, reason for offering himself up to the law. If, as he claimed, he had gone back to his regiment, his intention had been to return to duty. There was nothing in his history which suggested an interest in matters spiritual and, if one accepts his claim to have gone through some kind of conversion, it could only have happened, figuratively speaking, like Paul on the road to Damascus. One wonders if he confessed his crimes to senior figures in the regiment and was told to turn himself in and use biblical reasons for his sudden change of heart. The British Army has consistently refused to discuss his military record or to confirm whether he returned to the regiment at that time. There would surely be a record of the court-martial and what Walker Baker said in mitigation, if it ever took place, as he claimed.

The duty sergeant was astounded by Walker Baker's apparent willingness to confess until Walker Baker introduced a caveat. He would not reveal the names of his accomplices, he stressed. Nonetheless, he made a statement describing the murders he committed but nowhere in his expansive account did he give the impression that he was a man who could no longer 'bear the thoughts of what he had done'. He asked Sergeant Godley to keep his name out of newspapers and promised that in return he would reveal where bodies and weapons were buried. He would even 'name names'. That promise appeared to contradict one of his first statements to Godley that he would not name accomplices.

He was transferred to Salisbury police station for a further interview with a Detective Bridewell. He told Bridewell that RUC Special Branch already knew about him. 'Some of them are with us,' he added, referring to the UDA. He promised to reveal 'all the hits' in East Belfast, Derry and all of Belfast but that was dependent on him being allowed to serve a prison term in an English jail.

Within days, he was secretly transported to Northern Ireland where detectives further questioned him. He was charged and placed on remand in Crumlin Road prison in Belfast to await trial. Sometime between June and October he was spirited out of his cell at night and flown to England, accompanied by a Home Office Inspector of Prisons. That journey, which was listed on a classified file, was never made public. His lawyers and RUC detectives handling his case were not told about it. The Home Office holds the file, suggesting the involvement of MI5, though one source told me that Walker Baker was taken to England to meet personnel from MI6. What I find significant is not the particular intelligence service that wanted to interview him, but the fact that he never mentioned the trip when 12 years later he made disclosures about his life to politicians, priests and journalists. It would be tempting to conclude that he was taken to England for 24 hours and offered a deal. However, there is no evidence to support that theory. I believe, as a result of what I was told by a source in 2003, that MI5 wanted to question him about his allegations of collusion between RUC Special Branch and the UDA. They also wanted to know if Special Branch or Military Intelligence had been running him as an agent.

A senior police officer who saw the Home Office file on Walker Baker, in circumstances that I am not at liberty to reveal, was shocked that the secret trip had been kept hidden from so many people for so many years. What the police officer did not see was any written record of what transpired when Walker Baker was flown to England, who spoke to him and what the conversation was about. The police officer felt that a deal was struck with the assassin that he would be allowed to serve out his time in an English prison provided he shut his mouth and stopped making dangerous allegations about elements of the security forces. That is exactly what happened. His trial was speedily processed at a time when some suspects were on remand for periods exceeding 12 months. In October, he appeared in court and pleaded guilty, ensuring that he had no defence to offer and therefore no forum to outline his earlier claims of collusion. He was sentenced to life with a recommendation that he serve a minimum of 25 years. In mitigation, his lawyer, the renowned QC Michael Lavery, argued that Walker Baker had initially gone AWOL from his regiment after a drinking spree. He arrived in Belfast and was tempted by the lure of money in the UDA. He joined the organisation and trained its members. None of that mattered to Lord Chief Justice Lowry, whose belief was that Walker Baker was a cold-blooded killer who should be taken off the streets for a long time. On leaving the court, Walker Baker was transferred to Franklands prison in England.

From that moment, he faded into obscurity, even though his mother tried to persuade journalists to investigate his case after he told her he had been working for British Intelligence. She said he had told her he was a military agent the moment he returned home and joined the UDA. She added that the Army had issued his personal gun to him. No one listened to her pleas until the mid 1980s when her son began contacting journalists, priests, politicians and social activists from his prison cell.

He wrote to Father Denis Faul, who was so intrigued by what the assassin told him about collusion that he visited him in Franklands prison. Father Faul publicly stated that Walker Baker's allegations about British military involvement in the killing of Catholics should be investigated as well as his allegations about RUC collusion with loyalists.

The celebrated *Daily Mirror* journalist, Paul Foot, also spoke to the soldier-assassin, but Ken Livingstone, the British Labour MP, carried out major interviews with him in his prison cell. Livingstone concluded that his story contained substantive evidence of military and police collusion with loyalist paramilitaries. Among the many statements made to the Member of Parliament was one about RUC officers:

> We were led to believe that these officers handing over weapons were getting orders from higher authority. But you know the public was not aware weapons were going missing from RUC stations. The station where I lived was Mountpottinger. Ammunition was coming to UDA HQ or down to —'s house in — Street [*information withheld by author*] and he was handing over the weapons to us and we were using them for assassinations. When they came to raid —'s house they got a .45 revolver but it was never ever brought out in court that it was a police weapon. He got 12 months for having an illegal weapon in his house but it was never established that it belonged to the RUC.

During the period alluded to by Walker Baker, several weapons including two Sterling sub-machine guns were taken from the armoury at Mountpottinger station and were not recovered. The RUC only admitted to the disappearance of the weapons when confronted by journalists. There is sufficient evidence to connect individual policemen with collusion but Walker Baker provided no concrete evidence to connect Special Branch, MI5 or Military Intelligence with his operations or other UDA crimes. He did, however, provide details of a planned killing that confirmed what Livingstone had heard from Provisional IRA sources.

— of the Inner Circle Murder Squad was involved in that. The UDA went over to do an assassination at the Red Lion which is beside the Albert Clock in the centre of Belfast but a police Land-Rover came round the corner and — [*he refers to an RUC detective*] was parked in the car park just beside the Albert Clock. The assassination didn't come off because the Land-Rover came round the corner, so the guns were put in the detective's car and he drove them back through police and Army checkpoints to East Belfast and handed them back to us. But the assassination was carried out later with police guns and Sterling sub-machine guns.

One of the interesting facets of that story, if one is to believe it, is that there was a dirty detective but the uniformed police were clean. According to Walker Baker, it was the presence of uniformed members of the RUC that deterred the assassins from realising their objective. I believe that during a decade in his cell, ruminating about his life, Walker Baker used the time to concoct a host of conspiracy theories and embellish stories he had previously given to detectives. Yet I am left with a feeling that there was truth in some of the things he said, especially when he first walked into Warminster police station. But I contend that by the mid 1980s he had begun to wrap his early allegations in a tissue of fiction. As a consequence, it is almost impossible to determine where the truth lies in respect of his major allegations of collusion.

What most disturbs me about his story and his crimes is that he was able to operate with relative impunity under the noses of Special Branch, RUC detectives and police mobile patrols. He was a soldier when he killed and was therefore a trigger man in the ranks. That, however, does not support a conclusion that he was acting under British Army orders when he was in the UDA. There is no evidence to connect him with the MRF or any other counter-insurgency groupings, including the RUC department responsible for handling and running terrorist agents and informers.

One is, however, left puzzled by some of the unanswered questions about his life. How did he manage to go AWOL and remain in Belfast for so long when the Army knew that his home was in East Belfast? What happened between the time he left Belfast and resurfaced in Warminster police station? Who arranged for him to be spirited from his prison cell to England and who met him? What was discussed? Then, there is his prominence in East Belfast as a bodyguard to Herron and the Inner Council. Surely the RUC checked him out and discovered that he was a soldier, still in the employ of the British Army. If they did not check him out, why not? And if they did know his military history, why did they not interview him or inform the Army of his whereabouts? The RUC had plenty of informers in UDA ranks who could have given them specific information about Walker Baker and his crimes.

In late '80s and early '90s, after unsuccessfully campaigning to serve out his sentence in Northern Ireland, he was released. His desire to return to a Northern Ireland prison was one of those many imponderables in his story. Why should he have wanted to risk his life in a Northern Ireland prison when he had 'grassed' on the UDA?

The answers to all of those questions matter less than my belief that he was a cold-blooded assassin, who later struck out at authority with a plethora of unsubstantiated allegations. He was never subjected to psychiatric testing and my belief is that if a test had been conducted, the diagnosis would have been that he was an aggressive psychopath. His military training was a factor but only in that it served his grandiosity and his need to exert control over others, especially the vulnerable people he abducted and killed.

I am also inclined to believe that he was never truthful about the extent of his crimes but I accept that he knew where 'bodies were buried'. I have always felt that, like republicans, loyalists were involved in the scandal now known as 'The Disappeared' – people killed and secretly buried. While the spotlight for such crimes fell on the IRA, I was told that the UVF and UDA had engaged in a similar policy. The Milltown Cemetery killer, Michael Stone, told me in a prison interview that he knew where bodies were buried. I understood him to be talking about East Belfast.

Walker Baker stands out as one of the most lethal and brutal trigger men of the Troubles. Unfortunately, in the mid to late 1980s when he began to attract attention as a result of his startling allegations, people tended to ignore the man behind the conspiracy theories – a callous, inhumane enforcer with no respect for life. To believe everything that such a man says is tantamount to ignoring his willingness to conceal so many aspects of his life.

4

THE 'TEFLON' DON AND THE POLITICAL HITMAN

James 'Pratt' Craig and John McMichael were prominent UDA trigger men who could not have been more different in terms of their personalities and commitment to the loyalist cause. 'Pratt' Craig had all the trappings and excess of a Mafia boss of bosses, whereas McMichael resembled a consigliere, dispensing advice to the foot soldiers under his control.

Both rose through the ranks of the UDA during some of the most savage periods of violence in the 1970s and '80s. Craig's stomping ground was the Shankill area of West Belfast and McMichael cut his teeth in the east of the city and in parts of the countryside of Counties Down and Antrim. I met both men and closely studied their lives, establishing close links with McMichael whom I frequently interviewed. Their careers as killers and terror bosses were in some respects not dissimilar. They were both cunning and callous but other factors in their personalities put them on a deadly collision. A unique characteristic of their reign of terror is that they were careful not to leave their fingerprints on assassinations and other crimes. In the case of Craig, it was believed that police could never make a charge against him stick. Like the New York Mafia boss, John Gotti, he was a Teflon Don. McMichael hid his terror identity behind the carefully constructed role of politician while he ordered others to pull a trigger or detonate a bomb.

By the time I first met James 'Pratt' Craig, he was a stocky, married man in his early 40s and was overall UDA commander in West Belfast where he lived. During my first encounter with him in UDA HQ on the Shankill Road, I was struck by his expensive jewellery – a gold watch and bracelet – his designer clothes and his retinue of thugs. He reminded me of a character from early gangster movies. No matter how much he tried to appear cool and sophisticated, the veneer of a common criminal was evident. His 'bodyguards', who were more like admirers, secretly feared him. Their fawning was invested with knowledge that he could kill anyone within his inner circle who dared challenge his authority or betrayed his trust. When he spoke, they listened and nodded politely or laughed when he laughed. They were part of his 'family' and were accorded special privileges. He kept them well lubricated with alcohol and bought them holidays on Spain's Costa Brava. Craig was a master at dispensing largesse from the profits of his criminal enterprises. It bought allegiance from his retinue and, most importantly of all, silence about his operations. His private wealth was derived from racketeering, extortion and donations from middle-class businessmen who wanted to feel safe from his tendency to levy a 'tax' on all businesses. It did not matter to Craig whether small shopkeepers, bar owners or building contractors ran the businesses. And when it came to doing business across the political divide, he was willing to 'get into bed' with the enemy if it generated a profit.

There was a noticeable swagger when he strode into a bar or illegal drinking den, flanked by his entourage of bodyguards. But he personally was no pushover. He had all the attributes of a hard man or what the Mafia calls a 'wiseguy'. In John Gotti parlance he was a 'made man'. For Craig, that meant he was a fully fledged and sworn member of the UDA. His physical appearance conveyed his ability to throw a good punch and his prominent knuckles testified to his years as an amateur boxer and street fighter.

He had also taken a few punches and at times his face displayed puffiness. He had done some of his fighting in prison, a place for which he had little fondness. At the outset of the Troubles, he found himself incarcerated for assault and later commented that the next time he 'hammered' someone he would make sure there were no witnesses in a 'fit state' to provide evidence against him. His stint in prison was fortuitous because it brought him into contact with loyalist paramilitaries. He distinguished himself as a natural leader and became the self-styled commander of a group of UDA prisoners. His initial flirtation with terrorists convinced him the UDA was an organisation to provide him with power and cover for his criminal expertise. Until then, his illegal pursuits had only amounted to housebreaking, larceny and the handling of stolen goods.

Like so many criminally minded people who were drawn into the UDA in the early 1970s, he recognised the lax discipline in the organisation and the freedom it offered for 'extra-curricular activities'. In contrast to many of the younger recruits, he had life experience in the criminal world. He was adept at offsetting his lack of education with flamboyance, cunning and toughness. He was also a good storyteller with a penchant for boasting about how he had ruled the streets before the Troubles. When truth got in the way of a good story, he reverted to fiction. He possessed a shrewd understanding of the politics of his own community and that enabled him to closely link himself to the loyalist cause.

When asked how he maintained discipline among UDA personnel in the Maze prison, he replied with characteristic bluntness: 'I've got this big fucking hammer and I've told them that if anybody gives me trouble, I'll break his fucking fingers.'

In the Maze, he became a minor celebrity but also made every effort to demonstrate to republicans in the prison that he was a fair-minded negotiator. He had no desire to complicate his life by making enemies of people who might seek to kill him when he was freed and could be partners in future criminal conspiracies. His rise to prominence in the UDA began with his role in an anti-sectarian conference held in the Maze prison in 1972. The unusual aspect of that event was the fact that it was a British Government-inspired strategy to encourage paramilitaries on both sides to reach a pact to end sectarian killings. The belief was that prisoners in the Maze were a major power bloc on both sides. That was accurate, because men who had been imprisoned for their beliefs and actions were highly regarded within their respective terror groups. On the republican side, leaders like Gerry Adams were in the Maze and still exerted considerable influence on Provisional IRA strategy.

The Government, without making the matter public, decided that it would grant immunity to wanted terrorist leaders to attend the conference. When all interested parties, under the direction of a British Government representative, met within the prison, Craig proved to be a voice of conciliation. At the table were members of the Provisional IRA/Official IRA/UDA/UVF/Red Hand Commando and two clergymen to represent each community.

The stated aim of the conference was to map out an agreement to halt spiralling sectarian murders, especially in the Greater Belfast area. The loyalist contingent offered to commit to such a plan provided the Provisional IRA ended its targeting of off-duty policemen and members of the Ulster Defence Regiment. The Provisionals insisted that was acceptable but they reserved the right to kill policemen and members of the UDR in uniform. All sides appeared to agree on one thing – if the war continued, the UDA/UVF/Red Hand Commando would be entitled to shoot members of the IRA and vice versa.

The central issue of calling a halt to sectarian killings seemed in principle to have the support of all present until Sam Smyth, one of the loyalists' visiting delegates, expressed dissent. He declared that the conference was a sham. In his view, a three-year-old child or a 70-year-old woman in the Catholic community were legitimate targets. Craig took grave exception to Smyth's outburst and told him to 'keep his views to himself'. Everyone in the loyalist delegation saw the facial reactions of republicans and knew that Smyth had just signed his own death warrant. Within three weeks of the conference the Provisional IRA killed him. His murder ended any hope of a deal between the paramilitary factions, and sectarian killers returned to the streets.

Smyth's death taught Craig an important lesson. He realised that the Provisionals were capable of killing any loyalist leader. From that moment, his own mortality became his primary concern and he was determined to do whatever was necessary to stay off the IRA's assassination list. During his remaining time in prison, he developed a dialogue with members of both wings of the IRA. The contacts he made were part of a cunning strategy to ensure that republicans regarded him as a reasonable guy. The officials he met in prison made him feel a lot more comfortable and his friendships with some of them were to be important in the years ahead.

On his return to the streets, he quickly became a dominant force within the UDA in West Belfast, establishing a base of operations in the Shankill district. He soon created an inner circle of confidants to distance himself from actual operations, especially sectarian murders. From a legal standpoint, that ensured his primary role as a terrorist was obscured. However, his fear of the Provisionals was decidedly aggravated after several loyalists were assassinated. He realised that he needed to find a way to make sure he was insulated from their hit squads. What was required was a firm guarantee that he would never be on their target list. In furtherance of that objective, he used one of his inner circle to make it known to the IRA's Belfast Brigade that he had no intention of targeting them. It was a clever ploy because he knew there was an unspoken rule that leaders on both sides were not to be assassinated. Nonetheless, he wanted it from the 'horse's mouth' that he – not other UDA leaders – was recognised by the IRA as a UDA leader.

His other major concern was the RUC investigative force in nearby Tennent Street police station. The station had a detective branch responsible for investigating 'ordinary' crimes in parts of West and North Belfast but, with the onset of the Troubles, that role had changed to solving terrorist murders. Craig did not want police scrutiny of his terrorist and criminal activities. Like Seamus Wright, who learned he had a value when he became an MRF agent and then a double agent for the

IRA, Craig believed that police would turn a blind eye to his operations if he provided them with useful intelligence. He knew he had to strike a deal with RUC CID figures in Tennent Street, but on his terms. He had no desire to be run as an agent or informer. Instead, he would give Tennent Street detectives intelligence in a way that would not compromise him. Such a relationship would keep Special Branch and British Military Intelligence off his back. He was intimately familiar with the workings of intelligence agencies. For example, he understood the kickback for cooperation was that terrorists were allowed to be terrorists and to engage in 'ordinary' criminal activity of the type he preferred.

In contrast to CID, Special Branch handled informers on its terms. An informer or agent's cover depended on the person being a good terrorist or criminal and having status in either role. Special Branch officers preferred total control and expected agents to follow orders, so Craig opted for a looser arrangement. CID did not run agents and traditionally relied on informers who from time to time provided useful titbits of information. By 1972, CID detectives in Tennent Street were investigating terrorist crimes, mostly after the fact. They were keen for any help in closing files on sectarian murders. Therefore, if a criminal could point them in the right direction, they were prepared to overlook many of his indiscretions. That fitted Craig's scenario. He had no desire to play the agent role by alerting the authorities to crimes which were about to occur. His preference was to let CID know who had pulled a trigger after someone had been murdered. In that respect, he was selective about whom he named and, in most cases, it was someone he did not like or who was privately criticising his leadership. He also focused on compromising those who knew too much about his involvement in terror. He either set them up to commit a murder and then divulged their names to CID or simply waited until they had killed someone before he made a call.

After a time, several detectives at Tennent Street recognised his voice when he telephoned. He never gave his name but often asked to talk to a senior detective, who was in effect his handler. While researching this book, I spoke to that handler, who is now retired. He said Craig had helped him solve 12 murders. It is a staggering figure but the detective assured me that, in each case, Craig's information, mostly conveyed in telephone calls, was impeccable.

In order to gain an insight into the way Craig personally dealt with murder, one only has to examine an episode in a UDA club in the Shankill. He and his retinue were drinking in the club when a local man approached them. He produced a pistol and complained that it was 'useless' – it was 'jamming'. Craig reached forward and took the gun from him. He then levelled it at another man playing pool. There was a pause as Craig's fellow drinkers waited to see what he was going to do. He smiled, pulled the trigger and shot the pool player through the head, killing him. He then handed the gun back to its owner and told him to return it to a UDA arms dump. With a grin he turned to his buddies and told them 'to clean the place up'. As he continued drinking, some of his retinue disposed of the body and washed the blood off the floor. Several hours later, he telephoned the senior detective I mentioned and told him the location of the body. He was careful not to admit that he had pulled the trigger. The detective later told me: 'He personally killed people but not as many as he ordered killed. His information on killings was accurate and he was a valuable source. His help in solving 12 murders made a considerable contribution to our work in Tennent Street. Without his information, we might never have got the guys who carried out those killings. I knew he was a bad apple but you had to take the rough with the smooth to get the job done. It was give and take in relationships with highly placed informers.'

'Pratt' Craig not only pulled the trigger but also enjoyed watching people being tortured and killed. One of his associates said to me: 'Jimmy was a hard man and shrewd with it. You didn't take your eye off him or let him think you didn't like what he was doing. He was just as likely to put one in your head if he felt like it. He had snitches in the Shankill who told him everything people said about him. After a while some of us knew not to say anything that could be carried back to him. He was generous, mind you – some said to a fault. He liked to be seen to be the man who had everything and could throw money around and there were plenty of extended hands when he was about. But he had a frightening side to him and that kept everybody in check. He had seen things and what he told us sure scared the shit outta younger guys. He'd been there when some bad things were done in the clubs – y' know what I mean? He boasted about it.'

To an outsider, the source I have just quoted appears at times to talk in the abstract with phrases like 'some bad things'. I found that to be common among loyalist terrorists I interviewed. It was a mechanism they used, often unconsciously, to distance themselves from the reality of grisly murders. The phrase 'some bad things' alluded to 'rompering'. A similar use of language was relied on by the self-confessed 'maniac', Pastor Kenny McClinton, when he used words like 'grossest' to suggest extreme brutality.

Craig only boasted about what he had observed, or participated in, to his close circle. He was scared that, if he acquired a reputation of being a ruthless killer, news of it would reach the Provos. While Craig was acting out the role of terror boss and Mafia Don, John McMichael was also rising through the ranks of the legal terrorist organisation. In 1973, it mimicked the IRA and established a military wing, the Ulster Freedom Fighters. McMichael, in conversations with me, expressed admiration for the Provisionals and how they had successfully created an 'Armalite-ballot box' strategy. He believed the two intricately linked elements had provided important dynamics in the IRA's armed 'struggle'.

Danny Morrison, a former member of the IRA's Army Council but nowadays a novelist, was credited with devising the philosophy of the gun and the ballot box. He cleverly portrayed himself as a leading member of Sinn Fein while maintaining an important role in the military strategy of the IRA. McMichael wanted to emulate Morrison by becoming a prominent political spokesman for the loyalist cause while he masterminded terrorism. Like Craig, he had been a foot soldier and had done his fair share of killing but had never left his fingerprints on his crimes. I believe he was protected from prosecution because he provided a service to the intelligence world. In contrast to Craig, he did not play the role of informer but ordered terror in connivance with elements of the intelligence community.

He was also a man with a genuine desire to formulate a policy to end the violence, but only on his terms. While the IRA existed, he saw it as his duty to eliminate them and he was not discriminating when targets of opportunity were innocent Catholics. He outlined his concepts to me in a restaurant in Hillsborough in the early 1980s.

'We didn't have the professionalism of the IRA. We were always reacting to events and it was simple to just go out and select any Catholic. We were not getting the real people – the IRA and their supporters. I knew people in our own community would respect us more if we chose prestige republican targets. We knew the Brits wouldn't mind the IRA being killed by us, and would probably turn a blind eye to us operating in that way. We were constantly receiving intelligence files from contacts in the RUC, UDR and British Military Intelligence but nobody was acting on it. In border areas we used those contacts more than we did in the city. Down there it was simply a nod and a wink and our people would have all the necessary intelligence to do a hit. They would have files on the target, his address, his movements, as well as the movements of the security forces at the time we wanted to take him out. But it was all too haphazard. I also reckoned we needed more contact between the UVF and ourselves. In border areas there were lots of joint operations because people lived constantly under threat and there was no question of one-upmanship. Belfast and other major centres were very different. There was too much energy spent on racketeering and other pursuits. Some guys were in place from the early '70s and ran their own private armies. I had to be careful not to tread on too many toes. The Provos taught me a lot about the control needed over volunteers. They were good at the politics and the terror. I believed if we could develop a clear political strategy as well as a more sophisticated armed strategy that we would also be a formidable force.'

Those words came from McMichael the terror boss and not the affable, straight-talking loyalist political thinker who contributed to radio and television debates. He even attended political seminars in the Irish Republic. The comments he made to me are essential to an understanding of what he had been and the person he had become. They also encapsulated his ambitions as a terrorist and politician. He was unapologetic about the extent of collusion between elements of the State security apparatus and loyalist paramilitaries. He saw it as a vital ingredient in winning his war. The only window into his past in the above statement was his reference to the early killing of innocent Catholics. He had played the role of trigger man in the loyalist sectarian murder campaign but, by the time he spoke to me, he was determined to shape the UFF into a force like the Provisional IRA with a disciplined military strategy. He would take his finger off the trigger and order others to kill. The targets would be, in his words, the IRA and their supporters. He knew only too well that loyalists interpreted 'supporters' to mean any Catholic nationalist or republican.

His condemnation of private armies and racketeering within the UDA symbolised his antagonism towards James 'Pratt' Craig and other members of the UDA Inner Council. He did not confess that he had also been involved in the criminal world of the UDA. Others knew about his past as the following statement from a UFF source indicates: 'John changed his ways. In the early days he was a bit of a wild operator but he was always cleverer than the rest of us. He kinda educated himself. Some of us used to joke that he saw himself as the Gerry Adams of loyalism. He had his fair share of money when the profits were coming in. If anybody tells you that John got his money through honest means, he's pulling yer leg. Having said that, he was one of our best. Y' have to give it to him that he wanted to root out the touts and the criminals who were damaging the cause. He knew that people like Craig were running their own patch and creaming off profits from the organisation. Some people thought John had no right to criticise when he had been at that hisself but everybody has a right to change. Craig was giving the UDA a bad name and that wasn't all he was at, as everybody knows. But John knew Craig was not an easy target.'

My source was correct that McMichael recognised the dangers in confronting Craig. That was reflected in McMichael's comments to me about how dangerous it was to 'tread on too many toes'. The 'too many toes' were other self-styled brigadiers who resented interference with their criminal operations. Like Craig, they had power and deniability and McMichael was unable to pit himself against such a powerful collective. In public, he was deputy to UDA Commander Andy Tyrie, one of the 1973 signatories to the document which announced the arrival of the UFF. Tyrie, who retired from the UDA in the 1990s to run a business in County Down, did not like the spotlight. He allowed his deputy to become the public face of the organisation and the spokesperson for its political agenda. McMichael revelled in that role and was careful not to associate himself with the UFF, which was the major focus of his energies. As he suggested in his comments to me, he wanted to formulate a more clinical terror campaign through the intelligence available from the RUC, UDR and the British Army. His agenda suited Special Branch and secret parts of the Military Intelligence apparatus. It meant that he willingly became a function of a Military and Special Branch counter-insurgency strategy and, in doing so, became an agent. The high-profile targets he selected for assassination soon evidenced the beginnings of his ambition to make the UFF a more lethal force and demonstrated that he could rely on the security forces to assist in that endeavour.

Miriam Daly was a quiet, softly spoken woman with a razor-sharp intellect. She was born in 1939 in the Curragh of Kildare in the Irish Republic and excelled at school, eventually becoming a lecturer in Economic History at University College, Dublin. It was there she met her husband, Dr Joe Lee. He died prematurely and, several years later, she married Jim Daly. He was from Armagh but had been born in England to Irish parents. Though seven years younger than his wife, he shared with her an intense interest in politics. She regarded herself as a socialist and he toyed with the prospect of becoming a Marxist. In 1968, they both took lectureships at Queen's University in Belfast and lived nearby in the Stranmillis district. She became deeply involved in the civil rights movement and that is when their lives dramatically changed. She was a forceful speaker despite her demure appearance and quickly established herself as a prominent social activist. That brought her to the attention of loyalists and she received telephoned death threats and a bullet in the post. It did not deter her from campaigning but by 1974, she feared for her life and moved with her husband to the predominantly Catholic Andersonstown area in West Belfast.

In the six years she had been in Belfast, the civil rights struggle had been replaced with a long war and she and her husband gave their support to the concept of a 32 County Democratic Socialist Republic. By the end of the '70s, she and Bernadette McAlliskey, née Devlin, a former Queen's University student and Member of the Westminster Parliament, were members of the Irish Republican Socialist Party. It had originated from a split within the Official IRA and considered itself the true inheritor of the James Connolly socialist tradition, dating back to the nineteenth century.

Miriam Daly and her husband were core influences in the IRSP but by 1980 they had drifted away. The IRSP had become intricately linked with its military wing, the INLA, and was constantly riven with personal and ideological disputes. However, Miriam and Jim Daly were prominent public figures because of their efforts to focus political support on the rights of prisoners in the Maze. They were frequently photographed at rallies demanding political status for republicans in the H Blocks.

On the afternoon of 26 June 1980, neighbours saw her sitting on the porch of her home and reckoned that she was passing time until the return from school of her ten-year-old twin daughters. At some point, she was seen walking to a nearby shop to buy cigarettes and that was the last sighting of her alive. When her daughters entered the house, they found her tied to a chair. She had been shot five times in the head and spent cartridges were on the floor. Detectives who arrived on the scene concluded that the killer, or killers, had spent some time with her and had probably waited, hoping her husband would appear. Fortunately, he was attending a seminar in Dublin.

Forensic tests on the body indicated that a cushion had been placed against Miriam Daly's head to silence the sound of the fatal gunshots. Republicans predictably attributed the murder to the SAS because of the professionalism of the hit and the fact that the killers — police believed there was more than one shooter in the house — would have needed good intelligence to operate so coolly in a Catholic stronghold.

The Provisionals were correct that the killing bore the hallmarks of a well-planned assassination but the culprits were members of a UFF hit team, operating on orders from John McMichael. They had up-to-date intelligence on their target, knew the layout of her home and were assured that there would be no security forces patrols in the area. The killing illustrated the strategy McMichael outlined to me as his goal but came at a time when he had not fully developed it. However, it confirmed to me that he had already established close links with Military Intelligence and Special Branch. In the course of researching this book, I spoke to several former UFF operatives who said that, even as early as 1980, McMichael was in possession of RUC and Army data. He had sufficient 'contacts' to ensure that UFF operations were not compromised by police or military security in a given target zone. Daly, like McMichael's next target, Ronnie Bunting, was someone the intelligence community wanted eliminated. They were happy to have McMichael strike at the heart of republicanism.

Bunting, whom the Provisionals accused of setting up Jim Bryson, was a leading INLA strategist believed to have been instrumental in ordering the assassination of Margaret Thatcher's close adviser and confidant, Airey Neave. There was no proof to substantiate that charge but he would have known that the killing of Neave was planned. Ronnie Bunting was the son of Major Ronald Bunting, the loyalist 'cheer leader' of Paisleyism in the late '60s and early '70s, and was one of those 'rarities' in the conflict: a Protestant who was a committed republican socialist. He was astute, well educated and lived in Ballymurphy. Like Bryson, he had become a high-value target for loyalists and the intelligence community. The intelligence community had more than just a revenge motive to encourage them to collude in the murder of Bunting. The killing of Airey Neave was daring and it removed from the scene a hard-liner, whom Margaret Thatcher had considered a potential Secretary of State for Northern Ireland.

At 1 a.m. on 15 October 1980, Bunting and his close associate, Noel Lyttle, were in the Bunting home. They had been discussing strategy for several hours and decided to go to bed. Lyttle retired to an upstairs room where Bunting's 14-month-old son was sleeping. Bunting tidied the living-room, checked the locks on the downstairs doors and joined his wife, Susan, in bed at 1.30 a.m. Two of his other children, aged three and seven, were in an adjacent room.

At 3.30 a.m., Susan Bunting and her husband heard a loud banging downstairs. By the time they both got out of bed, gunmen wearing ski masks and khaki pullovers had smashed open the front door and were at the top of the staircase. Susan Bunting provided this account of what happened next: 'We both jumped out of bed but, by the time we got up, the men were already pushing in the bedroom door. We tried to force the bedroom door close but the shooting started and I fell back onto the bed. The next thing two men were in the room and started shooting Ronnie.'

She jumped on to the back of one of the gunmen but he continued to fire. She was also shot three times in the back and side. 'While I struggled with one of the men, the other left, casual-like, without a care. As he walked downstairs, he shouted something like: "C'mon, Geordie" or "Georgie." The other man left and, as he walked to the stairs, he turned and shot me in the mouth. I turned and saw Ronnie. He was dead.'

Meanwhile, Noel Lyttle had been shot as he tried to get out of bed. He died on the way to hospital. Despite the sound of the gunfire in an area normally under heavy security, the killers had no difficulty making an escape. What struck me about the killing was again the professionalism of the trigger men. They entered the house with ferocity, typical of men with a military-style background. They were cool and clinical and they clearly knew the layout of the Buntings' home. The time of the double murder was also intriguing. It occurred at the optimum hour for a successful stealth entry. When people are normally in a deep sleep, they are slow to react. The whole operation had required good intelligence and careful planning. It also needed the support of the security forces to ensure the killers reached and left their target zone without interference. The dress style of the killers hinted that they were military, especially the khaki pullovers and the ski masks. Terrorists rarely dressed in that fashion, preferring dark jackets and balaclavas.

For republicans, the killing was the work of the SAS and one can understand why they instinctively reached that conclusion. However, it was carried out by a hit squad under orders from John McMichael. I have since been told that at least two of the killers were members of the UDR. The killing was made easy because of collusion between the intelligence community and the UFF, through McMichael's direct contacts. It was suggested to me by a reliable UFF source that McMichael received advice on the planning of the double killing from two members of Military Intelligence. That would explain how the trigger men acted with precision and knew exactly where to find Lyttle and Bunting in that house.

Just like Billy Wright in his successful targeting of republicans, the UFF supremo had access to hundreds of dossiers compiled by RUC Special Branch and the British Army. And, he admitted to me, he recruited members of the UDR to train his hit teams.

In Unionist circles, he was regarded as the paramilitary voice of reason. When he produced a political document advocating dialogue between both communities, he was coached by leading Unionist politicians and lawyers in how to structure, script and present it. At his instigation, I introduced him to the SDLP leader, John Hume, in the BBC carpark in Belfast. That same day, after having a meal with him, I also brought him into the company of Eamon McCann, a highly respected writer and journalist. What transpired conveys elements of absurdity in a society in conflict. We consumed several bottles of wine with Eamon and had a pleasant political dialogue until Eamon bluntly confronted McMichael about his role as a terrorist. He demanded to know how many people McMichael had killed and the number of assassins he had under his control in the UFF. McMichael had not expected the verbal assault and began a tirade about the IRA, asking Eamon to stipulate the number of gunmen in Provo ranks. Eamon replied that the media had greatly exaggerated the numbers of IRA gunmen and, if he were to hazard a guess, it would be in the realm of 100 to 150. 'John, come clean. How many gunmen do you control?' said Eamon.

McMichael was in no mood for stepping outside his public role of politician by responding to the question.

Fortunately for all concerned, the exchanges on that evening were verbal, lubricated with a lot of alcohol. I am told that the following day, Eamon suffered, not from a hangover but from a dreadful feeling that he had overstepped the mark with one of the most dangerous men in Northern Ireland. In reaching that conclusion, he was correct. Perhaps McMichael had a hangover the next day and forgot what my writer friend had said. That is a reasonable conclusion since nothing untoward happened to Eamon in the years following the episode.

In the 1980s, the intelligence community knew the internal workings of the UDA/UFF. It had prior knowledge of killings and ran agents and informers in both the UDA and UFF. James 'Pratt' Craig, who had initially provided information to CID, was being run by E Department of RUC Special Branch, responsible for handling informers and agents. Another of their prime sources in the UDA was Tommy 'Tucker' Lyttle. They used him to supply disinformation to the media by encouraging him to become a major source for a local, veteran journalist. Men like Lyttle, Craig and McMichael were protected from prosecution because of their links to the British Army and Special Branch.

Craig's Special Branch contacts knew about his racketeering and the fact that he was establishing links to criminals within the INLA. It was an unholy alliance designed to avoid turf wars. Craig and his INLA associates extorted money from construction firms by ensuring the protection of the workers on building sites. Both he and the INLA reached agreement that the sites from which each of them extorted money would not be attacked or compromised. On several occasions, Craig and his INLA partners provided security for each other's sites.

The organisation that Craig most feared was the Provisional IRA and in the mid '80s he used one of his retinue to make an approach to the IRA's Belfast Brigade leaders. They responded to the overture and an IRA operative named Joe was assigned the task of dealing directly with Craig. Joe lived in Unity Flats close to Craig's base of operations. When the Provisionals wanted to kill the UVF assassin, John Bingham, they sought help from Craig. He provided intelligence on Bingham's habits and the layout of his home. By 1986, Craig's balancing act was leading him down a dangerous path and McMichael was asking questions about him. A later UFF investigation into Craig's links to the Provisionals revealed the following: 'Meetings with Joe were only attended by Craig or ——— of the UDA. They were held in the Capstan, Royal and King Arthur bars in Belfast city centre. The IRA contacted Craig after Gerry Adams was shot and asked him what was going on and what about the arrangements regarding top men. It is believed Joe made the call. Craig was stupid to tell other people about the call.'

Before the UFF ever learned about those meetings with Joe, Special Branch was aware of them and even secretly filmed Craig talking to Joe.

Craig had long ago begun to believe that he was invincible. He had managed to maintain control of the UDA in West Belfast and to keep his enemies at bay by doing favours for them. He also felt insulated from the security forces because they too were the beneficiaries of his studied dispensing of intelligence. At the same time, he personally ran his favourite UFF C Company in the Shankill, acting out the role of terrorist leader. It was an amazing double act but it could not last.

Across the city, McMichael heard the rumour that Craig was enabling IRA attacks on leading loyalists. It was true. One of the leading loyalists set up by Craig was Lenny Murphy, the infamous leader of the Shankill Butchers, a UVF gang of mass murderers. Murphy was shot dead by an IRA hit team from the Ardoyne as a result of information provided by Craig. McMichael suspected that there had to be collusion between someone in the UFF in the Shankill and the Provisionals and Craig fitted the profile of a shady, untrustworthy character.

Craig also set up for assassination 'Bucky' McCullough who had been one of his inner circle. McCullough signed his own death warrant when he began to criticise Craig for using UDA racketeering profits for personal use instead of the purchase of weapons. He also learned that money intended for the welfare of loyalist prisoners was finding its way into Craig's coffers. McCullough made public his views about Craig while the latter was briefly in custody on racketeering charges and threatened to expose him to McMichael. When Craig was released, he was told about McCullough's threats and arranged for the INLA to kill him. McCullough was later gunned down on the Shankill Road.

McMichael understood the power and autonomy of UDA commanders like Craig and knew it was dangerous to confront him on the basis of rumour. Even when McMichael received a report from a UFF operative in the Shankill that Craig regularly met his IRA contact, Joe, he was not sure how to react. Craig learned about McMichael's interest in him and immediately offered his UFF counterpart information on the INLA. Craig knew that if he was accused of consorting with the enemy he could easily argue that he was merely running an intelligence operation against his enemies. McMichael issued an instruction to Craig to cease all contacts with republicans but Craig ignored him. It was not long before

Craig learned on the UDA grapevine that his nemesis was building a dossier on him, which he hoped to present to the UDA Inner Council.

In the spring of 1987, McMichael was preoccupied with overall UFF strategy. That was when he appointed Brian Nelson, a soldier and former member of the UDA, to run UFF intelligence assets. Thirty-nine-year-old Nelson was an agent for the Army's secret Force Research Unit and, with access to high-grade information from his Military Intelligence bosses, began plotting killings with the UFF chief. McMichael took his eye off Craig and that was not a wise move. I was told, however, that he informed Nelson about his suspicions regarding Craig. He explained to the military agent that he had encouraged UFF operatives to 'drop information' to see if Craig picked it up and acted on it.

McMichael failed to understand that Craig was ruthless and well schooled in deception. He also neglected to take into account the fact that he was trying to corner a 'viper'. Craig had successfully eliminated most of his enemies within the loyalist fraternity and, as the McCullough killing demonstrated, he did not have to dirty his hands to do it. Facing possible exposure as an informer, Craig cleverly turned to the Provisional IRA to eradicate the problem but there was no guarantee that they would oblige and kill McMichael. They had deliberately avoided targeting loyalist leaders for over a decade. There were many occasions, as IRA operatives confirmed to me, when they could have killed the UDA Commander, Andy Tyrie. However, Craig had learned that the UFF attempt on Gerry Adams' life in 1984 had forced a rethink and they had, with his help, killed major loyalist assassins in West Belfast. The only problem in seeking the help of the IRA was that McMichael was regarded as a political leader of loyalism and not an organiser of terror. Craig had an ace card which would change their minds. He told his IRA contact, Joe, that the man behind the assassination attempt on Adams and other senior republicans was John McMichael. That information sealed McMichael's fate. Craig did not have to supply much information about McMichael because the IRA knew where he lived and that he owned a bar, the Admiral Benbow, in Lisburn. They quickly discovered that McMichael had lax security and often parked his car near his bar. The UDA supremo had believed that his public profile protected him from an IRA attack and that the IRA had not linked him to the attempted murder of Gerry Adams.

On 22 December 1987, the IRA planted a bomb under McMichael's car and it exploded as he got into the vehicle outside his home. He suffered horrific injuries and died on the way to hospital. Within 48 hours, McMichael's offices in Gawn Street in East Belfast were ransacked and documents taken. Later speculation centred on Craig but he was not the culprit. The raid was made to look like a burglary but was carried out by Brian Nelson on orders from his handlers in the British Army's Force Research Unit. They and Special Branch were anxious to remove incriminating evidence of McMichael's links to them. Craig attended McMichael's funeral and told mourners that the IRA would pay for the murder of his 'friend'.

McMichael's early demise angered Nelson and his bosses in the Force Research Unit, a variant on the MRF of the early '70s. From the 'raid' on McMichael's offices, Nelson and Andy Tyrie acquired McMichael's files on Craig but those files did not provide sufficient evidence to encourage the Inner Council to take action. In 2003, I asked a senior UFF operative why Nelson and others did not move swiftly to eliminate 'Pratt' Craig.

'It's easy with retrospect to say we knew it was Craig's hand in John's murder but to tell you the truth, most of us knew shit. Sure, we all knew Jimmy was a bit of a bastard but he wasn't the only one feathering his nest – which was part of the order of the day. Nobody was big enough to point a finger at him and he seemed as upset as everybody else did. Some of the lads said he even cried when John was killed and for days ran around in a rage saying he would get the bastards who did it. But then Nelson came up with videotape – well – fuck me, that did it – that's when the shit hit the fan. It began to dawn on us that he was dirty and it was agreed to put surveillance on him and talk to some of his people – you know with the kind of warning that if they held back and we found out that Jimmy was the man that they would pay. Looking back, I'd have to say that knowing what I know, Nelson and the people he worked for would have wanted Jimmy six feet under. The rest of us felt it had to be done right and the evidence had to be solid.'

The video Nelson gave to the UDA/UFF leadership was handed to his Force Research Unit bosses by a member of Special Branch who worked closely with them. It showed Craig meeting with an IRA leader in the Capstan bar in Belfast city centre. The recording had been made by specialists from E4A and E4B. They operated within the Special Branch E Department, which handled agents and informers. The bizarre aspect of that meeting in the Capstan bar was that Craig had provided Special Branch with prior notice of it. The Special Branch officer who made the videotape available to the FRU believed their thesis that Craig was out of control and expendable. In eliminating McMichael, he had struck a blow against their secret war, which McMichael had helped mastermind. Through McMichael, collusion had been effective in promoting the use of counter-gangs.

Other information about Craig, some of it forwarded by the security forces, provided the UDA's Inner Council with a more complete picture of

Craig's life. That can be see in the following section of a UFF document presented to Inner Council Brigadiers.

> [*Names and addresses withheld by author.*] In February of 1988, Craig was in a car stopped by a Security Forces patrol in Dunmurry. The other occupant was —, a top Provo Craig met in Crumlin Road jail. [*Author's note: If that was true, it shed light on the fact that the UFF acquired documents from Dunmurry police station in September 1989 relating to suspected members of the IRA.*] The Provo is the boyfriend of another leading Provo — — of —, Glen Road, telephone number —. Craig was also observed meeting — of Moira Street in the Short Strand . . .

On 10 October 1988, the UDA leaders evaluated all the written allegations against Craig but it was the videotape Nelson gave them that proved the most startling piece of evidence. Without much debate, there was a unanimous decision to kill the Teflon Don but all those present recognised that it would not be easy. He was a naturally suspicious man and had lately increased his security. There was no easy way of killing him within his stomping ground while he had his inner circle of admirers protecting him. They had not flinched from giving him unquestioning loyalty while he continued to dispense largesse. The death of McMichael and rumours from East Belfast that Jimmy Craig was dirty meant nothing to them. He was lining his pockets and theirs and also running C Company assassinations of republicans. He was no different from other UDA Brigadiers. They all ran rackets and terror. That was an accepted part of life in the UDA and Jimmy was a true loyalist. From the formation of the UDA there had been no love lost between the two competing parts of Belfast. Loyalists in the Shankill believed they lived in the birthplace of loyalist terror going back to 1966 and were much more militant than their counterparts in the East.

Brian Nelson, Chief of UFF Intelligence, suggested to the Inner Council that the only way to kill Craig was to lure him out of his lair. He had good reason to want rid of him. His FRU bosses had warned him that Craig was unpredictable and his links to the Provisionals and the INLA could prove costly to the UDA/UFF. If he could set up McMichael, what was to prevent him doing the same to Nelson or others controlled by the intelligence community? Special Branch, which had benefited from Craig's willingness to help in years past, was not informed of the plan to kill him. Perhaps, the plotters suspected that Craig had links to the RUC and they did not want anyone tipping him off. Another reason may be that, while the FRU and Special Branch worked closely together, the FRU did not always share intelligence with Special Branch and vice versa. In fact, FRU operatives felt that Special Branch was overly secretive. It had been long in the agent-running business and had seen many secret military organisations come and go. Special Branch officers had always felt superior to their English counterparts in groups like the FRU. They were indigenous operators with a more detailed knowledge of the complexities of both communities. Many amateurish Military Intelligence operations over three decades had cost the lives of informers and agents and that had not endeared the military spies to their Ulster colleagues. My evidence is that, if the FRU had told Special Branch about their intentions regarding Craig, Special Branch would have pulled the plan.

Nelson knew that Craig's weakness was greed, so an intermediary was used to convince Craig that if he travelled to a bar in East Belfast he could act as a fence and benefit from gold objects taken in a robbery. Craig was tempted by the offer and let down his guard. On the evening of 10 October, without his retinue to protect him, he travelled across the city to the rendezvous. As he waited in the bar for a criminal contact to arrive, two men entered with automatic weapons and opened fire. He died at the scene from multiple gunshot wounds.

Special Branch bosses were furious when they later learned that one of their own had passed the videotape to Nelson and that he had used it to get Inner Council permission to order the hit on Craig. Some senior members of Special Branch privately commented that they would not forget Nelson's 'treachery' in failing to consult them about the execution of one of their agents.

In the shadowy world that Craig and McMichael inhabited, it was inevitable that they would eventually collide but not perhaps in a way anyone could have anticipated. Craig had the potential to remain a Teflon Don if Nelson had not arrived on the scene. I was told that it was unlikely the Inner Council would have ordered his execution without the compelling evidence on the videotape. It served to harden other evidence of a more circumstantial nature. Underlying their initial reluctance to kill him was their recognition that he was truly one of them – a criminal and a terrorist. In the long term, his demise would change nothing. He would not be the last Teflon Don. Others would emerge with sobriquets like 'Mad Dog' and would be more successful criminals than Craig. Drugs would also become a major part of the UDA's operations. And the terror would not cease in Craig's stomping ground of the Shankill.

As for McMichael, the Political Hitman, he achieved his aim of emulating the Provisional IRA leaders he admired. Before his death, he had begun to resemble Sinn Fein leaders like Danny Morrison who had a secret terrorist role. Unlike the Provisionals, however, he never achieved his aim of creating their kind of discipline within the ranks of the UDA/UFF. His major problem in that regard was that the UDA was rooted in a culture of crime and reflex sectarianism. He had been part of both until he formed an admiration for the IRA and, in confronting racketeering, he ran foul of James 'Pratt' Craig. He told me in 1980 that he was wary of treading on too many toes and in treading on Craig's he went too far. His role in collusion with the intelligence community was another element in his downfall. On instruction from his intelligence sources, he had ordered the assassination of the Provisional Sinn Fein President Gerry Adams and that had returned to haunt him. The story of both Craig and McMichael sheds light on the dirty war and the unstable character of the UDA/UFF. In the wake of their deaths, things did not change but, as I will show in a subsequent chapter, through Brian Nelson, McMichael's vision of a more lethal UFF strike force became a reality.

5

PAEDOPHILE TERRORISTS

In any investigation of the grisly murders of the early 1970s, the killing of ten-year-old Brian McDermott deserves mention. A Protestant from East Belfast, Brian was seen playing in the Ormeau Park in South Belfast on a Saturday afternoon. That was the last sighting of the boy until parts of his charred, dismembered body were found on the nearby banks of the River Lagan. There was wild media speculation that he had been abducted by a black magic cult and killed in a bizarre ritual.

No one has ever been brought to justice for his murder but secret police and Military Intelligence files reveal that subsequent inquiries identified a possible suspect – a sadistic paedophile, John McKeague. Military Intelligence also examined the possibility that William McGrath, another homosexual pervert, could have been the culprit. Both men were leading loyalists whose lives crossed several times in their careers while they plotted terrorism and abused boys and young men. They were linked to the dark side of Northern Ireland with McKeague the more visible of the two.

McKeague rose to prominence in loyalist circles in the 1960s as a flag-bearer for Paisleyism and despite a conviction for buggery was accepted in the ranks of conspiratorial Unionists. In 1964, his name became associated with extremism when, in tandem with Paisley, he threatened to lead a march to tear down an Irish tricolour which was being flown outside Sinn Fein offices in Divis Street in the Lower Falls. The public display of the flag was in contravention of the Flags and Emblems Act but the authorities had chosen to ignore the breach of the law until Paisley highlighted the issue. In face of threats from Paisley and McKeague, the Unionist Government ordered the RUC to remove the flag. Riots ensued and police, backed by members of the paramilitary B Specials, quelled the disturbances.

The Divis Street riots were an important benchmark on the road to widespread communal violence in that part of the city where the Shankill and Falls ran parallel, with interconnecting streets. Catholics regarded the removal of the flag as yet another example of the determination of Unionism to silence the right of the nationalist community to freedom of political expression. Protestants viewed the riots as evidence of a resurgent republicanism on open display within the Catholic population. Meanwhile, in the shadows, a cabal of loyalist extremists was discussing the need for a credible force to combat the IRA which they believed was planning a return to physical force politics. That assessment was incorrect because the IRA, after the failure of its 1956–62 campaign, had divested itself of the belief that politics emanated from the barrel of a gun. However, truth and reality had little influence on those members of the cabal who were so infected with bitterness that they were never going to listen to reason. They deeply resented Catholic social action that was linked to demands for electoral reform and equity in the allocation of houses. When the Unionist Prime Minister, Captain Terence O'Neill, responded to Catholics with the promise of minor reforms, the cabal judged his actions to be capitulation and a trend which, if not halted, would lead to an erosion of Protestant political domination. Two of the conspirators, while driving a car, were stopped by police. Explosives were found in the boot of the vehicle and, though a report was made to the authorities, no action was taken against them. Robert McCartney, a leading lawyer and Unionist politician, believes a file on that matter still exists. It has always been McCartney's contention that the issue was covered up because of a connection between a member of the cabal and certain figures within the Unionist Government of the day.

The cabal consisted of a preacher, a lawyer, the paedophile John McKeague and members of the B Specials. They were convinced of the need to create a military-style organisation to assassinate key IRA leaders and to undertake actions aimed at destabilising the Unionist leadership of Terence O'Neill. By 1965 they had engineered the core of such an organisation to be called the Ulster Volunteer Force. In Belfast, its leader was the soldier, Augustus 'Gusty' Spence. Spence and a small band of men in the Shankill were not the driving force behind the UVF but merely the instrument for the cabal to realise its objectives.

In March 1966, Paisley warned that there would be 'an invasion' of Belfast from the Irish Republic to coincide with the traditional republican Easter 1916 celebrations. What Paisley intended to convey was that thousands of republicans would travel to Belfast for a demonstration of IRA triumphalism. However, his use of language was always shaped to convey something sinister. He told his followers, 'We mean business.' The implied threat in his words was his trademark.

While that language infused the political atmosphere with fear and suspicion, McKeague was busy meeting with members of the UVF. His predilection for boys and young men in a highly conservative Protestant community was common knowledge but his embrace of extreme political views negated any potential for criticism of his personal life. That was a growing feature of life in what was becoming a surreal atmosphere of sectarianism, which would eventually culminate in violence. Throughout the Troubles the phenomenon of non-recognition of the criminal and socially depraved elements of society was ignored. However, it was a dangerous ingredient. Men, who in a normal society would have been shunned because of their violent or anti-social behaviour, found acceptance because of their paramilitary roles as so-called defenders of their respective communities. It was as if the normal rules and definitions of sanity were pushed aside. Aggressive psychopaths operated without constraints. In a normal society they would have been under mental health care. The psychiatric unit of Downpatrick Hospital, with a medical brief to treat aggressive psychopaths, had to close during the Troubles because of a lack of patients. McKeague was one of those who slipped through the cracks of the mental health system.

Homosexuality was a non-topic in the mid 1960s when McKeague was publicly stirring up hatred and striding round the Shankill with young men at his side. Within the higher echelons of Unionism, there was a secret homosexual world that McKeague had access to. Sir Knox Cunningham, an Establishment figure and Westminster MP, was at the centre of a paedophile ring that held parties at a house in an English seaside resort. Boys and young men from the lower social classes in Northern Ireland were taken to those parties. Knox Cunningham was a friend of the well-known homosexual, Sir Anthony Blunt, the Keeper of the Queen's Pictures, who was eventually unmasked as a Soviet spy. He and Knox Cunningham had met at Cambridge. While McKeague was intellectually inferior to those men, he was allowed access to their inner sanctum because of their shared sexual appetites.

The dire warnings by Paisley of an 'invasion' from the Irish Republic did not transpire but that mattered little to McKeague and the other members of the loyalist cabal. One of the first actions of the UVF was tragic. A petrol bomb, thrown from a car at a Catholic-owned bar, landed in the home of 77-year-old Matilda Gould, a Protestant. She received burns to most of her body and died in hospital. Gusty Spence's UVF colleagues issued a statement admitting the death of the pensioner was a 'terrible mistake' and warned of violence to come. 'From this day we declare war against the IRA and its splinter groups. Known IRA men will be executed mercilessly and without hesitation. Less extreme measures will be taken against anyone sheltering them or helping them, but if they persist in giving them aid, then more extreme measures will be adopted. Property will not be exempted in any action taken. We will not tolerate any interference from any source and we solidly warn the authorities to make no more speeches of appeasement. We are heavily armed Protestants dedicated to this cause.'

That statement was a clear warning to Unionist Prime Minister Captain Terence O'Neill not to make any concessions to Catholics or speeches that the cabal regarded as 'appeasement'. The written threat was not penned by Spence, the leader of the Shankill unit of the UVF, but by some of the leading conspirators controlling him.

Spence and his unit met regularly in the Standard bar in the Shankill area and discussed whom they might kill. McKeague often dropped by and had a chat or talked strategy. He also travelled outside Belfast with Spence to talk to members of the blossoming UVF, most of them from the ranks of the B Specials.

The first person killed by Spence's unit was 28-year-old Patrick Scullion, a Catholic engineering worker. In later years, Spence became an articulate and often reasoned voice of loyalism but in 1966 he was a very different personality. He was impressed by those running the show, namely McKeague, a lawyer and a preacher. Like them, as he later told me, he was a bigot and that is clear from the following account of what transpired in Malvern Street on 26 June 1966, when four Catholic barmen crossed his path. The following is a statement made by 33-year-old Robert James Williamson, a member of one of Spence's units.

> I went to McDowell's bar [Standard] at the corner of Agnes Street, Shankill Road at about 8 p.m. I went with Gusty Spence and we attended a meeting of the Ulster Volunteer Force. The following men were at the meeting: Rocky Burns, Leslie Porter, Hugh McClean, Des Reid, Gusty Spence and myself . . . The whole lot of us left McDowell's [Standard] at closing time and went to Curry's house in Belgrave Street. Rocky Burns' coat was open and I saw a revolver sticking out his trousers. We had some more drinks there and, in fact, I had a lot of drink that night in McDowells. Some time after 11 p.m. I went to Watson's bar [Malvern Arms] in Malvern Street with Gusty Spence, Frank Curry, Porter, Reid and McClean. Rocky Burns did not come. We had a few drinks in there and then me and Porter and Reid went out in the direction of Glengormley. Reid left the car and came back with a parcel and put it in the boot. I never saw what was in the parcel but Reid told me it was gelignite. We drove to Craven

Street and I left them and went to Curry's house. I was standing outside Curry's house with Henry Johnston. I don't know where the gelignite went to. I went round to Watson's bar. I had a Luger gun in a shoulder-holster with me. It was loaded with six rounds of small-calibre ammunition. I joined two comrades I don't wish to name. I was told there were four IRA men in the bar. There were instructions given by one of my comrades to scare them. I took up position at the corner of Malvern Street and Ariel Street. My comrades took up their own positions. The four IRA men came out of Watson's pub. I moved towards the centre of the road. I drew my gun and fired towards the men, but low. Everybody was told to fire low. I mean my comrades. My gun jammed and I had to cock it and a round was ejected each time.

The statement was riddled with lies because it was an ambush to kill four innocent Catholics who had not realised that their lives were in danger by drinking in a Protestant district. It also illustrated the character of the UVF trigger men. None of them was a sophisticated thinker capable of masterminding a campaign of violence or building a terrorist organisation. That was the job of the preacher, the lawyer and McKeague. He was not well educated but was cunning and willing to undertake whatever role was assigned to him by his fellow conspirators. As for Spence, on the night of the shooting in Malvern Street, he demonstrated his ferocity by pursuing Liam Doyle, one of the barmen who later provided an account of what happened. 'I saw this man running after me. I saw flashes coming from him and he started to shoot into me. I was hit six times. I asked him why he was shooting at us as we were doing nothing. I pleaded with him not to shoot me and shouted, "Please, don't do that," or something like that, but the man made no reply and did not stop shooting.'

Spence later told me that when he was arrested and questioned about the episode, detectives wanted information about the lawyer member of the cabal. It proved that the authorities were well aware of the names of the leading conspirators yet no action was taken against them. While Spence and members of his unit awaited trial on murder charges, McKeague used the unit's gelignite cache to orchestrate a number of explosions which were blamed on the IRA.

Nowadays, many former UVF operatives seek to distance themselves from the McKeague era and deny there was ever any connection to him, but the facts speak for themselves. In August 1969, when Catholic areas of West Belfast were invaded by loyalist mobs with the connivance of B Specials and members of the RUC, McKeague was at the forefront of the assaults and directly involved in the burning of hundreds of Catholic homes. The Scarman Tribunal, set up to investigate the causes of violence during that period, condemned McKeague's role. In February 1970, McKeague and four other men were acquitted on charges of causing explosions the previous year. While their trial was in progress, two small explosions occurred in the vicinity of the courthouse. It was believed they were intended to influence the outcome of the trial.

McKeague's prominence and brazen homosexuality began to irritate some of the UVF leaders in the Shankill who felt that he was not right for their image. They also worried that he had a tendency to insert himself into too much of the organisation's decision-making process and that his connections to a wide range of loyalist groupings made it difficult to determine with whom his loyalty lay. By 1971, he was recruiting young thugs to carry out violence and they became known as Tartan gangs. They operated in West Belfast and in the east of the city where McKeague lived off and on with his mother and published a newsletter. Henry McDonald and Jack Holland in their book *INLA: Deadly Divisions* provided what I regard as an apt description of the McKeague I met and interviewed in the late '60s and early '70s: 'Blond-haired, clamp-jawed, tense, he always exuded menace and an angry intolerance, looking and behaving like someone who would have been a suitable recruit to Hitler's SS.'

He was also lean, sleazy and snake-like, his eyes slightly sunken. When he spoke, the menace was wrapped in slyness but there was no missing his capacity for sadism. It was not apparent to the UVF that by 1971 he had become an intelligence asset, providing information to Special Branch officers about other loyalists. I was told that they recruited him while he was on trial for causing explosions. He was not a difficult target for recruitment because Special Branch had sufficient information to blackmail him on the basis of his illegal sexual activities. By working for them, it enabled him to operate freely within the paramilitary world and not to fear prosecution for political or sexual crimes. In 1972, they handed him over to British Military Intelligence handlers though they still maintained contact with him.

He was a practised manipulator and the young thugs under his control were sometimes targets of his sexual appetite. However, all of them were directed to commit sectarian crimes. One of their first killings was on the evening of 13 March 1972. The victim was a 19-year-old Catholic, Patrick McCrory, who lived in Ravenhill Avenue in East Belfast. He had received a severe beating at the hands of McKeague's thugs who had warned him that they would 'get him'. He had become frightened of leaving his home and, on the fateful evening, answered a knock at his door and was shot dead. His girlfriend later identified two of the gang who had threatened him but no action was taken against them. That may well have been because it was not possible for the police to link them to his death.

Two months later, on 4 May, one of McKeague's Tartan gangs struck again but in North Belfast. The victim was a Catholic seaman just home on leave. He was abducted and taken to a house in the Protestant Tiger Bay neighbourhood. There he was beaten and stabbed 15 times before his body was dumped in an alley off Baltic Avenue. The killing had a ritualistic bloodletting dimension which would later figure in other murders ordered by McKeague.

Loyalists were not the only ones capable of such brutality. Two months later, on a Saturday evening, two Protestant friends, David Fisher, 30, and Hugh Clawson, 34, went to an illegal drinking club at Alliance Avenue in North Belfast. Both men lived in a small loyalist enclave named The River Streets, which had become notorious for harbouring UVF and UDA killers. After midnight on 1 July, Clawson and Fisher, after consuming a lot of alcohol, began walking home. The fact that they were inebriated probably lowered their awareness of the dangers lurking on their route, especially as it intersected with The Bone, a small Catholic district off the Oldpark Road. In that vicinity, vigilantes were on street corners and IRA gunmen in the shadows. There had been numerous loyalist attacks on The Bone and people there constantly lived in fear. As Clawson and Fisher walked down the Oldpark Road they were under scrutiny by a group of vigilantes who were members of an armed unit that operated independently of the Provisional IRA. When the two Protestants reached the edge of The Bone they were seized by members of that unit and taken to a nearby house where they were interrogated, beaten and burned with cigarettes. Their abductors had known from the moment they spotted them that they were strangers and likely residents of The River Streets. The interwoven sectarian geography of Belfast was burned into the minds of killers on both sides. The area from which someone emerged was enough to indicate their religion. Clawson and Fisher were not loyalist paramilitaries but any denial by them would not have changed their date with death. Before dawn they were led to a stretch of ground near Cliftonville Cricket Club and killed. Clawson was shot five times in the head and neck at close range and Fisher, three times. The unit responsible for their deaths was later incorporated in the Provisional IRA and its leader subsequently interned.

McKeague's personal life changed little in 1971. He continued to promote sectarianism through his newsletter and to direct the Tartan gangs. However, he ran foul of criminals in the emerging UDA who accused him of interfering with their extortion rackets by demanding money from people who were under their control. In a tragic twist of irony, his enemies lobbed a petrol bomb into his mother's home. Like Matilda Gould, who died from a similar attack in 1966, Mrs McKeague was trapped in the blaze and died. McKeague's detachment from the UVF and his contempt for the UDA forced him to rethink his paramilitary strategy. He decided to create his own paramilitary organisation and gave it the name the Red Hand Commandos. It was a grand title designed to indicate that, like the UVF, it was organised on a strict military and disciplinary basis. But, because of McKeague's sadistic tendencies, it was a group built for sectarian brutality. Into its ranks flocked members of the Tartan gangs and men similar in nature to its leader. Once again, he selected young men as much for bedding as for their potential for violence and cruelty. He acquired weapons through his contacts in the UVF, a fact that is strenuously denied by some members of the UVF but only because of later revelations about his homosexuality and involvement in the Kincora Boys' Home Scandal. In 1972 and later, he was seen as a committed loyalist and as long as he was killing Catholics no one in the ranks of the UDA/UVF condemned him or sought to publicly distance themselves from him.

One young man who came under his spell was Michael Stone, later nicknamed the Milltown Cemetery Killer. Stone had been in a Tartan Gang before he joined the inner circle of the Red Hand Commandos and received training in the use of weapons. The internal thesis of the organisation was that torturing suspected republicans – a euphemism for innocent Catholics who happened to fall in to the hands of the 'Commandos' – was preferable to a swift bullet to the head. Two killings stand out as ghastly examples of what McKeague wanted.

The first was that of Henry Joseph Russell, a Catholic who had just joined the UDR and who lived in the mainly Protestant town of Carrickfergus, outside Belfast. The Russell family had moved to Carrickfergus, hoping to avoid the sectarian strife in Belfast. Henry had joined the Royal Air Force at age 15 to become a nurse. With the onset of the Troubles, he bought himself out of the service and returned home to work in Purdysburn mental institution. On the evening of Friday, 12 July 1972, he left for the train to take him to Belfast. Once there he would customarily travel across the city, his route bypassing East Belfast. At two o'clock the following morning his body was found near the railway line at Larkfield Drive in East Belfast. He had been stripped to his underpants and burned with a red-hot poker – a cross was branded into his back. The rest of his body bore the signs of terrible injuries. He had also been stabbed but death had been caused by a bullet to the head. One of his mother's foster children later described Henry as a 'marked man' because he had believed that unknown persons had followed him for several months prior to his death. It was a ritualistic and sadistic murder and it did not matter that he was one of the few Catholics to join the UDR. What mattered most to his killers was his religion. The branding of a cross on his back could be interpreted as a comment about his religion or the belief of the killers that they had murdered him not just for Ulster but in keeping with the loyalist slogan, for God and Ulster.

The second murder, a carbon copy of the first, is one that has haunted me from the day I saw the body of the victim. He was Patrick Benstead, a grown man of low intelligence and childish ways. He often shopped for his family and liked being trusted with money for that chore. He lived in the Short Strand, a small republican stronghold on the edge of the major Protestant East Belfast. Where he lived may have convinced his killers that he had intelligence on the IRA. Another factor may have been that one of his relatives had faced arms charges.

On the Friday afternoon of 1 December 1972, Patrick Benstead was sent shopping and disappeared. At dawn the following day, a man walking his dog along Templemore Avenue came across his body lying in an alley at Crossley Street. Like Henry Russell, the body bore signs of torture. There were burn marks caused by a red-hot poker on the hands and soles of the feet. The letters 'IRA' were burned into his back and alongside them the number 4. The '4' may have signified that he was the fourth victim of his killers. Death was due to a single gunshot wound to the head. The body was stripped to underpants and socks. The use of a poker told police that the perpetrators were the same ones who killed Russell. Both men had been tortured in a house in East Belfast where a poker was heated in a living-room fire.

I have since spoken to a loyalist who was in the Red Hand Commandos in the early '70s and left the organisation to join the UVF, from which he also parted company after a dispute about a compromised operation in North Belfast. His view of McKeague was bitter and one could argue that it was motivated by something he preferred not to discuss. However, he offered me an insight into the way McKeague had operated.

'After all the stuff came out about McKeague, I never wanted anybody to know I was in the Red Hand because I knew what people would say – they'd say that I was queer and that's not true. John had his favourites and everybody turned a blind eye to that because it was all about action and it didn't matter to me who he fucked as long as it wasn't me. He knew not to play that game with some of us. I'd have put a bullet in his fucking head. A lot of us saw action but I never got involved in the nasty stuff. Fair enough, I did a few things when I was with them but nothing the

UVs [UVF] weren't doing at that time. John had a nasty side to him – he wanted to see the handiwork, if y'know what I mean. That sorta thing didn't interest me. He had a lot of headbangers around him but that was his style. He wanted to outdo the UDA – he hated them with a real passion. I didn't know then he was a tout but I'll tell you this. If he was giving the Branch [Special Branch] information on anybody it was the UDA. He had a lot o' contacts in the RUC because nobody bothered him. If there was a problem, he'd always say, "Don't worry, I'll sort that out." I left for personal reasons and let's just leave it at that.'

The phrase 'wanted to see his handiwork' indicated that McKeague personally participated in torture and murder. The source also made it clear that many people later denied any involvement with McKeague because of his paedophile reputation. One of the major influences on his life and the lives of many leading loyalists was a fellow paedophile, William McGrath, a British Intelligence asset from the mid 1950s. He was one of the most bizarre and shadowy figures of the Troubles. Balding, with dark-rimmed spectacles, he had a reputation as a crusading evangelist. He was born in 1916 and by the 1950s he was a rabid anti-communist. In the early '60s, as a member of Paisley's Free Presbyterian Church, he warned that the Marxist leanings of the IRA were warning signs of a forthcoming communist revolution in Ireland. Married to an English woman, who shared his political philosophy, he appeared to the world a happily married family man. At the beginning of the '60s he was living with his wife and three children in middle-class South Belfast.

People who met him or listened to him speak at Christian Fellowship rallies were impressed by his oratory and grasp of international politics. He was able to hold audiences spellbound and infuse them with fervour for his bizarre brand of politics and religion. He employed the archaic techniques of the Bible-thumping tradition, preaching dire warnings of God's wrath and dark days to come when blood would flow in the streets as communists tried to impose their godless doctrine on Britain and Ireland.

God, he told his audiences, had infused him with the dynamism to confront the communist menace, which was now rooted in republicanism. The Roman Catholic Church and the Vatican were frequent targets of his sharp tongue. He believed that Protestantism in Ireland was being systematically eradicated by the power of the Catholic Church in the Irish Republic. He saw merit in having a 'religious army' ready to wage war against the ravages of the Church of Rome and its Jesuitical hierarchy. The Jesuits, he told his followers, were the Vatican stormtroopers in a policy to undermine Protestant values. The rhetoric was evocative of the public and published pronouncements of Ian Paisley but they came from a man much more intellectually accomplished in the realm of politics, history and theology. While Paisley's influence was mainly with the working class, McGrath's reach stretched into the upper echelons of middle-class Unionism and down into the streets of the Shankill and East Belfast.

Unlike Paisley, he dabbled in concepts which went above the heads of many of his followers. He talked about the origins of the Celtic Church, which he so admired. It was, he argued, the last independent church to succumb to the power of Rome and the 'Pauline tradition', a reference to the apostle Paul and his seminal influence on the doctrinal development of the Roman Catholic Church. In McGrath's analysis, the Celtic Church had been the one true evangelical institution corrupted by Rome. He advocated that Protestantism, for its survival, had to return to the Celtic Church model.

His references to things Celtic confused uneducated Protestants who equated Celtic with the Irish Catholic tradition. They could not reconcile the concept of an earlier history with their own or the fact that Celtic tradition embraced the early origins of the peoples of Ireland, Wales and Scotland. McGrath was not averse to promoting his politico-religious agenda in the Irish Republic and spoke at gatherings in Dublin. He was also a member of the British Israelites, who helped shape some of his more outrageous assertions. They contended that Ulstermen would play a role in the rebirth of Britain, which was wilting under communism. They saw the Jews as instigators of the twin menace of capitalism and communism.

McGrath told rallies that the Queen of England was descended from the House of David and that one of the Old Testament prophets was buried in Ulster. That, he argued, was further proof that Ulster would return to the body of Christ. He even went so far as to claim that Ulstermen were descendants of the Lost Tribes of Israel. His emphasis of a connection to Israel and the Old Testament found willing disciples within Paisleyism, hence the fact that, during the Troubles, loyalists claimed affinity with the State of Israel and wore the Star of David.

In the 1960s, McGrath inserted himself into a wide range of loyalist groupings, especially the Ulster Volunteer Force. Like McKeague, he was closely associated with Paisley and even had his own Orange Lodge.

Behind his biblical rants and condemnations of Romanism, republicanism and communism, he was a pederast working for British Intelligence. Like McKeague, he sought out young men and boys, often using his ministry as a cover for his sexual proclivities. His connection to McKeague was through their shared, insatiable paedophile leanings and both knew Sir Knox Cunningham and other leading Unionist homosexuals. Collectively, they were part of what today would be called a paedophile ring. While researching my book *God and the Gun* I spoke to a source about this 'ring' and he explained that there were several Boys' Homes in Northern Ireland from which boys were picked up and taken to parties in Brighton, England. The following is a question and answer session with that source:

Q. Was money exchanged? Were these boys paid?

A. They were given beer money at a weekend for sex.

Q. A police investigation concluded that British Intelligence never knew about McGrath's activities at the Kincora Boys' Home. Did they know?

A. From 1972, there were policy files detailing the activities of Peter Montgomery [Northern Ireland aristocrat and friend of Lord Louis Mountbatten] and his rich friends in Northern Ireland. For anyone to say this matter was hidden from view is nonsense.

Q. There was a theory that elements of the intelligence apparatus permitted McGrath to abuse boys and provide them for others in the hope that they would be able to discredit or blackmail leading Unionists. Does that theory have any validity?

A. Yes. Of course they knew about people who would have been useful. They knew about the son of a member of the judiciary who brought — [*a young man who worked in a garage*] to orgies in the south of England at — [*name and address withheld for legal reasons*]. Young boys often appeared at these orgies.

Q. What age were the boys?

A. Sixteen and over. They were picked up by — [*name withheld for legal reasons*] and taken to England for orgies.

Q. Why was McGrath protected for so long?

A. Because he worked for the intelligence community. He knew people who were very powerful. If McGrath had been unmasked at an early stage, Blunt would have been named as a paedophile and no one could have been sure who else would possibly be named. There were top hats and royalty in that circle.

McGrath, unlike McKeague, had protection from the intelligence community before the Troubles began in earnest. As my source said, 'top hats and royalty', meaning the English upper-classes and people connected to the Royal Family, were part of a wider homosexual ring in which McGrath was an integral player.

However, in the crucial days of the mid to late 1960s, his dealings with the UVF were especially interesting because of the way in which he influenced the organisation in its infancy and those around it like

McKeague. He encouraged joint membership of the UVF and his own grouping, Tara, which promoted concepts like making the Roman Catholic Church illegal, ensuring cleanliness in Protestant districts, campaigning for integrated education and preparing every Protestant to bear arms and be in a state of readiness.

The Tara Proclamation stated that the organisation was not looking for 'trigger-happy gunmen' but responsible men 'prepared to defend their hearth and home and the glorious liberty that has come to us in the Gospel of Our Lord Jesus Christ'. McGrath advocated that Protestants should acquire a 'basic knowledge of guns and ballistics of fieldcraft and strategy. We need men of conviction, men of high principle, men of courage and of faith who are prepared to resist to the death if necessary, every attempt from whatever source, to unfurl the banner of the Evil One over this fair Province of ours.'

Most disturbing is that McGrath used religion to tap into the fear factor and siege mentality of the Protestant community and, within the law, cleverly advocated military preparations to defeat the enemy. The Proclamation left no doubt that the enemy was the rank and file of the Church of Rome – members of the other community in the Province: 'The situation is dark. The enemy is strong. Great and grievous difficulties will have to be faced, but all is not lost. Ulster is God's anvil on which is being forged the future not only of Ireland, but of all the British people of which we are a part . . .'

Chris Moore, author and journalist, stated in his excellent book, *The Kincora Scandal*, that McGrath set up Tara at the bidding of his British Intelligence handlers. Moore, who spent years delving into McGrath's secret world of sex and politics, made the following observation about the man he dubbed 'The Beast'.

'By "doomsday" he meant the point at which the union between Northern Ireland and Britain would be on the verge of disintegration. This, he said, would occur as a result of an invasion by the army of the Irish Republic, followed by the demand for the deployment of an international peacekeeping force. Tara would have in place a plan for a provisional government and a paramilitary force to support the existing security force. It was at Orange Order meetings that McGrath began to reveal the extent of the knowledge fed to him by unidentified "government" intelligence sources. It was at these meetings that he would tell those who challenged his views that they should never "question the word of an intelligence officer".'

McGrath politically indoctrinated many senior UVF figures as well as rank-and-file members in the late '60s: a fact that UVF leaders wanted to forget in subsequent years, especially when McGrath's sordid personal life was exposed. In 1971, when the UVF decided that it had enough information to show that he was a practising homosexual, the relationship between Tara and the UVF waned. It did not, however, end. In fact, contacts between McGrath and the UVF continued to the point when, in 1976, they both sought to buy and import weapons. The journalist Chris Moore believes that Sir Knox Cunningham bankrolled McGrath at the outset of the Troubles and I concur with that assertion. However, I also believe there were other financiers, including MI5, who employed him. While writing this book, I was astonished to discover that there were figures within 'aristocratic' circles on both sides of the Irish border who provided funding to loyalists for weapons. In one instance, a figure who lived in the Irish Republic with connections to royalty conspired with others to have weapons shipped into Northern Ireland.

Aside from McGrath's terror connections and spying, like McKeague it was the sordid side of his life that drove him to depths of depravity. In 1971, while living with his family in East Belfast, he became a house father at the Kincora Boys' Home, a short distance from his home. It was an institution under the aegis of Belfast Welfare and was designed to provide care for teenagers and young men in the 15 to 18 age groups. It opened its doors in 1958 and the warden in charge was Joseph Mains, a paedophile friend of McGrath. Mains and his deputy warden, Raymond Semple, shared boys with a paedophile circle which included McGrath and McKeague. Because of Kincora's proximity to his home, he was able, at a whim, to stroll along to bedrooms in the home at any time of the day or night and abuse some of the boys.

One of the ghastly aspects of what became known as 'The Kincora Scandal' was that McGrath and McKeague, as intelligence assets, were agents of the State. Colin Wallace, a former intelligence officer at British Army HQ in Lisburn, is on record as stating that Kincora featured prominently in secret intelligence reports. One report that he saw confirmed that the RUC knew about the abuse in the Boys' Home.

What Wallace was unaware of was that McGrath and McKeague had virtual immunity from prosecution because of the information they were supplying to their intelligence bosses. According to Chris Moore's investigation of McGrath, MI5 was the organisation that recruited and funded his political activities. They were also fully aware of contacts he made with Rhodesian and South African Intelligence Services in order to acquire arms for loyalists.

The veil of protection surrounding McGrath was finally lifted in January 1980 when an intrepid reporter, Peter McKenna of the *Irish Independent*, published a story about an official cover-up of a homosexual ring abusing boys in a Belfast home. McKenna, I am told, had been tipped off by a leading Catholic politician and spent months quietly investigating Kincora and McGrath. While he did not mention Kincora in his first report for his newspaper, he stated that a member of staff at the boys' home was a man with loyalist paramilitary connections. That was enough to identify McGrath and, from that moment, his sordid life began to unravel. Once the information was in the public domain, his intelligence handlers could not stop the police investigation that followed. Detectives like George Caskey who were given the task of investigating the history of Kincora were not the type of men to be pushed around or diverted from their job of bringing down those responsible for sexual crimes. Within two months, Kincora was closed and McGrath, Joseph Mains, the warden, and his deputy, Raymond Semple, were in cells awaiting trial. They were eventually given prison terms ranging from four to six years with McGrath getting the shortest sentence of four years.

One of the intriguing facets of McGrath's time in police custody was that he vehemently denied that he was homosexual or had abused boys in the Kincora Home. He insisted that he was a happily married heterosexual even when police confronted him with forensic evidence that he liked to be sodomised. He demonstrated to interrogators that he was adept at evading their questions and never flinched from his assertion of innocence. At no point did he compromise McKeague or other paedophiles in his 'ring'. As Chris Moore convincingly argues in his book, the wider story of 'The Beast of Kincora' and his paramilitary, as well as intelligence connections, did not surface during his interrogation or when he was sent to prison.

After being released from prison, he refused to give up his secrets and went to live quietly in a village on the County Down coast where he died in 1991. Those who ran McGrath made efforts to block the potential success of two public inquiries into Kincora. They may not have wanted the public to know the full extent of his role as an agent of the State and the part he played in the conflict, or as Chris Moore has revealed, his MI5 task to destabilise Northern Ireland to facilitate British withdrawal from Ireland.

McKeague had watched the trial of McGrath with some trepidation and after it ended he learned that he was the target for interview for a public inquiry into the Kincora affair. His handlers must surely have known that he was not in the same league as McGrath. The Tara chief was well skilled in anti-interrogation techniques and had been a long-term British Intelligence asset. McKeague was cunning and sadistic but not astute like McGrath. He told friends that he was not going to suffer McGrath's fate and do prison time. If necessary, he would give up important figures involved in the vice ring, some of whom had intelligence connections. But he had more secrets than those to give up, if he so chose.

In mid-January 1982, while McGrath languished in prison, detectives interviewed McKeague about Kincora. On 29 January he was in his shop in East Belfast when two members of the INLA walked in and shot him dead. The two INLA shooters had links to Special Branch and Military Intelligence.

Henry McDonald and Jack Holland wrote in their book, *The INLA: Deadly Divisions*, that a former British Intelligence officer told them McKeague threatened to go public about Kincora shortly before his death. That was an accurate assertion by their source. The sudden death of McKeague was an effort by senior figures in the intelligence world to rid themselves of a potentially bigger problem – the real risk that he would spill the beans on his terrorist crimes as an agent of the State.

The running of both men as agents lies within the immoral and extra-judicial character of the dirty war fought by parts of the State's intelligence apparatus from the outset of the Troubles.

6

DOMINIC 'MAD DOG' McGLINCHEY

When I first met Dominic McGlinchey, he looked impressive. He was six feet tall, and lean, with a receding hairline. In his 30s, his slightly rounded face gave him the look of a much younger man. In no way did he resemble the crazed psychopath staring out from the headlines of British tabloid newspapers. The press had used archetypal arrest photos, which made every suspect resemble an unshaven maniac. In the reflex news coverage of the Troubles, his tabloid sobriquet, 'Mad Dog', which he found slightly amusing, provided exciting copy and led to a tendency to blame McGlinchey for every atrocity.

However, he was a man who struck fear in his associates as well as his enemies. There was not a scintilla of guilt when he publicly admitted that he was a trigger man. Like so many terrorists I interviewed, he portrayed himself as an ideologue who never murdered innocent people. That was not how he was perceived within the security forces on both sides of the Irish border or by the families of those he killed with a clinical ferocity. He had many vicious idiosyncrasies, one of which was that when he pulled a trigger he preferred to be close and personal to a victim. He said that for him it was the most effective way to kill because he was not a trained marksman. It was a curious, if not self-serving way of portraying himself as a cool, cold-blooded assassin. It fitted neatly his profile of judge and executioner.

Dominic McGlinchey's history mirrored that of many young men of his generation who found themselves attracted to violence, often as a consequence of events outside their control and not because of a driving ideological commitment. He grew up in rural South Derry, which had a deep history of republicanism. In his childhood, he would have been aware of the IRA's border campaign as it fizzled out and finally ended in 1962. He would also have been conscious of a deep-rooted anti-Unionist feeling in his part of the Province. At primary school, he was regarded as a bright, though not an exceptional, student. In those formative years there was nothing in his character or demeanour to indicate the seeds of a violent future. On the contrary, he was a normal, inoffensive child.

By the time he was in his teens, civil rights marches, in tandem with Catholic agitation, were a constant feature of life and he told friends he wanted to be part of the protests. The reasons for such a decision are unclear and one can only conclude that he was reacting to events around him, and the idea of participating in marches offered glamour and a close identification with his own community. It was 1968 and he was 15 years old, hardly an age when he would have been able to understand the political complexities and many variables within society and the civil rights movement. He was inserting himself into a process which harboured political strains ranging from nationalist to left wing and physical force republicanism. He was not a member of the Fianna, the IRA's youth wing, but his subsequent presence in street protests brought him to the attention of RUC Special Branch. It had the task of photographing marches and riots in order to build files on 'subversives'.

After the formation of the Provisionals in 1970, he was merely one of thousands of young men on the streets confronting the security forces, especially in Derry. It was only a matter of time before the tall 17-year-old came to the attention of British troops. Following the first internment swoops, he and five youths of his age from South Derry were seized in an arrest operation and taken to a compound within the Ballykelly Army Base on the outskirts of Derry City. Like many detainees, he was held for five days and denied access to his family and a lawyer. During interrogation sessions he was roughly treated and questioned about people he had been seen with in riot situations. He was transferred to another compound at Magilligan and from there taken to the Long Kesh internment camp.

In the Nissen huts of Long Kesh, behind the barbed wire and searchlights, he found himself in the company of IRA veterans of the 1956–62 border campaign. Some of them ran political education classes and sessions in the strategies of guerrilla warfare. Republicans who met McGlinchey at that time described him to me as 'a big kid out of his depth'. He had been an apprentice mechanic before his arrest and lacked a basic grounding in the history and politics of Ireland. Many of the IRA men he met were those who had adopted a Marxist philosophy and the books they quoted and gave to McGlinchey to read were the works of the socialist, James Connolly, and European writers of the Left.

Years later, he would claim that Long Kesh was central to his political development and education. I tend to see that assertion as an attempt by him to insert himself in a lengthy process to explain his subsequent political development and commitment to violence. I believe the reverse was true and that the time he spent in Long Kesh was insufficient to greatly enhance his knowledge of history or politics. However, it did influence and contribute to the shaping of his life. Internment placed an impressionable 17-year-old in the company of much more astute and politically committed men. It also defined him as a terrorist in the eyes of the State and the security forces. I contend that the 11 months he spent behind the wire impacted a residual historical memory rooted in inherited values of opposition to the Northern Ireland State. Yet, even on his release in June '72, there was no apparent desire on his part to join the Official IRA or the fast-developing Provisionals. Instead, he began associating with young men who had not formed any direct connection to physical force republicanism. Two of his closest associates were Ian Milne and Francis Hughes.

Like McGlinchey, Hughes had left school at 16 and taken a job as an apprentice painter and decorator. He had no love for the security forces, having watched one of his brothers being brutally dragged from the family home during the first internment swoops. Nonetheless, it had not encouraged him to join the ranks of the Provisionals. He was only interested in girls, cars and motorbikes. His slight build, fresh-faced smile and reputation as a prankster were not the characteristics of a lethal trigger man in the making. Some of his friends later identified an event that occurred at the time he met McGlinchey, citing it as a turning point in his life.

He was returning home late one night from a dance when the car he was in was stopped by a British military patrol. He and a friend were taken from the car and questioned by the side of the road. Soldiers radioed their base with personal details about Hughes and received information that he was from a prominent republican family. Several soldiers then proceeded to beat and kick him and he sustained wounds that kept him confined to bed for almost one week. He refused to press charges against the soldiers, believing it would only lead to further beatings. At that time, assaults by soldiers rarely reached a courtroom and when they did, a presiding magistrate generally dismissed them.

It is impossible to say with any certainty that the episode described was the catalyst for Hughes joining the Provisional IRA. However, the behaviour of soldiers was often a contributing factor in the antipathy felt by many Catholics to the British Army. It is much more likely that the beating, coupled with his family history and his closeness to McGlinchey and Ian Milne, put him on a road to revenge. There is no evidence to suggest that either of the three sat down and debated the merits of joining the IRA or which wing best suited their ideals and objectives. In comments to his lawyer, years later, McGlinchey provided an insight into that period. 'You meet fellows who now say they had a political philosophy but they had not. You just went out and did it. When I was doing that at the start, I had no idea I was reacting against the State.'

McGlinchey appeared to imply that joining the Provisionals and becoming a part of their Long War was almost a typical thing to do. If that was so, then the violence that followed was motivated by revenge and directed at soldiers and policemen who were at the forefront of the implementation of internment and other measures aimed at defeating the IRA. Hughes and McGlinchey were from devout Catholic families and there was an inevitability that the Provisionals would be their organisation of choice. It was intricately linked to romantic nationalism with its roots in Catholic Ireland, and its Derry leadership of Martin McGuinness, a devout churchgoer, epitomised that religious dimension to the organisation.

Another factor in their decision to join the Provisional IRA was what McGlinchey called 'that colourful period', referring to the early '70s. What he meant was that young Provisionals quickly acquired a hero-worship status. Many were projected from the obscurity of otherwise ordinary lives into the role of 'defenders' of their community. In the surreal atmosphere of bars and clubs, conversation and music applauded past, and mostly dead, heroes – men McGlinchey and Hughes had only learned about in school. Suddenly the Provisionals awakened a sense that there were living heroes in the same blood sacrifice tradition of Easter 1916. They were young men who epitomised a willingness to die for a cause and to be wrapped in a green flag when the time came. 'To die were far more sweet, with Erin's noble emblem boys to be my winding sheet' were the words of one of the songs often played in clubs McGlinchey and Hughes frequented. Living 'heroes' determined to bask in the history of the past, which they all shared, impressed girls of their age.

There was a flamboyant dimension to the triumvirate of McGlinchey, Hughes and Milne. They were like gunfighters of the Wild West or characters from Dan Breen's memoir *My Fight for Irish Freedom*. Hughes made it clear that his heroes were the IRA men in the flying columns of the early twentieth century and he intended to emulate their exploits. At IRA training camps he demonstrated a natural ability in marksmanship and fieldcraft. He liked guns and learned how to take them apart, clean them and reassemble them while blindfolded. McGlinchey showed no such aptitude but proved to be a better organiser than his two friends.

Unlike their IRA counterparts in urban areas who were operationally limited by enclaves and sectarian geography, the trio of McGlinchey, Hughes and Milne had no such constraints. South Derry was for them an intricate maze of fields, lanes, country roads and ditches with which they were intimately familiar. Throughout towns, villages and isolated farms, they knew that they could rely on support in the form of food, places to hide and intelligence on the movements of police, British troops and soldiers from the UDR. Outdated maps in a terrain best suited to the guerrillas hampered the British Army. For decades, that area had been an IRA base of operations and a training ground. Ambushes could be mounted with ease and booby traps planted in hedgerows to kill members of a passing military patrol.

McGlinchey's stint as an operative ended within one year when he was arrested in a house in which weapons were stored. He was returned to Long Kesh and for 18 months made an effort to educate himself by reading and attending classes chaired by Provisional IRA leaders. On his return to South Derry to link up with Hughes and Milne, he was listed on security forces files as someone to be watched. He knew he was a marked man and that a knock on the door in the middle of the night would mean his return to Long Kesh. From that time on, like Hughes and Milne, he stayed at safe houses provided by sympathisers, and there were many of them in that region of Northern Ireland.

His commitment to the Provisional IRA was not as strong as it had been before his second stint in Long Kesh. While in the camp in 1974, the Provisional leadership, using a secret channel to the British Government, had intimated a preparedness to consider ending its campaign of violence. While details of the communications from the IRA's Army Council were not given to the rank and file in Long Kesh, the matter was discussed behind the wire. McGlinchey told Hughes he was concerned that some figures in the IRA leadership were not sufficiently committed to a war of liberation. Nonetheless, McGlinchey did not waver from his role as a trigger man and quickly became the Operations Officer for South Derry.

The new rank gave him freedom to select targets but he told Hughes and Milne he would be 'no armchair general' and would participate in operations. His targets, he added, would be off-duty members of the RUC and UDR who were vulnerable because they lived in remote, outlying areas. He stressed the importance of attacking police stations, especially in towns like Maghera, Bellaghy and Magherafelt where there was strong republican support and good escape routes. What made life difficult for the security forces was that he was an opportunist and ready to kill a 'soft target' outside his sphere of operations – generally an RUC recruit or

UDR reservist. With Hughes and Milne at his side, he wanted to leave the trio's imprint on killings and bombings. An operative under his control provided me with an account of the trio's collective mindset.

'They seemed to have no fear while most of us were scared stiff of being shot dead, wounded or captured by the Brits. Something I can't put a finger on bound them together. Hughes and McGlinchey were really close even though McGlinchey seemed a lot older. Maybe it was because he was in command. I got the impression that they wanted to outdo each other. They gained this reputation of being Robin Hood types and they loved it. I'm not saying they weren't committed to the cause – they were – but you always had the feeling that they lived and breathed action. Francie Hughes just adored guns and he really knew how to use them. McGlinchey was a tough guy and nobody gave him lip. What he said, went – simple as that. He wanted to terrorise the security forces the way they terrorised our people. Like, we didn't have any great political discussions about what we were doing. One of the things in our favour was that we were local lads and people were always willing to give us shelter and food. They'd say, "Good on you, boys." That sort of made you feel good about what you were doing. People would warn us when patrols were in areas because farmers were always out on the land and they missed nothing. Francie was more of a romantic than the rest of us. Sometimes, he was like a big kid – cracking jokes even when things were rough. I really think he saw himself as a Michael Collins or Sean Tracey. McGlinchey was the general. I don't think he ever flinched when he shot somebody. He and Hughes would boast about how good they were and how they were wanted men. I never heard them actually discuss the moment they killed somebody though once McGlinchey talked about being inches from a cop when he shot him. He said it was a strange feeling and that the cop looked at him as if he was already dead. That was all.'

One of the lethal components of the trio is that they personally knew Protestants of their own age who had joined the RUC and UDR but that in no way prevented them tracking and killing them. But not everything went smoothly in McGlinchey's operational role. He wanted to have the best-equipped units and his frequent requests for additional weapons were denied. He complained to senior Provisionals that units in South Armagh had 'better gear' than his teams. The IRA source I quoted earlier remembered McGlinchey's reaction to the IRA's refusal to provide more weapons.

'He had a point. South Derry, under his leadership, became one of the most lethal areas of operations. He was always complaining and what was most obvious about him was that he didn't like taking orders from people who were not out there like him – shooting and bombing. One of his major grouses was that places like Belfast had first call on the best gear. I liked him when I first met him but after a while I felt he was a bit arrogant whereas Francie was always a gentleman. Maybe McGlinchey had to be tough to get things done and keep people in line. I knew that sooner or later he would run up against the powers-that-be in the movement. Either that, or he'd end up on the Army Council.'

McGlinchey and Hughes were involved in scores of operations, including daylight attacks on police stations. In an attack on Bellaghy station, McGlinchey casually walked up to the concrete bunker outside the station and shot the policeman inside it. In another attack, using a technique perfected with Hughes, he placed a booby trap explosive device under a police reservist's car. When the reservist got into the car to take his daughter to school, the device exploded, killing both of them.

Efforts by the security forces to capture the trio proved fruitless. In 1976, in a desperate attempt to elicit public support, a wanted poster carrying their photographs was widely circulated in towns and villages. On 18 April 1977, their status in republican circles was further enhanced when they ran into an RUC mobile patrol. They were driving along the Moneymore Road at Dunronan when they spotted the patrol and quickly spun their car into a U-turn. It went out of control and became lodged in the side of a ditch. The trio exited their car and opened fire, killing two policemen and injuring a third. Stories quickly circulated, depicting them in a shoot-out in which they narrowly escaped only because of their military skills. The reality was that they were lucky on that occasion because they possessed overwhelming firepower and Hughes was a skilled marksman. They were essentially a hit-and-run team because they knew that in any major confrontation with an Army patrol they would be outgunned and unable to make a hasty retreat. The Army was also capable of calling in helicopters and reinforcements to close off areas.

Between intense periods of violence when troops were out in force looking for them, they fled to the Irish Republic and remained there for days and even weeks. At the height of their South Derry campaign, the IRA leadership, on advice from the Derry Commander, Martin McGuinness, sent them to hide out in New York. The tactic was to prevent their capture since such an eventuality would have been a major propaganda coup for the authorities. Their sojourn with Irish-American sympathisers was short-lived when they were wrongly accused of a robbery. McGlinchey wanted to kill the actual culprit but was told to 'lay off' because the person in question was an important fund-raiser in the USA. The episode led to the trio being granted a request to return home. Prior to his trip back to Ireland, McGlinchey got involved in a dispute between two bar-owners. A bar-owner in Queens, across the river from

Manhattan, gave me an account of what transpired. I have withheld the names of the bar-owners from his story.

'Eamon — approached Declan — and told him he wanted to buy him out of the bar they owned. Declan told him he had no intention of giving up the bar but Eamon said he would be back the next day with his lawyer to make a formal offer. Declan told him he was wasting his time but Eamon returned the next day with his lawyer and the relevant papers to seal a deal. As they walked into the bar, they saw Declan sitting at a table in the the back with a guy beside him. Eamon and his lawyer went up and sat down. The guy beside Declan said nothing but there was a folded newspaper in front of Declan. As Eamon's lawyer reached into his briefcase to take out documents, Declan reached forward and unrolled the newspaper. Inside it was a gun. He then turned to the lawyer and said: "You can deal with him," pointing to the guy beside him, who was Dominic McGlinchey. Eamon and his lawyer left.'

In 1977, McGlinchey ran into trouble on one of his cross-border trips after he hijacked a police car at gunpoint. That led to his arrest and a term in Port Laoise prison in the Republic. His sudden departure from the terrorist scene in South Derry did not hamper Hughes and Milne, yet some IRA operatives of the period believe that McGlinchey's absence deprived them of good operational advice. Hughes was top of the British Army's wanted list and SAS patrols were placed undercover in the South Derry countryside to capture or kill him. When intelligence was received that he was due to meet someone in a pub, an SAS team burst into the premises, firing into the ceiling. It was a strategy designed to force regular customers to go to ground. The SAS believed that, in such an event, the one man standing would be Hughes and he would reach for his weapon. To the dismay of the SAS, he was not there.

Stories about Hughes accumulated until it was difficult to distinguish between fact and fiction. The following text, written by a republican over two decades later, offers a flavour of what was in the mix in the 1970s:

> He led a life perpetually on the move, often moving on foot up to 20 miles during one night and then sleeping during the day, either in fields and ditches or safe houses; a soldierly sight in his black beret and combat uniform and openly carrying a rifle, a handgun and several grenades as well as food rations.

That text spoke to the legendary status which those around him were forming back in the mid to late 1970s, especially in the period after McGlinchey left the scene. For reasons I will make clear later in this chapter, it would not take much to further embellish his reputation in order to transform him into one of the best-known IRA men of his generation. The other members of the trio would never achieve the same standing in IRA folklore, partly because some of what was written about Hughes was true, namely that he operated in the IRA's favoured guerrilla tradition. While many members of the security forces, for reasons of political prejudice and understandable bitterness, will never admit that Hughes was a highly professional terrorist, some I talked to were prepared to admit that he was a deadly operative. Certainly, with McGlinchey as his boss, he was a more formidable figure. Not many Provisionals will denigrate the Hughes' legacy, though several I spoke to were dismissive of the 'Che Guevara' image of him in a beret and uniform, constantly armed for conflict. One Provisional said: 'No matter what you may feel about his politics, Francie Hughes would have fitted into other conflicts in the world – the Middle East, you name it. He was a superb operator and that was partly because he knew South Derry like the back of his hand and far better than the Brits who were after him or the RUC who lived there. There was no way he was running round in a black beret. Christ, he wasn't that stupid but he was luckier than most of us. Like McGlinchey he made his own luck most of the time but it was bound to run out sooner or later. There were too many people looking for him and you get tired of being on the run – you get careless. McGlinchey kept him under wraps. He killed a lot of members of the security forces – maybe not as many as McGlinchey – and he had guts but that's not enough to keep you alive or keep you from being caught.'

Luck had kept Hughes out of the clutches of the security forces but it ran out on the night of 19 March 1978. For some time, the SAS and other specialist military units had been perfecting the technique of inserting small units into the Northern Ireland countryside. Two or three men were helicoptered into areas to lie in wait for IRA units or to gather intelligence on the movements of IRA sympathisers. Units of two or three men with radio equipment ready to be used to call in reinforcements were secreted in hedges and ditches or specially constructed hides. Often a hide was a hole dug in the ground and covered with a camouflage of bracken. A small aperture was left for the use of a night-sight to survey the terrain.

On the night of 8 March, Lance Corporal Jones, who had been coopted from the Parachute Regiment to undercover duties, was in a hide with a colleague. They were tasked with maintaining surveillance on farmland several miles from the town of Maghera. Jones suddenly spotted two men approaching the hide. They were carrying rifles and dressed in combat gear. In Jones' estimation, they did not resemble what he understood IRA men to look like and were probably members of a UDR patrol.

Nonetheless, he chose to challenge them to reveal their identities. In doing so, he had to emerge from cover, revealing his location. Had he for a split second known that Francis Hughes was walking towards him, he would have opened fire.

In the darkness, Jones failed to see that one of the men was carrying an M14 carbine and had an ornate .38 Smith and Wesson pistol in his waistband. Those were Hughes' favourite personal guns. The moment Jones made his challenge, Hughes opened fire, followed by his companion. Jones was shot and mortally wounded. His fellow soldier was also hit but bravely fired several bursts from his Sterling sub-machine gun as Hughes and his companion fled. Hughes was shot in the thigh, the bullet shattering bone, but he kept moving, knowing the soldier still alive would radio for back-up. Hughes told his fellow shooter that he would slow him down and it was best they went their separate ways. As Hughes continued on foot, bleeding profusely, his progress slowed. He left behind his rifle and crawled through a hedge, but in doing so dropped his pistol. After several minutes trying unsuccessfully to locate it, he crossed several fields and found cover in a gorse bush. In order to halt the bleeding to his thigh, he packed the wound with soil.

Military reinforcements were quickly on the scene and recovered the terrorists' rifles. At daylight, using dogs, they picked up a blood trail which led directly to Hughes. As soldiers approached the gorse bush where he was hiding, they cocked their weapons and warned him that they would open fire. He crawled out, one hand in the air, and gave them a bogus name but RUC detectives who arrived within minutes knew his identity. He was taken by helicopter to a secure military wing of the Musgrave Park hospital in Belfast to undergo surgery. Blood loss and damage to the bone in his thigh at first encouraged surgeons to consider removing his leg but after major surgery that was unnecessary. However, after several operations, his left leg was shorter than the right, leaving him with a slight limp.

Months later, it was decided he was fit to be interrogated and was taken to Castlereagh where he proved to be resilient to days of questioning by experienced detectives. One detective, who was assigned to ensure that he was not physically abused, told me that Hughes was 'cocky' throughout the interrogation. For 72 hours, he refused food, believing it was spiked with drugs to make him talk, and only ate after his lawyer assured him it was safe to do so. His silence mattered little, but had he admitted to all the killings for which he had been responsible it would have allowed the RUC to close files that are open to this day. When he appeared in court, he was given a life sentence for the one crime the police could attach to him – the killing of Lance Corporal Jones. He also received 59 years for a range of other terror-related offences. Detectives told me that he personally killed at least 12 members of the security forces and injured many more. After sentencing, he was transferred to the H Blocks in the Maze prison.

On 15 March 1980, he followed Bobby Sands on hunger strike and died 56 days later. Through his death, he became a legend and finally emulated the dead heroes he had talked about to McGlinchey and Milne in the early '70s. In 2000, the British Imperial War Museum in London put his rifle and pistol on display. Alongside it were placed the other guns used on the fateful night Lance Corporal Jones was killed.

McGlinchey's life had changed dramatically in his time apart from Hughes. In Port Laoise prison, he reflected on his life of action and initially decided that on his release he would seek a role within Provisional Sinn Fein, the IRA's political wing. He knew that his notoriety as a trigger man would lessen his capability as an operative because he would be under constant scrutiny and that could impact negatively on other men he chose to operate with. The IRA leadership had also intimated to him that he could not return to a major operational rank. It preferred that he worked in the background, using Sinn Fein as cover to advise on overall military strategy. It was a logic applied to many senior IRA figures who found themselves compromised by being sent to prison. The more McGlinchey considered the option of a political role, the less he was enamoured of the idea. He told a fellow prisoner that he was unsure if he could sit in a Sinn Fein office, taking orders from Sinn Fein leaders who had never pulled a trigger. A significant factor, which impacted his uncertainty about his future, was a growing disillusionment with the Provisional IRA's Army Council. There are conflicting opinions about the exact reasons why he broke with the Provisionals when he left prison in 1982, but some observers believe the roots of his disenchantment lay in his experiences in Port Laoise. He had arguments with senior Provisionals from the Republic whom he called 'armchair generals'. From his standpoint, they had been sitting in the relative security of Dublin while he and Hughes were out shooting up the countryside of South Derry and risking their lives. A former Provisional described McGlinchey's time in Port Laoise.

'There was a gulf – historical you might say – between our people in the North and prominent figures in the movement in the South like David O'Connell and Rory O'Brady. It was a divide that had been in place from the Civil War. There had always been – until the Provisional movement really took shape – a tendency for leaders in the Republic to keep us out of leadership positions. In the North, we took over in the late

'70s because we were running the war. I wouldn't say volunteers from the North didn't respect volunteers from the Republic but many of us had a resentment of the movement's leaders of the early to mid 1970s. Had Dominic been in the Maze and not in a prison in the South, I think he would have remained loyal to us. I heard he ran up against the Old Guard in Port Laoise and it almost became physical. He was not a man to back down – that was his nature. There was a rumour he told O'Connell he was nothing but a fucking schoolteacher and armchair general. After that he was ostracised by other prisoners who saw O'Connell as a hero and an intellectual. Maybe that's why Dominic broke with us. It probably began as something personal and in prison those sorts of things can eat away at you and he probably felt isolated, which made it worse. He also had a chip on his shoulder about authority figures – that was part of his make-up. He thought he was better than the guys above him and in most cases that was true. But you have to toe the line in an Army. I also think he couldn't take the fact that when he got out he could no longer be the operator he was. Those of us who were compromised knew once we were released we were too high profile to get back into active service but that was all he had ever known. The prospect of being an armchair general didn't much appeal to him, considering the fact that he hated armchair generals.'

There was only one organisation capable of providing McGlinchey with the action he craved and it was the Irish National Liberation Army. In Port Laoise, he formed relationships with several INLA prisoners and, through them, conveyed to their leadership he was ready to break with the Provisionals. His reputation was enough to impress the INLA Command that he would enhance their operational capabilities. On his release from prison, he joined their General Headquarters Staff and moved to Dundalk with his wife, Mary, and their son, Dominic jnr. He quickly demonstrated his organisational skills by restructuring INLA cross-border units. He even encouraged some Provisionals who had operated with him in the past to join him.

It wasn't long before the INLA promoted him to Director of Operations and that role provided him with an opportunity to visit his old stomping ground of South Derry. Once there, he told the INLA units that he expected more from them. In particular, he wanted them to orchestrate a sustained bombing campaign. They would, he said, have the best weaponry and a large quantity of explosives. In a move designed to show the Provisionals that he was again an operational chief, he contacted leading IRA men, including Martin McGuinness in Derry. While there was a degree of arrogance in that strategy, it was also intended as a rapprochement because of ongoing friction between some members of the two organisations. He also perceived advantage in an exchange of ideas with the IRA and the opportunity for a sharing of intelligence. He did not want his units' operations to conflict with those of the IRA and felt that both groupings could benefit from closer contacts.

In terms of his ambitions for the INLA, he advocated that the organisation needed to develop a greater bedrock of support. His vision was influenced by his knowledge of how the IRA had built its reputation through a political agenda married to an effective military campaign. However, he had personal reservations about the IRA, believing their military effectiveness was sometimes constrained by the growing power of Sinn Fein. In his opinion, 'armchair generals' within the Provisionals' political apparatus often vetoed military decisions in order to facilitate a particular political strategy. He told colleagues that the INLA had no such hurdle to surmount and it was time to go on the offensive. An effective military campaign, he argued, would draw sympathisers from the Provisionals, and the INLA's political agenda could be finely tuned once Catholics realised that the organisation was capable of taking the war to the British. What he failed to understand was that the Provisionals had become a sophisticated terrorist organisation which had rid itself of many of the operatives of the '70s who had been motivated purely by revenge and tribal instincts. Secretly, they had maintained an ongoing dialogue with the British Government and had effectively fused their military and political wings. In contrast McGlinchey and the INLA were imbued with a residual desire for revenge. From the outset, I believe that he had a narrow understanding of the new organisation to which he had given his loyalty.

One of his major operational strategies was a campaign to assassinate Unionist political figures whom he believed were associated with anti-Catholic sentiments. The first target of his wrath was the Reverend William Beattie, a member of Paisley's Free Presbyterian Church and Party. That bid failed, as did others, but McGlinchey was not deterred from increasing the violent potential of the INLA. However, he soon discovered that it was not an easy task to control some of the men under his command or to prevent what he termed 'botched operations'. It was even more difficult to maintain a core of sympathisers.

An example of the INLA's callous disregard for life was an operation mounted in Divis Flats, a sprawling concrete 'jungle' in the Lower Falls area of Belfast. A booby trap device intended to kill a foot patrol of soldiers was placed on a balcony of a block of flats. When it exploded, it killed one soldier and two young boys. Residents of Divis, where the INLA had enjoyed support, demanded that INLA units leave the area. In a similar tragedy, a device placed in a motorcycle helmet killed a young Catholic. INLA gunmen also murdered two Protestants – a male pensioner and a Sunday School teacher in her early 20s. All those events confirmed the cowboy and reckless operatives under McGlinchey's control.

His focus shifted to the north-west of the Province where he had begun his terrorist life. His aim was to mount a spectacular operation in that area to increase his terrorist status and impress his former bosses in the IRA. In September 1982, he travelled to South Derry to meet senior figures in the INLA's Derry Brigade and bluntly told them that they 'were not pulling their weight'. While there he met Martin McGuinness to smooth over tensions which had developed between his units and those of the IRA. He assured McGuinness that they shared similar objectives and he was not opposed to joint operations. A former INLA operative told me that McGlinchey had a high regard for McGuinness and never tolerated any criticism of the IRA chief. However, the IRA had no desire to mount joint operations and felt that the INLA had too many ill-disciplined and sectarian figures in its ranks. In fact, the IRA considered punishing several of McGlinchey's men in the Derry area but decided that with McGlinchey in control, a feud would be bloody. They hoped he would keep his troops in line.

Just to prove he could still be a front-line operator, he led an attack on Cookstown police station and, armed with a Ruger rifle, killed a policeman. Two months later, carrying the same rifle, he shot dead another policeman in Markethill. Both attacks were carbon copies of operations he had once carried out with Francis Hughes and Ian Milne and were seen by some Provisionals as his attempt to prove to everyone that he had 'not lost his edge'. By November 1982, he was pleased to announce to anyone who would listen that the INLA had killed more members of the security forces in the 11 months of that year than their Provisional counterparts. He was again back at the top of the police and Army wanted list, with undercover soldiers hot on his trail. They had information that, while he had his base in Dundalk, he regularly used the same routes to cross the border into Northern Ireland. Special Branch and Military Intelligence chiefs warned undercover operatives if McGlinchey were encountered he would likely be armed and would not give up without a fight. In essence, the basic advice from that quarter was to shoot him on sight. The determination of the security forces to get him at all costs resulted in one of the most controversial episodes of the Troubles.

That episode had its origins in the trip McGlinchey made to Derry in November '82 when he told the Derry Brigade that he had not seen enough action from them and he wanted a 'spectacular'. They came up with a target that received his approval. The Brigade Intelligence Officer explained that soldiers from the Ballykelly Army base, where McGlinchey was interrogated when he was a teenager, frequented a disco at a local pub, The Dropping Well Inn. McGlinchey ordered surveillance placed on the pub and advised it should be bombed at a time likely to cause the most casualties. It mattered little to him that such an attack would claim civilian lives. In his opinion, it was justified collateral damage. He told the Derry Brigade that local girls – Catholics and Protestants – who attended a disco with soldiers were guilty of 'fraternising with the enemy'.

On 6 December 1982, a bomb concealed in a holdall exploded in the pub killing 17 people, 11 of them soldiers. Many were injured and one person died later in hospital. The atrocity was condemned by everyone, including the IRA, but McGlinchey and the INLA expressed no remorse. He said that the civilians killed in the blast should not have been there. They should have known, he added, that the pub was a likely target. In blaming the victims, McGlinchey became a hate figure, guilty of a twisted logic. In a bizarre statement, the INLA said the bomb had been placed at the base of a pillar to minimise the casualties. The reality was that its location succeeded in bringing down the upper structure of the pub, increasing the loss of life and injury. In the maelstrom of outrage across the British Isles, McGlinchey continued to try to justify the carnage. He declared, untruthfully, that the pub owner had been consistently warned that if he permitted soldiers to attend the disco, the premises would be attacked. The operation crystallised McGlinchey's ferocity and leadership. An INLA operative of the period described him to me as a 'conflicted personality'.

'He wasn't the mad dog the media talked about. He was very focused. People would listen when he talked. He had a grasp of international politics and often discussed the agendas of other revolutionary movements. He wanted to see the INLA as part of an international socialist brigade. He was also a hard man and when anyone stepped outta line – God help him or her. If he thought somebody in the ranks was an informer, it was a bullet to the head – no messing. He wouldn't have tolerated people doing crimes or drugs. He was clinical. He used to say the Provos were right to get away from the battalion structure and build a cell system. As for innocent people being killed, he would just say it was war. He didn't oversee every operation and he was blamed for lotsa stuff he wasn't involved in. I think the Brits deliberately portrayed him through the British media as a mad dog just so they could kill him without anybody batting an eyelid. As for all that stuff that he just wanted us to kill Prods, that's just not true. Sure, he took the view that if they killed our people, we should strike back but he didn't spend his time going round saying, "Let's kill all the Prods." He was not a holy Joe but his main targets were the Brit war machine.'

Clearly, those views were from someone with more than a subliminal admiration for McGlinchey and could have equally been applied to the loyalist trigger man, Billy Wright. The security forces knew they were not dealing with a mad dog, but a terrorist who had proved, from the early '70s onwards, that he was a dangerous and unpredictable individual. In the wake of the pub atrocity, intelligence bosses asked for every piece of intelligence on McGlinchey to be assessed and ordered handlers to talk to their informers in the border counties. They believed someone had to know something about McGlinchey's cross-border movements. Special Branch relied on its E4 Department, a version of the British Military's 14 Int, to find and trap him. E4 was subdivided into units dealing with surveillance, bugging, operating covert posts and collating data. It also had an SAS-type component, comprising a unit of policemen specially trained in close-combat killing techniques. The unit with the task of monitoring the homes and vehicles of known associates of McGlinchey was called E4a.

On 12 December 1982, two INLA officers, Seamus Grew and Roddy Carroll, died in a hail of bullets fired by members of E4a. Some of the shots were fired from close range and the double killing sparked a controversy, which became known as the 'RUC's Shoot to Kill Policy'. In an attempt to cover up the truth about the shooting, the British Government used the excuse of national security interest. The RUC subsequently leaked a story that the real target was McGlinchey and not Grew and Carroll. That was of course true and McGlinchey became aware there was an informer in the ranks of the INLA. Within months, he identified him as 43-year-old Eric Dale, a minor INLA operative who lived in Monaghan with Claire McMahon and her three young children.

On 3 May 1983, Dale heard a knock on the door of his home and looking out the window saw three armed men. He immediately told Claire McMahon to go to the sitting-room. She later recalled what happened: 'As Eric opened the door a masked man entered and came into the sitting-room. I was shaking and trembling and the masked man told me everything was all right and not to panic. The only people in the sitting-room were me and my three children.'

She was unaware that the face behind the mask was Dominic McGlinchey. He was dressed in a combat jacket and a shoulder holster resting on his chest contained a .44 Magnum pistol. He told her and her three children to be calm and allowed her to take her eight-year-old son Edward to the toilet. As she crossed the hallway she saw Eric Dale lying face down, surrounded by at least six masked men. When she returned to the sitting-room, McGlinchey told her they were taking Eric away to question him about guns and something that was missing. As he was led away, Eric Dale turned to her and said: 'I never harmed anybody.'

Four days later, his body, bound and wrapped in plastic, was dumped by the roadside between Newry and Dundalk. He had been shot in the head but his body bore the marks of torture. The INLA, on McGlinchey's instructions, issued a statement that Eric Dale had 'admitted under interrogation' that he had supplied the security forces with details of the movements of Seamus Grew and Roddy Carroll. The INLA also claimed he had provided other information leading to arrests and the seizure of weapons and explosives. The most pertinent part of the statement was an allegation that Dale had been making inquiries about the whereabouts of Dominic McGlinchey.

Dale was the man fingered by McGlinchey but he was not the only informer with knowledge of McGlinchey's movements. George Poyntz, a major spy within the Provisionals, was familiar with McGlinchey's cross-border forays and the homes of his associates. Was it Poyntz or Dale who informed, or was Dale a man willing to admit anything under torture? We shall never know. Poyntz was later spirited out of South Armagh by his handlers. I discovered that Poyntz met the UDA leader, James 'Pratt' Craig, at the former's instigation. He offered to provide Craig with information on leading Provisionals and to determine a time and place whereby a UDA hit-team could 'wipe them out'.

McGlinchey's torture of Dale and other suspected informers spread fear in the ranks of the INLA and when he became the organisation's Chief of Staff, everyone beneath him knew the price of treachery. At the height of his power in 1983, he spoke to the author and veteran journalist Vincent Browne of the *Sunday Tribune*. The interview was undoubtedly one of the most revealing of any leading terrorist in the Troubles. He told Browne: 'I do what I have to do and don't think about it thereafter.' Browne asked him if he saw the faces of his victims. 'Oh usually, for I like to get in close to minimise the risk to myself. It's usually a matter of who gets in first and by getting in close, you put your man down first. It has worked for me down the years. You don't really see nothing . . . Usually you don't see any blood . . . It is of course unpleasant.'

Those comments were made only weeks after INLA gunmen opened fire on a Protestant church congregation, killing three and injuring seven. McGlinchey denied involvement but one of the guns used was his favourite Ruger rifle. In order to distance the INLA from the atrocity, he ordered that a statement be issued from a bogus organisation, the Catholic Reaction Force, claiming responsibility. The statement said the attack was in revenge for the sectarian killing of Catholics. McGlinchey later told friends that he had not known in advance about the operation and his gun had been used 'for a purpose he had not intended'. Even if one accepts his denial, he was the INLA Chief of Staff and his demand for action was the dynamic for such sectarian carnage.

Security forces on both sides of the border were constantly on the lookout for him but in the Irish Republic the hunt became even more intense after he and several associates held policemen at gunpoint after being cornered. They stripped the policemen before escaping and the humiliation of the episode energised the search for him. Four months later, in the spring of 1984, heavily armed Irish police trapped him and he surrendered. The British Government immediately demanded his extradition for the murder of an elderly postmistress. The RUC believed that the case against him was solid because his fingerprints had been taken from a car used in the murder. He was extradited and convicted of the murder but one year later the conviction was overturned on appeal. In judicial parlance, a legal technicality saved him. The Lord Chief Justice, who heard his appeal, felt that the conviction was unsafe. He ruled that the fingerprints on the car could have been placed there at any time prior to or after the murder. Secondly, his membership of a Provisional IRA unit at the time did not necessarily support the Prosecution argument that he was the murderer. What the Lord Chief Justice could have said was that the Prosecution case had been bungled because it had not effectively anticipated the imponderables that led to the conviction being overturned.

Once again, McGlinchey had slipped through the net. To make matters worse, the British Government was obliged to return him to the jurisdiction of the Irish Republic. He was the first republican extradited and the outcome was farcical. The moment he was back in Irish custody, he was charged with his role in the armed siege which led to his capture by Irish police. He was convicted and returned to Port Laoise prison.

Languishing in his cell, his murderous past haunted him and he decided that when he was released he would give up terrorism and devote his energies to his wife and their two boys. Unfortunately, he had involved his wife, Mary, in his life of terror and together they had made enemies, especially because of their joint involvement in luring informers to their deaths. One evening while he was ruminating about his life, violence struck his household with the same ferocity he had used to dispatch many of his victims. Mary McGlinchey was in the bathroom of their Dundalk home with her two young sons when two gunmen burst in and shot her multiple times through the face at point-blank range. The style of the killing implied personal revenge. The Irish Government refused Dominic McGlinchey permission to attend her funeral, citing security concerns. From his prison cell he tried to find out who killed his wife, but few of his former associates were prepared to discuss the murder. His inquiries were hampered because the INLA had convulsed into splits and a bloody internal feud.

Some of those who met him agree he mellowed considerably after the death of his wife. On 14 June 1993, several months after he was released from prison, he quickly learned that even though he had decided to abandon a life of terror, terrorists were hunting him. As he took two children to a birthday party near Ardee in the Irish Republic, a gunman who had been tracking him moved in for the kill. McGlinchey later provided the following account of the attack: 'When I parked the car, I saw movement behind me. I thought it was a member of the Special Branch. Then I saw the sub-machine gun coming out. I made a run at the guy. There were two young girls in the car and I was afraid they might be hurt. By running at him, I got my hand into the breach of the gun. That is what saved me. He shot me in the hand and at the top of the forehead. One of the bullets lodged in my back.'

He dismissed a claim of responsibility from an INLA splinter group for the attempt on his life and told a journalist that his assailant was Billy Wright, aka 'King Rat'. He also said that 'it struck him as highly unusual that no loyalist group claimed responsibility'. McGlinchey was close enough to see the gunman and it is conceivable 'King Rat' was the assassin. If it was indeed true, there are several possibilities to explain the fact that the UVF did not claim responsibility. If Wright was acting on information supplied by British Military or Special Branch informers, the quid pro quo for getting a chance to kill such a high-profile target may well have been no UVF claim of responsibility. Instead, a bogus claim from an INLA splinter group would have served the purpose of exacerbating continuing splits within the INLA. Such conjecture is not within the realm of fiction in the context of the dirty war being fought at that time. As I pointed out in earlier chapters, men like Billy Wright and John McMichael killed on the basis of intelligence supplied by elements of the security apparatus. I also related how George Poyntz, the British Intelligence informer in South Armagh, offered to set up members of the IRA for James 'Pratt' Craig. Poyntz would only have done that on orders from his British handlers.

After the attempt on his life, McGlinchey told friends he expected to meet a violent end. It was a statement he had made many times in his terrorist career. One fact could not have escaped him. He no longer had a terrorist organisation to protect him. A former Provisional trigger man, who recognised McGlinchey's dilemma, told me civilian life can be more dangerous for a reformed gunman.

'McGlinchey was high profile and a lot of people wanted him dead. The Brits and the RUC certainly had a bead on him even if only out of revenge for killing a lot of their people. When he was operating with us and later in the INLA, he was always on the run. When you are on active service, you are constantly aware of your security. It's instinctive. You use safe houses. You never stay anywhere too long. You watch your back and you have other people watching it for you. Take all that out of the equation and you are as vulnerable as some of the people you used to target. That was McGlinchey's problem. He failed to understand that he'd become the sitting duck.'

His enemies were not going to forget his self-declared legacy of 30 killings in over 200 operations. In 1994, he was living in Drogheda between Dundalk and Dublin and made no effort to conceal his identity. One of his friends told me that he felt that loyalists would not venture that far south to kill him and, since he was no longer part of the INLA, no one in the organisation needed to fear him. By then, 'Mad Dog' had disappeared from the headlines and many of his neighbours did not know of his murderous past.

On the night of 10 February 1994, he drove his teenage son, Dominic jnr, to a shop in the Brookville estate in Drogheda to rent a video. On leaving the store, he failed to notice a red Mazda 323 with three men in it. For reasons never made clear, he stopped his car on the way home to make a telephone call in a public telephone kiosk. As he made the call, the red Mazda passed by, turned and then slowly made its way towards him, stopping beside the kiosk. By the time he turned to look at the car, the three men were alighting from it and walking towards him, each of them armed. Before he could react, they shot him ten times as his son watched.

It was later reported that as he lay dying, he shouted to his son: 'Jesus, Mary, help me.' In death, the man who had denied others the last rites wanted a chance at salvation.

A Drogheda detective who spoke to McGlinchey before his death, later said the former INLA chief told him: 'You either hide or you go on living as long as you can.' If that is correct, at 39 years old, McGlinchey knew he was living on borrowed time and was fatalistic. He had no control over his destiny or the fashion in which his life would end. More than 1,500 mourners attended his funeral in County Derry where he was buried alongside his wife. Among the mourners was the IRA supremo, Martin McGuinness.

Father Michael Flannagan told mourners he disapproved of the way the media gloried in McGlinchey's death and added: 'No one deserved to die like that. There's a little bit of good in the worst of us and a little bit of bad in the best.'

McGlinchey never achieved the republican hero status of his friend, Francis Hughes, even though they were not dissimilar in terms of their actions and propensity for violence. I put it to a former Provisional that the presence of Martin McGuinness at McGlinchey's funeral nevertheless indicated the high regard for him within the IRA leadership.

'That's true. They knew Francie would never have been a hero without McGlinchey's input in those early years. They won't say it publicly but they admired McGlinchey as a soldier. You could say, they knew that had he not joined the INLA he would have risen to the top in our movement. Our people never took much notice of the "Mad Dog" tag. That was part of the Brits' propaganda war because McGlinchey was a real threat. It was an attempt to criminalise him and make him seem like a psycho. They didn't apply the same tag to their soldiers who blew a lot of innocent people away on Bloody Sunday. The other thing is that Francie Hughes died on hunger strike and that made him a significant figure. I heard from people that before McGlinchey died he expressed regret about going over to INLA. He knew he made a bad choice. He was also too high profile to be operating and that gave the Brits an opportunity to make him a demon. Had he been with us, we would have stood him down from active service. He'd probably be still alive and part of the peace process.'

There are certain truths in the assessment of McGlinchey vis-à-vis the Provisionals but history will remember his boast that he killed 30 people. The victims of The Dropping Well pub and the Protestant churchgoers were not listed in his tally of 30. He was a man who craved action and not political compromise and it is unlikely if he had remained with the Provisionals, he would have risen to the role of Chief of Staff and been a part of peace negotiations. Had he not joined the INLA, he would probably have formed his own private army.

7

LEGAL TRIGGER MEN

At the outset of the Troubles, the predominantly Catholic New Lodge district of North Belfast was spared the attacks which were launched against parts of the Falls in the west of the city. However, as communal strife spread to many ghettos, the New Lodge developed a siege mentality. Loyalist areas, including the Shankill, Tiger Bay and the Shore Road, surrounded it, and Catholics shared the historical memory of the 1920s when many people on both sides were killed in sectarian warfare.

The New Lodge had a history of pro-IRA sentiment and, as in many Catholic districts, the Provisionals became the dominant republican force following internment in August '71. Their strength steadily increased as the UDA rose to prominence and North Belfast became a sectarian killing ground. The interwoven nature of that part of the city enabled loyalist hit squads to operate effectively because they were never far from their own neighbourhoods. It was easy for them to abduct victims or kill them in drive-by shootings. The Provisionals portrayed themselves as the defenders of the Catholic community and that doctrine suited many people in the New Lodge, even those who had previously given their allegiance to the Official IRA.

There were parallels between the New Lodge and an area like Ballymurphy. Both had a history of poor social conditions and a long-term resentment of the State. While the Provisionals may have initially seemed to be concerned about defence, they quickly moved to an offensive posture and by the end of 1972 areas like the New Lodge were the base for IRA operations, which included bombings and attacks on British Army patrols. The proximity of the New Lodge to the city centre enabled IRA teams to swiftly deposit car bombs and return to safe houses.

Increased IRA activity meant that by the beginning of 1973, the district was heavily patrolled by the British Army. More importantly there were Army observation posts that afforded 24-hour surveillance. On top of blocks of high-rise flats – Alamein House and Templar House – Army posts had cameras, electronic monitoring equipment and night-vision capability. Additionally, there were two 'Sangers' – concrete observation posts, and a semi-permanent sandbagged emplacement. Nearby was Girwood Barracks, the major Army base in the north of the city. It was, by military standards, a considerable presence with the capability to monitor people visiting and leaving the district's narrow streets and to photograph residents on street corners or when they entered and left bars and clubs.

Military Intelligence and RUC Special Branch built dossiers on everyone in the district, especially the male population, using intelligence gathered from the constant surveillance. Those suspected of IRA involvement had the letter 'P' placed alongside their names. I was told by a security source that a decision to allocate 'P' to a name might simply have been done on the basis of conjecture. In other words, if a person was seen talking to, or entering the house of a known Provisional that was sufficient evidence to warrant the person being deemed a Provisional. Jim McCann jnr and Jim Sloan, both aged 19, were on the Army's 'P' list and were members of the IRA.

They had grown up in the district and both attended the Star of the Sea Primary School before going to different secondary schools. McCann's father was a veteran of the Second World War and had escaped from a German POW camp. His background was not dissimilar to many Catholic men who joined the British Army in 1939–40. Some did so because of a family tradition and others because it was a way to earn a living. Despite the perception of anti-Britishness throughout Ireland, more Catholics fought in British regiments in the Second World War than their northern Protestant counterparts. The Irish component in British military history dated back to colonial wars of the 18th and 19th centuries when a large percentage of soldiers in the British Army was comprised of Irish, Scots and Welsh.

Jim McCann snr returned from the war, married and had eight children. The youngest he named Jim jnr and there was no evidence that he ever instilled anti-British sentiments in his son. By all accounts the boy was the quietest of his children. However, parental guidance had little impact on many young men at the onset of the Troubles. Peer pressure was a significant element leading many of them into paramilitary life. The role of the Army on the streets with its constant and often rough stop-and-search tactics was also a factor. The moment the Army decided that the Catholic population was the enemy, the ranks of the IRA swelled.

Jim McCann jnr and Jim Sloan were young men caught in an historical trap even though both had jobs which kept them off the streets. Sloan worked as an upholsterer and McCann in hotel kitchens. As close friends, they should have known the risks involved in membership of the IRA, especially in the summer of 1971 when McCann was shot in the back as he stood outside Sloan's home. It was an attempted assassination yet the crime was never investigated by the RUC. According to my sources, the police were told by the Military and Special Branch not to probe the incident. Such a move implied that the shooter was a soldier operating from one of the observation posts in the area. McCann spent a month in intensive care but his near-death experience did not disengage him or his friend from the IRA.

Sloan was also familiar with the risks in conflict and appeared to have been blessed with incredible luck. After leaving school at 15, he trained as an apprentice cook and his job took him to areas of the city where Catholics were not welcome. While working close to Belfast airport, he was stopped at a loyalist roadblock, hooded, abducted, interrogated and miraculously released. Later, while employed in East Belfast, he was badly beaten by a loyalist gang as he left his place of work. In 1972, he met a girl from Ballymurphy and married her and by the end of the year they were living in Lepper Street in the New Lodge.

On Saturday, 3 February 1973, the area was quiet and he promised his wife he'd be home before midnight as he left for Lynch's bar to have drinks with McCann. Tony 'TC' Campbell, a friend who had recently joined the IRA, was due to meet them but instead went to a parish disco to celebrate his 19th birthday. Just like that trio, there would be three others whose lives were about to collide.

Brendan Maguire, aged 33, was nicknamed 'Fat' because of his stocky build. Despite an asthma attack earlier in the day, his friend, Francie McAlorum, persuaded him to go to McLoughlin's bar on the nearby Antrim Road. Maguire, like many men in the district, was a docker and was well liked by neighbours. It was said 'he enjoyed his pint' and sang when he had one too many drinks. After a spell in McLoughlin's, he and McAlorum walked to the Circle Club for a nightcap and were seen there before 11 p.m. The club was situated at the corner of Edlingham Street and the New Lodge Road.

About the same time, John Loughran and his wife, Ann, were at home watching an Elvis movie. Ann was pregnant with their fourth child and was happy to have her husband home for the weekend. On weekdays, he worked as an asphalter with a French company based 100 miles away in Fermanagh. Earlier that Saturday, he had strolled through the neighbourhood and, at some stage, stopped to talk to residents. The area was a village and it was virtually impossible not to encounter childhood friends or acquaintances like Sloan, McCann, 'Fat' Maguire, 'TC' Campbell or Ambrose Hardy. Loughran was very popular because he was from a prominent boxing family. Like 'Fat' Maguire and Ambrose Hardy, he had no paramilitary connections. By all accounts he was a committed family man.

Ambrose Hardy, the youngest of 11 children, had gone to school with Jim McCann jnr and had bitter memories of the Troubles. Loyalist mobs had twice set fire to his family home when he lived on the edge of the New Lodge but this had not encouraged him to join the IRA. Locally, he was described as 'inoffensive'. He lived with his parents and enjoyed music nights in the Circle Club. Like Loughran, he was an asphalter. He was in the Circle Club when 'Fat' Maguire arrived shortly before 11 p.m.

After 11 p.m. Sloan left Lynch's bar and stood outside chatting to McCann. Across the road, Desmond Breslin left McLoughlin's bar with his wife and two friends. He saw McCann and Sloan but his attention was drawn to a dark-blue, four-door Ford Morris car which drove up the New Lodge Road and on to the Antrim Road. As a mechanic, he was familiar with car suspensions and was convinced the vehicle was weighted down with armour plating. 'I distinctly remember thinking that this was a military vehicle or had at one time been used as a military vehicle. I felt this way and was immediately able to discern the make of the car because at that time I was employed in a garage where we worked on those cars. There were some in the garage who were responsible for changing the colour on military vehicles from the standard military green to a dark-blue colour. Dark-blue was often chosen because it would cover the green. This car was that same colour of dark-blue.'

He was close enough to see the occupants of the car and provide a description of them. 'There was a man aged about 30 in the back seat in the passenger side. He was clean-shaven with a military-style haircut and was not wearing a mask or hood. He was wearing black clothing up to his neck, but had made no attempt to conceal his face. He was holding a standard sub-machine gun – either a Sterling or a Sten, but definitely a military-issue type of gun. In those days, everyone was familiar with the type of weapons carried by the military.'

Aside from Breslin and his friends, the only other people on the street were McCann and Sloan. Everyone else was indoors or ordering drinks as 'last orders' was called. Breslin continued to watch the strange car.

'I must have been 15 feet from the boys on the corner [Sloan and McCann] and as the car turned the corner, the man in the back opened fire on us . . . The car did a U-turn and came back up the Antrim Road. The gunman acted with military precision; he had held the gun properly when he opened fire and changed the clip in his weapon before the car even turned round. I have a vague memory of the gun being pulled in after the first burst of shooting.'

A second burst of shots was fired at a Chinese restaurant as the vehicle slowly travelled down the Antrim Road towards Girwood military base and Breslin saw the shooter put a new clip in his weapon. Back at Lynch's bar, Sloan and McCann lay dying on the pavement in pools of blood. Eight bullets had struck McCann and three had hit Sloan. The bullets were 9mm calibre, indicating they had come from a Sterling sub-machine gun, a standard military gun. The 'precision' Breslin referred to indicated that he was not the target. He watched with amazement as the car passed a Saracen armoured personnel carrier, drove up the Antrim Road and out of the area. He then ran to the aid of McCann and Sloan.

'They had been just about shot in half – they were in a bad way. When I saw them, I thought they were dead. I will never forget the surprise in their eyes. I guess no one expects it. They had just slumped and fell to the ground. They were lying next to each other, and one of them had his head on the other's shoulder. There was so much blood . . . The Saracen, which the car had passed, arrived back on the scene two minutes later. Three or four soldiers got out and were on foot.'

Many witnesses observed that soldiers in the Saracen made no attempt to intercept or to pursue the Ford Morris and soldiers in overhead observation posts did not react. At the time, the MRF was still functioning and it was months later that it became known as 14th Intelligence Company. Name changes were a regular feature of military strategy in the undercover war.

The gunmen's car had been observed making several passes through the New Lodge earlier in the day and soldiers in observation posts would have logged its presence. Those soldiers, had they so desired, could have radioed the Saracen and ordered decisive action. However, while regular soldiers were rarely part of undercover operations they were sometimes issued orders not to interfere when a covert operation was in progress. That is the only way to explain why they allowed the gunmen to make passes through the area, kill Sloan and McCann, fire at a Chinese restaurant, drive past them and leave the crime scene unimpeded. Of course, there is no evidence to confirm with any certainty that there were regular soldiers in the Saracen on that night.

The timeline of the events of that evening are critical to an understanding of what happened and the overall character of the British Army's action. The likelihood is that the shooting of Sloan and McCann occurred at 11.45p.m. and was the precursor to a wider military plan.

Soldier C (name withheld by the Army and Ministry of Defence for reasons of national security) later testified that he was the Commander of a mobile patrol in the area and heard automatic fire at 11.43 p.m. Soldier S (name also withheld for reasons given above) said that at 11.50 p.m. he was tasked by his Company Commander to take up position at the corner of Edlingham and Copperfield Streets. One wonders what the Army expected to happen in the wake of the drive-by shooting? C's rank and military history are unknown but he confirmed that he was armed with a 7.62 calibre, belt-fed, general-purpose machine gun, serial number A1051. It was capable of firing upwards of 600 rounds a minute and the belt had 160 rounds. It was too powerful a weapon to be deployed in the narrow streets of the area. It was fitted with a night-sight, indicating someone higher up the military command chain expected serious trouble. Did the Army brass anticipate another drive-by shooting by persons unknown? I pose that question more for effect than any genuine belief that it was a real possibility. Soldier S was positioned deep in the New Lodge to be ready for action. In the ammunition belt of his sub-machine gun, a blank round followed every fifth round to enable him to fire short, controlled bursts and prevent a trigger pull that would release anything from 10 to 50 rounds. In responding to orders, he joined Soldier Q at a sandbagged emplacement.

Soldier Q (name and rank withheld for reasons given above) said S was alongside him at 11.55p.m., approximately ten minutes after the shooting outside Lynch's bar. Q was armed with a 7.62 self-loading rifle, serial number 33547. It was also fitted with a night-scope and a magazine containing 20 rounds. According to his later testimony, he had an extra loaded magazine for the weapon. He and S built a small wall out of sandbags, which indicates that they were setting up a shooting platform because they took up separate lines of fire. S was positioned against the wall of 54 Copperfield Street and Q near the edge of the pavement. On reading their statements and discussing all the evidence with a former undercover soldier, it would be fair to conclude that they were a two-man team selected for a specific task.

Soldier Q, armed with the automatic rifle, made the following statement on which he was never cross-examined:

> At about 00.05 a.m. 4th February 1973, I saw a man standing in the alleyway between Spamount Street and Stratheden Street. This person fired a burst of about eight high-velocity rounds towards me. He then ran across Edlingham Street and I fired two 7.62 rounds at him and he fell on to the pavement with his legs on the road. After a few moments, he started crawling and then pointed his rifle at me. I fired four rounds at this person at the

same time S fired his gun. This man then slumped on to the pavement.

Soldier S, armed with the machine gun, provided a similar account and was never cross-examined. He saw Q shoot the alleged gunman and watched him collapse. He then looked through his night-scope and also opened fire at the same person.

> He turned and raised his rifle, pointing it in my direction. Thinking he was about to fire, I fired two 7.62 rounds. It then appeared that the impact of the bullets caused this man to roll over and he eventually came to rest approximately two yards from his original position. He then lay with his rifle lying on the ground.

They had just shot Tony 'TC' Campbell who had joined the Provisionals three weeks earlier. According to eyewitnesses, Campbell was heavily intoxicated that evening and, from my inquiries, the IRA would not have given him access to a rifle. He had not undergone the IRA's obligatory training in the use of weapons. A senior Provisional had this to say about Campbell: 'He was a novice. He had only just joined the movement and with plenty of experienced men in the New Lodge, we would not have given a rifle to a drunken kid. Secondly, after the shooting at Lynch's there was confusion in the area. McCann and Sloan were not on active service that evening because they were out drinking. That job was given to other people but when the shooting started, nobody really knew exactly what had happened. There were rumours that it was the military. Other people said it was loyalists. You don't strike back until you're sure of the facts and when Campbell was shot things became clearer but it took time to get some of our people together to decide what to do.'

The preponderance of eyewitness accounts confirms that shooting began from S and Q even before Campbell was killed. If that is true, the firing was designed to entice the IRA into a gun-battle. Campbell and others not connected to the IRA heard the shooting and were especially concerned by the screams of an elderly couple trying to make their way to Edlingham Street.

Patrick Johnston recalled that Campbell was determined to go to the aid of the couple despite pleas from people in the club that he should stay indoors. He ignored the advice and sprinted across the road but was shot. He then tried to crawl before a second burst of gunfire struck him. Seventeen 7.62 rounds hit him. That was nine rounds more than what Soldiers S and Q later admitted to discharging. One can conclude that they deliberately lied or they were not the only ones shooting at Campbell. If other snipers were firing from the observation posts on top of the two nearby high-rise blocks of flats, the British Army never admitted it. In fact, the Army refused to explain why S and Q provided incorrect information about the number of rounds they fired at Campbell.

The two soldiers' testimony that Campbell was hit at a relatively short distance by high-velocity rounds and then crawled to re-aim a rifle must be in doubt. The sheer impact of the bullets would have seriously incapacitated him. The only eyewitness evidence, which concurs with that of the two soldiers, is that Campbell tried to crawl after the first rounds struck him.

According to S and Q, within three minutes of shooting Campbell, they were back in action. Q had this to say: 'Another man appeared in the alleyway between Spamount Street and Stratheden Street. He fired one Armalite round at me and then started to walk across Edlingham Street, firing as he walked. I fired four rounds at him.'

S also fired his machine gun at the man: 'The gunman rose into the air and dropped near the first gunman.'

The image of a gunman strolling across a street, firing an Armalite at soldiers does not fit any episode which I witnessed while reporting the conflict. They had just shot and killed 'Fat Maguire' who had no IRA links. Malachy Cunningham had been with Fat Maguire when they looked across the street from the Circle Club and saw 'TC' Campbell's body move slightly, indicating he was still alive. There was a lull in the shooting, which encouraged Maguire and Cunningham to go to his aid. Cunningham, who did not know Campbell, later described what happened: 'Maguire and myself ran across Edlingham Street to Mr Campbell. I was a few paces behind Mr Maguire. As Mr Maguire reached the body, he knelt down, and, as he did so, a further burst of gunfire came up Edlingham Street. Mr Maguire said, "I'm hit", and slumped over the other body. The shots kept coming up Edlingham Street and I lay face down and started to crawl back from Edlingham Street to the safety of the New Lodge Road.'

To this day, it is impossible to access Maguire's autopsy report to confirm the number of rounds that struck him. Witnesses said the fatal round went through one of his eyes. Soldier S's account of the killing differed from that of his colleague, Q, and called into question their overall testimony of the events of that evening. Q said he fired at a gunman walking across the street but S remembered it differently. 'At 00.08 a.m., my location was once again the subject of enemy automatic fire, originating from the north-west corner of road junction, Edlingham Street–Stratheden Street. This gunman then broke cover and ran, in an easterly direction across the junction, firing automatic bursts as he ran.

As he reached the east side of the junction, I fired 2 x 7.62mm at him. As a result, the gunman was thrown sideways, into the air, finally collapsing on the ground, still clutching his rifle. He lay motionless, approximately two yards from the other gunman.'

Q had Maguire running across the street, firing, while S described him 'walking and firing as he walked'. Whoever helped the two soldiers compile their evidence failed to spot the glaring discrepancy. After shooting Maguire, S 'recocked' his machine gun and saw two women retrieve the bodies of Maguire and Campbell. He also alleged that he saw the women spirit away their rifles. Q supported his story.

John Loughran, who was at home watching the Elvis movie with his pregnant wife, Ann, heard the firing. His house was close to where Campbell and Maguire fell but he did not go outdoors. Malachy Cunningham, who was with Maguire when he was shot, crawled to Loughran's house and asked for help. He said Campbell was bleeding profusely but was still alive. Despite pleas from his wife, John Loughran told her, 'I have to go and help him.' Putting on a pullover, he went outside with another local man, Charles Carson. Neither of them had paramilitary links. Carson later offered this account of what happened when they reached the street: 'Mr Loughran crawled round the corner and caught hold of the body [Campbell]. I then braced myself to pull Mr Loughran backwards when another burst of gunfire came up Edlingham Street. Mr Loughran, though on his tummy, had his head raised, probably to assist him to pull the body backwards. As a result of this burst of gunfire, I saw Mr Loughran fall forward.'

Multiple eyewitness accounts support Carson's recall that the shots which killed Loughran were fired from the location of Soldiers S and Q. One of the many imponderables of that evening and early morning is that S and Q never admitted shooting Loughran. Perhaps their assertion that women had spirited away the bodies of Maguire and Campbell would have seemed incongruous if they had been obliged to account for the shooting of Loughran. Their statements were made in the knowledge of subsequent eyewitness testimony of how Loughran was killed. Essentially, if they had admitted to killing Loughran while at the same time claiming that the bodies of Campbell and Maguire had been spirited away, they would have had to concoct a story to explain why Loughran, a man with no paramilitary connections, was in that same location as the other people they killed. It would have defied belief that two women carried off a total of three rifles and three male bodies. A claim that three 'gunmen' were shot within feet of each other would have instantly raised doubts about what transpired.

After the killing of Loughran, Maguire and Campbell, IRA gunmen opened up on military posts in the district. In the Circle Club, 19-year-old Ambrose Hardy worried that his mother, hearing the shooting, would be terrified if he did not immediately return home. He had only gone to the club to buy cigarettes and had got caught up and began drinking after S and Q fired the first shots. He asked Lily McAuley for her white petticoat, which he intended to use as a flag of truce. She stepped out of her underskirt and handed it to him. Later, she recalled that he walked to the doorway of the club and extended his hand, waving the underskirt. There had been a short lull in the shooting, which encouraged Hardy to believe he could make it home under a flag of truce. He refused to listen to wiser counsel from older people in the club like Charles Smith, who subsequently admitted that it would have taken several men to physically restrain Hardy from leaving. 'We were all shouting, "Don't go out." Ambrose had just stepped outside the door – which was getting closed as quickly as he was getting out – and he was shot. It happened so quick that I don't even remember him being shot even though I was in the hallway.'

A witness who lived opposite the club saw Hardy wave the underskirt twice and then 'give the finger' towards the military observation posts on top of the nearby high-rise complex. The bullet that killed him entered the top right-hand side of his skull and tracked downwards through his body, exiting his back. Only a military sniper with a night-scope, positioned on the high-rise flats, could have made the shot. Autopsy evidence confirmed a high level of alcohol in his bloodstream – 120 milligrams per 100 millilitres. As with Loughran's death, the British Army never admitted killing Hardy.

With six dead and others injured, the British Army issued a statement that all six were IRA gunmen. Soldier S said he had only fired 28 rounds from his sub-machine gun in response to 250 rounds directed at him. Q claimed that he fired 53 bullets from his rifle, which was 13 in excess of the two magazines he admitted using. Each contained 20 rounds. Two years later, the Army admitted firing a total of 250 rounds and refused to explain who fired them.

Q's written testimony contained a claim that he stopped firing when S declared: 'White flag. Stop firing'. S did not mention that piece of detail in his statement. Both their accounts also conflicted in relation to the times they gave for the arrival of ambulances and what exactly happened when they moved into their sand-bagged shooting 'platform'. S alleged that they came under fire as soon as they were in position yet there was no mention of that in Q's account. Even more intriguing was that their later statements, presented in their absence to an inquest, were incomplete.

S's typed statement carried his signature and listed seven pages but the inquest was only provided with five. Q's statement was missing one page. There was no explanation why Q allegedly gave his statement on 4 February and S two days later. The lack of a proper police enquiry or military investigation at the time of the shootings underscored the inadequacy of the judicial process and the power of the British Army and Ministry of Defence to frustrate attempts by others to get to the truth. Female witnesses provided the following testimony to the RUC but their evidence was not followed up.

> Teresa McKinney: Finally, about 1 a.m. I went home. When I got home, I turned on a small transistor radio I had. I could hear the police radio on it as well as Army transmissions. That night, after I got home, I could hear the British Army on the radio. There is a soldier saying, 'There is a man coming out of the Circle waving a white cloth.' Then there was a response along the lines of, 'We got him.'

Kathleen McCormack lived on the 12th floor of Alamein House, directly under an Army observation post. In the course of that night, she also heard soldiers talking above her. She told police that she overheard soldiers saying, 'I got that one, you get the other one. No, you missed. Have another go.' She described what she understood to be 'banter' about who shot someone and who missed:

> When I heard about the killings by the British I realised that what I had been hearing the night before was the soldiers aiming at the men in the street. I was sickened to realise that what I had thought was some kind of game was actually the murder of these boys – certainly of Ambrose Hardy. Never once when I was listening to the soldiers did I hear them saying that gunfire was returned or that someone on the ground had a weapon. It was just the soldiers aiming and trading targets. I can hear the voices to this day.

Irrespective of whether these were credible witnesses, that was something to be tested by police investigators and it was not. More importantly, a third female witness, Alice Smith, made a taped recording of the military's communications. When that was made known to the RUC, she received a visit from what she described as 'special soldiers' who seized her tape. It has never resurfaced.

The shooting of Sloan and McCann spoke to the style of MRF assassinations of the period. A car similar to the one used by the trigger men was located two days later beside Tennent Street police station in the Shankill area. In it were eight 9mm bullet casings – the exact number of rounds used to kill Sloan and McCann. What happened to the other casings from bullets fired at the Chinese restaurant near Lynch's bar? Why were they not left in the car? By the time this car was found, the Army knew from autopsy reports the exact number of rounds fired at Sloan and McCann.

Was the car found near the Tennent Street police/military facility the one used in the shooting? I doubt it. I believe, in the wake of controversy about that night's events and the willingness of the IRA to admit that three of the victims were Provisionals, a similar car was left in the Shankill to suggest that loyalists and not the MRF were responsible for the drive-by shooting at Lynch's. Loyalists would not have left only eight casings in a car nor would they have operated with the cool efficiency of the trigger man in the back of the Morris Ford. I believe the initial killings were part of a undercover military strategy to force the IRA into a gun-battle, hence the setting up of Soldiers S and Q in a shooting platform within minutes of the shooting of McCann and Sloan.

I spoke to former loyalist operatives about the episode and they told me that the UDA and UVF were not involved. 'We would have bragged about it for years if we had done it,' said one loyalist. He also scoffed at the prospect that loyalists would have left only eight rounds in the vehicle. 'Nobody with any sense removes rounds and leaves just eight,' he added.

There was no forensic examination of the car and no clarification about its ownership or if it had been stolen. Since police had a full description of the vehicle for two days, it seemed particularly strange that it was found in the Shankill near a police facility. Perhaps that was the best way for the MRF to later plant a car to ensure it was found — in an area frequented by policemen.

No attempt was made to conduct a forensic examination of the scene of the shootings or to interview eyewitnesses. Only two forensic tests were carried out on the six bodies, namely those of Sloan and Loughran. A test carried out on Sloan by RUC forensic officer, John Martin, indicated 'lead particles on hands and clothing consistent with exposure to lead residue'. That was a conclusion affirming that Sloan had discharged a firearm, was close to someone who had fired a gun or that he had handled ammunition. However, that initial judgment was subsequently deleted from John Martin's statement to an inquest in 1975. Had it remained in place, lawyers representing families of the six victims would have subjected Martin, unlike the soldiers who were not obliged to attend inquests, to cross-examination. I unapologetically use the term 'victims' because nothing I have found in the Army's account of that evening suggests otherwise. On the contrary, I believe it was a case of legal trigger men operating outside the law.

In respect of the forensic test on the body of Loughran, his lawyers discovered that a finding of lead residue had been attached as an addendum to a statement provided by the RUC forensic officer, John Martin. The Lord Chief Justice for Northern Ireland subsequently dismissed the police forensic evidence against Loughran. If the Army was convinced that all six were gunmen, why were RUC forensic tests not carried out on all the bodies? Again, there is no answer to that and to many other questions the Army, RUC and Ministry of Defence need to address about the events of that evening and early morning.

Lawyers representing the families of the six victims were constantly denied access to documentation pertaining to the shootings. The following are questions I believe require answers in order to reach an understanding of what transpired.

How many soldiers were in the area that night? What do military logs and radio transmissions contain? What, if any, information was conveyed from the Saracen about the initial shooting? How many soldiers fired weapons? How many soldiers were issued with night-scopes since that was the first time they were deployed in that district? Were those soldiers from regular regiments? Why, according to eyewitnesses, were regular soldiers behaving in an unorthodox fashion earlier on that Saturday? Who took the statements from S and Q and why were they taken at different times? Where are the missing pages from their statements? Why did the RUC and Army carry out no extensive investigation in the wake of the killings? Why were there no documents showing that the car used by the initial shooters was forensically tested and its vehicle history determined?

I would also like to know if Soldiers S and Q were ever interviewed by the RUC and if not, why not? RUC files on this matter, if they exist, should be handed over to the judicial authorities to help clarify if police inquiries were hampered by the Army and subsequently by the Ministry of Defence in London. Documents related to the inquest into the death of 'Fat' Maguire were removed from the Public Records Office by an RUC officer, suggesting a cover-up or a deliberate attempt to prevent lawyers using that inquest transcript. Such a move could only have been made on the direct orders of the Chief Constable or Special Branch. It was just another example of the lack of transparency by the security forces. The Ministry of Defence has consistently refused to release documents required under the rules of the European Court of Human Rights.

In 2003, a panel of jurists released their findings into the shooting.

The panel included distinguished lawyers such as Eamann McMenamin of the Belfast legal firm Madden & Finucane, and Gareth Pierce of Birnberg Pierce & Co, London. The others were Don Mullan, an international human rights activist, Kate Akester, a lawyer and Chair of Mental Health Tribunals in London, Colin Harvey, Professor of Constitutional and Human Rights Law, University of Leeds, and Ed Lynch, an American civil litigator. They stated that their aim was to bring the matter before the European Court of Human Rights.

It has never been my tendency to loosely describe soldiers as assassins but I believe that in this case, and others in this book, the soldiers in question were legal trigger men whose activities have been deliberately covered up. Until controversial killings like those in the New Lodge and elsewhere have been opened up to honest scrutiny, there will be a lingering doubt about the willingness of the British Government to admit to past crimes.

8

KILLERS IN THE FAMILY

Hugh Leonard Thompson Murphy was only seven years old when he extorted money from other pupils at the Argyll Primary School in West Belfast. When he needed back-up he threatened other kids that he would set his older brothers on them. The brothers, William, ten, and John, nine, were pupils at the same school. It was 1959 and the three boys were living in Percy Street, one of several long streets linking the Shankill and Falls districts. Their parents, William Murphy and Joyce, née Thompson, were vastly different personalities. Joyce was assertive and William, a dock labourer, was hardworking but maintained a low profile. They were Protestants yet their family name suggested they were Catholics and that adversely impacted on the parents and their sons. Percy Street was one of many homes they lived in because each time they settled in a Protestant neighbourhood, rumours surfaced that they were hiding Catholic origins. In particular, it was alleged William Murphy was connected to Murphy families in Sailor Town in the docks. Joyce had no such problem and came from a loyalist background. She was hard on the political issues and resented the Catholic slur. At Argyll Primary School, her sons had to live with jibes like 'Murphy the Mick', which was more often than not applied to her youngest boy, Hugh Leonard. The term 'Mick', intended to mean Catholic, was applied affectionately within the Irish Guards Regiment to indicate someone of Irish descent but in Belfast it was used in the same pejorative manner as 'Taig'.

Hugh rarely called himself Hugh Murphy because he felt that was much too close to a Catholic-sounding name. He preferred to be called Lenny Murphy and that name stuck with him throughout his life. By the time he was 12, he was found guilty of burglary and larceny. He was attending a secondary school and continued to run extortion rackets by stealing other pupils' meal tickets and selling them on at a reduced price. No one called him a 'Taig' because he had his own gang and could always call on the support of his brothers when faced with overwhelming odds. In 1968, he left school having made little effort to learn even though he was regarded as a pupil with above average intelligence. That assessment may have related more to his innate cunning and deviousness than any genuine intellectual ability. He was quickly back in trouble and received two years probation for theft. One of the determining features of his character was an intense hatred of Catholics, which he shared with his brothers. With John, he visited discos and bars in the Shankill area and showed all the tendencies of a teenager out of control.

In August 1969, Lenny and John Murphy, along with a person, to whom for legal reasons I shall subsequently refer as Mr A, were seen helping mobs burn Catholic homes in Percy Street and adjoining streets. Their role, though minor, had the effect of elevating their status as committed loyalists. It also erased the tendency of people to imply that they were secretly from Catholic origins. Lenny, then only 16, had already been in UVF bars like the Gluepot and Bayardo. Sometimes, accompanied by his brother John, aged 18, and Mr A, he impressed senior loyalist paramilitary figures with his bitter opinions. In particular, he received nods of approval when he referred to Catholics as 'scum' and 'animals'. One loyalist of the period told me that it was obvious that Lenny and his brother John wanted to be 'super prods' as a way of excising any doubts that they had Catholic ancestry. One of the curious aspects of their name problem was that a Catholic family named Murphy lived in Sevastopol Street, 150 yards from the Murphy home. In that family, two of the males were called William and John Alexander, names that Joyce Murphy had given to Lenny's brothers. No matter what Lenny Murphy and John Murphy did to change perceptions through their professed hatred of the other community, there remained a perceived wisdom in the Shankill that their father, who steadily became a retiring figure in public, had something to hide.

The years 1970 and 1971 were crucial in the development of Lenny Murphy, his brother John and their associate, Mr A. Lenny became the most assertive of the three and John and Mr A, already members of the UVF, took him into the organisation's ranks. He immediately formed what was loosely called the Murphy gang with Robert 'Basher' Bates and Samuel 'Big Sam' McAllister. They were two thugs who were easily impressed by Lenny and his constant companions, John Murphy and Mr A. Bates, four years older than Lenny, had a short fuse and ran his own gang which he disbanded to become a Murphy associate. He had a criminal record dating back to 1966 with seven charges of assault and disorderly behaviour. 'Big Sam' was also a petty criminal who, from childhood, had been involved in a disturbing litany of crime. He was over six feet in height, heavily built and used his size to intimidate others. At Lenny and John Murphy's insistence, Bates and McAllister joined the UVF.

In the first six months of 1972 Lenny Murphy prepared for his terrorist career in a most unusual fashion by attending murder trials being held in Crumlin Road courthouse. Sitting in the public gallery, he listened to police giving forensic evidence and to lawyers debating the validity of evidence against terrorists. A detective who saw him in the court believed that he was also there to identify IRA sympathisers and supporters who sat alongside him in the public gallery. He was frequently dressed in a leather jacket and a scarf, which he casually draped over his left shoulder. In his jacket pocket he had a pair of leather driving gloves and would put them on any time he shook hands with a policeman. One detective I spoke to never forgot his eyes. 'He was like a smiling assassin. The one thing about him I could never forget were those eyes . . . those blue eyes that pierced you . . . He always had young girls around him, even in the courthouse.'

Lenny was a womaniser and enjoyed being seen around the loyalist clubs of the Shankill, chatting to whichever woman looked available. He was also a loner and was careful not to be seen publicly with known members of the UVF. He was slowly building his own 'Team' with the help of his brother, John, and Mr A. His first direct involvement in killing, in which his two close associates were present, was on Friday, 21 July 1972. That day a 34-year-old Catholic, Francis Arthurs, from Fallswater Street off the Falls Road, was travelling in a taxi from the predominantly nationalist Ardoyne area in North Belfast. The taxi was stopped on the Crumlin Road, which runs parallel to the Shankill Road. The mistake made by Arthurs was a classic one, in that the enclave from which the taxi emerged signalled to those watching the area that the occupant of the vehicle was a Catholic. Arthurs was drunk and unaware that the previous night a young Catholic couple, also travelling in a taxi, had been apprehended and murdered. When Arthurs' taxi was stopped he was bundled out of the vehicle and was hit over the head with a metal object. He was then taken to the Lawnbrook Social Club, a loyalist club off the Shankill Road. In the club were Lenny Murphy, his brother John, Mr A and members of other paramilitary organisations, drinking and making merry. Arthurs was in a 'romper room'. He was held in the rear of the club until revellers with no paramilitary connections left for home. He was then paraded before the remaining drinkers and beaten severely by all of them. The man seen to hit him harder and cause him more pain than the others was Lenny Murphy. Arthurs was not just beaten until he became almost unrecognisable, he was stabbed repeatedly in different parts of the body with a knife wielded by Lenny Murphy. At 4 a.m., after he had been interrogated and tortured, he was shot and his body dumped in a street less than a mile away.

A detective revealed to me details of Lenny Murphy's involvement in another murder which occurred around this time. Again, a knife was used and it was likely that John Murphy, his ever-present associate, was also present at that killing. At 20 years of age, with the support of his brother John and Mr A, Lenny had begun to make the knife a trademark of his gruesome handiwork. There were many people who would not have believed that he was capable of such brutality. His appearance did not suggest anything sinister about his character or his intentions. The only apparent thing was his pathological hatred of Catholics but that did not shock many loyalists in the Shankill area who identified with his sentiments. To most people, he was a hardworking shop assistant but his flamboyant lifestyle of drinking and womanising was paid for from the profits of robberies and racketeering. He was 5 ft 6.5 in. in height, of slim build, with a crop of curly dark brown hair, blue eyes and a sallow complexion. He had a long face with overly long ears, a small, turned-up nose and a rounded chin. There was a scar on the back of his left hand and several tattoos on both arms. The tattoos were of King William of Orange on a horse, the words 'Mum and Dad', the Red Hand of Ulster and 'Rem 1690'. The tattoos were typical of a working-class tradition though he often hid them from view. It was suggested that vanity was his motive for doing that since the tattoos were drawn in his teens and later conflicted with his flamboyant 'man-about-town' image.

While forming his own UVF unit, he kept a low profile, as did John Murphy and Mr A who often met in secret while Bates and McAllister were regularly seen on the street corners and in bars. When the unit got together, their chosen place was an upstairs room of the Brown Bear pub on the Shankill Road. Willie Moore, a taciturn loner who owned a black London-type taxi, also attended those meetings. By 1975, the 'Brown Bear Team', as it became known, comprised 20 young men, all selected by Lenny, John Murphy and Mr A. While Lenny allowed his two close associates to express opinions about operations and membership of the Team, he was the 'little general'. The names of some of the Team are worth mentioning because they illustrate the kind of people he chose for terror. There was 22-year-old Arthur McClay who committed his first crime at the age of 13 when he placed explosives in a letter box. Another member was Benjamin Edwards, 24, who liked flashy clothes and had the nickname 'Pretty Boy'. He was also a petty criminal. There was Norman

'Winkie' Waugh, a reticent loner with a slight speech defect. His features suggested low intelligence and local people said he 'was not right in the head'. The eldest member of the Team was Edward Leckey, 34, a criminal from the age of 15. The names ran off the tongue like a Mafia hit squad. There were several other misfits, one of them a part-time member of the Ulster Defence Regiment and the youngest, John Townsley, a tough individual regarded as mature for his age. All of these people would become known as 'The Shankill Butchers'.

The presence of John Murphy and Mr A was crucial to Lenny Murphy maintaining control over the others. He knew that if there was any dissension in the ranks, or a risk that a member of the Team was about to cooperate with the police, his close associates would warn him. The UVF later tried to distance itself from what became the Murphy cut-throat legacy but the leadership at the time was complicit in permitting him to engage in an orgy of murder of innocent Catholics. An example of their closeness to him was their request in 1975 that he root out undesirable elements in the ranks of the organisation in the Shankill area. That request was, to put it mildly, absurd.

Lenny Murphy's modus operandi was to call a meeting in the Brown Bear pub which was attended by his brother, John, Mr A and selected members of the Team. After consuming alcohol, they would agree to 'kill a Taig'. There was never any debate about the political merits of such a course of action or the overall political situation in Northern Ireland. On the evening of 24 November 1975, such a meeting took place. Willie Moore, the taxi driver, also worked as an apprentice butcher and he, at Lenny's request, arrived with butchery knives from his workplace. Those present drank until midnight, with Lenny explaining that it was better to use a knife because if they were stopped in a car with a gun they would be arrested. That was one explanation but another he had previously offered at one of their meetings was that the ultimate way to kill a man was to slit his throat. They all agreed to use Moore's black taxi so that if police stopped them he could say he was carrying passengers. Murphy's criminal mind covered every eventuality down to the fact that they would not have to travel far to find a Catholic to kill – someone walking along the street, possibly coming from a pub.

After midnight, Moore, 'Pretty Boy' Edwards, Archie Waller and Lenny Murphy set out to find a victim, with Murphy in possession of a sharp butchery knife. The route Murphy mapped out took them down the Shankill Road, across to the Crumlin Road and down the Antrim Road into Clifton Street, with a shorter return journey. The purpose of the route was that anyone walking after midnight would be easily spotted at a distance. More importantly, any person in the vicinity of the lower

Antrim Road and Clifton Street was likely to be a Catholic because the sectarian geography of the city determined that Protestants would not use those roads after dark. The likelihood was that it would be a thoroughfare preferred by Catholics from the New Lodge or Unity Flats. The taxi with Murphy and the others on board took the planned route with one or two slight variations devised by him. They avoided Clinton Street's main thoroughfare and entered an adjacent area of narrow, darkened streets such as Library Street and Union Street. Both streets were only 150 yards from the bottom of the Shankill Road and less than one mile from Murphy's home.

Elsewhere in Belfast that night, 34-year-old Francis Crossan was travelling across the city from a club near his home in the Suffolk area of South Belfast to North Belfast where his family had been intimidated out of their home one year earlier. On his way to the Holy Cross Bowling Club in the Ardoyne district, he passed the spot where his brother Patrick, a bus driver, had been the victim of a sectarian shooting several years earlier. People remembered Crossan drinking quietly in a corner of the club and later told police that he left ten minutes after midnight. There was no public transport and he made the fatal mistake of walking to the city centre.

Sometime after 12.30 a.m. Moore, in the driver's seat of his taxi, spotted a man walking towards Royal Avenue, the city's main thoroughfare. It was Francis Crossan. Murphy told Moore to stop the taxi alongside the solitary figure, then Murphy, Edwards and Waller rushed from the vehicle and Murphy hit Crossan over the head with a wheel brace. As Crossan fell to the ground his assailants dragged him into the taxi and drove off. Within minutes they were on the Shankill Road. Moore later revealed that Murphy kept hitting Crossan with his fists and the wheel brace and kept repeating: 'I'm gonna kill you, you bastard.' 'Pretty Boy' Edwards' recollection was that Crossan 'kept squealing the whole time'.

Murphy directed Moore to drive to an alleyway off Wimbledon Street in the Shankill district. By the time they reached their destination Crossan was quiet and Moore stopped the taxi to allow Murphy and the others to take Crossan's blood-spattered body from the vehicle. With Moore's help the four men carried him deep into the alleyway and dragged him along the ground until they were out of sight of the roadway. Murphy then took out a large butchery knife and stood over Crossan, who was lying on the ground breathing heavily, his eyes closed. Murphy set about hacking at Crossan's throat until the head was almost severed from the trunk. Finally, and triumphantly, he held the knife aloft. Murphy's hands and clothes were soaked in blood and there was also blood in the taxi. He ordered the others to accompany him to his home where they washed out the taxi and removed their bloodstained clothing. The knife was carefully wiped and returned to Moore for safekeeping. The autopsy on Crossan determined that death was caused by the throat being sliced in a manner which also severed the root of his tongue. There were massive blunt injury wounds on his whole body, suggesting Edwards and Waller had also attacked him in the back of the taxi. Moore later admitted that he repeatedly kicked Crossan as he lay in the alleyway.

At this time, Lenny Murphy was married to 21-year-old Margaret Gillespie and they lived in Brookemount Street close to his family home where his brother John resided with his parents. Mr A lived close by. John Murphy and Mr A knew all about Lenny's cut-throat exploits and encouraged him to further excesses. Lenny blooded other members of his gang, using them to hold down victims while he exerted considerable force in his attempts to sever victims' heads. He also ensured that he left no obvious clues at the scene of his crimes and no witnesses to his cruelty.

On Saturday, 26 February 1976, he allowed two women to be present at one of his killings – one of the women was well known to him and the other later fled Northern Ireland to live in Canada. That evening, in the Long Bar pub in the Shankill, Lenny was surrounded by the women, members of his gang, his brother, John and Mr A. For several hours he held court, bragging about his exploits and how he was going to 'kill a Taig' later that evening. At 1 a.m. Lenny Murphy, 'Basher' Bates, Willie Moore and a Mr C (name withheld for legal reasons) left the bar with the two women. Mr C secretly fancied Lenny's young wife but was careful not to display his interest in her. Outside the Long Bar, the two women joined Moore in the front of his taxi while the others got into the back of the vehicle. Murphy told Moore to drive to the Library Street area where they had abducted Crossan and later another Catholic, Thomas Joseph Quinn, who had also met Crossan's fate.

That same night, 24-year-old Francis Dominic Rice, an unemployed labourer, spent much of his time drinking with friends in a Catholic social club on the periphery of Belfast city centre. His journey home took him through Union Street. He was not drunk and was regarded as a man who could defend himself. As he walked into Upper Donegall Street, Moore's taxi pulled alongside him and Murphy leaped out of the vehicle brandishing a wheel brace. Rice tried to escape but was felled from behind and staggered on to the roadway. Bates rushed from the taxi and helped Murphy drag Rice, who by now was slightly dazed, into the vehicle. Moore drove the short distance into the Shankill area.

As the taxi travelled slowly along the Shankill, Murphy, Bates and Mr C kicked and punched Rice. While the two women turned to watch the assault, Moore observed it through his rear-view mirror. According to 'Basher' Bates, Murphy suddenly stopped the beating and searched Rice to ensure that he was a Catholic. On his person, Rice had a membership card for a club in the New Lodge district. Bates later said that was what sealed Rice's fate but I doubt it. I also believe that Bates lied in a perverse way to provide police with a motive for the murder. If I am wrong, then the only conclusion that one can reach is that Murphy's psychopathic instinct always preceded reason and only after he had severely beaten a victim did he seek to find out if the person was indeed Catholic.

Murphy told Moore to drive to his parents' home in Brookemount Street and, once he arrived there, he went into the house where his brother John handed him the knife which had been used on Crossan and other victims. The taxi was then driven in the direction of the Lawnbrook Social Club and, at Lenny Murphy's insistence, to Esmond Street. During this journey, Murphy taunted Rice with the knife and cut him about the throat and sides of the neck while he was being held down in the rear seat. Mr C sat on his chest and Bates held his arms. Moore later admitted that while Lenny Murphy was in his parents' home getting the knife, Bates and Mr C beat Rice and told him that he was going to be killed.

When the taxi reached Esmond Street, Murphy gesticulated to Moore to pull up at the entrance to the alleyway. Rice was conscious, Murphy having ensured the cuts to the throat and neck were not fatal. However, Rice moaned in pain when Murphy announced he was 'going to finish him off'. Murphy asked Bates and Mr C to help him take Rice into the alleyway and told Moore to drive the women to the far end of it. Rice was carried into the alleyway and then dragged a short distance and placed on his back. The three killers kicked him before Murphy went to work with the knife. It took Murphy several minutes as he slowly hacked through his victim's throat, only stopping when the blade touched the spine. From the taxi parked nearby, the women saw what was happening.

There were many killings during that period and the RUC, even with a team led by the experienced detective Jimmy Nesbitt, had no clue to the identity of the culprits. What remains surprising is that, with all the informers in loyalist ranks, no one gave up Lenny Murphy. He had created a reign of terror and UVF bosses feared him, though I also believe they were secretly happy with his gruesome handiwork. After all, killing Catholics was a significant focus of UDA and UVF policy from the early '70s onwards. The basic premise in both organisations could have been encompassed in the phrase 'the more terror the better'.

A month after the Rice murder, Murphy made his first mistake when he was arrested for a failed murder attempt on two Catholic women, one of whom was shot and injured. He burned the car used in the murder bid but was apprehended fleeing in another vehicle. Inside it were Bates and two men who cannot be named for legal reasons. There was also a pistol Murphy had used to fire at the two women. For reasons never explained by the police, Murphy was taken into custody and the others released. Before police could interview him, he asked to use the toilet in the police station and was caught trying to wash lead residue off his hands and clothing. When confronted about trying to remove evidence, he replied: 'That's the first mistake I've made.' Orders were then issued to arrest Bates and the other two men but the police had waited too long. Murphy's accomplices had time to change their clothing and shower. Police suspected Murphy of being the leader of what was being now called the Shankill Butchers gang but he laughed when asked about the killings of Crossan and others. Nonetheless, police had him in possession of the gun used in the attempt to kill the two Catholic women and found residue on his hands and clothing from a firearms discharge. While he was in custody awaiting trial, no attempt was made to trace his associates even though Bates, one of his inner circle, was with him when he was arrested. The police explanation was that they believed they had the cut-throat killer in custody and he was going to prison. The police were also burdened by other investigations and did not have the resources to mount a large-scale surveillance on Murphy's gang.

In prison, Lenny Murphy was visited by Mr A and John Murphy. Both relayed his instructions to the gang and his desire for a continuance of cut-throat killings, which he reckoned would fool police into thinking he was not the 'Master Butcher'. First, however, John Murphy and Mr A linked up Bates and other gang members with another UVF unit to attack a Catholic bar. After that operation, Mr A and John Murphy decided it was time to follow Lenny's orders. Moore and McAllister were given the job of 'killing a Taig'. At 10 p.m. on 1 August, six months after their gang leader was arrested, they set out in the black taxi with Moore driving. McAllister sat in the back with a hatchet under his coat. They had learned well from Lenny Murphy and soon spotted Cornelius Neeson, a 44-year-old married Catholic. Moore pulled the taxi alongside him and McAllister leapt out and savagely struck Neeson multiple times on the skull, killing him. It was not the kind of murder Lenny Murphy had ordered and that was made clear to the others by John Murphy and Mr A. At that time, Lenny Murphy made a plea bargain on a firearms charge and received a six-year prison term, knowing he would likely be released within three to four years.

Lenny was locked away in the Maze where Mr A, somewhat of a loner when not in the presence of the others, was told by Lenny that the cut-throat killings had to restart to keep police off his trail. He knew that Jimmy Nesbitt and his team of detectives were still looking at him as their prime suspect for multiple gruesome murders and other terrorist killings. Mr A and John Murphy held a meeting with the 'Brown Bear Team' and told them it was Lenny's wish that Willie Moore should take over the killing in his absence. Moore worshipped and feared Lenny but was also conscious that Mr A and John Murphy were ever present to ensure Lenny's orders were carried out and no one expressed dissent. Moore was the ideal substitute because he also hated Catholics, was cool and quietly ruthless. He had learned from Lenny Murphy how to operate in a tactically random fashion, avoiding any defined pattern of action, which might be detected by police. Moore later argued he continued the campaign of cut-throat killings because he feared Lenny, Mr A and John Murphy. There is no evidence to support his claim. It was true, however, that Lenny's two closest associates were always watching Moore.

On Friday, 29 October 1976, 24-year-old Stephen McCann and his 17-year-old girlfriend, Frances Tohill, walked from the Queen's University district to their homes in North Belfast. They were students and did not have money for a taxi. It was 2 a.m. and they unfortunately took a route which intersected streets where Lenny Murphy had abducted some of his victims. As they walked into Millfield, which crossed the bottom of the Shankill Road, Stephen had his left arm round Frances's shoulder and her right hand was buried in the pocket of his jacket. Frances later recalled that they chatted about the student party she had just been to and she thanked him for coming across town to make sure she got home safely. Frances later provided an account of what happened next:

'As we walked past the corner of Brown Street we were both aware of men standing on the corner with Millfield. We did not look at them directly and simply walked on. Something was shouted after us but I did not hear the exact words. We both turned to look round and at that moment Stephen was dragged from me. One man grabbed me from behind with his hand held over my mouth. I will never forget the feeling. I inclined my head so that I was looking into his eyes. I will never forget those eyes. It was a look of evil. I thought to myself, "Should I pretend to faint?" I decided it was the best thing and slumped to the ground. My attacker said, "Don't move. Don't scream." It all happened so quickly. I was terrified and confused. I did not know what to think. Stephen made no noise. I didn't hear him scream or shout. I lay on the ground. I heard nothing, not the sound of a car or the attackers escaping. After a few minutes, I got to my feet and ran in the direction of home.'

Her decision to slump to the ground saved her life; otherwise she would have been led away with Stephen McCann. The man holding her was Willie Moore. Stephen McCann was taken by Moore, 'Big Sam' McAllister, William Townsley and Artie McClay. They had not wanted to waste time carrying Frances Tohill when Moore's new Cortina car was parked some distance away in Brown Street.

The four Shankill Butchers had spent the evening drinking in the Lawnbrook Social Club planning the murder and, as Lenny Murphy had always done, they wanted to make a swift abduction. Stephen McCann was bundled into the back of Moore's car. On the way to Mr A's house in Brookemount Street where John Murphy also lived, Stephen McCann sat between McClay and McAllister. They beat him and questioned him about his religion. He neither screamed nor protested; he just admitted he was a Catholic.

At Brookemount Street, Moore got out of the car and went into Mr A's home where he collected the knife used in other killings and a .22 pistol. When Moore returned to the car, he gave the knife to McAllister who taunted Stephen McCann with it and ran it across each side of his neck, leaving long superficial cuts in the shape of symmetrical rings. Moore drove to Glencairn, one of Lenny Murphy's favourite places for dumping corpses. Moore, Townsley and McClay dragged their victim behind a community hall. Moore ordered him to sit down but Stephen McCann knelt, his head slightly bowed. At that point, Moore shot him once through the top of his skull, sending him sprawling sideways to the ground. Moore took the knife from McAllister and, watched by the others, cut his victim's throat back to the spine. Moore drove back to Mr A's home and returned the knife and gun and then left his accomplices at their respective homes.

The demeanour of Stephen McCann throughout his ordeal was that of a young man who knew from newspaper headlines that he was in the clutches of the Shankill Butchers and was about to die. There was something courageous about the way he accepted death. Only 12 hours earlier he had finished writing a song to be played at a peace rally on the day of his death. The murder confused detectives who had hoped that with Murphy in prison the Butcher killings were over.

Moore later admitted to the detective, Jimmy Nesbitt, that he had told Mr A they had 'a Taig in the car'. Moore's choice of language to describe the events leading to the murder were intended to play down the beating Stephen McCann received while in the car. 'The fellow was between Artie and Sam in the back seat and they hit him a couple of times. He wasn't unconscious but he wasn't shouting or anything . . . When he was lying on the ground I cut his throat. It was a butcher's knife I had, sharp as a lance and it just slit his throat right open.'

There was a casualness in the way the Shankill Butchers later talked to Nesbitt about their savagery. Moore did not admit to him that he knelt down to hack at Stephen McCann's throat and then rearranged the corpse. A police report confirmed that 'the body was lying on its back with the legs underneath; the head was lying back and the hands drawn upwards to the chest'. In other words, Moore had positioned the corpse to present as grotesque a sight as possible, with the throat wounds immediately visible to police arriving on the scene. McAllister lied about his role and claimed that the victim 'got a slap' while he was in the car.

Stephen McCann's lyric for the song he intended to sing at a peace rally on the day he died was testimony to the inner beauty of his soul. It was called 'Skies'.

> In our dreams we know a man
> Who knows what life and death are all about;
> Because he's seen them he can feel them,
> He has been there so he knows.
>
> We all live just for a moment
> But we know we die for ever more
> And all our dreams come true.
>
> The man we know so well has come to take us
> And to claim us
> And to bring us to the place where we belong
> And where we should have been the day we were born.
>
> But all my dreams are over now,
> I've lost the man who gave me life
> To use it or abuse it,
> I returned it to him broken
> And discoloured with my sins since time began;
> But he forgave me.

The Shankill Butchers killed not only Catholics but also Protestants who crossed their paths. 'Big Sam' McAllister, in a drunken brawl in the Shankill, beat a man severely and then killed him by repeatedly dropping a concrete block on his head. He then carried the body into a churchyard and went home. The victim was a member of the UDA and James 'Pratt' Craig, the UDA Commander in West Belfast, demanded that the UVF punish McAllister. The UVF had no desire to have a feud with the UDA and told McAllister he would have to be 'kneecapped' – shot in both knees. McAllister struck a deal with the UVF Brigade Staff that he would present himself at an agreed location to be shot in the arms, not the knees, and the shooting would only take place after his wife gave birth. Two months later he was shot in both arms with a .22 small calibre pistol. His wounds were minor and quickly healed.

Unknown to 'Pratt' Craig, Moore, Bates and McAllister also killed one of his close friends, Chris Moorehead, who was nicknamed 'Nigger' because of his dark complexion. Moorehead had the misfortune to encounter the three members of the Shankill Butchers while they were drinking and watching a football match on television in the Windsor bar on the Shankill Road. Moorehead walked through the bar to go to the toilet and McAllister, perhaps for racist reasons, said, 'There's the nigger', and followed him. Inside the toilet, McAllister held him in an armlock until Bates arrived. Moore then joined them after Bates produced a spanner and a knife. Moore later provided the following account of his role: 'I saw Nigger lying on the floor and there was blood everywhere. He was lying on his stomach with his head to the side. I was handed the big spanner and told to hit him with it. I hit him one blow which I think hit him on the shoulder. Altogether the three of us hit him to make sure we were all in on it.'

They left him lying on the floor and returned to their drinks and the football game. The body lay there overnight. The following day they returned to dispose of the body. Moorehead had received a knife wound to the throat, which was not the cause of death. He also had 18 lacerations to the scalp and bruises all over his body. Moore interestingly pointed to an important feature of Shankill Butcher crimes – the necessity for everyone to take part in the brutalising of a victim in order to make each player guilty and guarantee his silence. It was akin to the Mafia code of *Omerta*.

That was symbolised in the cut-throat killing of another Catholic, 52-year-old Joseph Morrissey. After he was attacked and abducted, Moore, McClay and McAllister drove to Mr A's home to get the knife and pistol used to kill Stephen McCann. Mr A told Moore he did not have the pistol and that he would just have to rely on the knife. It was Mr A's attempt to ensure that Lenny's orders were followed, namely that a knife was preferable to a gun. As Morrissey was being taken to their 'dumping ground' at Glencairn, McClay held the victim down in the back seat of the car while McAllister made superficial incisions on his neck and face and told him they were the Shankill Butchers. At Glencairn, Morrissey was still alive when Moore began cutting his throat. When he had finished, he tried to sever the head with a hatchet handed to him by McClay. The killers drove to Mr A's house where Moore was supplied with clean clothes and washed blood from his shoes. He left the knife and hatchet in Mr A's backyard. In later testimony, each of the killers in that murder tried to play down their respective roles but the autopsy evidence showed that Morrissey had suffered terrible torture before his throat was finally slit and that all of them were involved.

While Mr A, the eldest of the triumvirate which included Lenny and John Murphy, did not wield the knife or pull the trigger, John Murphy liked to think of himself as a serious operator. He was content to let Mr A discuss strategy with the others and to be available to supply or hide the knife and guns but personally wanted to show Moore that he could kill when required. In March 1977 he planned a bombing attack for the republican Easter parade celebrations which were due to take place. With Mr A's help, he persuaded the UVF Brigade Staff to let him borrow 'Tonto' Watt, their number-one bomb maker. However, Mr A decided that he had to be involved in the fine details of the plan and that was agreed. In the early hours of Easter Sunday morning, 10 April, the bomb, concealed in a beer keg, was placed along a route due to be used by republican marchers. John Murphy led the bombing team to the target and watched while they placed the bomb in position. It exploded later that day, killing a ten-year-old boy. There were no mass casualties because the timer of the device had been wrongly set. 'Tonto' Watt was later charged with the bombing and took to reading the Bible in prison.

By the time Lenny Murphy was released from the Maze on 16 July 1982, most of his gang were behind bars because they left a witness. In their admissions of guilt to detectives (for reasons too detailed to explain here) they refused to give up Lenny, his brother John, Mr A, Mr C and others in the UVF whom I cannot name for legal reasons. Twenty-four hours after Lenny Murphy strode smiling from the Maze prison, a party was held in his honour but his wife and nine-year-old daughter were not invited. She had taken up with Mr C, who had been courting her from the moment Lenny went behind bars. In fact, he learned of their affair after she returned from a Spanish holiday with Mr C. Lenny did not seem to mind because he was tired of marriage and told his brother John that he wanted to 'play the field'. John Murphy was the organiser of the party, which was held in the Rumford Social Club in the Shankill area. Mr A was also present with senior members of the UVF leadership. Before midnight, a tall, bearded, shabbily dressed stranger entered the club. He was 33-year-old Norman Maxwell of no fixed abode. He was a Protestant who lived in Salvation Army hostels and often ventured into clubs in the hope that someone would take pity on him and buy him a drink or give him money. Lenny Murphy took exception to Maxwell's intrusion and dragged him outside with the help of John Murphy and Mr A. Maxwell was then severely beaten and, as he lay on the ground, Lenny Murphy drove a car over him several times. He then put the body in the car and dumped the corpse off the Oldpark Road.

From that moment, he began rebuilding his Brown Bear Team with the help of his brother and Mr A. He also returned to his previous life of terror. At the same time, he acquired a permanent girlfriend, flashy clothes and a car. Three months later, he committed what detectives regarded as one of his most bestial murders. The victim was a Catholic, 48-year-old Joseph Donegan, an unemployed carpenter with seven children. After he abducted Donegan, using a taxi of the type Moore had owned, he took him to 65 Brookemount Street, a vacant house he had once shared with his wife. Murphy was in the company of a new member of his unit, 'Wingnut' Cowan, who had driven the taxi while Murphy brutalised Donegan in the back of the vehicle. By the time the vehicle reached its destination, the insides of the rear windows were bloody. They took Donegan into the kitchen of No. 65 but not without a serious struggle as Donegan fought for his life. Murphy left Cowan with Donegan in the kitchen and walked across the street to a house registered in his name and fetched a spade and a pair of pliers. It is worth noting that Brookemount Street was also the location of Mr A and John Murphy, who lived with his parents.

Lenny Murphy tortured Donegan by using the pliers to pull out his teeth which police later found scattered over the floor. I remember looking at a photograph of the teeth. Nearby was a discarded teddy bear, which had been owned by Murphy's nine-year-old daughter. While Donegan was still alive, he was taken to the yard of the house and beaten with a spade. Aside from 'Wingnut' Cowan, there was another man present whose name I cannot use for legal reasons. That other man also wielded the spade. Cowan later said that when he walked into the yard, he saw the man with the spade. He could also hear Donegan breathing heavily as he was beaten and from the smell knew that 'he had shit himself'. The beating continued until the shaft of the spade broke, by which time Donegan was dead. John Murphy and Mr A were both aware of the Donegan torture and murder and arrived to help with the disposal of the body. However, as it was being removed from the yard, a young couple walked by and Mr A decided to leave the body in the alley at the back of Lenny's former home.

There were only three teeth left in Donegan's mouth and the injuries to his whole body were unbelievably severe. Lenny Murphy was questioned about the Donegan murder but police could not pin it on him. He was, however, a marked man and the Provisional IRA knew his identity. With the help of the UDA leader, James 'Pratt' Craig, who wanted to keep the IRA off his back, Provisionals in Ardoyne learned about Murphy's routine. They discovered that he often travelled with his girlfriend, Hilary Thompson, to her home in Glencairn, the area where the Shankill Butchers killed and dumped many of their victims.

At 6.40 p.m. on 16 November 1982, Murphy drove with her to Forthriver Park, unaware that an IRA hit team was tailing him. As he stopped the car two gunmen armed with a sub-machine gun and a .38 Special revolver shot him 26 times in the head and body. Lenny Murphy's mother, Joyce, denied that her dead son was the leader of the Shankill Butchers. 'He couldn't hurt a fly,' she told journalists. What she failed to grasp was that Lenny Murphy swatted people like some people swat flies and her son John was no better than his brother. The UVF leadership gave Lenny Murphy a grand send-off. UVF personnel kept police and journalists at a distance from the home and the coffin, which was flanked by armed men in battledress. Joyce Murphy told the media that her son, Lenny, had been planning to leave Northern Ireland because of police harassment. Both statements were untrue. One of the ironies of the funeral was that the 'Master Butcher', as the journalist Jim Campbell dubbed him, was buried in Carnmoney Cemetery, yards from the grave of one of the Shankill Butcher victims, Stephen McCann.

John Murphy faded into obscurity, perhaps because he feared the same fate as his brother. However, the IRA did not know about the roles of John Murphy and Mr A. When I wrote my book *The Shankill Butchers*, I was unable legally to name John Murphy and had to refer to him as Mr B. That legal impediment was removed in 1997 when he died in a road accident in Catholic West Belfast. Some of the people who went to his aid before he died were the type he and Lenny would have selected for death years earlier. As for Mr A, his role in terrorism continued, albeit in a less pronounced way. In 1998, Lenny's eldest brother, William, was sentenced to two years in prison for admitting possession of ammunition found in his son's bedroom. His son, William jnr, was found guilty of battering a pensioner to death during a burglary.

By the late 1990s, all of Lenny Murphy's crew, including Willie Moore, 'Big Sam' McAllister and 'Basher' Bates, were back on the streets. Bates, who claimed to 'have found God' in prison was shot dead by a young Protestant in revenge for a killing he had been involved in during his time with Lenny Murphy.

The Shankill Butchers were amongst the biggest mass murderers in British criminal history and by my reckoning killed over 30 people. Lenny Murphy underwent a psychiatric test before one of his trials and was declared sane. The basis for that assessment may have been that his crimes were premeditated, yet I believe a more accurate definition would have been aggressive psychopath. What is staggering about the story of Lenny Murphy is that, in a section of a relatively small city by world standards, he managed to recruit so many people with tendencies similar to his own. It would be akin to the American serial killer, Ted Bundy, having been the leader of a gang of murderers in his likeness. The fact that John Murphy participated in his brother's gruesome life added an even more bizarre dimension to the overall story. And then, there was Mr A, whom I cannot name for legal reasons. When that legal impediment is removed, my book *The Shankill Butchers* will be even more horrifying for future readers.

In the 1990s, many senior UVF figures tried to rewrite history by declaring that Lenny Murphy had been out of control and the organisation had disapproved of his butchery. That was a clear attempt by the UVF to erase that element of its history. Murphy was admired in the ranks of the UVF and UDA. Billy 'King Rat' Wright knew him and spoke highly of him, as did men like the Cemetery Killer, Michael Stone, and the self-professed maniac, Pastor Kenny McClinton. The UDA leader John McMichael was furious someone in his organisation enabled the IRA to rid society of the 'Master Butcher'. McMichael's reaction was not simply motivated by his search for an informer in UDA ranks, since Murphy was a member of the UVF.

I contacted Lenny Murphy's ex-wife by telephone from the Europa Hotel in Belfast years after his demise. She spoke to me and appeared willing to meet. Over a period of hours, I had several conversations with her and she insisted she would need to speak to her boyfriend before talking to me at length. In a final telephone call with her, she said her boyfriend had arrived home and had told her not to discuss her life with Lenny Murphy.

Jimmy Nesbitt and his team of detectives failed in their bid to bring Lenny and his close associates to justice but they tried hard for many years. Nesbitt and the men in his team such as Cecil Chambers and John Scott were superb investigators but they were unable to break the code of silence imposed by Lenny Murphy, John Murphy and Mr A.

Nesbitt was a legend in the RUC and when I wrote *The Shankill Butchers* he helped me understand the inner workings of the group. Members of RUC Special Branch did not appreciate his efforts. When I published prison photographs in my book, which I acquired from a journalistic source, Nesbitt was wrongly accused of leaking them to me. I later heard from security sources that certain members of Special Branch tried to damage his career. Because he remained a friend of mine, Special Branch later cast suspicions on him in respect of documents I used in a subsequent book, *The Dirty War*. I obtained the documents in question from a disgruntled member of Special Branch. Jimmy Nesbitt eventually became Head of Regional Crime and retired in the late '90s. In my opinion, he was one of the most professional detectives of his generation. When I asked him in January 2003 to name the most frightening terrorist he had ever met, he replied: 'It was Lenny Murphy. I can never forget his cold, cold eyes.' Like a serial killer, Murphy had enjoyed playing mind games with Nesbitt but the detective brought down most of his gang.

Mr C also escaped the police net. He appeared to fade from the scene though his brother, who operated with the Shankill Butchers in several sectarian attacks, remained active while living off the earnings of a prostitute. People often asked if writing about the Shankill Butchers was stressful. I have to say that, even while writing this chapter, I felt a chill. It is difficult for me to erase the images I saw when investigating their crimes. The horror of autopsy and crime-scene photographs is impossible to convey in words. I admit I have had many nightmares over the years, which led me to understand the awful stress on detectives who dealt with the terrorism of the Troubles. They were faced with the ghastly nature of violence on a daily basis. Nesbitt's team in Tennent Street had over 200 unsolved murders at the time the Butchers were on their killing sprees. Nesbitt was also under a death threat from the IRA. Equally, I had security problems as a consequence of writing books like *The Shankill Butchers*, but so did other writers and journalists. It was a recognised risk when writing about conflict.

9

TERROR BOSSES

In July 1971, a month before the introduction of internment without trial, few people paid much attention to a statement in a loyalist news-sheet circulated in East and West Belfast. It was the birth certificate of the Ulster Defence Association.

> Being convinced that the enemies of the Faith and Freedom are determined to destroy the State of Northern Ireland and thereby enslave the people of God, we call on all members of our loyal institutions, and other responsible citizens, to organise themselves immediately into platoons of 20 under the command of someone capable of acting as sergeant. Every effort must be made to arm these platoons, with whatever weapons are available. The first duty of each platoon will be to formulate a plan for the defence of its own street or road in cooperation with platoons in adjoining areas. A structure of command is already in existence and various platoons will eventually be linked in a coordinated effort.

One of the men who helped draft that statement was Charles Harding Smith, leader of the Woodvale Defence Association. A tall, dark-haired, taciturn man, he was not given to small talk. Among his close friends was the paedophile, John McKeague. Following increased IRA violence in response to the sentiments and objectives expressed in it, the 'birth certificate' had a deep resonance within the Protestant/loyalist community. Many people in that community had a desire to see the emergence of a credible opposition to the Provisional IRA.

The language and the way in which the statement was crafted pointed to authors much more accomplished with the written word than Charles

Harding Smith, a man with a basic education. Behind the scenes, William Craig, a former Unionist Minister of Home Affairs and William McGrath, the paedophile leader of Tara, were among several figures who secretly discussed the need for a replacement of the B Specials. Among those present at one meeting were two men, one of them a lawyer who, in 1973, helped the UFF draft the document announcing its arrival on the terrorist scene.

Harding Smith had considered the option of merging defence associations like his own with the UVF but was advised against it by those I have mentioned. For its part, the UVF was not keen to fill its ranks with thugs, criminals and people whose loyalty could not be assured. It preferred to see itself as a disciplined, military-style body.

William Craig, known as Bill to his friends, was a very social person and a natural conspirator. He told Harding Smith and others that there was a need for a people's army because the UVF was non-representative of the aspirations of the Protestant community. Like Ian Paisley, Craig was one of the most influential figures at the onset of the Troubles. He dressed impeccably, was married to a German wife and lived in an impressive house with a flagpole in the front garden. He was a man who was hard on the issues, especially when they related to the nationalist population. When he had been Minister of Home Affairs in the mid to late 1960s, he treated civil rights marchers like common criminals.

Outwardly he resembled a successful stockbroker. At 5 ft 9 in. tall, he had a suntanned face and a somewhat portly figure. He spoke with a clipped delivery, which was distinctive because he tended to add 's' to many word endings. Some people believed that when he spoke, his speech was slurred because of alcohol. He was a heavy drinker and, on several occasions, he made public speeches after over-imbibing. In the mid 1980s, I spent an evening with him in the Linenhall bar in Belfast and talked to him about his political past. He was skilled at revising his own history but provided me with fascinating insights into the early days of loyalist paramilitary development.

According to him, from late 1970 onwards there was a deeply held view among Unionists that the disbandment of the B Specials had left Protestants defenceless. The B Specials, he said, had provided a sense of security and after the emergence of the Provisional IRA their loss became more acutely felt. He was keen to assure me that he was never involved in violence and only responded to people who sought his advice. In 1971, he became convinced of the need for organised defence. He did not feel that the UVF was the body to provide it. Protestants, he told his friends, had a right to legally defend Ulster and the UVF did not fit that objective because it was a proscribed body. I pressed him about the UVF, pointing out that surely it was the only body, given its place in the Troubles from

1966 onwards. He reacted defensively because he knew that I was aware of the fact that the UVF disapproved of him. However, he quickly reminded me that his objective was the creation of an umbrella organisation with a lower layer of local militias.

'When you say militias, do you mean platoons because that is the term you frequently used even before the UDA was formed?' I asked.

He smiled and again explained that he had envisaged a popular army with a legal framework – a defence organisation. In other words, he knew, as a lawyer, that it would be a crime to encourage people to join the ranks of the UVF. He was also conscious of the fact that Protestants possessed 100,000 legally held weapons and therefore had the means to arm a 'popular army'. I knew that he met with the UVF in 1970 and was rebuffed by them so he had discussions with the shadowy paedophiles, William McGrath, John McKeague, as well as Charles Harding Smith and Tommy Herron, the defence leader in East Belfast.

I asked him if McGrath advised Harding Smith and other militia leaders since he had been the UVF's mentor for several years. McGrath, I pointed out, was also fond of talking about 'platoons'.

'You will have to ask him. I'm sure that at the time he would have shared his opinions with many in the Unionist family.'

William Craig's concept of a loyalist army combining street defence groups like Harding Smith's was certainly designed not to rise above the law while flouting the spirit of the law. In public, Craig sometimes resembled a strutting Nazi apparatchik. He saw himself as a saviour of Ulster and was happy when surrounded by paramilitary trappings, which included men in leather jackets and a motorcycle escort. His desire for power frightened men like Harding Smith and Tommy Herron, who had no intention of placing themselves under his control. However, they were impressed with his advice. When it became apparent to him that Smith, Herron and others did not want his leadership, he created his own organisation, which he called Vanguard. His vision for it, as he confirmed to me, was to provide a focus for growing Protestant discontent. That, however, was not his only objective as he outlined when addressing a rally in January 1972.

> We in Ulster are intent on seeing that we have a constitutional organisation that can effectively preserve and maintain in Ulster the British heritage. It is not the Constitution that matters to us. It is the British way of life. Any tampering with our Constitution would merely be the beginning of the inevitable sell-out and would expose us more and more to the caprices of British politicians, who for the sake of expediency are all too likely to betray their friends.

Tacit in his remarks, which came three days before Bloody Sunday, was a subtle warning to the British Government of Edward Heath that there should be no 'tampering' with Northern Ireland's status within the United Kingdom. By then, his contacts had informed him Heath was considering abolishing the Unionist Government at Stormont. The UDA was in its infancy but Craig had detached himself from its formation.

In January and February 1972, there were the beginnings of a dual-track paramilitary process under the guise of legality. There was the UDA and Craig's Vanguard, which was out front with dire warnings of trouble to come. The curious thing about both organisations was that membership overlapped. Craig's narcissism drove him to create an organisation he could effectively control and, as he admitted to me, his judgment to move quickly was proven to be correct. He said that he realised then that it would take time to bind together local militias like Harding Smith's and Herron's and there would be inevitable turf battles. He had, he added, no stomach for dealing with some of the unsavoury characters in defence bodies. In a dangerous climate, he provided loyalism with an articulate justification for action, wrapped in a veneer of constitutional legality.

> We in Vanguard feel the time for talk is over. We want the Ulster loyalists to commit themselves to the course of action. We are finished with all this wishy-washy approach to the menace which threatens our Province, and by the time we all come together in an Ulster rally on 18 March every part of the world will know where Ulster loyalists stand and will know that the Ulster loyalist is capable of doing more than talk. Late as the hour is, and it is jolly late, I can say with confidence we are going to win this struggle . . . We are going to beat this conspiracy into the ground and we make no accommodation with the enemies of this country, of this democracy.

The night following that statement, two Catholics were shot from passing cars. Craig knew where his threats would fall. He was aware Harding Smith and Herron had the UDA ready for action. He had provided them with the thesis for such action. One month later, he displayed his true character in front of 75,000 loyalists assembled in the Ormeau Park in Belfast. Among them were the new leaders of the UDA. Before he addressed the 'troops', members of McKeague's Tartan gangs lined up in front of him with banners which read 'Shankill Battalion' and 'Shankill Tartan'. The Battalion banner was there to signal the UDA's approval of him as one of the guiding lights within loyalism.

When he addressed the crowd, he chose language which, if used on the British mainland, would have led him to a jail cell. He said that 'we will establish a more sophisticated intelligence service than is available at the moment . . . If the politicians fail, it will be our job to liquidate the enemy.' That was exactly what the UDA wanted to hear and he received resounding cheers. Two days later, he added more fuel to the fires of fear and hatred when he warned that 'we may be moving into a situation close to war'.

I asked him at our meeting in the '80s if he realised using words like 'liquidate' encouraged the UDA and UVF to kill Catholics. He responded that the times had required strong language. The IRA had to know there was 'a price to be paid' if their campaign continued. He neglected to mention that a month after the Ormeau Park rally he talked about the need for a 'shoot to kill' policy. 'When we say force, we mean force. We will only assassinate our enemies as a last resort when we are denied our democratic rights.'

In reality, his use of 'liquidate' and 'shoot to kill' was heard loud and clear in the ranks of the UDA and UVF. It had the effect of empowering both organisations to go about the business of killing members of the other community. Like other leaders in loyalism, he was vague when it came to defining 'enemy'. Years earlier, he had declared civil rights marchers the enemy. He knew that loyalists were incapable of making subtle distinctions between nationalists who had aspirations to live in a United Ireland and physical force republicans. He was, in my estimation, the dynamic for the surge in violence beginning in the early '70s and the carnage which followed. In that sense, I believe he fits the definition of this chapter. His words in 1972 were testimony to the man who initially argued for an army and platoons of men.

'We are determined, ladies and gentlemen, to preserve our British tradition and way of life. And God help anyone who gets in our way,' he told a rally in Enniskillen in February '72.

He was deliberately vague when he used 'anyone' just as he had been when he referred to liquidating the enemy. Those who listened to him knew exactly how to interpret that vagueness. The ability to do so lay deep in the historical memory of loyalism, just as republicans knew to whom the IRA was referring when it talked about the enemy – the Protestant Unionist State. For the UDA, there was no ambiguity in his words. They admired his articulation of their position but interpreted it with a more direct language, as shown by a letter in a UDA 'Bulletin' of the period. A woman allegedly wrote the letter.

I have reached the stage where I no longer have any compassion for any nationalist man, woman or child . . . What I want to know are where the hell are the MEN in our community? Have they any pride? Have they any guts? Why have they not started to hit back in the only way these nationalists bastards understand? That is ruthless, indiscriminate killing . . . If I had a flame-thrower, I would roast the slimy excreta that pass for human beings. Also I'm sick and tired of you yellow-backed Prods who are not even prepared to fight for your street, let alone your own loyalist people. When civil war breaks out, and God forgive me I hope it's soon, I, at least, will shoot you along with the Fenian scum.

Whether the letter did in fact originate spontaneously from a woman was irrelevant. What was significant was that someone in loyalist circles was trying to incite the UDA to kill Catholics. It was the kind of language, which men like Lenny Murphy and others would have used. A leader accompanying the letter noted: 'Without question most Protestants would agree.'

From 1972 onwards, William Craig became a minor player as the UDA took on the mantle of Northern Ireland's largest paramilitary body. However, as Craig had suspected, the merging of local defence groups would prove to be a difficult task and would lead to turf wars. As the UDA began its sectarian assassination campaign, anyone in the loyalist community who opposed it faced swift retribution. In March '72, Ingram 'Jock' Beckitt, a 37-year-old docker from Crimea Street in the Shankill area, felt that the UDA was filled with criminal elements. He made no attempt to conceal his views and his opposition to the new body became known to many of its leaders. A Scot by birth, he was a heavily built man whom locals described as 'an honest Prod'. He was also renowned for his brawling skills and was reputed to have fought six policemen to a standstill in a bar brawl. In all, his reputation was of a hard man who was a straight talker.

He and his brother, 'Pinky', were a well-known duo and were seen as community 'leaders' before the Troubles began. Overall, they had good relations with the local police because they were not criminally minded and were quick to defuse violent situations. It was reported that they had helped calm tensions after violence erupted in August '69. 'Jock' Beckitt was one of the original members of the UDA and his sister, Jean Moore, later became a signatory to the document which announced the formation of the UFF.

While drinking in bars and clubs in the Shankill, 'Jock' talked about 'miscreants' who were using their status in the UDA as cover for their criminal pursuits. At a meeting of Shankill militants on 26 March 1972, he pointed to a group of men and described them as 'not men at all – only a bunch of thugs and gangsters'. He warned everyone present that he would inform the police about their crimes if they did not cease.

Later that evening, in a Shankill club, 'Pinky' Beckitt voiced open support for his brother and was attacked and badly beaten by a group of men. When 'Jock' heard about the assault, he was outraged and headed for the club. When he arrived, two armed men were waiting for him and shot him the moment he went inside. Believing he was dead, they transported his body in a car to nearby Conlig Street to dump it in an alleyway. When they reached that location, 'Jock' regained consciousness and attacked his assailants. One of them shot him in the head, killing him. His sister, Jean Moore, accused a 'UDA faction' of murdering him. The two shooters, Thomas John Boyd and William Spence, were later executed in their homes. Both were known criminals. The murder of 'Jock' Beckitt shocked local people and Harding Smith, one of the UDA's founders, realised something had to be done to root out undesirable elements in his organisation.

One of the features of the early days of the UDA was that it had two significant areas of operation – West and East Belfast. Tommy Herron controlled the East and Harding Smith the West. Both men passed out military ranks to their underlings the way someone would hand out toffees. Cronies of both men became lieutenant colonels, majors and captains. The controlling body of the organisation was the Inner Council, a motley assortment of men with brigadier rank, with a chairman and vice-chairman. As I pointed out in an earlier chapter, the Inner Council met in two Belfast hotels.

Herron and Harding Smith were different in terms of personality, objectives and leadership qualities. Harding Smith was quiet, devious, ruthless and determined to shape the UDA along the lines of the UVF, which he admired. He wanted discipline and a defined strategy. Herron was also ruthless, with a propensity for criminality. Unlike his counterpart, he strutted round UDA HQ in East Belfast like a Mafia Capo, his legally registered pistol in a holster. As long as his cronies got action, there was no need to worry about where the money came from to keep them happy. He was bombastic and had a short fuse. Once, while I sat in his office to interview him, he pistol-whipped one of his minions for reasons he did not explain in my presence. Harding Smith was much more calculating and clinical, with a tendency to brood before making life-and-death decisions.

In West Belfast, he admired the UVF but not the Gusty Spence supporters in its ranks. Spence, the 'hero' of the 1966 Malvern Street shootings, had created a minor metamorphosis within the UVF as a consequence of his discussions with Official IRA operatives in prison and his own self-education. He developed a thesis that the Protestant working class had suffered under Unionist Rule in the same way as their Catholic counterparts. They had, he argued, been exploited by rich landowners educated at English public schools like Eton. In essence, he advocated that the UVF should move from an innately Rightist political position to the Left. He admired the Marxist theorising of the Official IRA and abhorred the romantic nationalism of the Provisional IRA. Naively, he believed he could instil within the UVF recognition that a Protestant left-wing ideology had merit. His views, through his meetings in prison with young UVF operatives who regarded him as a hero, found some fertile ground and filtered into the ranks. To the horror of senior figures in the UDA in West Belfast, some of their personnel through frequent contact with the UVF in the Shankill began to debate Spence's left-wing philosophy.

UDA Lieutenant Colonel Ernie Elliott, Harding Smith's second-in-command in Woodvale, began reading works by Karl Marx after discussions with UVF friends. In clubs, he delighted in quoting phrases and passages from Marx and explaining how Marxist concepts could be applied to the 'loyalist struggle'. Some of the men under his control were impressed but the majority who heard him were deeply suspicious and confused. Rumour began to spread that he had communist tendencies and he had met members of the Official IRA. The latter rumour was true. At a meeting with Official republicans he felt he was their intellectual equal and enjoyed conveying that belief to members of the UDA in the Shankill district.

Those rumours reached the ears of RUC Special Branch and were passed to British Military Intelligence. Within the British Army's HQ in Lisburn, there were Cold War warriors infected with paranoia. News that communism was infecting the ranks of the UDA worried them. The prospect of the UDA embracing a left-wing philosophy of the type espoused by the Official IRA rang alarm bells. It may now appear ludicrous that such a reaction was engendered but one has to understand the international political character of the period and the situation in Northern Ireland. Senior figures in the British military apparatus did not see the UDA posing any threat to them but even the remote possibility of a rapprochement between part of that organisation and the Official IRA was not a scenario they had anticipated or were prepared to contemplate. The Information Policy Unit, a British Military Intelligence grouping with a disinformation agenda – a function of what was termed Psyops –

was brought up to speed on the information about Ernie 'Duke' Elliott's 'communist tendencies' and his links to the Official IRA. Within the IPU, there was an MI5 element and when the matter reached the ears of that service, a plan was conducted to discredit Elliott. It was decided to use the paedophile agent, William McGrath, to covertly circulate stories in loyalist ranks that Elliott was a criminal and a communist.

Harding Smith was in London facing arms charges when the disinformation campaign against Elliott was launched. On acquittal, Harding Smith returned to West Belfast where Elliott had been running the Woodvale Defence Association in his absence. He quickly learned from underlings that while he had been out of circulation, criminal activity had increased within the UDA areas under his control. There had been, he was told, robberies and the hijacking of liquor trucks to supply illegal drinking clubs. Elliott had made no effort to curtail the crime-wave and had financially benefited from it. No one mentioned that in East Belfast, under Herron's leadership, crime was an integral part of UDA policy and most of the members of the Inner Council were beneficiaries of racketeering and extortion profits.

Harding Smith's close associates, men who shared his ultra conservatism, warned him that he had to act decisively to stop the rot. His vision of a highly disciplined body would not become a reality and the UDA was in danger of being banned if criminality dominated its agenda. Its leaders might even be interned. He was informed that the police, who had good relations with the UDA, were unhappy about coming into the Shankill and other UDA-controlled districts in the west of the city. There had been a comfortable relationship with the RUC whose members had ignored extortion levies on local businesses and other activities. If lawlessness continued, the RUC might take a deeper interest in the UDA and that would be counterproductive. It would also restrict the UDA's capacity to operate as a paramilitary body.

Harding Smith called a meeting of the West Belfast leadership but did not invite Ernie 'Duke' Elliott. At the meeting, there was unanimous agreement that a 'clean-up' was required. Those present, who had been responsible for the crime-wave, fingered Elliott as the guilty man. It was easy to do because the perceived wisdom flowing from the British disinformation campaign was that Elliott was a top criminal. Others at the meeting voiced the rumour he was a communist and had met the Official IRA. They also cited his penchant for quoting from the works of Karl Marx and Che Guevara. Harding Smith responded that he would give them a 'clean-up' on condition he had complete authority to act as he saw fit. All present promised him their support and he told them action would be forthcoming and swift.

On 7 December 1972, an abandoned mini-traveller car was spotted in a street near a notorious loyalist enclave known as The Village in South Belfast. The name, The Village, did not fully convey its history as a place that harboured many vicious UDA and UVF gunmen. Police and soldiers called to the scene noticed a cardboard box in the back of the vehicle and were cautious. They expected to find a bomb. There was one but it was not made of explosives – it was a political 'device'. A military bomb expert placed a small charge at the rear of the vehicle and blew off the doors. A rope was carefully placed round the box and it was dragged clear of the car. As the box hit the roadway, a body fell out of it. The victim was Lieutenant Colonel Ernie 'Duke' Elliott and he had died from a shotgun blast to his head.

He had been abducted the previous night with another man. That man was found wandering along Ainsworth Avenue, a short distance from where Elliott's body was discovered. He had been badly beaten and told police that he and Elliott had been drinking in UDA clubs in the Shankill, then they decided to travel across town to Sandy Row, a predominantly loyalist district situated approximately half a mile from The Village. To get there, they had crossed the Lower Falls near Divis Flats. According to the story from Elliott's unnamed companion, he and Elliott had been in the official car of the Woodvale Defence Association. They stopped at traffic lights on the edge of the Lower Falls and three masked and armed men approached the car. The men knew Elliott and separated him from his companion.

RUC detectives were not impressed by the story. If, as the mystery man suggested, he and Elliott had on the spur of the moment decided to go to Sandy Row, it was unlikely the IRA would have had three men loitering at traffic lights to abduct Elliott. The route allegedly taken by Elliott and his companion was one that UDA personnel would not have chosen because of its proximity to 'enemy' territory. Additionally, police could not comprehend why the IRA would have killed Elliott and not his companion. RUC detectives quickly made it known to journalists that they did not believe the mystery man's account of what transpired and that loyalists had murdered Elliott. They added that Elliott had probably not left the Shankill and was killed there. His companion, they believed, was beaten and released with orders to provide police with a bogus story that the killers were members of the IRA.

The UDA in East Belfast preferred the mystery's man account and immediately killed Joseph Kelly, a 47-year-old Catholic. He was on a bus, returning from work. As it stopped at Castlereagh Street in East Belfast, two young gunmen boarded the vehicle. Kelly was sitting downstairs reading a book when one of the gunmen shot him six times in the head at close range. Clearly, his regular travels through East Belfast had come to the attention of the UDA or a loyalist in his workplace had informed the organisation about his routine. Within days, another Catholic, 16-year-old James Joseph Reynolds, was riddled with sub-machine gun bullets. Both had paid with their lives because no one, particularly Harding Smith, was willing to take responsibility for the execution of Elliott. The two Catholics might have died anyway in a climate in which UDA hit teams were constantly searching out victims.

Dave Fogel, a senior UDA officer, later claimed Harding Smith had been trying to integrate 'evil men' into the UDA – members of the UVF. The allegation was true but was not related to the decision to kill Elliott. His execution symbolised the 'clean-up' Harding Smith had promised. No other notable UDA figures were targeted at that stage and Elliott's friends kept a low profile. His departure severed any hope of contact between the UDA and the Official IRA and ended any political discussion which could be interpreted as promoting a left-wing ideology in the UDA.

Harding Smith faced greater problems than 'Duke' Elliott's alleged criminality and communist tendencies. Across the Lagan River in the east of the city, UDA racketeering was eroding popular support throughout the Protestant community. Tommy Herron knew that Harding Smith had removed Elliott and Herron had no intention of suffering a similar fate. He distrusted Harding Smith and the young militants who surrounded him. After Elliott's death, an uneasy alliance developed between the factions in both parts of Belfast. In the background, Harding Smith jockeyed for power and became joint UDA vice-chairman, superseding Herron in rank and, de facto, Jim Anderson who had been sole vice-chairman while Harding Smith was in London on arms charges.

One of Harding Smith's first acts as joint vice-chairman was to order the arrest of Elliott's friend, Dave Fogel. He was taken to a house in East Belfast, paraded before Harding Smith and questioned about a deterioration in law and order. Fogel answered that outsiders had misrepresented the facts and that there had been a smear campaign aimed at him in the same fashion that rumours were spread about Elliott. After the questioning, he was released but he knew that his fate was sealed. On 22 January 1973, six weeks after Elliott's murder, he fled Northern Ireland and sold his story to the *Sunday Times* newspaper. In it, he claimed that the turmoil in the UVF was due to Harding Smith's return. He issued the following condemnation of the UDA:

> There is a power struggle going on and I don't want to be a part of it. We are mixing with dangerous and evil men out for their own gain and not for the interests of ordinary working-class people – the Protestant people of Ulster.

It was clear his comments were aimed at Harding Smith, especially when he added that a 'vicious and evil smear campaign' was being directed at Tommy Herron. Fogel was correct because Harding Smith and conspirators like the Tara leader, William McGrath, were circulating stories about Herron being 'soft on Catholics' because he had been baptised Catholic in St Anthony's Church in East Belfast. It was also said he had republican relatives, one of whom was a member of the Provisional IRA.

Someone, and I do not believe it was a person in the UDA, had carefully researched Herron's family history and discovered facts about his origins. Unlike Lenny Murphy, his name did not imply a Catholic background and, until that time, his associates had not known that he was baptised Catholic. Like Murphy, however, from the outset of his role in terror he had been determined to be more sectarian than those around him. He was what Gusty Spence called a 'Super Prod' – a person who chose to be more extreme to hide his Catholic roots.

Within the Military Intelligence hierarchy there was a generally held view that Herron was a dangerous individual. On several occasions, much to the consternation of the British Army Command, he had threatened major confrontations with troops. Within the Army mindset was a conviction that there could not be two enemies on the ground. The prospect of the Army being forced to confront the largest loyalist paramilitary organisation as well as the IRA did not sit well with British generals. In contrast, the Army regarded Harding Smith as a typical loyalist militant whose enemy was the same one the troops were combating. Another concern for Military Intelligence analysts was that Herron was wild, unpredictable and his criminal pursuits were endangering the UDA's legal status. No one in the military wished to see the UDA proscribed because in such a scenario the security forces would have been forced to target the organisation and intern its leaders and rank and file.

I put that analysis to a former Military Intelligence officer who commented: 'We did not see the UDA as a problem and it was not a problem we wished to deal with. We had enough on our hands with the two wings of the IRA at the outset and especially the PIRA after the Officials declared a cease-fire. No one wanted to envisage a situation in which our troops were caught between two warring factions – one was enough, thank you very much. The UDA in East Belfast was somewhat of a problem because Herron was not a man to listen to reason. He was liable to go off half-cocked. There were concerns that his leadership role would force Number 10 to deal with the UDA and no one wanted that.'

Herron reacted to Harding Smith's antagonism and rumours reaching him that there could well be a coup against him. Behind the scenes he marshalled his own supporters. On 21 January, the same day Dave Fogel fled to London, 200 UDA commanders met and reaffirmed their support for Herron. They condemned people who were circulating rumours about him. Herron then issued a personal statement that the rumours were being spread by 'a man who was seeking to break up the organisation and take power for himself'. The man, he added, 'was not even a member of the UDA'.

Herron's statement came ten days after Harding Smith became chairman of the UDA. The man he referred to was Harding Smith but he rightly anticipated that if he divulged his name to the media, he would be seen to be the person splitting the organisation. However, he was assured that the rank and file of the UDA knew to whom he was referring.

The gulf between the two terror bosses illustrated the confusion and turmoil within the UDA. It had grown up almost spontaneously and therefore was loosely structured. Local commanders wielded virtually unchecked power. They came together as a body only within the Inner Council where overall policy and strategy was thrashed out in a democratic fashion after considerable alcohol was consumed. The positions of chairman and vice-chairman were not intended to carry executive authority but merely the roles of spokespersons and chairing of meetings. In other words, they were intended to be *primus inter pares* – and no more. The reality with Herron and Harding Smith in place was otherwise.

At the end of January, the majority of members of the Inner Council persuaded Harding Smith and Herron to put aside their open hostility for the betterment of the organisation. Within months, it was clear that the enforced accommodation between the pair had broken down. Crime and extortion had remained unchecked and Harding Smith believed it was eroding the UDA's capability to launch an offensive against the IRA and the Catholic population. Like the Mafia, the UDA had rapidly gained a near-monopoly of all thefts in Belfast. Raids on shops were carried out with military precision, creating an underground of stolen goods. The RUC was too busy dealing with terrorism to respond to the rise in crime with the result that crime became an institutionalised feature of life. Men like Herron who benefited from crime were like aristocrats in their own areas.

At the beginning of June, Harding Smith flew to Toronto to talk to loyalists who had settled there and were raising funds and purchasing weapons for the UDA and UVF. The other man at the centre of the UDA controversy, Tommy Herron, decided to stand for election for a new Assembly in the province. The news was music to Harding Smith's ears. According to UDA rules, Herron was obliged to resign his vice-chairmanship. He announced that he had done so but he continued to run the UDA in East Belfast out of its HQ on the Newtownards Road. He also gave statements to the media and appeared to be still in command. Jim Anderson, a leading member of the Inner Council, resigned in disgust but, when he learned Herron might really resign, he announced he was reconsidering his decision. Harding Smith made it known he wanted Herron to leave the UDA but Herron was made of sterner stuff than Dave Fogel. To Harding Smith, and figures in Military Intelligence, a removal from the scene à la 'Duke' Elliott was beginning to seem the only way that Herron would go.

In East Belfast, Herron levied a weekly tax on every householder for the 'protection of property'. Shopkeepers, publicans and bookmakers were forced to pay large sums to stay in business and if they refused they knew that a bomb or bullet would be their punishment. UDA men who had been unemployed before joining the organisation openly flaunted wealth and that angered many in the Protestant community.

Harding Smith's trip to Canada had a dual purpose, one of which was to allow for a major development to take place in his absence – a development that Inner Council members, including Herron, had been informed about. At the end of May, with other militants in West Belfast, Harding Smith had shaped a strategy in which the UDA's military capability would be detached from the political structure, much in keeping with the Provisionals dual-track process of Sinn Fein and the IRA. The effect, he hoped, would be to leave the UDA insulated from the Law when its gunmen carried out attacks. The UDA would de facto claim those attacks, but under another name. It would therefore not be tainted with the charge that it was a terrorist body. Harding Smith and his close associates believed the UDA as constituted was not an effective military machine and corruption in the ranks was weakening its terror effectiveness.

On 7 June, while he remained in Canada, a story appeared in the *Irish News*, a leading daily newspaper, claiming militants had taken over the UDA in a bloodless coup. The following day, it was revealed that the militants had set up a new headquarters on the Shankill Road and two UDA leaders, John Haveron and Tucker Lyttle, were being held there. Lyttle, unknown to the UDA, was a Special Branch informer. From UDA HQ in East Belfast the story of a coup was denied but later in the day a spokesman from that HQ said Herron was being held captive in a bar. A TV camera crew was allowed into the bar to film Herron sitting in a chair flanked by masked men. Asked whether he was being held voluntarily or against his will, Herron replied: 'I suppose you could say a bit of both.'

He did not appear unduly concerned and neither did the wives and families of the three men being held. Astute observers of the conflict realised that the episode appeared to have been stage-managed with Herron's approval. Little did they know that he had no choice but to be a part of it. Within 48 hours, Herron and the other two UDA operatives were released. Then, early on 9 June, a Dublin-based journalist of the *Sunday World* newspaper was summoned to UDA HQ on the Shankill Road and was given a long statement. It was a well thought out and eloquent apologia of militant Protestant opinion, announcing the creation of the Ulster Freedom Fighters. It criticised press bias during the Troubles and the misunderstanding it had shown in relation to Protestant reaction to the events of the previous four years. It explained in some detail the ethnic origins of Ulster Protestants and listed grievances it believed the press had overlooked. It was signed by Andy Tyrie and Jean Moore, the sister of Ingram 'Jock' Beckitt. Tyrie would later become chairman of the UDA with John McMichael as his deputy. Jean Moore had been the head of the women's section of the UDA, which never matched the IRA's female wing, Cumman na mBann, in terms of effectiveness and terrorist expertise.

I was later informed that the 'birth certificate' of the UFF was written for the organisation by a lawyer with deep connections to loyalism. That made sense because the signatories to the documents, and others in the UDA leadership, would not have had the skill to craft such a statement. The lawyer in question was involved in the early days of the UVF and was a seminal figure in the cabal, which helped form the UVF in the lead up to the Malvern Street shootings in 1966. He was the person whom detectives most wanted to know about when they interviewed Gusty Spence in the days after the Malvern Street episode. He was a close associate of McGrath and a clergyman. One has to read the full statement to realise that it was not written by Andy Tyrie, Jean Moore or Harding Smith.

We accept that the press of the world is sick of the sound and sight of Ulster, sick of our orgy of destruction, sick of our rancour and sick of our brutalities. Why, therefore, you ask, should you be interested in the self-delusive ravings of a band of extreme Protestants? A band of men cast in the role of wicked 'heavies', the 'bad guys' of the story, the narrow-minded bigots of Ulster, the cause of all the present troubles?

Mountains of words have been written about us in the past four years and our role in the affair is cast by the press in a certain way and all comments about us are based on these assumptions:

That we are narrrow-minded. That we are fanatical. That we are similar to the IRA. That we hate all Catholics. That we are repressive 'right-wing' fascists. That we cannot be reasoned with.

With all that has been written about the Scots-Irish of Northern Ireland, you would have thought that someone would have eventually grasped the essential truth of it all. The real cause of the bloodshed, the real cause of the hatred. We think you, the press, have done nothing of the sort, and it is high time that you did; for, if nothing else, we do feel you owe our people a little latitude. Just this once.

It seems a lifetime ago that our competent, if partisan, government came under fire from a civil rights movement which, it has to be admitted, did have a justification for many of its grievances. Cast inevitably in the role of St Bernadette came a pint-sized lady of fiery oratory and poverty-striken background. How the press loved this little lady, pictured her swinging prettily in a garden as her victories over the repressing, misruling Unionists were announced.

You, the press, made a heroine of this girl and you bear a heavy responsibility for what followed. The blundering, incompetent and seemingly repressive antics of our leaders confirmed your attitude that she and her associates were right and that we were wrong. The B Specials, the reactions of our police forces, and the so-called ambush of Burntollet, hardened your views which, in turn, hardened ours, and the die was cast.

It is such a pity that you do not consult your history books, for the real truth lies there, repeated over and over again, like a gramophone record. We are a hybrid race descended from men who colonised Scotland from Ireland in the fifth century, and who then colonised Northern Ireland from Scotland in the seventeenth century. Our existence was not placid in Scotland, but that was heavenly compared to our life in Ireland. For four hundred years we have known nothing but uprising, murder, destruction and repression. We ourselves have repeatedly come to the support of the British Crown, only to be betrayed within another twenty years or so by a fresh government of that Crown. What is happening now mirrors events in the seventeenth, eighteenth and nineteenth centuries.

We are not good at propaganda and extolling our virtues or admitting our faults. We just stick to our points of view, bow our heads and pray for it all to die down for another fifty years or so. Gradually, however, we have come to realise that this time other factors have come into the age-old conflict of the Scots-Irish versus the Irish-Irish, or if you prefer it that way, the Protestants versus the Catholics in Ireland.

Traditionally the English politicians let us down – betrayal we call it. The Catholics try to overwhelm us so we are caught between two lines of fire. Second-class Englishmen, half-caste Irishmen, this we can live with and even defeat, but how can we be expected to beat the world revolutionary movement which supplies arms and training, not to mention most sophisticated advice on publicity, promotion and expertise to the IRA?

We do not have large funds from over-indulgent, sentimentally sick Irishmen in America who send the funds of capitalism to sow the seeds of communism here. We do not have the tacit support of the government of southern Ireland and we do not have the support or interests of the British people.

We are betrayed, maligned and our families live in constant fear and misery. We are a nuisance to our so-called allies and have no friends anywhere. Once more in the history of our people we have our backs to the wall, facing extinction one way or another. This the moment to beware, for Ulstermen in this position do fight mercilessly till they or their enemies are dead.

We would like to remind you of a few salient facts: the Russians who condemn our people have millions in slave labour camps and their Government is the biggest mass murderer since Adolf Hitler. Edward Kennedy, the heroic swimmer of Martha's Vineyard, is hardly in a moral condition to criticise his pet rabbit let alone us. The ruler of Libya is a raving fanatic. If the Unionist Government of Northern Ireland was corrupt, it was as pure as the driven snow compared to the Government of John Mary Lynch. If the press likes scandals then let them examine the private fortunes of Government ministers in the Lynch republic. Fortunes made out of a divine intuition about future planning permissions. If the Protestants in the south of Ireland are so content, why do their numbers dwindle and why do they never complain?

If the Southern Irish Government wants us then it will have to win our hearts, rather than have us as bitterly hostile losers in a bombing war of attrition tacitly backed by them. Their own history should tell them this will never work. Your troubles destroyed their tourist industry, and a few well-planted disease-ridden animals could very rapidly destroy their economic growth. They too are not immune from trouble, and they should not support evil men of violence lest it rebound heavily upon them.

The British Army in Ulster has good soldiers who are being set up like dummy targets. The orders of the politicians are tying both hands behind their backs. The British public says: 'Send the soldiers home.' We say: 'Send the politicians and the officers home and give us the men and the weapons – or, why not send the soldiers home and leave us the weapons and we will send you the IRA wrapped up in little boxes and little tins like cans of baked beans.'

The politicians who rule our lives from England do not understand us. They stop the Army from defending us properly and us from defending ourselves. We do not like these flabby-faced men with pop eyes and fancy accents. We do not like Heath and we do not like his 'side-kicks'. We had to stomach Reggie until Poulson saw him off, and Lambton and Jellicoe went in a more interesting way. We should really like to see wee Willie waddle off to cut the throats of his colleagues in Westminster and leave us to sensible ideas and policies which will work.

We ourselves are not perfect. We ourselves do not always see eye to eye, but the time is coming when the Scots-Irish of Ulster will have to reconsider their future actions. The bloodbath could very soon be a reality, and you who condemned us for it could have precipitated it unjustly on decent people because they gerrymandered a few constituencies to avoid giving power to people who were educated and dedicated to destroying a way of life.

You turned an adulterous little slut into a revolutionary saint; a soft-voiced priest fanatic was called a moderate, and you gave a terrorist organisation all the publicity it desired. It was not an Irish leader of the IRA who said we were all fit to be bombed but a sick little pop-eyed Englishman with a false name and no Irish connections whatsoever. We the Scots-Irish are fighting for survival. We think we have been greatly wronged and we think you should watch the events of the next month with extreme care.

That document contained the most eloquent statement of militant loyalism and its thinking during the Troubles. It was not issued as a UFF text but as a policy document of a new UDA leadership. That was of course disingenuous because hours later, the UFF emerged. As I pointed out, there was no one in paramilitary ranks capable of writing such a lucid and frank exposition of what constituted Protestant patriotism. It was substantially correct historically and, just as Spence had indicated in his lectures to young UVF men in prison, the document accepted the legitimacy of some civil rights grievances. The author acknowledged that there had been gerrymandering but justified it in terms of the need to preserve the integrity of the Unionist State. The use of language and structure implied an intelligent hand in the writing and formulation of the text. Words like 'rancour', 'self-delusive', 'latitude', 'partisan', 'hybrid', 'placid', 'over-indulgent', 'maligned', 'intuition', 'tacitly' and 'precipitated' were not common in the vocabularies of working-class loyalists. The statement was clear, concise and argued the case point by point in a logical and cogent style. It suggested that, for the first time, Protestant militants had begun to formulate a coherent ideology quite separate from, and in many ways opposed to, the traditional Unionism they had unquestioningly supported for 50 years. Harding Smith's personal relations with the UVF in West Belfast enabled him to persuade the lawyer to undertake the writing of the document.

Several hours after the journalist received the statement, a bomb was thrown into a Catholic bar at Unity Flats near the bottom of the Shankill Road. A barman picked it up to throw it outside and it exploded, blowing off his hand. His action saved the lives of dozens of customers on the premises. Fifteen minutes later, the UFF telephoned the *Belfast Telegraph* newspaper and made its first claim of responsibility for a terrorist attack. Hours later, UFF assassins struck again. They abducted a Catholic, 35-year-old Daniel O'Neill, and shot him through the head. At the location where his body was discovered, police found marks on the grass where he had tried to crawl before he died.

Harding Smith carefully planned the emergence of the UFF, ensuring he was out of the country when it took place and that Herron was held captive while militants appeared to mount a 'bloodless coup'. In some ways, it was a farcical strategy and one wonders for whose benefit. The intelligence community knew exactly what was happening because of the informers and agents it had in UDA ranks. One can only conclude it was intended for public and political consumption and to legally insulate the UDA leadership from the emergence of a 'new' terrorist organisation. It ensured nationalist demands for the banning of the UDA would have less effect because terrorism would now be claimed under the 'flag' of the UFF. That ideally suited British Military Intelligence and RUC Special Branch. As I have illustrated elsewhere in this book, elements of the State security apparatus used the UFF to carry out assassinations of republicans and suspected republicans while the UDA remained a legal body for two more decades.

On Harding Smith's return from Canada, he held a secret meeting of the UFF and called for more attacks against the IRA and the Catholic population. He also told those present that there was 'unfinished business'. The organisation, he warned, would not function with popular approval unless there was a 'clean-up', a term with which he had increasingly become familiar. When it was achieved, a new leadership could be installed in East Belfast. Everyone present understood he was referring to Tommy Herron.

On 15 June 1973, six days after the UFF announced its presence, two youths, not wearing masks, called at Herron's house in the Braniel housing estate in East Belfast. His wife told them he was not at home. They produced guns and forced their way past her. The only other adult in the house was Mrs Herron's brother, 19-year-old Michael Wilson, who was Herron's bodyguard. He was asleep upstairs, recovering from injuries he received a week earlier when Catholic women in an enclave at the bottom of the Newtownards Road beat him with hurley sticks. The gunmen burst into the bedroom and shot him through the head. He died instantly. Before they left, the gunmen told Mrs Herron that had her children not been in the house they would have shot her too. The gunmen then made their escape on foot through the predominantly Protestant estate. Despite subsequent claims that the IRA was responsible, the truth was the gunmen were sent across town from the Shankill with orders to kill Herron and his wife. Killing his wife, Harding Smith believed, would make it look more like an IRA attack. Police later discovered that a car used by the gunmen was hijacked in the Shankill earlier that day.

The following night, the UFF discussed the possibility that Herron would finger Harding Smith for the murder and retaliate. In order to offset that happening, they chose a macabre smokescreen. They decided to kill a Catholic and claim that it was in revenge for the IRA's murder of Wilson.

Elsewhere in Belfast that night, 16-year-old Daniel Rouse from the Catholic Andersonstown estate was returning home from a night out with friends. He got out of a taxi several hundred yards from his home and failed to notice a dark-coloured van at the side of the road. Two men got out of the vehicle and bundled him into it. Shortly after midday the next day, a caller representing the UFF telephoned the *Belfast Telegraph*. He said that a youth from Riverdale, Daniel Rouse, had been kidnapped and shot twice. 'He is dead. He was shot twice. He was killed in retaliation for the IRA's murder of Michael Wilson. There will be plenty more of this happening.' Daniel Rouse's body was found face down on a grass verge at Dunmurry Lane in South Belfast. The following day, the

UFF killed another Catholic, 25-year-old James Kelly, whose body was left in a ditch. Again, the UFF telephoned a Belfast newspaper. The caller announced, 'We have just assassinated an IRA man on the way to Larne. We gave him two in the back and one in the head. He is dead. This is in retaliation for Wilson.' The victim was not a member of the IRA but that did not matter to the UFF. The strategy to create the perception in loyalist ranks that the IRA killed Wilson seemed to work.

In true UDA tradition, even when they killed their own and blamed it on the IRA, Wilson was given a massive funeral attended by Harding Smith and other members of the Inner Council. The Reverend Ian Paisley officiated at the service during which mourners unanimously condemned the IRA for murdering a 'true loyalist'.

The IRA, in retaliation for the killings of Rouse and Kelly, abducted and shot a mentally retarded Protestant teenager. He was David Walker from the Belvoir housing estate in East Belfast. He was bundled into a car, driven to O'Neill Street in the heart of the Lower Falls and taken into an alleyway. Once there, he was shot in the head and chest. He was still alive when found but died on the way to hospital. In typical tit-for-tat fashion, the UFF killed a 26-year-old Catholic man in the Oldpark. He was hit by five bullets as he stood at the door of his home.

Within days of Wilson's murder the rifts within the UDA were clearly spelled out in an article in the *News Letter*, a daily newspaper read mainly by Protestants. The story contained accurate information, indicating that the journalistic source had to be Tommy Herron, or those around him. Herron, despite UFF attempts to indicate otherwise, knew that he had been a target for assassination and that the gunmen who shot Wilson were not members of the IRA.

> There were firm reports last night that the split in the ranks of the Ulster Defence Association is widening. Disputes that now beset the once powerful paramilitary movement have recently been underlined by the emergence of the Ulster Freedom Fighters. This is a breakaway group which, within the first days of its existence, has claimed responsibility for two murders and two explosions. Anonymous telephone callers have said its members have killed to avenge the death of Michael Wilson on Friday. The UDA is considering strong action against the UFF which, it believes, 'is creating a situation where the UDA could be proscribed as an illegal organisation'. The East Belfast section is under fire from many directions. Younger members within the section feel the leadership has allowed the movement to deteriorate. The West Belfast hierarchy also feels the order of

priorities on the other side has been lost. They believe East Belfast members are more intent on lining their own pockets than protecting the Protestant population. There have been allegations that a 'protection racket' – with Protestant publicans and shopkeepers forced to 'pay up or else' – is in force. Former vice-chairman, Tommy Herron, has admitted that UDA men were paid for protecting property in East Belfast. But he is adamant that there is no protection racket and claims the people involved were happy to pay the money. This has angered the hardline Ulster Volunteer Force as well as militants within the UDA. The 'freedom fighters' align themselves more closely with the outlawed UVF on the grounds that it is a far more idealistic body than the UDA. Some security chiefs are now convinced that Michael Wilson, Tommy Herron's brother-in-law, was killed by militant Protestants as a warning to the UDA to get back in line . . . Tommy Herron resigned his position so as to stand as a candidate in the Assembly elections. He still acts as spokesman for the organisation.

Whether it was Herron or one of his henchmen who spoke to a *News Letter* journalist, the message was clear. Herron wanted Protestants to know that he was not a racketeer and that the UFF was in danger of creating an environment in which the UDA might be banned. He was also telling Harding Smith that he knew who killed his brother-in-law and that he was the intended target. Harding Smith did not respond and allowed things to cool off, even praising Herron's leadership at Inner Council meetings. However, his determination and that of the UFF to get rid of Herron did not weaken. Three months later, Herron was lured from UDA HQ in East Belfast by a telephone call from a female with whom he was having an affair. He drove with her into the countryside unaware that screws holding in place the back seat of his car had been loosened and a gunman was concealed in the boot. When Herron stopped the car, the gunman pushed down the rear seat and shot him dead. Herron's legally held gun was still in its holster under his left armpit when his body was found. Harding Smith and the UFF immediately blamed the IRA and, true to UDA custom, Herron was accorded a massive funeral.

One year later, Provisional IRA Internal Security personnel were interrogating two informers, Vincent Heatherington and Myles McGrogan, when both men revealed that they had met one of Herron's killers. They named Gregory Brown, a UDA operative from East Belfast. The two informers, whom the IRA later murdered, were 'Freds' – agents recruited by the MRF two years earlier. They said they had met Gregory Brown in the Palace Barracks Army base where the MRF ran its operations until 1973 when it went through a name change and became 14th Int. Gregory Brown told them that he shot Herron. The IRA passed the information to the UDA, who executed Brown. For complex reasons I explained in my book *The Dirty War*, the IRA did not kill Heatherington and McGrogan for several years.

After the IRA executed Heatherington, David McKittrick, the respected writer and *Independent* journalist, raised intriguing issues about the Herron murder. He did not know at the time what I later learned about Heatherington and McGrogan and their connection to Gregory Brown through Military Intelligence. Nonetheless, McKittrick's sources were excellent and that was clear in an article he wrote on 8 July 1976 for the *Irish Times*, almost three years after Herron's demise and following the murder of Heatherington. He inferred a connection between the murders of Gregory Brown and Heatherington.

'The killing has been admitted by the Provisional IRA which claims that Heatherington was shot because of complicity with the security forces, but the story behind his death is much more complicated than that. A strange story lies behind these facts and it looks as though the full details will never be known. It begins with the death of Tommy Herron in 1973 for which no one has been brought to trial.'

RUC Special Branch was intrigued by the connection made by McKittrick and by the fact that, in a separate article, he carried a claim that Gregory Brown, an RUC detective, a Catholic and a woman had murdered Herron. Two Special Branch officers paid McKittrick a visit and, by his account, were 'particularly interested in the alleged involvement of a policeman in Herron's death'.

Within two years of Herron's murder, Harding Smith, who survived several attempts on his life as feuding continued in the UDA, decided to leave Northern Ireland. He had created enemies in the UDA because of his ruthlessness and there were others in the wings like James 'Pratt' Craig prepared to kill him to take his power. He settled in Skipton, Yorkshire, and worked as a lorry driver. Nothing more was heard of him and he died in 1997. The media in Ireland paid little attention to his passing. His enforced exile was motivated by his intimate knowledge of the ruthlessness of the organisation he had helped create. It leaders were never free from purges and turf wars. He and Herron had been two of the most notorious terror bosses of the conflict – men whose propensity for violence was similar. They merely differed in terms of their personalities and objectives. I firmly believe that Herron's death, while ordered by Harding Smith, was carried out by people with links to

British Intelligence. Herron was not only a target of Harding Smith but also other people in the shadows with a wider view of the conflict and grander designs.

While researching this book, I learned that Herron and Harding Smith were separately present in UDA clubs when innocent Catholics were tortured – in UDA parlance, 'rompered'.

10

STONE COLD ASSASSIN

In January 2003 Michael Stone, contrary to rumours that he was living in Spain, was sitting in a house in East Belfast working on paintings for a new exhibition. The notorious loyalist trigger man had turned his talents to art after being released from the Maze prison in the 1990s as part of the terrorist release programme dictated by the peace process. In May 2003, he published his memoirs, promising to reveal everything about his life as an assassin. As I expected, there was an outcry from the families of his victims, who have a right to claim the royalties from his book sales on the principle that a convicted killer should not benefit from his crimes. I knew that in an autobiography he could never be truthful about his life and I was proved right in my judgment when I read his book.

In the years since I wrote my book *Stone Cold* I have learned a great deal more about his history and why he subsequently attacked me in the *Sunday Life* newspaper after the book's publication. There were aspects of his past that he was determined to hide for the sake of his image and there were people that he was frightened to discuss with me at the time. He was especially incensed when I linked him to the late terrorist leader, John McMichael. In the course of this chapter I will explain why. Secondly, his association with a British Military agent was an element of his life he carefully kept hidden in the course of our discussions in the Maze prison and in letters we exchanged. Stone is still regarded as a loyalist hero. The truth about him is critical to an understanding of the level of collusion between the security forces and the UFF as well as the interconnections between various elements of the loyalist paramilitary apparatus. There are also important similarities to be drawn between him and other trigger men in earlier chapters of this book.

When I first met Michael Stone in the Maze prison in August 1990, I was struck by his innate narcissism. He was determined to impress with stories about the flamboyant social life he had led, the women who had admired him and his professionalism as an assassin. He assured me I was not looking at the 'real' Michael Stone but the 'incarcerated' Michael Stone. The 'real' Michael Stone wore Boss suits, went to discos, had girlfriends, one of whom was a Catholic with whom he had a child. He had fathered other children, some in a marriage, and loved them all equally. Women found him irresistible. At that first meeting, he did not resemble the wild man seen on television screens throughout the world in 1988 when he attacked the IRA leadership at a funeral in Milltown Cemetery in Belfast. His hair was now longer and tied in a pony tail. His body testified to daily prison workouts and he told me that he could easily snap a person's neck. After that first meeting, I felt that Stone had many of the personality characteristics of the Shankill Butcher, Lenny Murphy. However, I was only beginning to get inside his head and I reserved judgment.

I talked to him about his family background and the fact that I had been told by loyalists he was from a mixed marriage and his father was Catholic. That did not please him and he assured me it was untrue. My sources told me the perceived wisdom in the loyalist community was that his father was Frank Stone, a Catholic from the Ardoyne area of Belfast, and his mother was Ivy Susan from Birmingham, England. They had lived in the Highfield housing estate in 1969 and moved out after Catholic families were targeted by mobs. Stone wrote to me to dispel the rumours he had Catholic roots:

> As you know, my name is Michael Anthony Stone, date of birth 2/4/55. My natural parents were Cyril and Mary Stone. They met and married in Birmingham where my natural father was stationed. Cyril was in the Royal Corps of Signals. Like so many of these 'soldier-girl' relationships it lasted two years and sadly it was over. The marriage ended, my natural father brought me back to his family in Belfast and to his one sister Margaret who lived in the Braniel in East Belfast.

I conducted a search of birth and marriage registry documents in Belfast and Birmingham and learned that Stone's information was accurate. In his parents' marriage certificate, his father was listed as Cyril Alfred Stone. His profession was given as lorry-driver with a chemical manufacturer and there were no references to him being in the Royal Corps of Signals. More interestingly, his mother was Mary Bridget Sullivan and was born in Birmingham. Her name confirmed Irish Catholic roots, a fact Michael Stone never acknowledged to his loyalist paramilitary colleagues. He was aware of the import of his mother's name. In Northern Ireland, names and surnames denote a specific religious persuasion. Loyalists knew his father had married someone with a Catholic name. It was the only way one could account for the perceived wisdom that Michael Stone was from a mixed marriage. His dilemma had parallels with Lenny Murphy's life, though in the latter's case it was an erroneous belief that the Murphy family was concealing Catholic family links.

In his letters to me, Stone was truthful about the length of his parents' marriage. His mother was 19 when she married his father in 1953 in a London registry office. They parted after two years, remarried others and had children. She literally left Cyril holding baby Michael and walked out of the family home in Birmingham never to see her son again. Unable to care for the baby, Cyril took him to his sister, Margaret, and her husband, John Gregg, in the tiny coastal hamlet of Ballyhalbert on the shores of Belfast Lough. In his formative years, Michael Stone regarded them as his natural parents. In 1959, the Greggs moved to the Braniel housing estate on the edge of East Belfast. They were typically Protestant working-class people with a home full of photographs of relatives who had served in the British Army. John Gregg worked in a Belfast shipyard, the hub of loyalist solidarity.

When Michael Stone entered primary school, his aunt informed him about the existence of his natural father but his mother was an 'unmentioned subject'. His father sent letters and birthday cards but his aunt kept them from him, storing them in a cupboard with the aim of giving them to him when he reached maturity. He told me the Greggs were 'working-class loyalists'. It was his way of defining them in terms of loyalty to the British Crown and Ulster. Childhood for Michael Stone was similar to that of many boys in both communities. He was regularly taken to church, well clothed and fed. He was an average student and transferred to Lisnasharragh Secondary in 1966. When I asked him about his understanding of the political and religious character of Northern Ireland at that time, he responded: 'I knew I was truly British. I was after all English and my father had served in the Royal Corps of Signals. Maybe my mother was Catholic but my father was Protestant and I was reared in the Protestant faith.'

By the end of 1966, his heroes were the same as those of 'King Rat' – the UVF trigger men who shot Catholic barmen in Malvern Street. He also shared with Wright a penchant for thuggery and was constantly in trouble. In 1968, as civil unrest gripped Belfast, he was the leader of the Hole in the Wall gang. He was physically tough and enjoyed intimidating other boys of his age. One of his contemporaries provided the following description, which could just as equally have been applied to Lenny Murphy.

'Stone was either called Flint, after the television programme *The Flinstones*, or Stoner. Other kids feared him because he could be really vicious. He really fancied himself and took an interest in all the girls in the area. Most of us were very shy about girls but not Flint. He would go alone and stand outside Grosvenor High just to watch the talent. I remember he had an Alsatian and he would take it with him for protection, or because it gave him an air of authority. He used violence to impress and was likely to attack some innocent kid to prove how important he was.'

In August '69 when hundreds of Catholic homes were set alight in West Belfast, Catholic families were forced out of estates like the Braniel where Stone lived. He disbanded his gang and joined the Tartans, assuming the leadership of the Braniel Tartan, a bunch of sectarian thugs who were part of an organisation established by the paedophile, John McKeague. The transition from thug to sectarian thug was not a difficult one for Stone to make as tribal tensions increased. From that moment, he was well on his way to much more than vicious attacks on Catholics in East Belfast. In 1972, aged 17, he joined McKeague's Red Hand Commandos who were responsible for some of the grisly murders of that period. At the same time, he came to the attention of UDA boss, Tommy Herron, who also lived in the Braniel. Herron asked him to join the UDA. As I pointed out in an earlier chapter, Herron had reason to hide his Catholic roots. Perhaps he felt an affinity with the young Michael Stone who was known to be from a mixed marriage. If that was not the reason, Stone's propensity for violence must have impressed him. Herron knew Stone was under McKeague's control but that was not an impediment to UDA membership. In the early '70s, membership of paramilitary organisations overlapped.

The UDA, with its criminal tendencies, suited Stone and he soon went on a crime spree. On his 17th birthday he was found guilty of handling stolen goods. He was given a conditional discharge by the courts and ordered to pay compensation. He did not do so and ended up back in court for stealing guns and ammunition from a sporting shop. He was jailed for six months and sent to the Maze, which held many internees at that time. On release from prison, he returned to the ranks of the UDA and the Red Hand Commandos. In the UDA, he was impressed by Albert Walker Baker, Herron's killer bodyguard, and associated with older men with blood on their hands.

According to Stone, he formed a relationship with a Catholic girl in 1974 though he never produced any evidence to confirm it. She had a child, he said, but he did not tell his loyalist colleagues. They would have been angry that he was having sex with a Catholic. When recounting this story he gave me the impression he was boasting. I suspected he was trying to impress me with a revelation that a loyalist trigger man was capable of 'pulling a Catholic' female and having a child with her. He told me he was impressed because she was middle-class and he stole a car to enhance his standing with her. He was caught but only received a probation sentence. I was unable to trace such an offence on his police file. I understood stealing or hijacking a car was hardly a crime for which a probation sentence appeared adequate. Nonetheless, it was possible he received a minor sentence. The court system was overburdened with terrorist cases and ordinary criminal activity was not given a high priority. The description of the Catholic girl as 'middle-class' mirrored what he told me about his mother whom he had never met. He said she was middle-class and had left his father for the 'bright lights', as though that made her a more interesting and colourful figure in his mind. His attitude to women and to fathering children reflected some deep desire to prove to himself he was not like his parents. In contrast to them, he would have lots of children and love them all equally. His unique narcissism came through in several statements he made to me.

'I used to go to the Beaten Docket and other bars in expensive gear. I drank with Catholics but they only knew me as Michael or Stoner. It was great knowing they were unaware they were standing beside someone who could blow them away. I have to admit I was always a flirt. I enjoyed being with women, be it night-clubbing or out for a meal. My way of life, i.e. my illegal activities, dictated the way I lived. I always ended it before it had a chance to become permanent. This was a selfish attitude but for obvious reasons I had to adopt a "no one keeps tabs on me" policy. You won't believe this but women never told me at the outset they were pregnant. I could have told them all to have abortions but I didn't agree with abortion. You may find it hard that someone like me who has frequently taken life could be against abortion. Really I was. I value human life but not the lives of the people I've killed. Well, maybe one or two who got in the way of an operation. I couldn't sanction abortion.'

During his wandering Casanova period, one of his close friends in the Red Hand Commandos, Samuel Ferguson, bombed two Catholic-owned bars in East Belfast. Stone was a typical East Belfast paramilitary. When not involved in violence, he took to crime. On 29 July 1975, he was convicted of driving without a licence or insurance and sent to prison for six months. On his release, he was re-arrested and returned to prison for committing an earlier, similar offence. When I asked him about his criminal tendencies, he attributed his crimes to terrorism and not to any desire on his part to benefit from crime or because he was instinctively criminal.

In 1976, he married Marlene, an attractive Protestant girl, and, according to him, decided to leave behind his criminal-terrorist past and settle down to family life. To earn a living he took a job as a bouncer and was soon charged with attempted murder for a vicious assault on a man outside a dance hall. He was held in custody but the charge was downgraded to inflicting bodily harm. He brought his pregnant wife to court as a ploy to seek leniency and succeeded by not receiving a prison term. As for his marriage, he found it impossible to remain faithful because of his fondness for clubbing and his conviction that women 'threw themselves at him' and his inability to resist their overtures.

Stone has never revealed anything about his role as a terrorist between 1972 and 1976. In the light of his history, one has to assume that he did so to avoid being questioned or charged with unsolved killings of the period. When questioned by me about those years, he displayed vagueness, at times implying that membership of the UDA and Red Hand Commandos was akin to membership of a local library. You could visit the establishment simply when you felt the need to do so. He studiously avoided any detailed discussions with me about John McKeague's leadership of the Red Hand Commandos. By the time he spoke to me, McKeague was dead but his paedophile legacy had surfaced. It is my contention Stone did not wish his past to be too closely connected with McKeague. Equally, Stone admitted to me that he had known William McGrath, the 'Beast of Kincora Boys' Home'. He had also been a member of his organisation, Tara. Again, Stone did not elaborate on his knowledge of, or association with, McGrath. The latter was still alive when I first spoke to Stone in 1990.

It is clear Stone spoke to me only about murders which the police were able to connect him to, and not about periods in terrorist life when he appeared idle. He told me he lived an enforced isolation between 1976 and the early 1980s when he returned to the UDA and joined the ranks of the UFF. While researching the present book, I discovered he had lied to me in 1990–91. He only joined the UFF at the instigation of its leader John McMichael, and only after McKeague was assassinated in 1982. This fact further reinforces my belief he remained in the Red Hand Commandos until that time. However, nothing is known about his operations on behalf of McKeague. In 1983, McMichael was busy reshaping the UFF to make it a more lethal killing machine and would not have taken Stone into its ranks unless he was a proven operator.

Also in 1983, Stone traced his father and went to England to meet him for the first time. He did not warn him of the visit and simply turned up on his doorstep. 'I was suddenly looking at this tall man but I didn't see him as my father. He looked embarrassed,' Stone told me. There were photographs of his mother, who was 'a good looker' and 'really attractive'. He did not perceive Cyril as his father. He was a 'big uncle'. His father was reluctant to discuss the break-up of the marriage to Mary Bridget Sullivan and told his son she left him for a 'better life'. One year after the meeting with his father, Michael Stone left his wife and their three children for an 18-year-old girlfriend, Leigh Anne.

His career in the UFF began in earnest in 1983 after a meeting with John McMichael in the town of Comber, County Down. They were photographed together in a car by members of 14th Int. and years later Stone was shown the surveillance photo while in police custody. When I wrote about this episode in *Stone Cold*, members of the UFF were angered by my mention of McMichael and blamed Stone for telling me about his connection to the revered terrorist leader. Stone was ordered to issue a public denial that he had ever been connected to McMichael. I subsequently asked a loyalist source why the UFF had been angry that I had linked McMichael with Stone.

'You have to remember that the image of John McMichael as a UDA political leader is sacred to some people. They have no wish to see him linked to terrorism because he carefully avoided any such link when he was alive. It may seem a moot point but they are very touchy about the McMichael image. When they thought that Stone had blabbed to you they were furious and told him to deny it. That message was sent into the Maze to him.'

The text in my book that triggered UFF anger, and forced Stone into a retraction of what he had told me, revealed the truth about his relationship with the 'Political Hitman', John McMichael. The venue for their meeting in 1983 was the car park of a bar-restaurant on the edge of the town of Comber, the place where the photograph was snapped by intelligence operatives. When Stone arrived at the meeting place, McMichael was seated in his car. Nearby, a UFF bodyguard was in another vehicle with instructions to watch all movement; a precaution to ensure neither man was being followed. The bodyguard was told to note the registration numbers of cars entering the car park. It was mid-afternoon, the restaurant was closed and the bar attracted little custom. McMichael, with the aid of a UFF source, was able to check car registrations through the RUC computer. He invited Stone to sit beside him in his car. McMichael's bodyguard remained in the car park while the UFF boss took Stone on a drive through the nearby countryside. During the trip they were photographed. It was suggested to me by a long-time intelligence source that McMichael may have set up the secret photo shoot for his own intelligence handlers. My source's thesis was that the intelligence community wished to know more about Stone and place him on file as a possible recruit for their terrorist operations. However, there is no proof to sustain such a theory. During the drive, McMichael made it clear he required Stone to undertake a 'sanction' and the target was an IRA intelligence officer from West Belfast.

According to Stone, he asked for proof his intended victim was IRA and McMichael told him the UFF possessed security forces' files on the target. Stone agreed 'to do the hit', provided he was given access to the files to reassure himself the target was a Provo.

Stone told me he received detailed RUC and British Army surveillance notes on 35-year-old Paddy Brady, a Catholic from St James's Crescent on the Upper Falls. The documents claimed Brady had been seen with known IRA activists and was a member of Provisional Sinn Fein. The surveillance notes also contained details of Brady's family life and the names of his wife and daughters. The most critical information was about his place of work and daily routine. He was a milkman, using his private car every morning to travel to Kennedy Bros Dairy on the Boucher Road in South Belfast. There, he picked up a fully laden milk float and drove back to West Belfast. The journey took five minutes.

Stone used the information to watch Brady and decided the optimum time to kill him was early morning when there were few people on the streets. McMichael also gave Stone a video of Brady standing, arms folded, on the speakers' platform at a Provisional Sinn Fein annual conference (Ardfheis) in Dublin. In the classified notes, there were recurring phrases – 'republican sympathiser', 'drinks with known PIRA', 'suspected of passing information to PIRA'. In truth, the only thing any of those phrases indicated was that he was a man with republican aspirations but the composition of all the phrases created a lethal juxtaposition. Stone chose to kill Brady with a shotgun loaded with size 4 cartridges. He also requested a revolver in case the shotgun jammed. His choice of the shotgun was motivated by his knowledge that, unlike a pistol, revolver or rifle, a shotgun left no important forensic evidence. Those other weapons left rifling on bullet casings. Bullets from a victim could be traced back and matched with the weapon that fired them. A shotgun cartridge, even if left by accident at the scene of a crime, was not easy to trace to its weapon of origin. Stone provided the following explanation for his use of a shotgun.

'At close quarters this is a fearsome weapon. If you are not close enough to do a head job with a pistol, a shotgun blast to the head is lethal. It's good if you are mobile and ready for a quick getaway. I favoured a shotgun when working close to a target.'

His target, Paddy Brady, was not a member of the IRA but was a committed republican. He was also treasurer of his local community centre and a member of 11/E5 Branch of the Allied Transport and General Workers Union. He was a typical target for the 'blanket surveillance' which the police and Army mounted against republicans and republican sympathisers. He was also a 'special' target for those in the intelligence community who were supplying McMichael with information, knowing the purpose for which he would use it.

At 4.30 a.m. on 16 November 1984, Stone and two other members of the UFF selected by McMichael drove to West Belfast to kill Brady. They saw him getting out of his car and pulled alongside him. Stone wound down the window of his car, levelled the shotgun and fired twice – once at his victim's body and then at his head, killing him instantly. Like Lenny Murphy, Stone went home, burned his clothes, had a bath, scrubbed his body and cleaned out his ears with cotton wool to remove any lead residue traces. He boasted to me about his mental training for the murder as if to convey his self-image of a professional assassin.

'I knew his weight and that was one of the reasons I chose the shotgun. I reckoned he was so big that if I only got shots off from a pistol, and they were only body shots, he might survive. I was intending to do it all quickly. I planned to immobilise him with one round to the body, and then shoot him in the head as he was going down. The shotgun at close range from the car was the best weapon. With a revolver I would have been obliged to get out, thus losing time and the initiative, and taking too many risks. Fair enough, if he'd run I'd have had to go after him. He was big and I thought carefully about the most effective option. I opted for an automatic shotgun and size 4 cartridges. It wasn't simply because it was a good weapon, it wasn't easily traced.'

The shotgun was a Remington 5-shot and may well have been a legally owned weapon which had been borrowed or stolen. The way Stone bragged about the murder was not dissimilar to the manner in which Lenny Murphy talked about his crimes. Murphy knew the law well and how not to leave forensic evidence which would put him at the scene of a killing. I am not sure if Stone actually went through the thought processes he outlined, though he could have learned killing techniques from others in the UDA, Red Hand Commando and UFF – men like Albert Walker Baker who had a military background. The elite SAS employ a technique similar to the one outlined by Stone. A shot to the body is often intended to put down a target before the killing round is fired into the head or heart. One feature of the murder, which was reminiscent of Lenny Murphy's modus operandi, was the 'mind game' Stone played with detectives. He left three cartridges on the rear seat of the vehicle as his 'calling card'. It was an act of bravado equal to his narcissism. He continued to use the shotgun as his weapon of choice and each time he killed someone, he left size 4 cartridges to let police know they were dealing with one assassin. It was a technique that US Special Forces used in Vietnam. They left an Ace of Spades card on the bodies of Viet Cong. Stone was an assassin who desired recognition from police in much the same way a serial killer leaves a 'signature'. In Lenny Murphy's murders it was the slitting of his victims' throats. While there is not sufficient space to outline all Stone's killings, it is important to focus on April 1987 and an aspect of his terror career he chose to hide from me in 1990.

In April 1987, John McMichael appointed British Military Intelligence agent Brian Nelson to the rank of chief of UFF Intelligence. I was reliably informed Stone met Nelson with McMichael. When I spoke to Stone in 1990, Brian Nelson was still operating as a terrorist agent and orchestrating killings for the British Military, using UFF teams of hitmen. In my conversations with Stone, he deliberately avoided any mention of Nelson and McMichael's connection to him. In retrospect, I am still puzzled by a statement Stone made to me at one of our meetings in the Maze. He said: 'Someday I could tell you a story that now you would not believe.' Was he talking about Nelson and the fact that the British agent was running him as a terrorist agent?

British Intelligence knew of Stone's existence from the time he was photographed with McMichael in Comber. Equally, the photograph and Stone's role in the UFF would have been conveyed to the Force Research Unit by 1987. There were other photographs of Stone on intelligence files. One was of him in a car with John McMichael in South Derry. The photograph was slightly blurred and was taken while McMichael and Stone were returning from a trip to Derry City where Stone planned the assassination of the IRA leader, Martin McGuinness. That bid was aborted.

Another intelligence photograph showed Stone walking his two Staffordshire bull terriers in the grounds of Belfast Castle. Alongside him was John Bingham, a notorious UVF trigger man. Bingham was accompanied by his golden labrador.

In 1987, Nelson and his intelligence bosses were aware of Stone's targeting of Owen Carron, a well-known republican. The plan to kill Carron was aborted at the last minute because he had a court appearance. After the IRA murdered John McMichael, Stone was involved in the attempted assassination of another republican at a time when Brian Nelson was running his assassination campaign at the instigation of the FRU. Stone was therefore a cold, experienced assassin run by British Military Intelligence, probably without his knowledge.

However, he is most remembered for the Milltown Cemetery attack in March 1988 when he tried to kill the Provisional IRA/Sinn Fein leadership. In researching this book, I learned Stone lied to me about the planning of the cemetery attack. I can only conclude it was to protect Nelson and therefore himself from Nelson's long reach. He told me that on the evening of 16 March 1988, the night before he went into Milltown Cemetery, the UVF supplied him with a 9mm pistol (serial number L44788) and seven grenades. He neglected to tell me those weapons and a Ruger pistol with ammunition speed-trips were given to him on the instructions of the British agent, Brian Nelson.

The following day, funerals were held for three IRA operatives killed on the orders of Prime Minister Margaret Thatcher by SAS teams in Gibraltar. Nelson, his FRU bosses and presumably people at Cabinet level in the British Government were informed about what was about to take place in the cemetery. Stone was going to take out the IRA and Sinn Fein leadership at the graveside. When I asked him how he entered the cemetery, he told me he went in through the front gate with thousands of other mourners. That was another lie. He approached the cemetery from the M1 motorway and he was not alone. Since writing my book on him, I have revisited the evidence of an eyewitness who watched him walk up through the cemetery with three other people. One witness, John Jordan, a taxi driver, was there that day as part of his professional role in assisting a US ABC network camera crew. He was sitting in a van with a camera mounted on its roof and saw three men and a woman enter the cemetery from the M1 motorway. He thought they were members of a film crew but wondered why 'they were a bit late' to cover the funeral. 'They were cutting it a bit fine,' he later remarked. One of the three men was Stone, who walked past the van in which Jordan was sitting and stared at him. The other persons walked across the cemetery and later exited on the Andersonstown side. After Stone launched grenades and started shooting, he threw a grenade at Jordan's van. Stone told me about seeing a van in the cemetery and believed it was a vehicle of the RUC undercover unit E4a. Why did he believe that? He said the van had antennae on top of it. He lied. The van at which he threw a grenade had a camera mounted on its roof. His explanation was: 'I reckoned the van was positioned there to record events in the cemetery. There was a general lack of security presence, and the van was a means of providing one.'

Police later interviewed a witness, a Protestant with no paramilitary connections, and appeared uninterested in his account of how Stone entered the cemetery in the company of others. The RUC was supplied with footage of those who had accompanied Stone leaving the cemetery. The footage was retained as evidence and its whereabouts is unknown.

During the cemetery operation, Stone waited until the third IRA coffin was lowered into the republican plot before he reached into a pouch straddling his chest and took out two RGD-5 grenades with seven-second delay fuses. He threw them at the grave and then reached for his guns. During the mayhem that followed, he ran off, pursued by mourners. Cameras throughout the world captured images of him shooting at mourners as he ran towards the motorway. Three young men were killed and others were injured in grenade blasts. He was seized on the motorway by mourners and beaten before police arrived on the scene and rescued him.

He told me an escape plan was in place and a UFF car and driver was waiting for him on the M1 motorway but the driver panicked and left. Stone miscalculated the courage of mourners who pursued him even though he had killed some of them and thrown grenades at others. Before he reached the motorway, an unmarked van, which had been there for some time, took off and I have since been reliably informed that it was permitted to pass through military roadblocks unimpeded. Stone was close to making good an escape but I am still not convinced he would have chosen the route he took had his life not been in jeopardy. The strangers who were seen entering the cemetery with him left by another route, which also led out of the cemetery to the motorway. Was the van there to observe Stone and then pick him up with others on the motorway? It is a possibility not to be discounted. I also believe, had Stone not been caught, the televised coverage of him would not have led to his immediate capture. He resembled a wild man and his photograph was not in regular police files. There was a kamikaze element to the operation but it almost succeeded. Some sources I talked to speculated that Brian Nelson and his British Intelligence bosses believed Stone would not survive the operation. They were equally confident if he made it out of the cemetery and was captured, he would not give up Brian Nelson. Anyway, the narcissistic assassin wanted to be in the limelight. He wanted fame and he got it when he survived the cemetery attack. That was enough for him not to seek a deal with the authorities by giving up his accomplices. I do not believe he was suicidal but that Nelson convinced him the escape plan was foolproof. Nevertheless, he knew there was a price to be paid if he was caught and a prison term was one he was willing to pay just for the notoriety.

Hours after police rescued him, he received a hospital visit from 'strange men'. They stood in his room talking and staring at him. Were they members of the FRU there to discover if he was likely to 'sing' to RUC detectives? Stone was subjected to a psychiatric assessment before his trial and, like Lenny Murphy, was declared to be sane. However, as happened in the evaluation of Murphy, Stone's psychiatrist was not familiar with many of the details of his family background and terrorist career. I contend that, had the psychiatrist been in possession of all the relevant details, Stone would also have been defined as an aggressive psychopath. Perhaps he would have been recommended for mental health care.

11

JOHNNY 'MAD DOG' ADAIR

PART 1: FROM SKINHEAD TO TERRORIST

On the evening of 11 February 1993, a Provisional IRA hit team hijacked a car in the Ardoyne area of North Belfast. Armed with a high-powered rifle and pistols, they drove into the heart of the Shankill district in West Belfast. When they reached Glenfarne Street, they parked their car and within minutes had taken over the house at number 54. Two members of the team remained downstairs. Their companion, with a rifle, took up position at the open window of an upstairs bedroom. He kept his finger on the trigger as he scanned nearby Hazelfield Street, his gaze constantly focused on number 10. From time to time, he put the rifle to his shoulder, peered down the gun's sights for several seconds, and then relaxed. After two hours, he told his companions his target had not appeared and they had spent too long in enemy territory. They abandoned the mission and returned to Ardoyne.

Their operation was similar to the one mounted by the IRA when they tracked down and killed Lenny Murphy, leader of the Shankill Butchers. On this occasion, however, their target was a man who was also ruthless and cunning, but more powerful than Murphy had ever been. He was Johnny 'Mad Dog' Adair, Officer Commanding the UFF throughout Northern Ireland and not, as some believed, only the boss of the UFF's C Company in the Shankill area of Belfast. It was not the IRA's first attempt on Adair's life and would not be the last.

One month later, on a Saturday morning, the IRA placed 'spotters' on the Shankill Road to watch for Adair. They had orders that, once they had determined his location, they should make a telephone call to a house in the Ardoyne where a three-man hit team was waiting. The team was armed with an automatic rifle, a shotgun and a pistol. The gunmen's journey to the Shankill would only take a matter of minutes. At 1.15 p.m. they received a call that Adair and an associate were having a conversation in a parked car in Berlin Street. Within seconds, the IRA men were in a hijacked car on their way to the Shankill Road. As they drove into Berlin Street, they saw Adair still talking to someone they did not know. They drove towards his car and when they were level with it, one of the IRA men opened up with an automatic rifle. Adair and his companion suffered only minor injuries in the attack. I later interviewed an IRA man who was knowledgeable about the attempts on Adair's life. 'That bastard had more lives than a cat. We had people on him all the time and he knew it so he was extra careful. But we reckoned that he would not expect us to return to the tactic we had used in February so we waited six months to let him believe he was in the clear – to sorta make him let his guard down.'

On 15 September, the IRA unit which had targeted Adair in February returned to the same location – number 54 Glenfarne Street. Just as they had done on the previous mission, they played a waiting game with the rifleman upstairs watching Adair's home at number 10 Hazelfield Street. The assassins were in the house a short time when the doorbell rang. One of them opened the door and admitted a friend of the occupant, who immediately reached for a legally registered pistol which he had on his person. In the next few minutes there was a stand-off between the stranger and the assassins. They slowly exited the house and fled, fearing that a shoot-out would alert the police, as well as Adair and his associates.

The INLA was also planning to kill Adair and the following month, on 19 October, two gunmen, armed with a rifle and a sawn-off shotgun, were told to cruise his neighbourhood. If they spotted him they were to open fire and, if there was an opportunity to kill him in his home, they were to do so. The gunmen were in a car hijacked earlier in the day in the Falls area. As they drove into Daisyfield Street, close to his home, an alert policeman in a mobile patrol became suspicious. When the patrol approached the gunmen's car, it was driven off at speed. Within minutes, the police forced it to stop on the Crumlin Road. The gunmen made no attempt to use their weapons and surrendered.

By 1993, Adair was the most wanted man in Northern Ireland and would remain so until 2003. The media had given 'Mad Dog' his sobriquet, and it was one he enjoyed because it was indirectly inherited from the IRA/INLA trigger man of repute, Dominic McGlinchey. At 30,

Adair had risen quickly through the ranks of the UDA/UFF and, unlike loyalist terrorists before him, he exercised total control of units across the province with a ruthlessness characteristic of loyalist terror bosses of the early 1970s. It was believed he had ordered more killings than his idols: Billy Wright, John McMichael and Lenny Murphy.

'Mad Dog' was born John James Adair on 27 October 1963. His home was in the Lower Oldpark area of North Belfast. He was one of seven children. Not much is known about his childhood except that it was spent in a tough neighbourhood in which large Protestant districts surrounded tiny Catholic enclaves. The Lower Oldpark stretched on one side to the Cliftonville Road, and on the other to the Shankill and Crumlin Roads. In 1970–71, a large number of Catholic homes were attacked and families forced to flee. When sectarian assassinations began in earnest in 1972, the Oldpark, from that year onwards, was the scene of some of the most vicious murders of the Troubles. It was in that part of the city that Clawson and Fisher, two Protestant men, were tortured and shot dead. Another killing was that of Thomas Madden, a Catholic who was strung up in a slowly tightening noose and butchered. There were 147 stab wounds on his body, indicating that someone had slowly chipped away at his flesh like a sculptor carving from a block of wood. In that tribal environment, Adair was subjected to militant loyalism and developed an intense hatred of Catholics. Unlike Billy Wright, when Adair reached his teens he did not immediately gravitate towards paramilitary ranks. Instead, he founded a gang of skinheads, much like the Tartans run by the paedophile terrorist, John McKeague. The friendships he established in his gang were to follow him into a life of terror.

He was small in stature but assertive. He and his fellow skinheads burgled homes and shops and stole cars. Profits from their crimes were spent on wild parties and alcohol. They also experimented with solvents, which was a precursor to more serious drug use as Adair grew older. In the lawless atmosphere of the late 1970s, he and his gang mounted attacks on Catholic youths in the area. According to people who knew him at that time, he was a 'little general'. He came to the attention of the RUC and was arrested on several occasions for disorderly behaviour, assaults on police and rioting. The thuggish dimension to his life was complemented by his resentment of authority and lack of concern for the effects of his actions on others. In the light of his overall history it is reasonable to conclude that, had he been given a psychological test at that time, there would have been sufficient evidence to indicate a troubled and dangerous personality. In his late teens, there was an episode that may have contributed to his increasing hatred of Catholics. Somewhere in the Oldpark area, he was ambushed by Catholic youths and subjected to a severe beating.

His police file, which lists numerous offences for that period, shows that he first came to the attention of the RUC when he was 14 years old. However, there is nothing in that file to indicate when exactly he became a paramilitary. The only date mentioned anywhere is 1983, when he was charged with hijacking a car. He was 20 years old and, by my reckoning, was already in the ranks of the UDA/UFF. His police file is blank for the period 1983 to 1987, though he later boasted that he was involved in 'some dirty stuff' during those years. The phrases 'dirty stuff' or 'dirty ones' were widely used loyalist euphemisms for sectarian murders, mostly of a brutal nature. In 1988, he was appointed second-in-command of the UDA's C8 team and that was not a rank he reached without proving himself to the UFF. So, one can reasonably conclude that his terror career began some time between 1983 and 1988. A confidential police file records: 'During 1989, the subject was very active in UFF ranks and was involved in several murders and attempted murders.' His reputation quickly spread throughout the UFF, not only because of his terrorist operations but because he liked boasting about his exploits to anyone who would listen. A UFF operative of that period provided me with a description of Adair as a young terrorist.

'Johnny had that "little man syndrome". He was small and stocky and had a barrel chest. He would wear big boots and a Wrangler jacket and jeans. He strutted a lot like a fucking cock hen. People would laugh behind his back at the cut of him but not to his face – no fucking way. He had a short temper and could handle himself. He liked to think he was really strong – physically, I mean. He'd puff his chest out when he came into the club and was always on a short fuse but he was some operator. He seemed to have no fear – no fear. He seemed a bit reckless but he was shrewd. One thing everybody knew about him was that he was loyal – that's something you'd have to give him – loyal to his friends. He wasn't somebody you wanted as an enemy. Friends he had when he was younger were always a part of his inner circle – the ones who had been close to him when he was a fucking skinhead. Can you imagine? Johnny, a skinhead? But then again, he was a rough diamond. Sure, he hated Catholics. All you had to do was listen to what he wanted to do with them – crazy stuff, I tell you.'

In 1990, he was presented with an opportunity for advancement in the UFF when 'Winky' Dodds, the UDA's West Belfast Brigadier, was imprisoned. It was an ideal rank for the ambitious Adair because it came with the right to control UFF units in that part of the city. His police file confirms that he got the job and also became Commander in charge of the UFF in West Belfast. The RUC was keeping a close eye on him and, on 8 August of that year, he was charged with three murders, twenty counts of possession of firearms, a threat to kill and committing grievous bodily harm. He was held in custody for four months but released when the charges were dropped. There is nothing in his file to show why the Prosecution Service did not pursue the charges. One would be entitled to conclude that, even then, no one was prepared to testify against him.

During his incarceration, the UDA's Inner Council appointed Jim Spence to the rank of Brigadier, West Belfast. That did not please Adair and, on his release from custody, without seeking approval from the Inner Council, he resumed the role of Commander of the UFF in the west of the city. He ordered sectarian murders and Spence was unable to control him. Friction between them reached boiling point and Spence turned to the Inner Council with a plea for them to rein in Adair. Some members of the Council expressed alarm about Adair's recklessness, but others admired him. The result was a power struggle in the governing body and those who approved of Adair's terrorist credentials won the day. Spence was told to back off but the most significant aspect of the Inner Council debate was that Adair was made UFF Commander for Northern Ireland. The most important effect of the ruling was that he was automatically awarded a seat on the Inner Council.

With such power and position, he was entitled to shape UFF strategy and policy. He quickly set up teams of trigger men in other UDA Brigade areas, with special emphasis on Belfast. The way it worked was that individual Brigadiers tasked teams but he had authority to initiate killing sprees or call them off.

His prestige as a terror boss grew after he ordered the setting up of hit teams in South and East Belfast and they successfully carried out sectarian killings. He focused much of his energy on C Company in the Shankill area and regarded it as his personal killing squad. He had suddenly become the most powerful figure in the UDA/UFF with no one in a position to challenge his authority. He ruled with an iron fist and, like Lenny Murphy, whom he admired, he instilled fear in the lower ranks. Everyone in the UDA/UFF understood no one crossed him and lived. In April 1993, he solidified his power-base by appointing himself the UDA's West Belfast Brigadier after Jim Spence was imprisoned. His police file noted his upward mobility.

Consequently, Adair has become the single most powerful member of the UDA/UFF by a substantial margin. His murder campaign was subsequently extended throughout Belfast and despite periodic brief respites remains at a high level. Increased levels of policing and improved briefing of uniformed personnel in Adair's target areas has had the effect of reducing the capabilities of Adair's teams. However, these units still maintain the ability to mount successful attacks regularly throughout Belfast.

Like the Shankill Butchers, who met in the Brown Bear pub, drank a lot and then decided to kill a 'Taig', Adair and his C Company associates followed the same pattern. A UFF informer relayed to his Special Branch handler a story which conveyed the casual way Adair and his inner circle treated human life. The Special Branch handler's account of the story found its way into Adair's confidential police file.

> It emerged that the C Company UFF team were present on a Sunday evening in a Shankill Road club with the intention of engaging in a session of drinking. Upon the arrival of the first round of drinks the mood of the party was jovial when one of the assembled dozen or so members shouted, 'Let's bag a Taig.' Although this command was intended in jest, Adair picked up on the suggestion and within five minutes had detailed every member of the team to play a specific role in the murder attempt, which had now become a reality. Incredibly, 15 minutes later, the operation was underway and it was only then that the team realised that they hadn't actually discussed a target. At this point it was decided to drive into a local Catholic area and shoot the first male person they encountered. Approximately 25 minutes after the first suggestion, the entire team had returned to the club and resumed drinking, the celebration of the murder being led by Adair.

Adair wanted to establish himself as a genuine successor to John McMichael by targeting members of the IRA and Sinn Fein. However, when any of his teams were unable to find high-priority targets, they had instructions not to leave a Catholic area without 'a kill'. 'King Rat', who visited him in the Shankill on several occasions, impressed Adair. In 1994, during one of his visits, he told 'Mad Dog' never to get caught with a gun in his hands. In other words, the UFF leader should follow his example and order killings but never be near the scene of a murder.

It was advice Adair liked and he told the other members of C Company what Wright said to him. Adair's other hero was the Milltown Cemetery killer, Michael Stone, whom he visited several times in the Maze prison. During a visit on 15 January 1992, he donated money to Stone and again gave him money when he visited him on 28 September 1993. There were also visits on January and February of the following year. His admiration for Stone knew no bounds and was reciprocated even though Stone made a pretence of being in favour of the peace process. They both shared a sectarian mentality and innate narcissism. With Stone, he discussed strategy and asked about the latter's connections to Ulster Resistance. Adair was looking for a new arms supplier and knew that Ulster Resistance had a share in a large consignment of guns smuggled into Northern Ireland from South Africa. The weapons had come from Lebanon and were passed to the UVF/UFF and Ulster Resistance by BOSS, the South African Intelligence Service. Adair was keen to know whom he should approach in Ulster Resistance to find out if the organisation was prepared to sell him guns from its arsenal. Stone, who once trained Ulster Resistance personnel, knew the right people to contact. In four visits to Stone, Adair donated £150 so that the killer could buy luxuries. In all, he made 68 visits to loyalist terrorists in the Maze between February '92 and March '94, donating a total of £510 to them. While he was dispensing largesse to lifers, he was taking payments from UFF men on remand in Crumlin Road prison. His frequent visits to Crumlin Road and the Maze were also designed to show the UDA/UFF that, unlike previous leaders, he never forgot his men.

His loyalty, as he liked to describe it, was extended to former skinhead friends who were given prominent roles in C Company. It made him feel safer to have friends watching his back. They would inform him of dissension in the ranks. In turn, they were fiercely committed to him. The solvent abuse, which he shared with some of them in his skinhead days, soon led to more serious drug-taking. Adair loved partying and money from racketeering and extortion was used to buy drugs for celebrations following murders by C Company trigger men. Adair's drug of choice was Ecstasy. He and his inner circle quickly realised that there was money in drug sales and decided that they should have a piece of the action. That decision was followed by other UDA Brigadiers and a decade later led to bloody turf wars. But, at the outset, even from Adair's standpoint, other criminal pursuits were providing him with a comfortable lifestyle. In Hazelfield Street where he lived with his common-law wife, Gina Crossan, and their three children – Jonathan, nine, Natalie, seven, and Chloe, two – he had the trappings of a terrorist godfather.

The security measures at his home characterised his need for protection and confirmed that he was no ordinary citizen. The front door was made from PVC and had three Chubb dead-bolt locks. Behind the door was a thick metal plate. There were also steel shutters inside the front and back doors. The downstairs windows were bullet-proof and there were security lights to the front and rear of the building. A CCTV camera/monitor system covered the front of the house. RUC surveillance focused on the CCTV monitoring system because it resembled a model designed and constructed at the Police Authority workshop in Lislea Drive, Belfast. Detectives began to look closely at his inner circle, suspecting that one of his associates had access to the police facility, which made the system, or to someone who worked there. An entry in his RUC file noted that photographic surveillance was concentrated on 'what goes on beyond mere sightings' of two of his associates. They were Paul Orr of 134 Silverstream Avenue, Belfast, and Alan Hill from 28 Woodvale Avenue in the Shankill area.

On 19 February 1994, detectives, who were part of an inquiry team with instructions to take down Adair, decided to have a closer look at the CCTV system. They went to his home, seized it and arrested him. He was taken to Castlereagh holding facility and interrogated. He stated that the security system was supplied and installed by Alan Hill. It was 'arranged and paid for' by his friend, Paul Orr, at a cost of £1,100.

Orr was immediately arrested and admitted he had bought the CCTV equipment. Detectives went to his home and found £824 in cash and documents relating to UDA prisoners at the Maze and Crumlin Road prisons. According to the police notes, in the search they found other documents containing 'details pertaining to UDA/UFF affairs' and finance provided to prisoners. As for Adair, detectives wrote: 'It can be established that security at John Adair's home was arranged and paid for by an associate who is presently charged with UDA membership and in whose name was found evidence of his handling and control of UDA finance.'

Detectives then switched their attention to Alan Hill and discovered he was employed at the Police Authority workshop in Lislea Drive in Belfast. He was arrested and admitted stealing the CCTV equipment and installing it in Adair's home. A search of his work-room locker unearthed a piece of paper with Adair's home telephone number and a car registration – VRM LIW 4719. Detectives searched vehicle registration records and learned that the number was for a blue Mazda owned by a republican living at Campion Way in Derry. When Hill was asked why he had the number, he replied he had obtained it through his close association with police officers. One has to wonder how many other vehicle registration numbers he acquired while working in a police facility.

In Adair's day-to-day life, he bore little resemblance to one of his predecessors, James 'Pratt' Craig, who wore designer clothes and had a penchant for expensive jewellery. 'Mad Dog' liked to dress like a thug and preferred to spend his ill-gotten gains on alcohol, drugs and holidays in Spain with his close associates and his common-law wife. He rented self-catering apartments in Tenerife so he could lie in the sun, get a tan and drink copious quantities of Bacardi rum. Like Stone and Lenny Murphy, he boasted to his friends that women found him irresistible. The truth was he had several lovers. He did not want people to think of him as a married man even though he had a common-law wife and three children. He constantly told everyone he did not have a 'steady relationship'. In keeping with his self-image of a ladies' man, he wore T-shirts to show off his chest and biceps. He even installed exercise equipment in his home for daily work-outs. A noticeable feature of his personality was his bizarre sense of humour. He printed personal business cards and handed them out like confetti in bars and clubs. He also gave them to police and soldiers when he was stopped at roadblocks. The cards carried the inscription:

Ulster Freedom Fighters
West Belfast, 2nd Battalion
YE HA
FUCK THE IRA

The interior of his home was perhaps the most obvious symbol of his role as a criminal. He told police he and Gina Crossan survived on social security payments, which was laughable. The living-room was furnished with a black leather sofa purchased from Wrights International at a cost of £1,650. The floor was parquet-tiled and there was a large tank of exotic fish. There was also a Hitachi remote-controlled teletext television, an Amstrad Satellite System, a Dini midi hi-fi and 100 compact discs. As part of the security system, the room had a monitor showing images of the front of the house. The crescent-shaped light in the centre of the room was attached to a large fan.

The kitchen, where he liked to sit with his associates and plan terror, was furnished with a table, chairs and a black leather settee. There was also a ghetto-blaster and a television. No expense was spared in the purchase of appliances. The white, built-in kitchen had cost £3,000. There was also a built-in fridge/freezer, a Hotpoint hob, an oven with an extractor fan, a Creda washing machine, a Sanyo microwave oven and a Creda tumble-dryer.

Upstairs were three bedrooms. Bedroom one contained a Samsung video recorder, Matsui television, Hitachi security monitor, bar bells and weights, white body armour, Diatron telephone, midi hi-fi and a centre light with a large fan. Bedroom two had a Hitachi midi system and a centre light with a large fan. Bedroom three had a Sharp's television and a midi hi-fi system. The bathroom with a bath and shower was fully tiled.

It was his 'little palace', but it was certainly not financed with social security cheques. Department of Social Services records show that, from 23 April 1990 until 31 January 1994, he received income support of £36.70 weekly. Gina Crossan was in receipt of weekly payments totalling £55.65, rising to £71.45 in April 1994. She also had child benefit payments of £15.50 weekly, which were increased to £26.20 on 6 April 1994. Additionally the DHSS paid her over £5 per week for being a single parent. During the period I have just outlined, Adair admitted to police that he had six personal cars. Some were bought with cash and others financed through companies. However, police records show that between 1991 and 1994, he owned 12 cars, which included a Rover, Audi, Peugeot 309 GTE, Orion Ghia, Mazda 323 GT and a Sierra Sapphire. His expenditure confirmed he was a criminal godfather and detectives studying his spending concluded the only way to take him down was to convict him of racketeering. Their file on him showed that, in terms of terrorism, he was untouchable. Like Lenny Murphy, he was so feared that no one was prepared to give evidence against him. Each time detectives arrested his associates, they were rebuffed. That was in total contrast to the RUC's previous targeting of UFF leaders. There had rarely been such a wall of silence.

A crucial ingredient missing from the Adair inquiry team's efforts was an input from Special Branch, which suggests Special Branch had its own agenda in respect of the terror boss and C Company. One has to take into account the fact that Special Branch and Military Intelligence had run a lot of informers and terrorist agents in C Company over two decades. They may not have wanted Adair compromised. Earlier, I included a Special Branch note, which appeared in a police file about Adair. It was the only one and related to an informer Special Branch had within Adair's inner circle. Surely the informer, had he been made available to detectives investigating Adair, could have helped them in their search for a reliable witness? Throughout the Troubles, Special Branch did not share its informers or agents with CID. It was secretive and no one ever knew its agenda, except those who worked closely with British Military Intelligence and MI5 in the running of certain informers and terrorist agents. Even then, Special Branch did not share everything with its intelligence collaborators in the undercover war.

The unanimous view within the RUC inquiry team tasked to investigate Adair was that his ability to thwart justice set him apart from previous UFF militants. Associates offered immunity from prosecution and a new life outside Northern Ireland used to say they would go to prison before they would risk his wrath. A confidential police report lamented the problems facing the inquiry team: 'It is agreed by about the entire membership of the West Belfast UDA/UFF that they fear Adair more than any of his predecessors.'

Adair's life was terror 24/7 and he spent a great deal of time studying police operational methods and the response of security forces to the operations of his trigger men. As a consequence, he constantly changed strategy and the locations of targets when he realised there was a high police presence in a particular Catholic area. I believe he learned a great deal from his contacts with 'King Rat' and Michael Stone. For example, his hit teams were ordered to destroy their clothing after each operation. They were advised to shower, wash their hair and scrub their skin to remove traces of lead residue from firearms discharges. Adair also learned a great deal about police surveillance techniques and it was noted in his police file: 'Adair is much more surveillance aware than others and has frequently spent a considerable amount of time "cleaning" himself of surveillance prior to engaging in UFF activity. Therefore, it can be seen that the subject is thorough in the extreme and also remarkably shrewd with regard to his awareness of his own position.'

One of the methods he used to distance himself from killings was to ensure that when they happened, he was seen in public. At the time of a murder, he would visit a bar or club, which later provided him with multiple witnesses of his whereabouts. Much more significantly, he learned the basic rules of the judicial system and how they related to what he was entitled to say, without incriminating himself, during police interviews. He also discovered how the law could, and could not, adversely impact on comments he made in asides to policemen whom he met in public. His knowledge of legal principles guiding police in interviews was extensive. Consequently, he became self-confident and arrogant when he was formally questioned. No one is certain how he acquired such a detailed knowledge and learned to use it effectively to keep himself out of prison.

Of all the terrorists I have investigated, he was the most brazen. Murphy and the Butchers operated in darkened streets, but he personally made forays into Catholic areas, often on foot, to check out addresses and targets. Between 14 April 1991 and 18 March 1994, there were 39 recorded sightings of him in 'enemy' territory. They were listed on his police file as DTs and the first was numbered DT: 1364/91. It confirmed he was observed walking along Flax Street in the Ardoyne at 12.40 a.m.

On 14 April 1991, when he was stopped and searched in a Catholic district, he was found to be wearing white body armour. On 3 January 1991, a Constable Sawyer making his way into the Ardoyne saw him. The police note of the incident said he remained in the area for approximately ten minutes. A Constable Mawhinney, who saw him in the Falls district at 2 p.m., signed a DT: 2248.

The majority of the DT sightings proved he entered Catholic areas mostly in daylight hours when there were plenty of people on the streets. Therefore, he was less obtrusive. The middle of the night was recorded on several DTs. One was registered by a Constable White and stated that Adair was on foot in the Ardoyne at 3 a.m. The areas listed in police and military sightings included parts of North Belfast where the Shankill Butchers had carried out many of their killings, but he also travelled to West Belfast – Andersonstown, Ballymurphy and Poleglass. On all the occasions when he was stopped and questioned, he was unarmed.

His willingness to carry out surveillance was testimony to an insatiable desire to be personally involved in the killing process. He wanted also to impress his associates and the security forces whom he believed shared a common enemy with him. He showed no fear when he was stopped and questioned by police or soldiers. Confidential police documents, which contained his remarks at checkpoints, offer a frightening insight into his personality.

On 7 March1992, he was stopped at 8.15 p.m. while driving a Montego car, registration WXI 7969, along the Crumlin Road. A search of the car revealed an ordnance survey map. Asked why he had the map, he laughed and said that it was to 'find his way round republican areas'.

DT: 5065/93 recorded that he was questioned at Shankill Road and Boundary Way. He was in a Cavalier car, registration DBZ 8689, with an associate, William Dodds. He boasted to a police sergeant at the checkpoint that his car had armoured doors. He also told the sergeant he had briefly been detained by police in Scotland and was on his way home. I learned that 'King Rat', who had an arms supplier in Glasgow, arranged Adair's trip to Scotland. Wright had suggested that, if Adair could come up with the money, his supplier would provide him with a consignment of Ruger pistols.

At 7.30 p.m. on 15 October 1993, one of Adair's hit teams killed a pizza delivery man in the Newington area of North Belfast. The victim was a Catholic and was shot in the face at point-blank range. Two hours later, Adair drove his Rover 214 up to a police checkpoint near his home. 'Who shot the pizza man?' he smiled. 'Who's killing all these Taigs?'

Three days later he was stopped and questioned while driving the same car with William Dodds beside him. When he was told by police to 'have a nice day', he responded: 'I will have when I spill some Fenian's blood.' Several days later, he made the following remarks to Constable S. Doak: '— — [*name withheld by author*] is afraid to live in the Ardoyne and is calling the shots from the New Lodge. I'll put a bullet in his head.' He boasted at another checkpoint that he was 'away to plan a mass murder'.

The following list is from DT files. They will help the reader better understand Adair's feeling of invincibility and hatred. They may lead the reader to wonder how he was able to remain at large. In each incident, a police officer wrote down what Adair said to him. I have withheld names of some people mentioned by him.

DT/BK3: 'You'd better hurry, there's been a shooting.'

DT No. N/A: 'I may visit a Sinn Fein man's house.'

DT: 4081/92: Stated the next republican target had an outside toilet.

DT No. N/A: Stated that if it were not for him all the Prods would be dead.

DT: 6188/93: Stated that he heard through the grapevine it's going to be a bad month for sectarian murders.

DT: 7134/93: 'You are playing with death. Watch yer car.'

DT: 7134/93: Stated he was looking for the instigators —, — [*two names withheld*]. He suspected he might catch them at a girl's house in Rosapenna or Lower Cliftonville.

DT: 1408/93: Stated that he was going 'up to take a look at the Donegal Celtic. I'm told there's a lot of bad boys drink about there.' Asked whom, he said: 'You should know. Yous are in collusion with us.' Commenting about police suddenly appearing and stopping him, he said: 'Aye, it looks like I'm going to have to change my plan, but you weren't about when we popped up the other day.'

DT: 1139/90: Boasted of being a gunman.

DT: 1074/91: Stated they were going to see Martin O'Prey. [*Author's note: John Thompson, an associate, was in a car with Adair when that comment was made. O'Prey was shot dead in his house in the Lower Falls four months later by loyalist gunmen who entered through the back door. He had been a leading member of the INLA breakaway organisation, the IPLO.*]

DT: 1990/93: Stated he was checking on a sick Sinn Fein Councillor X, who lived at [*name and address withheld*], opposite

—. 'Also John — is a dead man.'

DT No. N/A: 'This is harassment. Go to West Belfast and do it there.'

Asked what he knew about West Belfast, he stated: 'I know more than you know —, — [*two addresses withheld*].' Stated: 'You know who lives there.' Asked about his rocket team [*Author's note: Adair's C Company had several Russian-made RPG7 rocket launchers*], he stated: 'That's only a sideshow. The next one's for the Ardoyne.' [*Author's note: By sideshow, he was referring to a rocket attack on Sinn Fein premises in West Belfast.*] Went on: 'It will only be a decoy. The next one is a big one. A five-hundred pounder for the West.'

DT No. N/A: Inquired of police if — [*name withheld*] was still driving a Ford Escort. Described — [*name withheld*] as a 'vicious bastard'. Said — [*name withheld*] had just returned from Castlereagh after seven days for the double murder in Ligoniel. Stated: 'That bastard drove the car.' When asked how he knew this, he said: 'Intelligence Officer.' Adair questioned police about IRA suspects' vehicles in Ardoyne. Also inquired who drove a black taxi and said he was involved in PIRA.

DT No. N/A: Made it clear he was furious about the bombing in the Short Strand and the RPG in the Markets. He said he would be killing as many PIRA as possible, shortly. He asked for info about — [*name withheld*] and knew the address. He said he wished to personally kill — [*name withheld*]. He was frustrated that the recent attacks against Sinn Fein in the Ardoyne and Andersonstown had not been more successful. He said it was a waste of soldiers' time searching his car, as he was not stupid enough to carry stuff on him and added that he has people to do that for him.

DT No. N/A: I'm protecting the public of Great Britain. I'm looking for yer man —. [*name withheld; he had referred to the same person in an earlier DT.*] Remarked about preferring an AK to an SA80. [*Author's note: The AK47 and SA80 were automatic rifles. The latter was used by British troops.*]

When he made all of those comments, he knew policemen were not taping them. He often chose a form of language and, sometimes, a vagueness, which did not make his comments actionable under law. During five of the DT stops, William Dodds accompanied him. Twice he was with John Thompson and once with a man listed as Fitzgerald. On Adair's file there were 206 registered police sightings of him in the company of known terrorists, as well as men on remand for terrorist offences, and convicted terrorists. Appendix Six of a confidential police assessment of the sightings of Adair in Catholic areas contained the observation: 'There can be little doubt that Adair's frequent forays into Republican areas have a more sinister connotation and leaves [sic] little room for doubt that he is in fact targeting future victims for his murder gang.'

He was confident the police and military knew he was a UFF terror boss but that did not deter him. Within Appendix Six, investigating detectives in the Adair inquiry team focused on a *Guardian* newspaper article by the journalist Maggie O'Kane. It was published on 19 October 1993 and entitled 'For God and Country'. It purported to be an interview with a UFF Commander in West Belfast, nicknamed 'Mad Dog'.

Detectives building a case against Adair were intrigued by what she had written about him and considered it accurate. She had revealed he kept a photograph taken with Michael Stone outside the Maze. The photograph which police later seized, was taken in September '92 when Stone was released under the peace accords of the Good Friday Agreement. William Dodds was also in the photograph.

Maggie O'Kane wrote that Adair had the photograph lying beside the gear-stick of his personal car. In her article, she also referred to Adair as 'Mad Dog' without mentioning his real identity. She was unaware a police report of an interview with Adair contained the following response to a question put to him about his nickname: 'I'm "Mad Dog". The difference between me and McGlinchey is that he killed policemen and I kill Taigs.' On several occasions, after he was stopped at checkpoints, he signed a waiver document with the following admission: 'Johnny 2nd Batt. UFF.' His desire to be recognised as 'Mad Dog', the ruthless terrorist leader, extended to the interview he gave to Maggie O'Kane.

The more detectives examined her article, the clearer it became Johnny Adair was the subject of her piece. The following year, while being formally questioned, he admitted he had given the interview to Maggie O'Kane. But, in 1993, what she wrote fascinated the Adair inquiry team. She portrayed him with great accuracy. Detectives selected passages from her report which they believed defined their target. They hoped some of her material could be useful in a case against him, provided they could show in court that Maggie O'Kane's 'Mad Dog' was their man. Her description of her interviewee certainly pointed to Adair:

His short blond hair has highlights. He stands about five foot seven inches tall in his white-striped training shoes and has the body of a stocky full-back beginning to go to seed. He wears a gold earring in his right ear and a light denim shirt covers tattoos in honour of the Ulster Freedom Fighters.

Investigators were especially interested in the fact he had made admissions to her. One, in particular, caught their attention.

> He drives into Belfast's Catholic ghettos to kill with a six-inch cardboard cut-out of a Celtic football player swinging gently from his back windscreen, partly as a decoy, partly because it amuses him. He selects the targets himself . . .

Detectives scrutinising her article highlighted the phrase 'selects the targets himself' and underlined it. They later commented about the article in a preliminary document about Adair's role in terrorism:

> The above information could only have come from the subject of the article, which as stated, can only be John Adair. Members of this inquiry team seized from Adair's home, during the 11th of January 1994, a six-inch cardboard cut-out of a Celtic football player.

The article hit a high note when she referred to her interviewee as a member of the UDA's Inner Council. The assertion about Inner Council membership immediately alerted detectives to his identity. Her journalistic skills were impeccable and, in the light of what is revealed in this chapter, she got close to the truth about the Godfather of Terrorism. Her report was not the only one detectives carefully examined while building their case. They read and re-read an article by the veteran journalist, Alan Murray, which appeared in the *Irish Independent* that same month. It was published under the headline 'Face to Face with the UDA's Top Assassin'. In Appendix 7(a) 9.10 of the inquiry team's case against Adair, they reflected on Alan Murray's insights. Like Maggie O'Kane, he did not reveal the identity of the 'Top Assassin'.

> At another point in the article, reference is made to an incident whenever Adair and a man described as 'IRA O.C. North Belfast' had an altercation at Clifton Street. The article implies a connection between that incident and a gun attack on the home of a relative of the IRA member that same night and a subsequent attack on his mother's home. Adair is quoted as stating, 'if they

> attack people on the Shankill Road and are charged, then the UFF
> will note the address and hit the house. Their mothers, their
> fathers or brothers and sisters will pay a price.'

The members of the investigating team also noted the incisive and colourful way in which Murray described the 'Top Assassin'. 'He is a bundle of nervous energy and talks fifteen to the dozen, racing along, flinging the names of IRA men across the room. The addresses he personally knows because he has targeted their homes.'

The articles by both journalists became an integral element in the overall thinking and strategy of the secret police investigation. Both interviews confirmed Adair was confident about talking to the media because he was convinced he was untouchable. Detectives understood that bringing him to justice would require a substantial body of evidence. It was time to refocus their strategy. He knew how to bend the law when it came to concealing his terrorist crimes but how good was he at laundering money and hiding his role in racketeering and extortion? There had to be another way to take him down and investigators unanimously decided to go after his finances to prove he was a godfather. If they could link racketeering with all their circumstantial evidence of his terrorist activity, they could define him as a terrorist godfather. The two articles would be included in the mix and there were also the sightings and statements he had made during interviews and at vehicle checkpoints. It was, in effect, a 'catch-all' strategy and was permitted under Section 27 of a 1991 piece of legislation aimed at men like Adair. In the minds of some investigators, there was a genuine belief that such an approach was unlikely to succeed because its objectives were too broad. Adair was a master of deception and extremely cunning.

One of the lead investigators, Detective Sergeant Johnston 'Jonty' Brown, a detective in the mould of Jimmy Nesbitt who cracked the Shankill Butchers case, had studied Adair closely for years prior to the setting up of the inquiry team in 1993. Brown was thorough, honest and incisive. He knew from personal experience how Adair enjoyed 'playing games' with police. On 10 August 1992, the UDA, after two decades, was proscribed. That same day, Adair, accompanied by associates James Spence and Curtis Moorhead, strode into Tennent Street police station where 'Jonty' Brown met him. As the detective listened, the three men smiled and declared they had just resigned from the UDA. A short time later, Moorhead was convicted for UFF acts of terrorism. Adair's unsolicited admission of UDA membership came as no surprise to 'Jonty' Brown. Undercover surveillance tapes of UDA HQ at 275A Shankill Road showed Adair frequently visited the HQ. After proscription, the HQ was renamed the 'Welfare Wing'.

Once the inquiry team began rethinking its strategy, 'Jonty' Brown said he had the ability to get closer to Adair to compile more damaging evidence against the terror boss. 'Jonty's colleagues saw advantage in such a strategy but were concerned for his safety. Like 'Jonty', they knew he would be walking into a 'wily lion's den'.

PART 2: TAKING DOWN 'MAD DOG'

Detective Sergeant Johnston 'Jonty' Brown was no ordinary cop. He had joined the RUC in 1972 and throughout his career he had learned a great deal about terrorists, especially men like 'Mad Dog' Adair. He had deliberately established a rapport with Adair from the moment the UFF terror boss took over C Company in the Shankill. During all his conversations with him, he had listened intently and, over three years, had built a dossier, writing down everything he learned in notebooks and journals. The evidence he had was devastating but no one at the top of the RUC hierarchy appeared to have an appetite for seriously targeting 'Mad Dog'. Perhaps, if they had done so, prior to the arrival of the inquiry team in 1993, many lives would have been saved. Within the team, there was an urgency to take down Adair and 'Jonty's' fellow detectives felt empowered to use any legal means to achieve their objectives. 'Jonty' had got closer than anyone had to Adair, and his colleagues on the team unanimously supported him when he recommended to their bosses that they should covertly wiretap future conversations with 'Mad Dog'. 'Jonty' pointed out to his team leaders that Adair's weakness was his 'propensity to boast' to police officers and soldiers. They gave 'Jonty' the 'green light' to target Adair by visiting him in his home or talking to him in the street. On each occasion, 'Jonty' was accompanied by another policeman. Jonty's ability to get Adair to talk about terror was astounding. It reminded me of the technique used by FBI Special Agents to bring down the Mafia families in New York. During meetings with 'Mad Dog', 'Jonty' Brown was in uniform, sometimes accompanied by another detective, also in uniform. The objective was to make their target comfortable, even if that meant exchanging pleasantries and allowing him to feel he was in control. Every effort was made to convince him they had no ulterior motive. They were aware of his conviction that the UFF and the security forces were battling a common enemy. I acquired transcripts of five recorded conversations though, I suspect, there were many others. Notes attached to the following transcripts of those recordings are not the author's.

Adair: I've tried my hand at everything but no good, so I had to go to terrorism and build my way through the ranks. A couple of dirty ones and a couple of good ones, to the top of the ladder, untouched too. In the whole of the Northern Ireland, the ball's at my foot. If I go, it goes. I say 'stop', it stops. If I say 'make the bombs or scare the peelers for 48 hours', the ball's at my foot. I've some fucking power, I'll tell you. How did I get to the top? Scratching my balls do you think? Do you think I bluffed my way to the top?

[*N.B. The reference to 'scaring the peelers for 48 hours' is a reference to a 48-hour period between 2 and 4 July 1993, when the UFF in the Shankill carried out a substantial series of attacks on the police, using both firearms and explosive devices.*]

Uniformed Officer: Is there a cease-fire at Christmas?

Adair: No, there's no cease-fire. Not while I'm here. They tried to have a cease-fire while I was in Castlereagh. [*N.B. A reference to his arrest and detention at Castlereagh Police Office between 28 October and 2 November 1993.*]

Uniformed Officer: Did anything happen while you were in Castlereagh?

Adair: No . . . sure, fuck, if I go away for 48 hours, there's not a shot fired. I went to fucking Spain and there wasn't a shot fired. [*Holiday in August 1993*] All the fucking wee men were taking drugs and going mad.

[*N.B. Police can prove from recording that during Adair's last two periods of detention and when he was on holiday, no UFF-related terrorist incidents occurred in the Belfast region.*]

In response to a reference to the Uniformed Officer that persons had been in the Shankill to target him, he stated to an associate present: 'Why did our vigilantes not get them?'

After one of the attempts on Adair's life, Stephen Larkin, a Provisional IRA suspect from the Ardoyne, was arrested and charged with attempted murder. Following his appearance in court, Adair acquired his address and sent trigger men from C Company to attack his home. They fired into the house but Larkin's mother, who was inside at the time, was uninjured. Adair's constant desire for revenge reached a crescendo on Saturday, 23 October 1993. On the afternoon of that day, Thomas Begley, a Provisional IRA volunteer, walked into a fish and chip shop on the Shankill Road carrying a bomb in a holdall. The bomb was comprised of Semtex explosives and a timer. The shop was situated beneath UDA HQ. The bomb exploded prematurely, killing Begley and ten innocent Protestants. The IRA had mistakenly calculated that Adair and other UFF/UDA leaders were due to hold a meeting in upstairs rooms of the building. The meeting had taken place before Begley arrived with the bomb and UFF/UDA personnel, with the exception of three men, had left the premises.

The following day, in the debris of the bombed-out building, detectives from the team investigating Adair found a 1993 A4 diary. It contained references to the UFF and an extensive list of addresses and telephone numbers of journalists, solicitors and prisons. Of particular interest was a list of suspected police informers, some of whom were serving sentences for UFF-related terror. One address in the diary, which appeared to confirm its owner, was Adair's. It was written alongside his home telephone number. Some detectives felt they had the basis for questioning him and the task fell to 'Jonty' Brown and another detective who visited Adair's home. Below is a transcript of the subsequent interview. I have included it in the form in which it appeared in the inquiry team's file. Adair's speech was indicative of an angry man and illustrated his lack of sophistication.

> Adair: At the end of the day do you see, if the UFF, I'm just saying this, or the UDA were ever in there, sure they [*PIRA*] were always fucking killing innocent people before they were getting to them [*UDA/UFF*] members and see when they were getting to them, they weren't even killing any of them'ns. You see, of the three people that was in UDA Headquarters, there was only three slightly injured so there you are.
>
> [*N.B. Refers to 275A Shankill Road as UDA Headquarters.*]
>
> Adair: These auld gutless ones send two wee lads down with a fucking Semtex or whatever, put it outside UDA Headquarters.
>
> *When questioned if the bombers were after Adair himself, Adair stated:* I know what happened. They spotted me going in earlier. Whoever it was on the Shankill Road spotted me and 'Winkie' going into it earlier on. [*i.e. UDA HQ*] You read the statement there [*PIRA claim of responsibility*], there's three statements. There was somebody on the road yesterday, either a man, male or female, in the cafe or standing about the Road who witnessed me

and 'Winkie' Dodds going in but all we done was went in, picked up a pass . . . [*Interruption*] . . . no, listen, I'm talking about IRA, you wouldn't know them. Sure a fucking girl nine months pregnant, you'll not know her. Whoever it was now they're right, they're right what they said, their statement, their first statement was they identified known members of the Ulster Freedom Fighters goin' in till there and they brought their plan forward, whatever they meant by that, so whoever was there, there's Adair and Dodds away in now and we're in. We just collected a pass to go up and see McCrory and we left. We weren't in more than five minutes but whoever watched us knew that we'd went in and thought maybe the UFF's having a meeting.

[*N.B. Adair states the IRA statement was correct . . . because someone had witnessed him and Dodds. Adair is confirming that he and Dodds were the known members of the UFF identified by whoever was watching the premises.*]

Adair: But they'll [*PIRA*] have to answer for what they do, shortly after. You mark my words, I get my hands on a good fucking bomb, it's going right into there [*Republican area*] no fucking doubt about it . . . Nobody will stop me from detonating them anywhere.

[*N.B. Threat to carry out bombing attacks in Republican areas.*]

Adair: If I applaud, respect the fellas for doing it . . . but I know it wasn't a sanctioned operation.

[*Re: Arrest of 2 X UFF suspects following a shooting attack at the Boundary bar (Catholic bar) on the afternoon of the Shankill bombing.*]

Three weeks later, Adair was at home when he had another visit from two members of the inquiry team. One of Adair's associates, Norman Green, was present. The following is a transcript of their exchanges:

Adair: Are we gonna get peace? Not while I'm about. I have to tell you, I'll never have peace . . .

[*LATER*]

That's it, we don't want peace.

[*LATER*]

Adair: Let's have a look at that Ruger [*police officer's pistol*]. I'm getting a few of them. Let's see . . . Norman, here's these weapons we're getting. Ruger, there it is. Fuck sake show him! We're getting a load of these . . . that's them there . . . paid for and all.

[*N.B. While Adair's reference to buying a quantity of Ruger*] *revolvers might be put down purely to banter, the significant thing here is the acceptance by all present that Adair would be in the market for firearms and Adair's own understanding that police would accept this.*]

Some killing power. That's the first weapon I ever used . . . and it near blew the fucking, it near pulled me away. I was about nine stone . . . no, it was the first weapon I ever used. It nearly pulled me into the house with it.

[*LATER*]

Adair: Fuck the Third Force. Look at the gear, ammunition I'm getting in the minute.

In response to the above, Norman Green, an associate of Adair's states: You've got more gear than Tennent Street barracks has.

Adair: There you are, I have.

[*LATER*]

Adair: Aye it is, it's very quiet at the minute, isn't it? That's 'cause they've cooled my temper, that auld Council [Reference to UDA Inner Council]. They said 'look', they talked a wee bit of sense till me.

[*LATER*]

Adair: So, would I want peace? We all would. Nobody wants to run seven days a week targeting Provos, killing innocent people, targeting Sinn Feiners, nobody wants to do that . . . all their lives. No, we want to go home and watch *Coronation Street* like all the rest of them. We're all human. We've balls and heart like the rest of youse. We wanna go away to the beach at the summer . . . Do you honestly think I want this war to go on? I want peace as much as the next man wants it, know what I mean, but I'll not sit back and let our fucking people get fucking walked on, do you know what I mean?

In response to a reference that Adair would have difficulty getting access to the amounts of money he now has in the event of peace Adair stated:

I don't need money. I get £80 a fortnight on the 'Bureau' and I get a few quid day to day. As long as I've got petrol in the car, food in the cupboard, I don't give two fucks. Certainly I get a few quid if I do the odd robbery. We do the odd robbery, it's known, isn't it? If the odd businessman comes up and says, 'There's a cheque for twenty grand', there you are, know what I mean, we don't need the money.

It was clear from secret recordings and comments he made to police at checkpoints that he believed he had nothing to fear from the RUC and the British Army. He was convinced they approved of his campaign of violence against the other community. I contend, through his contacts with Stone, Billy Wright and other members of the UDA's Inner Council, he was aware of collusion between elements of the State security apparatus and loyalist paramilitaries. I am astounded senior security figures did not immediately act against him once they were in possession of the covert recordings in which he clearly linked himself to terror. One of the features of the taped conversations was that he felt comfortable talking to uniformed policemen and soldiers. Throughout the Troubles, it was more often uniformed members of the RUC who passed information to loyalist paramilitaries.

A careful analysis of his speech patterns confirms the comments made about him by the veteran journalist, Alan Murray. Adair lacked a formal education and his use of language was that of an uneducated thug. He talked in a staccato style, clipping words and running thoughts into each other. In that sense, he was different from Billy Wright and John McMichael. They were more articulate and exhibited a higher level of learning. Missing from the transcripts of the covert recordings are the comments by 'Jonty' Brown and other detectives who accompanied him. Those absent contributions would have helped the reader better understand the style used by the investigators to coax Adair into making incriminating statements. Several short transcripts do, however, offer a brief insight into how 'Jonty' Brown operated. The following recordings were marked 'TSUs' on confidential police files. I have included them here in the form in which they were documented.

TSU 166/94

Policeman: You're quiet. There's something going on when you buggers are as quiet as this. There's some ulterior motive . . . a plan.

Adair: The Ulster Freedom Fighters in the past 72 hours have been involved in four attacks.

Policeman: I'm only interested in the Tennent Street area.

Adair: You can't keep this going to the same plan or you lose men. I'm prepared to lose the odd man but . . .

TSU 182/94

Adair: I'm a busy man.

Policeman: Busy man? What are you busy doing?

Adair: Job.

Policeman: What sort of job?

Adair: All sorts of things.

Policeman: Well, fill me in, Johnny. Tell me.

Adair: Fighting to keep Ulster part of Britain.

Policeman: Is that what you're fighting for?

Adair: That's all that's there.

TSU 208/94

Adair: What's happening? Is all quiet?

Policeman: At the minute, aye.

Adair: Some UFF cell running about now. They're very tight.

Policeman: What do you mean by tight, Johnny?

Adair: Well, they're slaughtering a lot in West Belfast.

The inquiry team's file was set out as a 'Preliminary Report: TERRORIST INVESTIGATION – JOHN JAMES ADAIR'. It comprised the following headings:

Circumstantial Evidence – sightings at UDA HQ, West Belfast

Association with convicted members of the UFF

Prison Visits/Finance

Michael Stone photograph

Sightings in Republican areas

Newspaper Articles: *Guardian, Irish Independent*

UFF Shooting Attacks on known Republican figures

Finance

Direct Evidence – Membership of the UDA/UFF

Comments/Admissions

The evidence contained in the document ran to over 100 pages. It cumulatively demonstrated that detectives, the majority of whom were regarded as the RUC's 'best', were convinced there was no simple antidote, within the existing legal framework, to the Adair problem. In contrast, the racketeering aspect of the investigation, while it is interesting to analyse, was not as legally potent. The Terrorist Finance Unit based at Stormont on the outskirts of Belfast helped with that part of the inquiry. A list was compiled of every item in Adair's home and given a valuation. An Ulster Bank account held by Adair and his common-law wife, Gina Crossan, was examined. In particular, scrutiny was directed at transactions made through that account, leading to the conclusion: 'The financial transactions involve the cashing of cheques through third party accounts for the benefit of, we believe, John Adair. Given the amounts and the companies involved, these monies may well be the proceeds of racketeering.'

Investigators compared the value of the items in his home with social security payments he had received over a three-year period. They detected what they called a 'shortfall of £37,524'. A confidential memorandum to Detective Chief Inspector McArthur said the 'short-fall figure' was a 'minimum figure and the actual amount is much greater'. 'It is abundantly clear that Adair is in receipt of money from a source other than his common-law wife's social security benefits. I can only conclude that Adair has access to, and control over, substantial sums of money.'

One of the difficulties in prying into his financial transactions was that detectives were unable to establish his home at 10 Hazelfield Street as his legal address. When questioned about the matter, he said he stayed at several addresses. Asked if there were other addresses he would care to list, he replied: 'Not at the moment.' He further stated that food and accommodation were provided free in those addresses. He added he did not have a wife or steady relationship but he did have a girlfriend. A further memorandum was sent to Detective Chief Inspector McArthur, reflecting yet another tenuous link in the attempts to prove he could only finance his lifestyle through crime. 'Adair has claimed that he drives three to four miles per day. Is there surveillance or any other evidence, which can be used to prove or disprove this?'

From the correspondence, one can see that investigators were looking at the minutiae of his life. They wanted to know his exact daily mileage in order to calculate the miles travelled in one year and the cost of petrol for his car. I think it would not be unreasonable for the reader to conclude that some parts of the investigation appeared to be focused on frivolous matters when the concentration should have been elsewhere. Nonetheless, he lied about every aspect of his finances, so much so that detectives again wrote to Detective Chief Inspector McArthur stressing the need for evidence to prove his guilt beyond a reasonable doubt. There was almost desperation in their words. Inherent in my analysis of police documents is a conclusion that the RUC's best on the inquiry team sometimes felt 'impotence'. They did not believe they had enough to constitute what would be required for a successful racketeering prosecution and, to some extent, their strategy was too broadly focused. But, it is also fair to concede that their legal advisers were not always on their side. When it was discovered Adair had filed a false loan application for a car, legal advice to the inquiry team was that conspiracy to defraud was difficult to prove. Under the 1969 Theft Act, the law would require a complaint from the lender and involve the prosecution of the car dealer, who was privy to the fact Adair supplied false information. It was considered unlikely the lender would be prepared to make a complaint against 'Mad Dog'.

The RUC Department, which provided assistance to the racketeering part of the investigation, was C1(3). Its staff told the inquiry team leaders that Adair knew they were on his trail and that they had made inquiries at his bank on the Crumlin Road. In response, he had allowed his account there to remain dormant. I was told he was tipped off after C1(3) investigators discovered he had been using other people and aliases to cash cheques at the Ulster Bank. A subsequent memorandum to Detective Chief Inspector McArthur lamented the problems facing the joint investigating teams. 'The financial information standing on its own establishes that Adair was living beyond his means. However, we still have to show its relevance to him directing the activities of a terrorist organisation.'

'Mad Dog' was aware of every move against his finances and carefully concealed his ill-gotten gains. The one aspect of the investigation to which he was oblivious was the wiretapping. However, there is also an unusual aspect to Brown's work. Special Branch had access to the recordings but not in the way one would expect, namely through a sharing of information. Special Branch had wired Adair's home. One of their listening devices was concealed in an overhead fan light in the living-room. While 'Jonty' Brown was having one of his cosy chats with Adair and members of his inner circle, Adair laughed and said 'Jonty' was probably wired. 'Jonty', without knowing there was a Special Branch bugging device above where he was seated, jokingly said there was probably a listening device in the fan light. Special Branch was furious and later told him so, adding that he could have compromised their operations. What operations, one might ask. How much did they know about the terrorist leader and why were they not sharing their intelligence with the inquiry team? Again, that is one of the typical imponderables which so often emerged in my investigations of the undercover war, especially in respect of operations involving Special Branch and British Military Intelligence. As I disclosed in earlier chapters, the UFF in the Shankill area, in particular C Company, which had also been under the control of James 'Pratt' Craig, was heavily penetrated throughout the conflict by the intelligence apparatus. The British Intelligence terrorist agent, Brian Nelson, who was appointed by John McMichael to the role of Chief of UFF Intelligence, took a particular interest in the killing capabilities of C Company before Adair became its Commander.

Among the evidence compiled by the inquiry team were items found in a search of Adair's home on 11 January 1994. A plaque was recovered, bearing the inscription: 'Presented to John Adair in appreciation of your sterling work – 1991'. There was also a photograph of three armed and masked men and two documents carrying Adair's signature, followed by '2nd Batt. C Coy. UFF'. In a police file alongside the items was a surveillance note that police had observed him personally painting a mural on a gable wall near his home. The mural depicted a masked terrorist brandishing an RPG 7 rocket launcher. Underneath was the inscription: 'UFF Rocket Team on Tour in West Belfast, 1994.' His intention was to make reference to rocket attacks on two Sinn Fein offices.

His self-image was vital to him and during a police interview in February 1994, he told policemen they should not look disapprovingly at him when they sought to link him to criminal activity. Like previous UFF/UDA terror bosses linked to crime, he tried to distance himself from allegations that he was a career criminal. He wanted loyalists and the security forces to see him in the same light as Billy Wright, John McMichael and Michael Stone – a patriot and hero. As he told the *Guardian* journalist, Maggie O'Kane, 'Stone is a hero, a real hero.'

Prior to the February police interview, members of his C Company robbed a post office on the Shankill Road. The sub-postmistress and her family were held hostage and warned not to subsequently cooperate with police investigators. After the robbery, the sub-postmistress discovered that, while the robbers were ransacking her home above the post office, they stole personal items of jewellery with a sentimental value. The detectives questioning Adair in February after the robbery reminded him he was the Commander of C Company and was therefore responsible for the robbery. How could he say on the one hand he was a soldier and be involved in organised crime? Adair feigned anger and said he had known nothing about it. 'I will see the family get their stuff back,' he declared. Twenty-four hours after he was released, a member of C Company walked into the post office, placed an envelope on the counter and left. Inside it were the stolen items of jewellery.

Part of the police strategy to lessen his influence on violence was to arrest and detain him for short periods because killings ceased while he was out of circulation. Throughout multiple interviews, while in custody, he displayed a bizarre humour. When once asked by a police interrogator if he knew why he was being questioned, he replied: 'To keep me off the streets so that the Catholics can do their shopping.' In response to a question about how he felt being held in custody in Castlereagh, he answered: 'It's great . . . a clear head and nothing going on every half hour – time to plan for the next couple of weeks.' One interrogator glibly inquired what he would do if he won a million pounds. He responded that he would 'buy a lot of gear'.

Castlereagh police office files contain a wealth of information gleaned from the questioning of Adair. Book 12 holds a transcript of an interview, which took place in the wake of investigations into the terrorist role of the British Military terrorist agent, Brian Nelson. The man with the role of lead investigator of Nelson and of the history of collusion between the security forces and loyalist paramilitaries was John Stevens, Deputy Chief Constable of Cambridgeshire, England. Stevens' first inquiry – there would be three – led to the rounding up of UDA leaders, among them Tommy 'Tucker' Lyttle, who subsequently died in prison. He had been a friend of John McMichael and James 'Pratt' Craig and had also been a Special Branch informer. Adair knew him well. The following is an extract from Book 12, written by one of Adair's interrogators.

> When asked what he thought of the Stevens Inquiry, he said he had done a good job, had got rid of all the 'shite'. He said that all 'Tucker' Lyttle and his crowd worried about was money. In Lyttle's time, there would have been one hit, about 50 robberies and a bit of extortion. Now there was a lot more hits and maybe one robbery. There was only one man who stood in the old days – John McMichael – he had four brains and that was good. There was one other and that was Andy Tyrie. He [*Adair*] said the UFF were doing a good job. Speaking about the Shankill bombing and subsequent UFF attacks, he said: 'The Prods had to even the score for the bomb on the Shankill.'

In another interview, Adair told a detective he could not understand why republicans were targeting him when there was '— [*name withheld by author*] in Newtownabbey and — [*name withheld*] behind the bar in the Times bar'. Adair was referring to members of the UDA Inner Council.

An interview in Book 4 contains statements by Adair which any legal novice would deem incriminating. However, Adair refused to sign interview notes, believing that in doing so he would be verifying their authenticity, and therefore according them prosecutorial value:

> He said, unprompted, that his visits to Castlereagh allowed him to clear his head, think of things and get matters in order. He said the last time he was lifted for seven days, there wasn't a shot fired by the UFF, but when he got out he got the boys together and told them that if he disappeared from the scene again, they are to carry on. He said that he was 60 per cent sure that there would be an incident from C Company while he was in custody, maybe even tonight. Having denied being a UDA godfather, he stated that he enjoyed deciding what would be the news tonight or tomorrow. He said he had projected the UFF to a very high

level. He said he was worried about a C1(3) inquiry regarding his financial status, that it was dragging his wife, Gina, into it and she is innocent.

On the same day in Castlereagh, an entry in Interview Book 7 described him discussing UDA/UFF members of the Inner Council:

> Still speaking about Joe — [*name withheld by author*] and his position within the UDA/UFF, he laughed and said Joe — would ring him up after shootings and ask him was that them people in the top right. Joe — was referring to the UFF emblem being at the top right-hand corner of the UDA badge. He said that Joe — and the rest of the Inner Council are old ginnies but he needs them too. He added that they can't all be soldiers – need thinkers, strategists, but it is the military that keeps up the pressure on the IRA and the system. When it was put to him that he had murdered people, he laughed and replied that he had never murdered anyone. With a smile, he said, 'Or I've never been caught.'

In 1995, the inquiry team's written report provided a compelling case that he was a godfather of terrorism. The report demonstrated a relentless search for evidence and the high standards of professionalism within the team. The inquiry was one of the most difficult tasks the RUC's Criminal Investigation Division had ever undertaken. Detectives were meticulous. However, the most potent element in their case was not the racketeering evidence but the recorded conversations.

That was recognised by the Prosecution lawyers, Pat Lynch and John Creaney, one of the most experienced Senior Counsel in Northern Ireland. On the basis of their recommendation, Adair was charged with terrorism and, in keeping with legal principles, his defence lawyers were permitted to learn about the substance of the case against him. In the summer of 1995, 'Jonty' Brown attended a meeting with the prosecution team in the home of the Junior Counsel, Pat Lynch. John Creaney and Lynch told 'Jonty' the most compelling part of their case was the body of evidence gleaned from secret recordings. It was clear to Creaney that Adair feared those recordings being used in open court, especially because he had spoken about, and lambasted, other members of the UDA's Inner Council.

The prosecution lawyers wanted to press home what they saw as the cutting edge of their case. They told 'Jonty' senior RUC figures had approved the prosecution's recommendation that he provide another statement but, this time, including all his notes of conversations with Adair prior to the setting up of the inquiry. 'Jonty' did so and when his second statement was inserted in the prosecution court filing, Adair pleaded guilty to directing terrorism. His decision was influenced by two factors. Firstly, 'Jonty's' notes combined with the wiretaps would have sent Adair down for 25 years to life if he had decided to contest the charges. Secondly, he feared the prospect of 'Jonty' going into the witness-box and divulging everything he had said in private, especially his remarks about his fellow terror bosses on the UDA Inner Council. The thought of going into prison and being portrayed as a 'loud mouth', who gave up UFF secrets and condemned the organisation's leadership, had attendant risks and Adair knew it. He took the only option available and pleaded guilty. In other words, for not wasting the court's time in a lengthy trial, he was given a reduced sentence of 16 years. Unfortunately, the covert recordings, and other material revealed in this book, did not become public knowledge. Equally disturbing was the fact he only remained behind bars for three years and was released, under licence, as part of the staged terrorist prisoner release programme within the peace process.

True to form, he returned to the Shankill to reclaim his status within the UDA/UFF. Adair and his C Company trigger men had not forgotten 'Jonty' Brown and singled him out as the man whose evidence had put Adair behind bars. I spoke to 'Jonty' about the problems he faced in 2000.

'My involvement in the Adair case was a bridge too far. My family became the targets. It was to be open season on Rebecca and me and the boys. In January 2000, informants close to Adair told me that he dreamed of getting back at me for putting him away. He was planning to have his C Company men seize my eldest boy Adam as Adam jogged around our little village with his friends. In March 2000, C Company members hijacked a Citroen car in the Shankill and drove to Ballyrobert to kidnap Adam. Their plan was to seize him and tie him to a lamp-post, kneecap him and put a placard around his neck with the sign "Drug Dealer" etched on it. It was just good fortune that on that particular evening we had taken Adam and his friends to a local technical college to choose a course of study. The UFF men were frustrated and abandoned their hijacked car not far from my home. They left some bullets in it with a note to "put Jonty's head up his hole". When the UDA threaten you as a police officer you can live with that but when they threaten innocent children that is an entirely different matter. I can't overstate the debilitating effect that had on my wife, Rebecca, and myself.'

Within one year of his freedom from custody, Adair was returned to the Maze prison for breaking the terms of his release, which required he remained apart from terrorism and racketeering. In his absence C Company, like many other parts of the UDA, devoted its energies to the drugs trade. Overall, the UDA/UFF resembled the New York Mafia families. In 2002, 'Mad Dog' was back in the headlines where he liked to be. He walked through the gates of the Maze to freedom and was no sooner back in charge of C Company than sectarian killings began again in North and West Belfast. At the same time, turf wars over criminal profits dominated meetings of the Brigadiers on the Inner Council. Just like the Cosa Nostra, the men at the top of the UDA had nicknames – 'The Egyptian', 'The Bacardi Brigadier', 'The Mexican', 'Doris Day' and of course 'Mad Dog'. Within the UDA's governing body there was a growing consensus that Adair's desire for sectarian terror brought too much heat on the organisation in the form of police and media scrutiny. The UDA's alleged commitment to a ceasefire and the peace process was in jeopardy and overall criminal profits were down. There was a real danger the authorities could move against all the Brigadiers and place them in custody, or worse, put them in prison for several years. Tensions between Adair and those opposed to him led to bloodletting.

Adair ran the Lower Shankill the way John Gotti ran part of Brooklyn in New York in the 1980s. Just as Gotti would meet and discuss strategy over drinks, Adair ran his operations from two pubs and the kitchen of his home. With his friend 'King Rat' dead, he linked up with elements of Billy Wright's Loyalist Volunteer Force in Belfast. It was a move designed to give him greater firepower in any confrontation with Inner Council Brigadiers. As internecine warfare continued, he told journalists his enemies in the UDA had placed a one million-pound bounty on his head.

In the Shankill, UFF militants on both sides of the dispute fought for control of the neigbourhood and attacked each other's homes. Adair and his enemies leaked damaging stories about each other to journalists. Each side claimed it was the other that was guilty of racketeering and running drugs in Protestant districts. Adair, dressed in his customary T-shirt, jeans and Wrangler jacket, his head shaven, happily posed for press photographers whenever an opportunity arose for him to be centre stage. He preferred to be photographed with his Alsatian dog, Rebel, which he referred to as 'auld Rebel' to signify the dog's age and its loneliness each time he was incarcerated. In an interview with an *Irish Times* journalist, he talked at length about his dog. When I read his comments about 'auld Rebel' I laughed. It was comical, and I had to remind myself Adair was directing terrorism when he was not discussing the temperament of his Alsatian.

During media interviews, John White, a UDA leader who professed a commitment to peace but who had a very dark and sinister past, often accompanied him. White was one of those evil figures of the 1970s in the mould of Lenny Murphy. On 26 June 1973, he and several UDA killers brutally murdered a Catholic Senator, Paddy Wilson, and 29-year-old Irene Andrews, a Protestant, who was employed as a secretary. The two were drinking in McGlade's bar in downtown Belfast beside the offices of the *Belfast Telegraph* newspaper. McGlade's was a haunt for journalists and politicians and that evening, Wilson, a married man, had a lot to drink. Peter McKenna, the *Irish Independent* journalist who later broke the Kincora story, was there and observed Irene Andrews 'coming on strong' with Wilson. Perhaps she and the Senator had been intimate before that night. On this occasion, Wilson rejected her advances and her request that he should drive her home. He turned to Peter McKenna and asked him to pretend there was a telephone call for him which demanded his immediate attention. It was, Wilson believed, his only way to detach himself from Irene. Peter agreed. But the ruse did not work. Later that evening, Wilson left the bar with her. She lived off the Crumlin in a loyalist district not far from the Shankill. What transpired from the time they left the bar until their bodies were discovered remains a mystery. There was speculation that they had been seen together on other occasions and that was why they were targeted. Other theories were that they were observed driving to her home before they travelled to a lovers' lane on the mountainside above Belfast. One theory was that their killers came upon them by chance as they prepared to leave the lovers' lane or began to have sex. Detectives later found her pants in her handbag. I tend to believe a loyalist source who told me years later the victims had been followed from McGlade's bar to the mountainside. When their bodies were found, he had over 30 stab wounds and she had been stabbed 20 times in the face, head and chest. The double killing was consistent with a frenzied attack but forensic evidence indicated it was committed with thoroughness. Wilson was dragged from the car and held on the ground while he was killed. One of the killers held Irene Andrews beside the car and made her watch. After Wilson was murdered, the killers turned on her.

John White was one of the killers wielding a knife. Even after he was convicted for the crime, White refused to name his accomplices and contended he was innocent. He could have fingered Davy Payne who died while this book was being written. For years after the double murder, Payne boasted about how the RUC had tried and failed to connect him to it. White and Payne were close friends of the UDA terror boss, Charles Harding Smith at a time when some of the most horrendous crimes were committed in North and West Belfast. White became a part of the peace process in the early to mid '90s and tried to distance himself from the double killing, telling journalists he had no part of it. In 2002, he was closely linked to Adair, even after the UDA Inner Council expelled 'Mad Dog' in September of that year. In media interviews, he acted as Adair's spokesman.

Adair's reign of terror ended on 10 January 2003, when the Secretary of State for Northern Ireland decided enough was enough. He revoked 'Mad Dog's' release-licence and committed him to the Maze prison, recommending he should not be released until 2005. Martin Breen, a reporter with the *News of the World*, interviewed Adair 24 hours before his arrest. Adair told him there would be 'retribution' for the stance taken against him by Inner Council leaders. 'They have to take the rough with the smooth,' he warned – a clear statement in Adair-speak for assassinations. Breen's story was front page with the headline: 'Mad Dog: Come and Get Me'. Alongside those words was a photograph of a puffy-faced, shaven-headed Adair with a gold earring in his right ear. He was wearing his favourite Wrangler jacket. In the interview, he claimed UDA Brigadiers had not only expelled him the previous year but had also tried to kill him. Weeks after the article appeared, a UDA Brigadier opposed to Adair was gunned down and killed while driving through the centre of Belfast.

The *Sunday World* newspaper, under the editorship of Jim McDowell, a fearless investigative journalist, had carried many stories about Adair's life of crime and the feuding within UDA/UFF. Three days after his licence was revoked in 2003, the newspaper ran a story under the headline 'Dubai Johnny'. Underneath was a report that, within 48 hours of Adair's departure from the scene, 18 top UDA figures jetted off for a holiday in Dubai to 'celebrate "Mad Dog's" incarceration'. It was a fitting complement to other stories which in the past had Adair jetting off to Tenerife.

Within weeks, John White fled Northern Ireland to stay with Adair supporters in Glasgow, 'King Rat's' favoured city, where he had, according to his sister, Angela, secret contacts. On leaving, White vowed, 'I will return', the phrase General Douglas McArthur had used when forced to leave the Philippines after the Japanese invasion.

In 2005, 'Mad Dog' will walk free from the Maze prison unless, in his absence, the authorities unearth information and persuade former associates to give him up for his crimes. If Northern Ireland has not changed politically by the time he returns to the streets, the security forces and the population at large will once again be faced with racketeering and murder. While there are many within the UDA/UFF happy to see him incarcerated, there are others who regard him as a hero, just as he admired Lenny Murphy, Michael Stone, 'King Rat' and John McMichael. Imprisoning Adair will not radically alter the dynamics of an organisation which has, from its birth, been imbued with tribal revenge and riddled with criminality.

As I pointed out at the beginning of this chapter, a medical assessment of Adair during his troubled teens would have indicated he had serious psychological problems and was likely to prove a danger to society. While writing this book, I spoke to professionals in the United States who have studied aggressive psychopaths and the psychopathology of serial killers. They agreed with me that Adair's statements suggested a disturbed, even deranged, personality. He fitted into the tribalism of his own society and was able to give vent to his basic instincts of hatred, revenge and a desire for notoriety. The manner in which he played games with police investigators and was happy to be seen targeting victims, knowing his finger would not be on the trigger, reminded some of those I spoke to of the traits of many US serial killers.

What is perhaps most disturbing about him, and others like the Shankill Butchers and John White, is that so many of them exhibited the same disturbing tendencies within an area a quarter the size of Brooklyn in New York. In the case of the Shankill Butchers, it shocks many who have studied their history of murder, that an aggressive psychopath like Lenny Murphy could find over 20 young men, imbued with the same perverse tendencies, in a tiny district of a city small by international standards.

The backdrop of deep tribal antagonism was a reality which enabled dysfunctional men on both sides to give vent, not only to anger, but also to basic animalistic instincts. Within loyalism, the lack of a clear ideological commitment was a factor in reflex, revenge violence. There was little military discipline within loyalist ranks and the sheer size of organisations like the UDA allowed for them to be taken over by men with only criminal objectives. Such an analysis is not to excuse violence on either side of the political and religious divide but to seek an answer to why the UDA, UVF and Red Hand Commando encouraged not only the deliberate killing of non-combatants, but also the savagery of 'romperings'. The UVF leadership knew the Shankill Butchers were responsible for multiple grisly murders, and so did the bosses of other groups who encouraged such heinous acts.

It is convenient to seek explanations for the crimes of men like Adair and Murphy only within the context of tribal warfare. I believe, at some time in the future, a study will be conducted to examine and seek reasons for the grisly phenomenon of the conflict and its manifestations in killings by paramilitaries in both communities. Within such a study, the interrogation and torture of informers by the IRA and others should be taken into consideration.

One of the most important features of the investigation of Adair was the role played by the inquiry team and the special contribution of 'Jonty' Brown. He not only displayed courage but, as I said earlier, he manifested the same attributes which had made Jimmy Nesbitt, the lead detective in the Shankill Butchers case, one of the RUC's best investigators. Both these men are now retired but 'Jonty' Brown has become a very controversial figure. Prior to leaving the police force, he faced the wrath of Special Branch, a matter I will deal with in the following chapter. His confrontation with some of the shadowy men in the intelligence community derived from his innate honesty as an officer of the law. The day he publishes the story of life in the RUC, from the troubled 1970s to the 1990s, a veil will be lifted from the undercover war.

12

A MURDEROUS MILITARY AGENT

Brian Nelson's Military Intelligence bosses portrayed him as the original boy scout. Acccording to them, he was loyal to the British Army even when he was Chief of UFF Intelligence and ran hit squads. He saved many lives and warned his intelligence superiors about the UFF targeting of 217 Catholics. That was simply the fiction to minimise his role as a murderous agent in the employ of the British Ministry of Defence. His crimes as a terrorist agent spanned more than a decade of the Troubles. He was a member of the British Army's Black Watch Regiment who travelled to Northern Ireland to join the UDR in the 1970s. His decision to return to his birthplace had striking similarities to the career of Albert Walker Baker. Nelson's history from the 1970s until the late '80s is a mystery. What is not in doubt is that he joined the UDA/UFF and was an agent for British Military Intelligence. Much more is known about his role in the years 1987 to 1990, which characterised one of the darkest periods in an ongoing dirty war. His murderous actions were no mere aberration or an uncustomary strategy on the part of intelligence agencies, namely Military Intelligence, MI5 and Special Branch.

Many respected writers and journalists agree Nelson's past reflected a dimension to the conflict which had its roots in the MRF policies of the early 1970s. In 1987, after a period of R & R in Germany, Nelson was persuaded to return to Northern Ireland. By then, the use of terrorist agents had become the cutting edge of intelligence apparatus strategies. Those strategies involved assassination and were central to a counter-insurgency philosophy that contravened the rule of law. Killings of suspected republicans were sanctioned in the mistaken belief that the media and the public would never learn about them.

From the early 1970s, the intelligence community operated unhindered because there was little serious scrutiny of its tactics. For journalists, it was politically incorrect, if not risky, to point an accusing finger at the excesses of the regular Army and the men in the shadows running informers and agents. Fortunately, only a few journalists became willing conduits for disinformation or actual agents. The majority of journalists genuinely made efforts to expose aspects of the dirty war and some were subjected to ridicule and discredited. Efforts to provide the public with news of what was happening behind the headlines were often hampered by news organisations.

When I worked for the BBC from 1973 to 1992, I learned that RUC Special Branch had access to in-house security personnel and were permitted to examine the personal files of editorial and production staff. I appointed a female journalist as a researcher, only to discover that Special Branch officers secretly pulled her file. Her boyfriend, whom she later married, was a leading member of Sinn Fein. He was, I subsequently discovered, a member of the IRA's Army Council. She was a highly professional researcher and did not compromise the editorial process or those working with her. Irrespective of whether Special Branch had a right to check her out, their unfettered access to BBC personal files concerned me. In BBC Northern Ireland, some personnel files had bogus details on the career backgrounds of several people with ties to the intelligence community. A major problem facing BBC journalists in Northern Ireland was the reluctance of several senior editors to move beyond their own inherited prejudices. When I joined the BBC newsroom in Belfast in 1973, I was somewhat perplexed to learn that statements from the Army 'Press Desk' and the RUC Press Office were never challenged and there were no BBC reporters with contacts at street level. In the reflex news environment of the time, broadcasting in Northern Ireland lacked a serious investigative element, which limited the public's knowledge of the conflict. The inherent dangers of relying on the Army or RUC to control the flow of information was brought home to me when I worked for the *Irish News* and *Belfast Telegraph*. In 1973, while I was a reporter with the *Belfast Telegraph*, I telephoned in a story about a grisly sectarian murder. I saw the victim's body and the wounds of torture. My news editor rang the RUC Press Office for a comment and was told the victim had not been tortured – the killing was just 'another senseless shooting'. I later discovered the RUC was trying to play down the ghastly nature of the sectarian murder campaign carried out by the UDA and the UVF. When I wrote about 'romperings' in loyalist clubs, that story too was denied by Army and RUC spokespersons in their press facilities. The editor of the *Telegraph*,

Eugene Wasson, refused to believe in the existence of 'romper rooms'. I was not discouraged and wrote the Penguin Special, *Political Murder*. I have to admit I never experienced censorship in the *Belfast Telegraph* or the *Irish News*.

Reporting on the Troubles was difficult for most journalists. Robert Fisk, one of the foremost journalists of his generation, ran foul of the BBC in Northern Ireland when he wrote a book questioning the failure of the BBC to act as an independent body during the UWC Strike of 1974. His book was accurate but was condemned and there was an unwritten BBC rule he should not be interviewed. Within the Corporation, censorship was characterised by the willingness of some senior editors to accept 'guidance' from British Government figures based in Stormont Castle. BBC editors in Northern Ireland were frequently susceptible to the overriding authority of management in London, who acted on their instincts to pander to the Government of the day because the Corporation was constantly in need of Government support to maintain or increase the level of its licence fee.

At the time of the Anglo-Irish Agreement, a senior BBC executive reminded me I was employed by the British Broadcasting Corporation and should understand where my allegiances lay vis-à-vis the Agreement. The advice was designed to persuade me not to give Unionists airtime to voice their opposition to the Agreement. I was 'carpeted' for permitting Harold McCusker, a Unionist MP at Westminster, to question BBC coverage of the Agreement and to argue that it neglected to properly reflect the views of his constituents. I was not shocked by any of those developments because I was severely criticised for sanctioning an interview with Jack Hassard, a Protestant member of the Police Authority who had resigned his post. He said the RUC had failed to properly investigate the alleged abuse of republican suspects during interrogation. BBC senior editors, and some journalists, complained that the interview, without the on-air presence of an RUC spokesman to answer Hassard's charges against the force, resulted in a biased story. In the view of my critics, my editorial judgment was flawed because, in BBC parlance, the story lacked 'balance'. I responded that the RUC had refused to provide a spokesperson. At a BBC editorial board meeting, I reminded my critics that balance did not have to be achieved in one interview. I had a journalistic obligation to reflect the opinions of a highly respected member of the Police Authority on a matter of public interest. I expressed concern that the imposition of an editorial rule, whereby a story could not be investigated if the RUC refused to provide comment, constituted handing the police an editorial veto. It was a dangerous form of internal censorship. Some of it derived from ignorance but there was also a culture within the BBC reflecting the prejudice existing outside the walls of Broadcasting House in Belfast.

In 1992, while employed by the BBC as a television programme editor, I was interviewed at my home about a controversial shooting which had taken place two years earlier. In my book *The Dirty War* I had revealed that the shooting dead of three men was the result of a cynical British Military Intelligence operation. Knowing what I know now, it was ordered by the same kind of men who ran Brian Nelson.

The dead were common criminals – members of the Hole in the Wall gang. They were shot by an Army undercover team at the junction of the Whiterock Road and Falls Road in West Belfast. One of the criminals was shot at point-blank range as he sat in a car outside a bookmaker's shop. His two associates, carrying replica weapons, were gunned down while robbing the shop. British Military Intelligence knew the men did not have real guns because 14th Int. personnel were bugging a house next door to where the gang was holed up.

Prior to the triple killing, RUC detectives, who had an informer in the gang, warned Special Branch the criminals only used replica weapons. In fact, they rarely operated in republican areas because the IRA had shot one of them through the arms, legs and ankles. The gang came to the attention of the intelligence community when they handled weapons and documents stolen by joyriders from one of two cars used by operatives of 14th Int. – the successor organisation to the MRF.

The first theft took place outside the Europa hotel in Belfast when a male and female, both members of 14th Int., decided to have sex in a room of the hotel. They left their vehicle outside the hotel and joyriders from the Falls area seized it and stole weapons and documents from the boot. The joyriders sold the stolen items to criminals who then gave them to the IRA. The second episode happened after other joyriders stole a Vauxhall Astra in the centre of Belfast and drove it to the carpark of the Homestead, a pub located at Drumboe between Belfast and Lisburn. They intended to dump the Vauxhall and swap it for a car in the car park. At the Homestead, they spotted a Nissan Bluebird and broke into it. Inside the boot there were two holdalls containing documents, a Heckler & Koch sub-machine gun with four loaded magazines, a 9mm Browning pistol with three loaded magazines and a stun grenade of the type used by the SAS. The joyriders decided the Nissan was too hot to handle and drove off in the Astra with the holdalls. They torched the Astra in the Andersonstown area and sold the contents of the holdalls to the Hole in the Wall gang for £200.

RUC detectives learned from their informer in the Hole in the Wall gang about the sale of the stolen items and, within two days, the sub-machine gun was recovered from a garage in Lurgan. There was no sign of the other items but the Browning pistol was located about a week later. Detectives felt it was only a matter of time before they recovered all the items. However, when Special Branch and 14th Int. were told detectives had an informer and knew where the Hole in the Wall gang was based, CID was removed from the case. The two intelligence agencies then mounted their own surveillance on the gang. There was a suspicion within intelligence circles that criminals were buying immunity from IRA punishment squads by giving them documents stolen from military vehicles. It was decided the criminal fraternity should be taught a lesson. The subsequent killing of three members of the gang was, in my opinion, calculated and cynical. It was ordered in the knowledge that the three men were planning the robbery of the bookmaker's, using replica weapons. The gang member who was shot at point-blank range in the car was in effect executed.

BBC Northern Ireland's *Spotlight* department decided to investigate the circumstances leading up to the triple killing. That was why I was interviewed at home. The programme was completed, but it was not broadcast on schedule. When it was televised, my contribution had been removed. It did not come as a surprise to me. The reporter who interviewed me had secretly warned me that, contrary to his wishes, my interview was cut. He was angry because I had been the only writer to investigate the triple killing. The broadcast documentary lacked significant details provided by me. Whether or not the removal of my material, without a reasonable explanation, constituted censorship, might seem debatable. However, there was a lack of editorial transparency – an ingredient central to good investigative journalism. The episode was not an isolated incident during my 18 years in the corporation.

Journalism in the British Isles has survived the ravages of the conflict, especially in prising open a window into the undercover war through a sustained investigation of the history of Brian Nelson. Notable among the journalists who pursued the Nelson story were: John Ware and Peter Taylor of the BBC; David McKittrick, *Independent*; Henry McDonald, *Observer*; Jim Cusack, *Irish Times*; Neil Mackay, *Sunday Herald*; John Murray Brown, *Financial Times*; Jim McDowell and Hugh Jordan, *Sunday World*; Ed Moloney, journalist and author, and the reporting staff at the *Belfast Telegraph*, *Irish News*, *Sunday Life* and *News Letter*. Through their combined efforts, which were often punctuated in some cases by the Ministry of Defence's resort to D notices to kill stories, they ensured that the story remained in the headlines. It was a tale central to an understanding of the philosophy underpinning the dirty war.

Brian Nelson was born in the Shankill area of Belfast in 1947 and grew up a committed loyalist. After serving with the Black Watch Regiment, he returned to Northern Ireland in the mid 1970s and that is when his role as a terrorist agent began. Until intelligence files are made public, and that is unlikely, one can offer several reasons why and how he was recruited by British Military Intelligence. He may have been identified by an MRF-type 'trawling' of British regiments for Ulster-born soldiers to work undercover. Alternatively, he might have been spotted as a potential agent when he joined the ranks of the UDA/UFF. In the light of his history, I prefer the first theory. Whatever the method used to recruit him, he possessed all the attributes required of a terrorist agent. He was a loyalist with military training and he was familiar with the mindset of the men of violence in his own community.

In 1986, while he was with his wife and family in Germany, there was a consensus within MI5 and British Military Intelligence on the need for an agent in the top ranks of the UFF. John McMichael had been a useful conduit for acting on British Intelligence targeting information but there was a need to move operations up a notch. McMichael had become wedded to the prospect of a glittering political future and was spending less time on military strategy. By taking his eye off military operations, he allowed parts of the organisation, especially in West Belfast, to concentrate on racketeering. Worse still, James 'Pratt' Craig was helping the IRA to assassinate leading loyalists and Inner Council Brigadiers were busy lining their pockets from drugs, extortion and rackets. The intelligence apparatus needed someone to keep the pressure on the IRA. In intelligence circles, there was a general belief that the only way to detach the IRA from its bedrock of support was to prove it could not protect the Catholic population. The objective required a robust sectarian murder campaign. There was also value in eliminating senior IRA operatives and members of Sinn Fein to weaken the organisation. Some intelligence analysts argued that a credible loyalist threat would force the IRA into serious talks with the British Government. Finally, if the IRA could be drawn into tribal warfare, the entire community would fear a return to the bloody sectarian days of the early 1970s and pressurise all paramilitaries to lay down their weapons. In future peace talks, it would be important to ensure the IRA was not the main player, otherwise republicans would be in a powerful position to dictate the details of a political settlement.

To an outsider, such a philosophy will appear outrageous, but it has to be understood those running the undercover war from the early '70s operated within a surreal vacuum. There were no effective political or judicial controls on their activities and they were immune to other perspectives. One organisation which felt it needed an effective terrorist agent running UFF operations was the Force Research Unit. It was another of those shadowy bodies spawned by Kitson's theories on counter-insurgency and Black Ops.

I learned about its existence in 1989 while doing research for my book, *Stone Cold*. I believed, as did one of my sources, it was called the Future Research Unit. I became aware of an FRU operation in which armed and masked men abducted a Catholic Queen's University student. He was taken to an unknown facility and tortured. Wires from a battery were attached to his genitals and each time he failed to answer questions about fellow Catholic students satisfactorily the battery was switched on. After several hours, he was unceremoniously dumped from a vehicle in the centre of Belfast. When he told RUC detectives what happened, they suspected he had probably been abducted by loyalists but they were puzzled that he had not been murdered. One detective drew the attention of his colleagues to a description the student provided of the battery used in his torture. It was a special battery used in British military vehicles. A secret police inquiry was launched and detectives visited British Army installations but received little cooperation. Regular Army officers pointed out they had no control over Military Intelligence activities and preferred not to get involved in a police investigation. When one of the detectives, through sheer perseverance, discovered the existence of FRU units, the police inquiry was shut down.

The Force Research Unit, with its motto 'Fishers of Men', was a highly classified grouping known only to Special Branch, MI5, the RUC hierarchy and the British Cabinet. In January 1987, its boss was Colonel Gordon Kerr, a Scotsman described to me as 'an arrogant man with grandiose ideas'. His Army career began with the Gordon Highlanders in 1971 and his first tour of duty, during which he had an intelligence role, was in County Armagh in Northern Ireland. He was university-educated and quickly rose through the ranks. In the mid 1970s, he took courses with the Intelligence Corps and was promoted to Captain. After stints at the British Army's Staff College and the Intelligence Wing in Ashford, Kent, he reached the rank of Major. He was posted to Berlin and returned to Britain in 1986 to take over the Force Research Unit. Like the MRF of the early '70s, FRU personnel were recruited from many branches of the Armed Forces. Its HQ was in a section of Thiepval Barracks, Lisburn, which also housed the offices of the MI5 Northern

Ireland Controller, leaders of 14th Int. and a senior representative of RUC Special Branch. According to a retired Special Branch officer, 'everyone was singing from the same hymn sheet' when Kerr arrived on the scene. The moment news reached Thiepval that Nelson was being pressed back into service, everyone was thrilled. Kerr appeared to have no reservations about Nelson, whose file indicated he was cocky, unpredictable and often indiscreet. My source provided descriptions of Nelson and Kerr.

'Nelson was confident – a bit too pushy at times but he was good. He knew that he had an edge over the Brit element because he was a local and fitted in. He knew exactly how people in loyalism thought and acted. You could say he knew his own value. He had extensive knowledge of paramilitary life and was well respected by the people above him – in the UFF, that is. I told one or two of our people that the only way he would ever get into trouble was if he let his mouth do too much of the talking. We were never that comfortable with him – not that we were running him, if you see what I mean. As for Kerr – well, he was something else. He was typical of the Intel Corps – full of himself, but he did not have the grasp of the situation our people had. He thought he could do whatever he wanted. He was thorough in the sense that he had a mania for putting everything on file – not always the best thing to do. He had a lot more people to satisfy than us. He fitted in to what was an ongoing thing so it's not as if he suddenly went haywire. He probably thought he was doing his best and it's not as if anybody on high told him to get off the tightrope.'

Across the intelligence spectrum, there were multiple bodies running agents and informers, but they did not always share intelligence. It was part of the culture of the secret war. Keeping secrets allowed for deniability when things went wrong. Nelson's return was seen as a good move. It would erode competition among agencies and ensure everyone combined their efforts in the targeting of republicans. Nelson had no qualms about resuming his agent role. A former intelligence operative told me Nelson was thrilled when he was informed his services were vital to the war against terrorism. First he had to be trained for the role his bosses had mapped out for him – Chief of UFF Intelligence. In January 1987, following a meeting with Kerr and a member of MI5 in a London hotel, he was sent to Ashford in Kent to learn computer techniques – the compiling, storing and sharing of intelligence data.

Why were intelligence chiefs so confident Nelson would be automatically appointed to the role of UFF Intelligence Coordinator? It was a post which permitted him to select victims and task trigger men to kill them. The answer is that Special Branch, MI5 and Military

Intelligence were controlling informers and agents in senior levels of the UDA/UFF. John McMichael, the UFF leader, was well connected to the security forces and may have been more than a conduit. As an agent he would have been in the ideal position to insert Nelson into the role required by the intelligence apparatus. McMichael was also second-in-command of the UDA to Andy Tyrie and was a member of the UDA's ruling Inner Council. I spoke to a former senior UVF gunman about the positioning of Nelson. My interview with him appears below. I began by asking if the UDA/UFF leadership knew Nelson was a British agent when he returned to Belfast in April 1987.

> A. For starters, you have to understand that Nelson was not seen as anything but a committed loyalist – that's my reading. If you look at it arse about face – I mean now that everybody knows what he was – you miss the point. You don't see the real picture. I think, when he came back in '87 that people in the UDA knew his pedigree. He was one of our own.

> Q. How much did they know?

> A. [*Laughs*] You're asking a Blackneck?
> [*At the outset of the Troubles, UDA men called members of the UVF 'Blacknecks' because they wore black pullovers which, when later worn with leather jackets, became the UVF's dress style for media photographs.*]

> Q. You must have heard something about Nelson?

> A. I heard on the grapevine he was a serious operator. I also heard he was close to John McMichael and Andy Tyrie. You know they ran the show.

> Q. Could either of them have known he was a military agent?

> A. Look here, there was always a connection between the Crown Forces and our people in the war against the IRA. Nobody scrutinised it too much. You don't bite off the hand that feeds you. That didn't mean we tolerated informers because that was a different thing. That was somebody selling you out. The UDA had more of a problem with informers than us because they had head-bangers and too many criminals. Those guys were easily turned by the RUC.

Q. What I'm trying to get at is an understanding of how an agent was likely to be viewed.

A. I know exactly what you're about. As I said, you don't bite off the hand that feeds you. If you take information from a member of the Crown Forces and it's good and keeps coming, you don't turn your back on it, especially if it serves your purpose. Am I making myself clear?

Q. Are you saying that if Special Branch or Military Intelligence had been running someone in the UVF, you would not have known the person was an agent and, even if you did, it would not have mattered to you?

A. [*Laughs*] Listen. If a guy has information that helps you target the enemy you are not going to worry no matter where he is getting it from. Are you gonna say that guy's an agent because he has good sources? No fucking way. The means is just as vital as the end. It doesn't matter who provides information as long as it fulfils your objectives.

Q. So, no one would have suspected or thought of investigating Nelson's sources and loyalties as long as he did the job?

A. I'll go with that. What he was doing was killing the enemy, so who cared?

Q. Even if the information could only have come from the intelligence community?

A. If the Crown Forces wanted people dead and wanted us to do it, we were the people to do it. We had the same enemy.

Q. If McMichael and Andy Tyrie appointed Nelson is there any way they would have known his employers were the Ministry of Defence?

A. John was a very shrewd guy. Not too much got by him. You'd have to be very sure of somebody to appoint him to the job they gave Nelson. I'm getting to your point. You'd have to know what he'd done in the past for you. I'd say you'd know if he was well connected to the Branch or intelligence personnel. You might know he's well connected, if you get my drift, and that might suit you.

Q. What if McMichael or Andy Tyrie were so well connected that other people persuaded them to make Nelson their targeting man?

A. I don't wanna go there.

Q. But you said nothing mattered but the objective.

A. Yes, but in any organisation you like to be in charge of your own destiny.

Q. Let me try and understand that. You're saying that it's fine to have close relations with the intelligence community, especially in the lower ranks, but leaders of organisations should not be controlled by what you call the Crown Forces.

A. [*Angry*] Look, I can't speak for the UFF. Let me tell you that John McMichael was a patriot.

Q. I wasn't questioning his patriotism. I just wanted to know if some people in loyalism believed he was an agent.

A. All right. The danger about having someone like Nelson running an organisation is that people outside its ranks own it. That's not good. I know what you're getting at about John. I heard some rumours – but they were only rumours – that John was bumped off to let Nelson run the show and people with an agenda had 'Pratt' Craig tip off the Provos about certain things so they went after John. By the time Nelson was back on the scene in '87, John was trying to wrest back control and instil discipline. Some people thought he'd let things slip because he'd been bitten by the political bug and saw himself as another Gerry Adams. It's dangerous waters and best left alone. I've nothing more to say to you on this subject.

I was informed that Brian Nelson met John McMichael and Andy Tyrie on his arrival in Belfast in April 1987. Assuming both men were unaware of his other intelligence role, he must have been very persuasive or his record in terrorism was sufficient for them to sign off on him becoming the UFF chief of targeting. Whatever their reasons for approving him, he had been well briefed by his other bosses about what the UDA/UFF expected from him.

The FRU set him up as a mini-cab driver, which permitted him to travel freely throughout the city, particularly in republican areas. Colonel Gordon Kerr appointed two supervisors as his handlers. One of them was Sergeant Margaret Walshore, nicknamed 'Maggs'. She was described to me by a Special Branch source as a 'hard case'. The role of the handlers was to set up a weekly rendezvous with Nelson to allow them time to brief him, to retrieve information from him and provide whatever intelligence and assistance he required. From the outset, he enjoyed boasting about his exploits. As an indigenous agent, he wanted to prove to his handlers he had an edge over them. He recounted stories about his trips into the Falls, Andersonstown, Ardoyne and New Lodge. Like 'Mad Dog' Adair, he was arrogant and cocky. He desperately wanted to play a personal role in the killing process and did so by undertaking surveillance on republican suspects and checking their locations and addresses.

In late spring of '87, McMichael told him about his ongoing investigation of James 'Pratt' Craig and identified the best UFF operatives, most of them from the Shankill area. McMichael gave him more than 1,000 security forces files; the accumulation of years of collusion. The files contained surveillance notes, maps, photographs and the addresses and family histories of known members of the IRA and Sinn Fein. They also comprised intelligence on suspected republicans and people who had been seen in the company of republicans. Nelson, through his own surveillance work and feedback from UFF gunmen who had unsuccessfully tried to use the information he provided, realised many of McMichael's files were out of date. Some people in the files were dead, dozens were in prison and others had moved home a decade earlier. Nelson was frustrated and relayed his feelings to the FRU. Colonel Kerr arranged for all of the files to be transported to his HQ at Thiepval. They were given to FRU analysts who checked them against their computerised records. Irrelevant files were set aside, others were updated and Nelson was provided with a new batch of documents. He then meticulously created his own filing system. Each target was accorded an index card with a photograph attached to it. The card contained a target's address, known haunts, friends and daily routine.

On 22 December, the Provisional IRA assassinated John McMichael. Nelson quickly acquired all McMichael's personal files, including one on James 'Pratt' Craig. McMichael's departure allowed Nelson even greater independence. Michael Stone, one of McMichael's favourite trigger men, quickly came to Nelson's attention. As I pointed out earlier, it was through Stone that Nelson and the FRU almost achieved their goal of wiping out the IRA/Sinn Fein leadership in Milltown Cemetery in March 1988. When the plan failed, Nelson turned to the UFF in North and West Belfast. Two of the killings he ordered in May and September illustrated the cynical nature of his work. In May, UFF gunmen shot Terry McDaid, mistaking him for his brother, and, four months later, 21-year-old Gerard Slane was shot seven times in front of his wife in their home. Both victims were Catholics. They were not members of Sinn Fein or the IRA. When Nelson was unable to find UFF gunmen to carry out a killing, he turned to the UVF. He also supplied the UVF with up-to-date files on members of Sinn Fein in return for a quantity of explosives.

A month after the murder of Gerard Slane, James 'Pratt' Craig was lured into East Belfast and killed. As I stated in the chapter on Craig, Nelson provided the UDA Inner Council with a secretly recorded Special Branch videotape of Craig meeting a leading IRA man. It was the compelling evidence which encouraged UDA leaders to approve Craig's assassination. In the wake of McMichael's death, Nelson had carefully studied the late UFF boss's notes on Craig. One thing was clear. Craig was a threat to Nelson's operations because of his links to the Provisionals and the INLA. In particular, Craig had assisted the IRA in killing Lenny Murphy, John Bingham, McMichael and other loyalist hard men. Nelson and his FRU bosses suspected Craig was just as likely to buy himself immunity from RUC detectives by revealing information about killings orchestrated by the FRU and Nelson. The FRU decided Craig was expendable. They argued that with him out of the way it would be easier to deal directly with C Company because Craig had always insisted he controlled his own turf and no one used his people without his approval. Four months after his death, UFF trigger men from C Company, acting on Nelson's orders, gunned down a Catholic solicitor, Pat Finucane. It was a killing which would eventually haunt Nelson and those running the State's undercover war.

Finucane, a Catholic, was one of the most brilliant lawyers in Northern Ireland. He was analytical and meticulous and possessed a genuine desire to seek justice for all his clients. He was fortunate to have a formidable staff in the firm of Madden & Finucane. One of his colleagues was Eamann McMenamin, a gifted civil rights lawyer. Like the vast majority of solicitors in the Province, Finucane was guided by the principle that every accused, irrespective of his or her religion, had a right to a fair hearing. The majority of his clients were from within the Catholic community but it was not a factor of his making. From the outset of the Troubles, people charged with terrorist-type offences gravitated towards solicitors from their own community. It was an innately tribal aspect of the society and was not fostered by the legal professions. Nor did the phenomenon in any way detract from the integrity of lawyers on both sides. There were many exceptions to the rule. Finucane's friend, Pascal O'Hare, was part of the defence team representing the Shankill Butchers, and Desmond Boal, a close friend of Ian Paisley, was Senior Counsel for republicans.

Only a few solicitors crossed the line and became intricately connected to paramilitaries. When writing *The Dirty War* I uncovered documents about a solicitor who regularly received cash from the UVF. In return, he visited UVF prisoners when they were being interrogated and, if they were cooperating with the authorities, he informed the UVF leadership. Finucane represented republicans but was not in the pay of the IRA, nor did he act to suit an IRA agenda. The security authorities perceived him as a threat because he successfully defended men they preferred to see incarcerated for a long time. Finucane knew the judicial system was often loaded against his clients. It was virtually impossible to force Special Branch officers, RUC interrogators, members of MI5 or soldiers to appear in court to be cross-examined on statements they made to prosecution lawyers. The interrogation process and the use of informers made it difficult to construct a reasonable defence. The Crown Prosecution Service frequently withheld documentation from solicitors for 'reasons of national security'. At a higher level, the Ministry of Defence relied on a range of ploys to keep undercover soldiers, agents, informers and Special Branch officers out of the courts.

Finucane had extensive knowledge of the workings of the intelligence apparatus and told clients not to discuss their cases while in custody or on remand. They were only to talk to him or a solicitor in his firm. He had learned from bitter experience that Special Branch, in order to learn his defence strategy, had placed informers in the company of his clients while they were in custody awaiting trial.

One of his major skills was his methodical approach to his job. He told his staff success depended on recognising there was always a 'paper-trail'. During inquests, which many lawyers viewed as a meaningless process, he cleverly saw value in the vast array of documents connected with deaths. For him, the documents were the genesis of a trail. For example, if an RUC inquest document was listed as 5A, he went in search of 1A, etc. His instinct was analytical, not conspiratorial. He always wanted to know what was contained in documents withheld from inquests. To achieve this end, he used the full resources of the law. The large numbers of hidden documents he acquired enabled him to force members of Special Branch into court – something they deeply resented. No Special Branch officer wanted to be questioned about the shadowy world in which he worked or to perjure himself to hide evidence. As a consequence, cases against some of Finucane's clients were dropped to protect the identities of members of Special Branch and the Military. A friend of Finucane provided me with a description of how he operated.

'He was very methodical and clinical. Sometimes when he received documents under disclosure, he was astonished by what they contained. Bureaucrats in the RUC who handled his requests had never before been asked to produce documents. By mistake, they often included papers of significance. Special Branch officers did not like being cross-examined because they had never had to face questioning under oath. The more success Pat had, the more enemies he made.'

When he won compensation for a republican client, he would sometimes laugh and tell the client to book a holiday and send a postcard to the Special Branch officer in the case. Some clients followed his advice. If he believed the judicial system had failed any of his clients, he sought redress in the European Human Rights Court, bringing further scrutiny to the activities of undercover operatives.

One of his enemies was MI5, the internal Security Service. In 1988, three years before his death, MI5 had a personal file on him. Alongside his name was the letter 'P' to indicate MI5 regarded him as a member of the Provisional IRA. Several other Catholic solicitors were named in the same file but there was no 'P' against their names. The MI5 definition of Finucane was based on bogus information provided by RUC Special Branch. However, that in no way shifts blame from MI5, which had its own informers in Northern Ireland and should have known better. It also had a Controller working alongside the FRU and other parts of the intelligence apparatus at Thiepval Barracks, Lisburn. The defining of Finucane as a terrorist was the beginning of a dangerous process. It provided the basis for mounting surveillance on him and ultimately led to his murder.

His telephones were bugged and a covert observation post was set up opposite his Belfast offices. Film was shot of everyone entering and leaving his offices and their identities checked with terrorist files at Thiepval Barracks. His home in North Belfast was watched and he was followed on a trip to the United States. While in the USA, a dossier was compiled on everyone he met and where he stayed. The FRU also built a profile of him, starting with his days as a student at Trinity College in Dublin. In 2003, an RUC detective, who went to Trinity with Finucane, tried to tell me Finucane had IRA connections but failed to provide evidence to substantiate his claim. The same detective had been present at the interrogation of Francis Hughes, who later died on hunger strike.

Pat Finucane knew he was being watched and accepted it was one of the risks of his profession. However, a court case in late 1988 decided his fate. Instead of hiring Counsel, he decided to personally defend a former hunger-striker, Patrick McGeown, who was accused of involvement in the killing of Corporals Howes and Wood – both FRU operatives. Finucane believed the Crown case against his client was based on flimsy evidence. More than 30 people had been charged in connection with the double murder and many were acquitted. In order to undermine the Prosecution, he cleverly relied on a British Army video filmed from a helicopter on the day the soldiers were dragged from their car, beaten and shot. His strategy succeeded and he left the courtroom hand-in-hand with a grateful client.

Special Branch, which had helped build the combined intelligence data on Finucane, met with the RUC Chief Constable, Sir John 'Jack' Hermon, in the autumn of 1988. They stressed urgent action should be taken against Finucane and other Catholic solicitors. They singled out Finucane and two others, one of them Paddy McCrory (who has since died), a highly respected solicitor. Special Branch chiefs told Hermon that Finucane and other Catholic solicitors were getting access to sensitive documents and the process had to be interdicted. Hermon asked for a detailed report on the matter. The RUC Chief Constable was one of the controversial figures of the Troubles. He was fiercely supportive of the undercover war and resented any scrutiny or criticism of his force, including Special Branch. In 1984, he had deeply resented the English police officer John Stalker's investigation into allegations of a shoot-to-kill policy and the activities of the E4 department.

In 1988, the Ministry of Defence also believed that Catholic lawyers were a problem and were not legally entitled to ask for sensitive documents under disclosure. That was a view at variance with the law. MOD legal advisers and intelligence chiefs were frustrated when classified documents were handed over. They knew it invariably meant the Prosecution had to drop charges to prevent the documents being introduced as evidence in open court. In such an event, the media would have been free to scrutinise the documents and pursue stories related to them. When charges were dropped against Finucane's clients, he was free to pursue civil actions against the RUC and the MOD.

When Hermon received the report from Special Branch, it contained a false accusation that Finucane had smuggled a gun into Crumlin Road prison to assist an escape by Provisionals awaiting trial. The Special Branch document had transcripts of wiretaps on the lawyer's telephones and details of the videotaping of other lawyers. For example, Special Branch had filmed

Paddy McCrory, one of those lawyers on the MI5 file, having lunch with Pascal O'Hare in the Kitchen Bar in the centre of Belfast. There was nothing sinister in the meeting. It was two well-known lawyers having a chat.

RUC Chief Constable Sir John 'Jack' Hermon took the report to London where he met senior figures from the Ministry of Defence. No record of his meeting with them is available or ever likely to be made public. Directly stemming from it, Douglas Hogg, the Junior Home Office Minister, made a statement in the House of Commons. He declared that 'there are a number of solicitors in Northern Ireland who are unduly sympathetic to the IRA'.

There can be little doubt that Hogg was briefed about the identity of the solicitors he referred to. It was a reprehensible act on his part, even though some of his parliamentary friends later claimed he was misled. His House of Commons statement effectively endangered the lives of all Catholic lawyers. It was heard loud and clear in loyalist circles. Pat Finucane's son, Michael, later described Hogg's comments as 'more chilling' than the other threats his father received. It provided loyalist paramilitaries with a justification for killing solicitors deemed by the British Government to be 'fellow-travellers' with the IRA.

In December 1988, Special Branch arranged for the arrest of leading loyalist trigger men who were taken to Castlereagh on the pretext that they were going to be questioned about terrorist crimes. But Special Branch had a more sinister objective. During questioning, one trigger man asked his interrogator: 'Who the fuck is Finucane?' In the history of interrogations at Castlereagh, it was not unusual for a Special Branch officer to arrive in a room and place a photograph of a republican suspect in front of a UFF or UVF gunman. A comment would then be made to the effect: 'Why have your people not targeted him?'

At the beginning of January 1989, Brian Nelson placed Finucane on his target list and supplied C Company trigger men with a copy of a newspaper photograph of Finucane outside court with his client, Pat McGeown. Nelson was so intensely committed to killing the solicitor, he personally carried out surveillance on his Somerton Road home in North Belfast. That was only discovered years later when investigators travelled to Canada and interviewed a couple who had lived beside Finucane in 1989. They were shown a photograph of Nelson and recognised him as a man they had observed in the days prior to the assassination of the solicitor. They astounded investigators by telling them they saw Nelson cleaning windows in the row of houses where Finucane lived.

On the evening he died, Pat Finucane was sitting down to a meal in the kitchen of his home. His lack of security allowed three UFF gunmen from C Company to burst into the hallway of his house. With a fork in his hand, he rushed from the table to block the gunmen, pushing closed an opaque-glass door linking the kitchen to the hallway. As he reached the door, he was shot and fell. One of the killers pushed open the door even though Finucane's body lay against it. In the kitchen the killers shot him repeatedly in the face and chest in front of his wife, Geraldine. In all, 14 bullets hit him. The killers acted with ferocity. Detectives, who later arrived on the scene, concluded that the killers had shot him repeatedly out of a personal revenge. The gunmen knew the hit had the approval of the authorities and took their time shooting him. The murder of Finucane had the hallmarks of other killings I have outlined in this book – Bunting, Lyttle, Miriam Daly, etc.

The solicitor's death renewed calls from Catholic politicians and the Irish Government for an inquiry into allegations of collusion between the security forces and loyalist paramilitaries. In the wake of the murder, the Nelson saga became murkier. At the home of Tommy 'Tucker' Lyttle, a close confidant of the UDA leader, Andy Tyrie, a journalist was given documents which demonstrated collusion between the security forces and the UDA/UFF. Brian Nelson was present at the meeting. Lyttle subsequently claimed the leaking of documents was aimed at damaging the RUC for targeting loyalists. A long-time friend of John McMichael and Andy Tyrie, the UDA chairman, Lyttle was a Special Branch asset for almost two decades. From a casual observer's point of view, the handing over of sensitive intelligence files to a journalist was counter-productive. It exposed a linkage between loyalist terrorists and their sources of information. It had the immediate effect of raising public awareness of collusion and led to the appointment of the English policeman, John Stevens, and his first inquiry into the undercover war. One may ask who ultimately benefited from the handing over of those files and the answer is MI5. Three years later, it was given the primary role in security and intelligence gathering in the United Kingdom and told to reorganise and clean up the intelligence apparatus. In the aftermath of the Cold War, MI5 had plenty of spare capacity to undertake such a task.

A retired intelligence officer told me that, after Finucane's murder, staff at MI5 HQ in London believed the dirty war in Northern Ireland would sooner or later unravel. They suggested an inquiry would clear out 'the dead wood' within the intelligence apparatus. The RUC as a police force would be cleared of wrong-doing and the UDR would take the biggest hit. The result would be the merging of the UDR with a standard British Regiment. British Army oversight of the UDR was vital if it was to survive the ravages of two decades of criticism from Catholics and the Irish Government. Military Intelligence would also be dealt a blow but that was no bad thing since it had too many 'cowboy' operators. Special Branch and groups like the anti-terrorist squad at Scotland Yard would come under the control of MI5 and everyone would be satisfied. If those were MI5's objectives, to some extent they were realised. However, MI5 failed to anticipate that attempts to cover up Nelson and the FRU's role in killings were bound to fail. My source made the observation: 'In 1988, personnel in the Security Service in London had become concerned about the way things were being run in Northern Ireland. Over the years, they had run their own agents in Ireland and didn't share them with others. The Northern Ireland Controller was worried about the operational policies of the FRU, 14th Int. and RUC Special Branch. I think those calling the shots in London were naive in believing they could manipulate the situation and initiate a clean-up that benefited them without any fall-out. The leaking of the documents was not at Nelson's instigation and it opened up a can of worms. I heard that MI5 big-wigs believed Stevens could be contained and they were wrong because the arrival of Stevens created a momentum and before long the media had their teeth in the story. But Five will survive the storm and there will be sacrificial lambs to satisfy the hounds.'

Stevens and his team of investigators quickly focused on the UDA/UFF and rounded up men like Tommy 'Tucker' Lyttle. As 'Mad Dog' Adair later pointed out in one of his interrogation sessions, the arrests of men like Lyttle benefited the UDA/UFF. It removed men who were informers and armchair generals and allowed for the emergence of young militants like Adair. Lyttle tried to cut a deal with Stevens and was turned down. In the meantime, Nelson was tipped off by the FRU and two handlers were sent to his home to collect all his computerised files and index charts. He was spirited out of Northern Ireland and his documents were removed to Palace Barracks. The choice of Palace Barracks to hide FRU files was to ensure that if there were a search of FRU HQ at Thiepval Barracks in Lisburn, incriminating evidence would not be there.

Stevens' personnel raided UDA HQ and found Nelson's fingerprints on documents but Nelson was at the Army Intelligence Wing in Ashford, England, being debriefed. The MOD knew, sooner rather than later, they would have to hand him over to Stevens. First, they needed to prep him about how to deal with Stevens and his investigators.

FRU boss Colonel Gordon Kerr believed his organisation would weather the storm and return to business as usual. He told colleagues everything would be fine after Stevens exhausted his search for incriminating evidence. Kerr forgot several important details about his agent. Nelson's file indicated he was cocky, unpredictable and often indiscreet. Nelson was not going to take a fall for anyone. As one of Kerr's staff later put it, Nelson was an 'unguided missile'. On orders from his superiors, Nelson flew back to Belfast and turned himself over to Stevens. He was placed in Crumlin Road prison and subjected to myriad questions. MI5 officers were also interviewed and signed statements claiming they were unaware of collusion with loyalist paramilitaries. It was a deliberate lie. MI5 knew that two of Finucane's killers were Special Branch agents.

While Nelson was being interviewed, Kerr suddenly began to feel the heat. He photocopied all the FRU's 'Secret Books' and lodged a copy with a German lawyer. It was insurance in the event the 'legal hammer' should ever fall on him. Like Nelson, he had no desire to be a sacrificial lamb. Stevens discovered Kerr was a typical bureaucrat and filed everything. He asked the Colonel to hand over all his documentation. The request was ignored for nine months. It was a calculated ploy by the intelligence top brass to allow them time to find out what Nelson was divulging to the Stevens Inquiry team. The withholding of the documents also gave Kerr time to sanitise his files so as to ensure that when he eventually handed them over, the information contained in them exactly matched Nelson's confessions to Stevens' investigators. It was a cynical manipulation of the judicial process and it had the backing of people at the very highest levels of the intelligence world and the British Ministry of Defence. Every effort was made to hamper Stevens and his staff, including the firebombing of their offices inside a secure police facility. The firebombing destroyed a considerable amount of evidence which Stevens and his team had collated.

On January 1990, Nelson made a statement to Stevens implicating himself in murder. He asked for an immunity deal in return for providing information on what he called 'other matters'. Stevens referred the request to the office of the Director of Public Prosecutions and it was rejected. Secret visits, of the kind made to Albert Walker Baker in 1972, were made to Nelson in his cell in Crumlin Road prison. Among those who saw him were intelligence personnel and representatives of the Army's legal department.

By the time he appeared in court in 1991, a deal had been done behind the scenes. The deal followed efforts at the highest levels of the British Military and the MOD to persuade judicial authorities to let him go. It was never an option in the light of the public scrutiny of his arrest. Nonetheless, the legal deal was regarded by the MOD as an ideal smokescreen to conceal the past. Two murder charges were dropped and Nelson pleaded guilty to a lesser charge of conspiracy to murder. His guilty plea was to prevent a hearing of the evidence and to thwart the media from investigating the FRU. It worked. Colonel Gordon Kerr took the witness stand as 'Colonel J'. He told the judge, Sir Basil Kelly, a former Unionist Attorney General under the old Stormont regime, that Nelson was a 'courageous man'. He stressed Nelson had always been loyal to the British Army and not the UDA. He had saved the lives of over 200 people, including Gerry Adams, the Provisional Sinn Fein leader. It was a carefully stage-managed performance by the FRU chief who also told the court no guidelines existed for the running of agents. In the context of Northern Ireland, he argued, agents were bound to become involved in criminality. Moral responsibility, he said, lay with the system, which had not found ways of coming to terms with the problems faced by an agent.

The judge was clearly impressed by the Kerr gospel and testimony. He sentenced Nelson to ten years in prison. To no one's surprise, Nelson was granted the right to serve his sentence in an English facility. Within three years, he was a free man living with his wife and family in Germany and later in England. One has to ask why Nelson was not charged with the murder of Pat Finucane and why the Director of Public Prosecutions did not seek an investigation into the killing after Stevens told him Nelson admitted involvement in it? An equally important issue is why the DPP did not authorise Stevens to mount a separate inquiry into the murder. Why were efforts not made to use Nelson as a Prosecution witness against a range of UFF trigger men whom he had used in more than ten murders?

Inaction on all those fronts can be attributed to the determination of the Ministry of Defence in London to hide the truth and hope the Nelson saga would fade in the public arena, as well as in the journalistic world. In 1992, Finucane's widow, Geraldine, decided she wanted the facts known. Through Madden & Finucane, her late husband's firm, she served a writ on the MOD for the unlawful killing of her husband by Brian Nelson. It was a clever legal ploy because of the way it played out and what was revealed. Nelson learned of the writ and the real possibility that he could eventually end up in court being cross-examined about the Finucane murder and other matters. He had no intention of becoming a sacrificial lamb and let it be known to the MOD that if they did not settle with Geraldine Finucane he would blow the lid on all his terrorist crimes as an agent of the State. The MOD had no desire to see the history of Nelson's involvement in terror being played out in a civil suit. It allowed judgement to be made against Nelson. In layman's terms, the MOD accepted responsibility for Nelson's murder of Finucane. By early summer of 2003, damages had not been assessed for the unlawful killing of Pat Finucane. However, Geraldine Finucane's legal strategy forced the MOD to silence Nelson and accept blame for his actions. The MOD's capitulation to pressure illustrated how desperate they were to ensure that Nelson kept his mouth shut. Clearly he was a 'loose cannon' who held the key to even more damaging revelations about his MOD career.

Thanks to superb investigating by John Ware at the BBC the lid was lifted off the Nelson saga before a third Stevens Inquiry was completed at the end of 2002. The likelihood is that much of the undercover war will never be opened up to scrutiny. There will, however, be sacrificial lambs as a result of the three inquiries. After the first Stevens' investigation, Gordon Kerr was awarded the military version of the Order of the British Empire and promoted to Brigadier. In 2002, John Ware tracked him down to Beijing where he was British Military Attaché, a very senior diplomatic post. Kerr refused to talk to Ware.

In 2003, I discovered that several Special Branch officers had travelled to the Irish Republic and secretly provided detailed statements about their undercover roles to Irish Government legal representatives. Like Kerr and Nelson, the Special Branch officers wanted insurance – allies in the event they should be sacrificed on the altar of political expediency. In 2002 and 2003, senior figures in RUC Special Branch warned that if they were made scapegoats for two decades of the British Military's secret war, the British Government would be opening a 'Pandora's Box'. Perhaps that is exactly what needs to happen. Special Branch should not be the only organisation, or considered the only one, which had 'bad apples' in its ranks and was engaged in a dirty war in which the rule of law was set aside. Thanks to journalists in Britain and Ireland, the story will not be buried and demands for transparency will continue to be heard.

Brian Nelson died in the spring of 2003, taking with him to the grave the story of the years we know little about and his killing spree on the orders of the Force Research Unit. His passing will make it easier for some of the guilty men to single him out as the major culprit as a means of hiding their own guilt. His death was timely for those determined to ensure that he never gave up his secrets. As he showed when Geraldine Finucane went after him, he had the power to threaten the MOD to settle with her. No doubt there will be conspiracy theories about his death, especially in the light of the fact that many intelligence agencies throughout the world have the capability to make deaths appear to be the consequence of suicide or of a particular illness. In this case no such evidence has been found, but how fortunate it is for many in power that Nelson has taken damaging evidence to his grave.

Detective Sergeant 'Jonty' Johnston Brown featured prominently in the third Stevens Inquiry. He provided critical evidence of the role of Special Branch in the murder of Pat Finucane. His courage in breaching the wall of silence surrounding undercover operations earned him threats from Special Branch officers and UFF trigger men. However, many policemen respected his willingness to tell the truth. His actions were exactly what the RUC required to restore public confidence in policing and the rule of law.

In the spring of 2003 there was a media feeding frenzy, not about the possible outcome of the Stevens Inquiry number three, but about an alleged British spy codenamed 'Stakeknife', who, it was claimed, had been in the upper echelons of the Provisional IRA for almost two decades. The intense media scrutiny of the Finucane murder and the history of collusion which Stevens had investigated for 12 years was taken off the front pages of newspapers.

For journalists throughout the British Isles and in the USA, 'Stakeknife' was a juicy, more enticing yarn with the potential to eclipse the Stevens' revelations about FRU-sponsored assassinations. 'Stakeknife' was a tale which had been in cold storage waiting for an injection of information to give it a new lease of life. It provided an opportunity for parts of the British Intelligence apparatus to limit damage caused by the Nelson affair and to erode the media's appetite for more information on the murders of innocents like Finucane. The dynamic for invigorating the story of an elusive spy codenamed 'Stakeknife' began with an allegation that 'Stakeknife' was 57-year-old Freddie Scappaticci, a builder living in the Andersonstown area of Belfast.

A journalistic argument for going public about the identity of 'Stakeknife' was that Scappaticci had a dubious past and was unlikely to sue. If he did, the argument went, his past would limit libel damages. The unsubstantiated allegations about him alleged that, in the role of 'Stakeknife', he was responsible for the deaths of many innocent people and had compromised major IRA operations over two decades. According to other printed reports, he had been a member of the IRA's Internal Security Department – a body with the role of hunting down informers in the IRA's ranks. Scappaticci was indeed an IRA mole-hunter and that was a fact in the midst of some wild media speculation. IRA personnel involved in that aspect of the dirty war were enforcers. Suspected informers were often tortured for information before being shot, their bodies dumped in alleyways or border roads.

Few journalists asked what British Intelligence operatives hoped to achieve by outing a man whom they claimed was one of their most valuable agents in the IRA. As such, if it were true, he was an employee of the British Ministry of Defence. At best, it was a curious anomaly that the MOD should expose Scappaticci when they had gone to extreme lengths, including the contravention of the judicial process, to protect Brian Nelson. I wondered if the 'Stakeknife' story and the naming of

Scappaticci were designed to divert attention from other issues. In my experience an ingrained feature of the dirty war was the policy of the intelligence apparatus to leak bogus information, truths and half-truths.

I came across the 'Stakeknife' story several years ago in the United States in the context of private assertions by a journalist-writer who said sources he had nurtured within the Northern Ireland security apparatus told him they had a high-ranking mole in the IRA. The journalist-writer further alleged that the IRA had decided to end its campaign because it had been so deeply penetrated by terrorist agents, in particular by a mole in the higher echelons of the organisation. I was dubious about those claims because they did not accurately reflect the reasons why the IRA first declared a ceasefire and later talked about decommissioning. I also knew that there had been many informers and moles in the ranks of the IRA but not one single terrorist agent or informer responsible for crippling the organisation's potential to continue its campaign of violence. I believe the information conveyed to me in the USA was the genesis of what became the 'Stakeknife' saga.

When the 'Stakeknife' story hit the headlines in the UK and in New York in the spring of 2003, I detected a reluctance on the part of some journalists to ask who was likely to benefit from the revelations. For my part, I understood such a question was an integral element of any serious journalistic investigation. There was a simple answer. British Intelligence, especially those who ran the dirty war. As soon as the story about 'Stakeknife' broke, it eroded ongoing journalistic investigations into the history of the three Stevens' inquiries. Stevens, much to the concern of the men in the shadows of the Intelligence environment, had opened a window into their world and what lurked there was unpleasant and devastating. Journalists were encouraged to question the secret policies implemented by British Intelligence services over three decades. A friend suggested to me that 'Stakeknife' was a story about the fog of war and not a smokescreen created by British Intelligence. I replied, 'The so-called fog of war is often a smokescreen designed by some of the combatants to hide their role in a conflict.' Throughout the British Isles, and in North America, the 'Stakeknife' revelations focused attention on the IRA and its past use of enforcers within its Internal Security Department. Those enforcers sometimes killed innocent Catholics wrongly accused of collaborating with the security forces. Families of victims shot as informers quickly demanded a public inquiry to determine if 'Stakeknife', as alleged in media reports, had sacrificed innocent people to protect his spy role. In other words, had he deliberately identified innocent men as informers and killed them to obscure his agent status? It was not an unreasonable demand from the families of victims. Innocent people had been sacrificed to protect terrorist agents. Earlier in this book, I dealt with an IRA operative murdered to maintain the credibility of Brendan Davison, who had been a terrorist agent working within the IRA Internal Security Department. In that sense, there was nothing new in the story of 'Stakeknife' until Scappaticci was identified as the elusive spy.

Those responsible for the 'outing' of Scappaticci knew their story had legs. It had an element which would prove true with a little journalistic investigation. Friends telephoned me in New York to ask me what I thought about the 'astonishing revelations'. I told them to reserve judgment because propaganda, lies and half-truths were weapons in a dirty war. I warned that one element of truth in a story can often be the mechanism for deception. I then spoke to a retired CIA source who had worked in the Middle East, and asked him for his analysis of the 'Stakeknife' saga.

'Modern conflict is as much about conditioning public opinion as any other strategy in the war against terror. Of course, it's imperative that you damage the enemy's reputation and that can be achieved with carefully crafted stories. The stratagem can only be successful if you understand how the media operates. As a rule, the media is fickle and will devour a story that has the right elements. The story has not got to be true but it has to have elements of truth – enough to give it a punch. If it falls flat, you damage the likelihood of your journalistic sources accepting future stories from you. If you are deliberately manufacturing a story it must have ingredients that will emerge with some media investigation. That is enough because stories about terrorism or espionage are never going to be fully exposed. Everyone knows that and accepts it. That's where you have the cutting edge of success. A cardinal rule when people in my business examine stories in the media from unnamed sources is to ask what is the intended effect – what did the terrorist who briefed the reporter hope to achieve? That is important because it can help us identify a specific terror organisation or the source of the article. It's not rocket science but a measured analysis. The media is always looking for a new angle on a story and media deadlines are time critical so it's not difficult to insert material into media outlets, knowing it will not be subjected to too much rigorous scrutiny. Journalists have a hard time because time is a luxury. If I give you a story which is 50 per cent true, I would expect you to at least run with it and make your own inquiries. Even if you do not print it, you will have spoken to other people and the story will become common currency. Somebody will pick it up once it's out there. If I drop below 50, you're gonna be suspicious. But, if I give you something which is 80 per cent true, you're gonna buy me a Martini. Why? Because in the world of terrorism it is not always possible for journalists to substantiate every allegation, so there is a degree to which journalists and their editors compromise to beat up on the opposition by getting a story out first.

'Linkage is all important in crafting a lie – linkage means that your story should be perceived to be reasonably interconnected with others out there because those other stories are an accepted reality. That will tend to give the story I leak to you a greater impetus and ring of truth. Not all half-truths are lies and it is often necessary to cleverly construct half-truths to get your point across or divert attention from something you would prefer not to be scrutinised. The apostle, Thomas, was the first forensic scientist because he wanted evidence and he was right on the button. He asked if he could put his finger into Christ's wounds. There are not too many apostles like that in the media and even fewer on the streets. Why do you think propaganda is a major tool in the war against terrorism? It is about winning hearts and minds away from the terrorists and if that has to be achieved with some manipulation of the facts, so what? The end goal is what matters.

'This "Stakeknife" you talk about may be a figment of someone's creative imagination. Equally, he may exist and to protect his real identity someone else is fingered. There is always the possibility the "Stakeknife" story is true but intelligence services rarely sacrifice their own people. It's not good for business – for recruitment, if you get my drift. You have to look deeper for what the story means, what it conveys and what it's likely to achieve. You may not find the right answers but your search may warn you to be careful about what you instinctively believe. I should also tell you that this "Stakeknife" story might not be intended for immediate effect. It could be out there to produce longer-term consequences for those who have leaked it. What you read 24/7 or see on the screen may not impact your life but it can have a debilitating effect on your particular commitment to an ideal or arouse deep suspicions you have about a particular ideology.

'When people talk about a world of mirrors, they fail to grasp that the mirrors are a two-way device. There is another aspect to all of this that you should consider and that is the appetite out there for such a story. There may well be an environment in which people will more readily accept it. Put simply, if an agency deliberately created this story, the prior analysis will have indicated that the environment was right and it would therefore have a degree of credibility.'

Scappaticci's past role as an IRA enforcer was the element of the leaked story of 'Stakeknife' which encouraged journalists to make the alleged link. The tale then opened up the murky world of IRA enforcers and how they interrogated, sometimes tortured, and more often than not killed those suspected of betrayal. It also provided a linkage to other stories in the public domain: the use of terrorist agents and their roles in assassinations, torture and betrayal. It dove-tailed with the story of 'the disappeared' – suspected informers who were executed by the IRA and whose bodies were never located. The story of 'the disappeared' caused serious embarrassment to the IRA and lost it much public support. At the time of the controversy, I pointed out that loyalist paramilitaries were also guilty of secretly burying people they had murdered but no police investigation was launched into 'the disappeared' in the loyalist community. Michael Stone, the Milltown Cemetery killer, told me he knew of 'holes in the ground', a reference to secret burials. He never mentioned that fact when he published his memoirs in 2003. The linking of Scappaticci to 'Stakeknife' reawakened interest in 'the disappeared' as well as the use of IRA enforcers.

In 1989, when I wrote *The Dirty War*, I was aware Scappaticci was a leading member of the IRA's Internal Security Department. I was investigating the killing of Joseph Fenton, a 35-year-old father of four from the Andersonstown district. The IRA claimed he had been working as an agent for Special Branch and MI5 for at least five years. Fenton was indeed an agent who had been recruited with threats and blandishments. He ran an estate agency in West Belfast and had done favours for the IRA. When his business began to fail, the intelligence services targeted him and provided him with money to keep his company afloat. His handlers encouraged him to provide the IRA with homes on his 'For Sale' lists for use as safe-houses and places to store weapons. Those homes were then bugged and over several years major IRA operations were compromised.

By 1988, time was running out for Fenton. Four IRA operatives were seized in a house provided by him and IRA Intelligence personnel suspected he was an informer. They investigated his professional life and uncovered his sudden ability in 1982–3 to set up Ideal Homes, his property firm. They were fascinated by the fact that after it was set up he led an expensive life, but within five years was again in debt. In July 1988, the RUC arrested him and accused him of money-laundering for the IRA. His arrest may have been a ploy to distract attention from his work as a spy. Alternatively, RUC detectives may not have known he was employed by Special Branch and MI5. By then, however, his usefulness as a spy was waning. His friends detected a noticeable decline in his ability to run Ideal Homes and his increasing dependence on alcohol. He could no longer cope with the constant risk of being unmasked. By the end of 1988, his business was in bankruptcy and he was working as a cab driver. The IRA later conceded that, for some time prior to his death, he had not been in a position to cause them much damage. By then he was of little value to his handlers but while he had been actively working as a spy he had seriously damaged the operational capacity of the IRA's Belfast Brigade. During his period of success, his handlers went to great lengths to ensure the IRA did not suspect him and sacrificed other agents to achieve their objective. When Fenton, on orders of his handlers, passed information to the IRA, he did so through an IRA officer who was appointed by the Belfast Brigade Staff to ensure his business was not targeted by criminal elements. A senior IRA figure responsible for the unmasking of Fenton gave me an account of how Fenton operated.

'Fenton took the heat off himself by providing the IRA, through the officer who was protecting him, with information which the IRA recognised was vital. He offered the names of two informers who were operating within the Brigade area. They were a husband-and-wife team, Gerard and Catherine Mahon, who were in their 20s. IRA Intelligence acted on the information and placed surveillance on the couple. Their house was used as a dump on occasions and it was wired by British Intelligence. We learned that later. They also tampered with IRA explosive devices that were occasionally stored in their home. They were interrogated, admitted their guilt and were court-martialled. They did not mention Fenton because they did not know of his treachery but he knew them. We now know through the interrogation of Fenton that he was told to give us them to remove suspicion from himself. When a guy is supplying information of that calibre, the tendency is not to suspect him. As time went on, however, and the Belfast Brigade lost men and weapons and eventually a mortar factory, the suspicion heightened and it pointed towards Fenton. Fenton knew that time was running out and he bolted. The IRA thought it had lost him but he returned to Belfast within a short time. He claimed that he had gone to England to watch a big fight. When he was finally interrogated, he told us that his MI5/Special Branch handlers told him to return to Belfast after he bolted. They told him to say that he was at a big fight. They must have known we would not accept that kind of reasoning. They were willing to sacrifice Fenton for a purpose. The reason why we know they were prepared to sacrifice him is that after we shot him we discovered an extremely sophisticated bug in a house which Joe Fenton had provided as a safe-house. In that house, members of the IRA discussed Joe Fenton's fate and the evidence against him. Therefore, his handlers knew that IRA suspicion was so great that he was likely to be found guilty and executed. They were still prepared to send him back. They sent him back to cover their tracks because they had someone equally important in place. They expected the IRA to be preoccupied with Fenton and to believe that Fenton was alone. That is always the way the Brits operate. Fenton was only a pawn to them. By sending him back they were allowing us to think that we had our man.'

The murders of Gerard and Catherine Mahon took place three years before Fenton was abducted. They were shot in an alleyway in the Turf Lodge area of West Belfast. Gerard Mahon was shot first but his wife broke free from her captors after seeing her husband shot through the head. As she ran, she was shot in the back. The Mahons' handlers and their intelligence superiors also sent Fenton to his death. He was deemed expendable, yet, even in his last hours, he was a tool for British Intelligence to learn more about the IRA's knowledge of its operations. The bug in the house where he was interrogated and tortured allowed his handlers to listen in real-time to his interrogation and pleas for mercy. They wanted to know how much their enemy knew about them. The only way to do that was to send Fenton back to Belfast to be interrogated. They were unwilling to prevent his murder because it could have exposed them and another agent. The questions put to Fenton by IRA interrogators provided insights into how the IRA had unmasked him and their operational methods for rooting out informers. It was critical knowledge for an intelligence apparatus which wanted to insulate its agents from IRA scrutiny.

There was an equally important reason for allowing Fenton to die. MI5 and Special Branch hoped his death would encourage the IRA to believe it had successfully caught the main agent in its ranks. But the two agencies had an even bigger spy whom they wanted to protect. He was Sandy Lynch, the IRA officer tasked by the Belfast Brigade to be the contact man for Fenton. For intelligence chiefs, Lynch was a much better prospect. Unlike Fenton, he was a senior IRA operative and capable of doing much more damage to the terrorist organisation. Lynch may not have been aware Fenton was a spy until the IRA began investigating him. I later learned Lynch told his handlers about Fenton's predicament. It is astonishing that Lynch, while he was the conduit between Fenton and the IRA's Belfast Brigade, passed intelligence from Fenton to the IRA. Some of that intelligence, provided by Fenton's handlers to keep him on good terms with the Belfast Brigade, included the names, addresses and vehicle numbers of uniformed policemen and detectives.

Lynch was unmasked by the IRA less than two years later and taken to a safe-house by IRA Internal Security. Scappaticci was among those in the house with the task of interrogating him. However, when Lynch finally made a tape-recorded confession of his guilt, Scappaticci was at home watching television. A tape of the interrogation was sent to Danny Morrison, a leading Sinn Fein figure who was also a member of the IRA's Army Council. Lynch, unlike Fenton, was an IRA officer entitled, under the IRA's *Green Book* Rules, to certain procedures. His fate had to be decided by a 'court' of his peers. And when a judgment was made it had to be conveyed to the 'Competent Authority'. In the case of Fenton the 'Competent Authority' was Danny Morrison.

IRA *Green Book* Rules 17 and 18:

17. The President of the Court shall be responsible for forwarding
to the Competent Authority:
a) The written records or other records of the proceedings of the
court and all documents connected with the trial.
b) The findings and sentence of the Court.

18. The oath to witnesses shall be administered by the President
of the Court.

On the evening Lynch's fate was decided, Morrison, after listening to the tape, made his way to the house where Lynch was held. As Morrison reached the house, British troops swooped and rescued Lynch. Morrison was found hiding in a house next door. During Morrison's trial, Lynch named Scappaticci as one of the men who interrogated him. Morrison was convicted of illegally imprisoning Lynch and jailed. Scappaticci was arrested and interrogated at the Castlereagh police office but was not charged. Afterwards, he fled to the Irish Republic and remained there for over a decade.

When it was leaked to the media that Scappaticci was 'Stakeknife', journalists quickly unearthed the fact he was named in the Danny Morrison trial. The information was enough for some journalists to conclude he was indeed 'Stakeknife'. Several press stories then alleged he was not in the house on the night that Lynch was rescued because he had betrayed Danny Morrison. Such speculation did not take into account the possibility he was not charged with the Lynch abduction and interrogation because it suited the intelligence services. By not charging him, suspicion was in fact cast on him and the IRA's Internal Security Department was temporarily weakened. He was questioned by the IRA but satisfactorily assured them he was not a spy.

None of what I have written seeks to excuse the IRA's use of enforcers or to depict Scappaticci as a boy scout. My aim is to raise doubts about what we often take for granted, namely what we read about the dirty war in some newspapers. The Fenton story, alone, symbolises the shadowy world of agents, double agents, enforcers and State intelligence services. There were many agents in the mould of the elusive 'Stakeknife', if he ever existed. For some journalists to jump to conclusions was akin to accepting the word of people whose business it is to confuse or distract us from asking for accountability about a lengthy dirty war.

One thing was clear to me about the 'Stakeknife' story. It instantaneously increased the public appetite for more information about the IRA's brutal interrogations and executions of informers, many of them innocent of the crimes alleged. It distracted public attention from the Stevens Inquiries, the torrid history of the FRU and the use of Special Branch informers in the murder of Finucane. It could be argued that the 'Stakeknife' story was created to minimise the damaging effects of the Stevens investigations on the whole intelligence community. It shifted the media focus to the IRA – a partner in the peace process, with an equally violent role in the dirty war. One could reasonably assume 'Stakeknife' was intended to weaken the IRA at a time when it was refusing to decommission its arsenal. The unsubstantiated 'Stakeknife' revelations created deep suspicion in IRA ranks. Some of its leading operatives considered breaking with the organisation and transferring their loyalties to an IRA offshoot. Throughout the history of republicanism, splits always weakened the IRA. As my CIA source pointed out, a fabricated story may have a long-term objective or, in my opinion, multiple aims. Some observers subsequently claimed the 'Stakeknife' story emanated from a disgruntled former intelligence operative but that was far from the truth. The leaking of the story originated from multiple sources.

13

MEMORIES DARK AND BLOODY

Several years ago, a New York Irish-American non-profit organisation sought my help in raising funds for the victims of the Omagh bombing. As part of a benefit, I encouraged five Broadway actors to read pieces from *Stones Don't Die*, a work of mine still in progress. When I was writing this book I decided that I should include some of those pieces for the reader since they reflect my inner feelings about the conflict. The individual pieces are about events and people mentioned in this book.

In 1972, 23-year-old Patrick Benstead, a mentally retarded Catholic from East Belfast, was abducted, tortured and then shot.

TO PATRICK

> They stoked fire into the palms of your hands;
> branded you like a maverick.
> I saw you naked,
> face down in the garbage,
> socks holed and torn,
> a bullet lodged in your skull.
> I thought I heard your
> screams into ears clotted,
> watched by eyes red, white and blue.
> God was twisted into Ulster,
> but you still spoke to me.

On 26 June 1973, 29-year-old Irene Andrews, a Protestant, and Paddy Wilson, a Catholic politician in his late 30s, were stabbed to death in a lonely lovers' lane above Belfast.

ILLICIT IN DEATH

Juice was in the genitals,
coloured Orange and Green.
Eyes never found the rear-view mirror,
but pillows waited at home.
Shadows marched in vengeance,
Plunging, there was no
Hockney pool for a splash.
This was a canvas shredded.

Joseph Donegan, a 47-year-old Catholic father of seven children, was abducted by Lenny Murphy, the infamous leader of The Shankill Butchers and tortured to death.

TO JOE

Alcohol cleaned the wounds
for travelling dentists.
It was another time, no teddy bears
in the madness.
The signature was in the action,
hardly in overalls.
Blood was in the excreta,
waste in eyes dehumanised,
and you spoke from the earth.

This is an account of a my meeting with John Bingham, the loyalist trigger man. It was bizarre because he had previously threatened me, then apologised and invited me to his home.

WHEN PIGEONS DIDN'T DIE

John stuck a gun in my mouth because he didn't like what I'd written about him. 'Next time, I'll blow yer fuckin' brains out,' he told me.
    'What were you thinking about at that moment?' asked a friend.

'It's difficult to find words when your teeth are pressed against metal,' I replied.

Days after the threat, John telephoned me. 'Sorry about that business,' he began, 'I'd like t' make it up to y'. Come up t' my house and have a drink with me. Look . . . if you're worried about yer safety, I'll personally guarantee it. Mind you,' he laughed, 'don't be tellin' the RUC where you're goin'.'

The invitation was so bizarre I agreed.

'Sit down,' he said on my arrival, pointing to a worn sofa while reaching for a bottle of whisky and two grubby glasses. Laughing, he told me he preferred Scotch to Irish whisky. Nervously, I accepted his offer of a drink.

'I was fuckin' angry with you the other day,' he remarked, lowering his first whisky measure and quickly replenishing his glass. When the whisky in the bottle eventually dropped below the level of the label, he reached under a cushion, withdrew a pistol and brandished it in the air. There was grease residue on the barrel where plastic once covered it and the earth hid its past.

'It's beautiful, isn't it?' he said with the glint of a cowboy in his worn eyes. He caressed it, sliding his fingers along the greasy barrel. 'It's a real piece of art, isn't it?' he grinned.

In his unwillingness to suffer, he omitted to tell me about the gun's past. Releasing the magazine into his left hand, he smiled and slammed it back into the depths of the grip. I knew the gun barrel had found other eyes: eyes closed in pain and terror, waiting for a final sound since death has no voice.

'A real work of art,' he murmured, as though there was no connection between the gun and his intent. He returned the gun to its plastic wrapping and emptied the remains of the whisky bottle into his glass.

'I'm a pigeon fancier,' he declared. 'Would you like to see my racing pigeons? I've some out the back.'

'I'd like to but I have an appointment,' I said, gingerly.

'Hummm,' he grunted. 'It'll have to be another time, I suppose. By the way, don't believe what other people are sayin' about me. I couldn't hurt a pigeon.'

As we shook hands at the front door, he pulled me close and his voice was low and chilling. 'You ever write about me again and I'll blow yer fuckin' brains out because you're no pigeon,' he hissed malevolently before grinning and closing his door.

Marty O'Hagan was the *Sunday World* journalist who exposed the terror role of 'King Rat'. Members of 'King Rat's' Loyalist Volunteer Force murdered him on 28 September 2001.

TO MARTIN O'HAGAN

We lived with conflict, you and I,
wrapped in a war over space,
clothed in a history made by others.
We lifted stones and peered under them,
knowing St Patrick left behind vipers,
venomous and angry in ignorance.
A firestorm was in Manhattan
with another God in the mix.
Ours was in bullets waiting for you.

BULGARIA/OMAGH '98

I was pruning roses on the terrace of Dora Kumurdjieva's house in Bourgas on the Black Sea. A black silk bow and her photo reminded me of the 40 days of mourning for her. I placed the rose clippings in plastic bags tied tight, knowing life had left them withered and choked by neglect. Omagh had its own plastic bags and black silk bows with flowers severed at the stem. 'The killers will blame it on the telephones,' I told myself, remembering the village of Claudy nestling in the Sperrin mountains one July morning in 1972. On that day, little Katherine Aiken was washing the window of her father's shop, and Mrs Brown was in the alley looking for her cat. My friend, the poet, Jimmy Simmonds, remembered that Artie Hone was on his way to a neighbour's door and Mrs McElhenney was serving petrol. I can't remember the name of the fifth person who was on Main Street but Jimmy knew there were people and not pigs squealing in the Village Square when a strange car exploded. Jimmy just imagined the moment, the dust and the terrible dead. The killers claimed they were in Dungiven trying to telephone a warning but the lines to Claudy were engaged. Years later, remnants of clothing from the dead and injured were still attached to overhead wires in Main Street. The images of Claudy revisited me in the summer of '98 when republicans again pushed the historical button of madness, leaving memories, which should never fade.

STILL LIFE OMAGH

It was streaked red,
not Bourgas tiles warmed,
slotted neatly into rooftops.
It was a photo, blackened white,
rising from a crumpled headline.
A Ford was now a soft-top,
twisted and ragged.
The edges severing softness,
assembled in line,
marketed in dust and plastic.

GLOSSARY

ARMY COUNCIL – The seven-man body elected to run the Irish Republican Army. It is bound by *The Green Book* of rules, which insist that it meets at least once a month. Members are required to be active service personnel and four members can constitute a quorum.

B SPECIALS – Part-time members of the Ulster Special Constabulary formed in 1920. B Specials gained a reputation for being anti-Catholic. To Protestants they were the first lines of defence in protecting the State from the IRA. They had massive armouries containing pistols, rifles, sub-machine guns, grenades and .50 heavy calibre machine guns.

CUMANN na mBANN – Female wing of the Irish Republican Army.

E DEPARTMENT – An RUC Special Branch department, which operated within the Royal Ulster Constabulary. It was subdivided into three sections:
E3 – responsible for handling agents and informers.
E4 – specialists in methods of entry, wiretaps, bugging and videotaping.
E4a – a covert team used in surveillance but trained in SAS-type assault and killing techniques.

FIANNA na hEIREANN – The junior wing of the Irish Republican Army. Its recruits ranged in ages from 11 to 17.

FREDS – Term given to indigenous terrorist recruits within the British Army's undercover squads in the early 1970s.

FBI – The US Federal Bureau of Investigation. The FBI had teams of Special Agents who worked closely with British Intelligence, Special Branch and the RUC in tracking down members of the IRA in North America. In contravention of the US Constitution, members of the RUC secretly operated with the FBI on the streets of New York and other US cities. Likewise the FBI sent operatives to Northern Ireland to liaise with the British security apparatus.

FOUR FIELD SURVEY TROOP – The cover name for a shadowy British Intelligence unit within 3 Brigade Detachment. The British Ministry of Defence destroyed all documents relating to its history and activities. Roger Freeman, an Under Secretary for the British Armed Forces, claimed it had been involved in map-reading and reconnaissance. He admitted all paperwork relating to it had been shredded.

14 INTELLIGENCE & SECURITY COMPANY – An elite and secretive British Army unit set up in the 1970s. It took over the work of the MRF when that organisation was subjected to public scrutiny and 'disbanded'. It was sometimes referred to as 14th Int., 14 Independent Company and DET.

FRU – Force Research Unit, sometimes referred to as Field Research Unit or Future Research Unit. It was a shadowy British Military Intelligence organisation running terrorist agents and sanctioning assassinations of republicans or Catholics suspected of being republicans.

GARDAI – Members of the GARDA SIOCHANA, the Irish Republic's police force.

GHQ – General Headquarters Staff. In both the IRA and INLA this body ran and planned ongoing operations.

HANDLERS – Intelligence officers tasked with running terrorist agents and informers.

H BLOCKS – A term used for the Maze prison, which replaced the Long Kesh internment camp. The Maze was built in the shape of an H and divided into Blocks, housing paramilitaries from both sides.

INLA – Irish National Liberation Army. A breakaway group from the Marxist-oriented Official IRA.

IO – Intelligence Officer.

IPLO – Irish People's Liberation Army – a breakaway group from the INLA.

LONG KESH – A disused airfield with Nissen huts, which became an internment camp after internment without trial was introduced in August 1971.

LOYALIST VOLUNTEER FORCE – A breakaway group from the Ulster Volunteer Force. Billy 'King Rat' Wright formed it.

MI5 – The United Kingdom's Internal Security Service. Contrary to its brief, it illegally operated in the sovereign territory of the Irish Republic.

MI6 – The United Kingdom's Foreign Intelligence Service. Sometimes referred to as SIS – Secret Intelligence Service. Contrary to its brief, it operated in Northern Ireland and considered the Irish Republic to be within its terms of reference. In the early to mid 1970s, it had a dispute with MI5 over who was responsible for running British Military Intelligence officers in Northern Ireland. In response to leaks from MI5 about its operations, it responded by leaking damaging stories about its counterpart to the media.

MRF – Known as the Military Reconnaissance Force and the Mobile Reconnaissance Force. The IRA called it the Military Reaction Force. Brigadier Frank Kitson, the British Army's foremost counter-insurgency expert, formed it in the early 1970s. Specialists with SAS-type training staffed it, as well as soldiers detached from different regiments and 'Freds' – indigenous terrorist agents.

OC – Officer Commanding.

OFFICIALS – Name given to the IRA after the movement split into two organisations in January 1970. It was driven by Marxist ideology in the 1960s and was an integral element in the civil-rights movement. It announced a cease-fire in 1972 and its political wing, Sinn Fein, became the Workers Party, which fought elections in Northern Ireland and the Irish Republic. It engaged in feuding with the Provisionals and never decommissioned its arsenal. It also received monies from Eastern Europe during and after the Cold War.

ORANGE ORDER – The most powerful body within the Protestant–Unionist community. It was infused with a territorial imperative which encouraged its leaders and rank and file to believe that it could parade anywhere in Northern Ireland, especially through Catholic neighbourhoods. It was the dynamic for uniting Protestants, who regarded it as the symbol and voice of their tradition. From the beginning of the Troubles, its insistence on marching through Catholic districts each summer to celebrate the defeat of James II of England by the forces of William of Orange in 1689/90 led to serious outbreaks of rioting.

PROVISIONALS – Provisional Irish Republican Army. It was formed in January 1970 after the IRA split and it took on the mantle of romantic Irish nationalism. It received money and weapons from Irish Americans, the Palestine Liberation Organisation and the Libyan regime of Colonel Mu'ammar al Qadhafi. Most of those who died on hunger strike in 1982 were Provisionals.

RED HAND COMMANDO – Loyalist terror group formed by the paedophile, John McKeague, who was also a British Military/Special Branch agent.

RUC – Royal Ulster Constabulary, Northern Ireland's police force.

SDLP – Social Democratic Labour Party. The majority party within the Catholic community in Northern Ireland. It disavowed violence to achieve its goal of a United Ireland.

SINN FEIN – Political wing of the Provisional IRA.

SPECIAL BRANCH – RUC department dealing with intelligence-gathering, data-collation and the running of terrorist agents and informers. Throughout its history, it was a secretive organisation, extremely protective of its information and sources. From the outset of the Troubles, it was the major organisation gathering intelligence on the IRA and was involved in dubious operations. After 1992, it was placed under the direct control of MI5.

SAS – Special Air Service. It emerged from the Long Range Desert Group during the Second World War. It is Britain's version of the Green Berets and is regarded as one of the most elite regiments in the world. Its operations and the identities of its soldiers are protected under the guise of National Security.

STORMONT – The seat of the majority Unionist Government of Northern Ireland.

SUPERGRASS – A terrorist recruited by the authorities to betray his fellow terrorists in return for a new life outside Northern Ireland.

TARA – A shadowy loyalist paramilitary group established by William McGrath, an evangelist and notorious paedophile. It had links to the Red Hand Commandos and the UVF.

TOUT – Northern Ireland slang for an informer or a terrorist agent working for the British security apparatus.

TCG – Task Coordinating Group. An umbrella organisation comprising representatives from the main intelligence and undercover organisations.

UDA – Ulster Defence Association. The largest loyalist paramilitary organisation. It was formed in the early 1970s.

UFF – Ulster Freedom Fighters. It emerged in June 1973 and declared itself the military wing of the UDA. It mimicked the Provisional IRA strategy of having a political wing and a military wing.

UDR – Ulster Defence Regiment. At the outset of the Troubles, it was set up to replace the B Specials but its history, until it was merged with a British Army Regiment in 1992, mirrored the anti-Catholic record of the Ulster Special Constabulary. Many of its members were in the UDA and some provided intelligence to loyalist paramilitaries in their targeting of innocent Catholics. Some UDR soldiers were directly involved in terror operations on behalf of the UVF and the UFF.

UNIONIST PARTY – The majority Protestant party. It held power, unchallenged, for over 50 years.

UVF – Ulster Volunteer Force. It emerged in 1966 and was formed by loyalists, including several politicians, leading clergymen and a prominent lawyer. The shooting of four Catholics by a UVF gang in Malvern Street in the Shankill in 1966 is regarded by many as the starting point of the present Troubles.

APPENDIX 1

THE GREEN BOOK

What follows is the constitution, aims, objectives and disciplinary procedures of the IRA. Known as *The Green Book*, it is the IRA's official handbook. It has not been edited or altered in any way. Any errors of grammar or of sense can be attributed to the original.

CONSTITUTION OF OGLAIGH NA hEIREANN

1. Title:
   The Army shall be known as Oglaigh na hEireann.

2. Membership:
1 Enlistment in Oglaigh na hEireann shall be open to all those over the age of 17 who accept its objects as stated in the Constitution and who make the following pledge:
   'I — (name) — promise that I will promote the objects of Oglaigh na hEireann to the best of my knowledge and ability and that I will obey all orders and regulations issued to me by the Army Authority and by my superior officer.'
2 Participation in Stormont or Westminster and in any other subservient parliament, if any, is strictly forbidden.
3 Enlistment shall be at the discretion of the Army Authority.

3. Objects:

1 To guard the honour and uphold the sovereignty and unity of the Republic of Ireland.

2 To support the establishment of an Irish Socialist Republic based on the 1916 Proclamation.

3 To support the establishment of, and uphold, a lawful government in sole and absolute control of the Republic.

4 To secure and defend civil and religious liberties and equal rights and equal opportunities for all citizens.

5 To promote the revival of the Irish language as the everyday language of the people.

4. Means:

1 To organise Oglaigh na hEireann for victory.

2 To build on a spirit of comradeship.

3 To wage revolutionary armed struggle.

4 To encourage popular resistance, political mobilisation and political action in support of these objectives.

5 To assist, as directed by the Army Authority, all organisations working for the same objectives.

5. Army Control:

1 The General Army Convention shall be the Supreme Army Authority.

2 The Army Council shall be the Supreme Authority when a General Convention is not in session.

3 The Army Council, only after Convention, shall have power to delegate its powers to a government which is actively endeavouring to function as the de facto government of the Republic.

4 When a government is functioning as the de facto government of the Republic, a General Army Convention shall be convened to give the allegiance of Oglaigh na hEireann to such a government.

5 All personnel and all armaments, equipment and other resources of Oglaigh na hEireann shall be at the disposal of and subject to the Army Authority, to be employed and utilised as the Army Authority shall direct.

6. General Army Convention:

1 A general Army Convention of Delegates (selected as set out hereinafter) shall meet every two years unless the majority of these delegates notify the Army Council that they it better for military purposes to postpone it. When a General Army Convention is postponed, it shall be summoned to meet as soon as the majority of the

delgates shall notify the Army Council that they deem it advisable.

2 An Extraordinary General Army Convention and that the urgency of the issue for the Convention does not permit of the selection of delegates as prescribed, that the delegates to the previous General Army Convention constitute the Extraordinary General Army Convention. When for any reason a delegate to the previous General Army Convention has become ineligible, or is not available, the Battalion Council shall elect a delegate in his/her stead. Every active Volunteer in the Battalion shall be eligible to stand as a delegate.

4 When the Army is engaged on active service, no Unit or General Army Convention shall be held until a reasonable time after hostilities has terminated, unless the Army Authority decides otherwise.

5 An Executive of twelve members shall be elected by ballot at the General Army Convention: at least eight of these members shall be delegates to the Convention: Four members may be elected from active Volunteers who are not delegates. The next six in line shall, however, be eligible as subsitutes to the Executive in order of their election. The Executive shall always have six substitutes in readiness.

6 No members of the Executive may also be a member of the Army Council and members of the Executive subsequently elected to the Army Council will resign from the Executive. Vacant positions on the Executive arising in such a way shall be filled by those substitutes next in line from the Convention elections.

7 The following shall be entitled to attend and vote at the General Army Convention:

Delegates selected by Battalion Convention.

Delegates selected by General Headquarters Staff and Staffs of Brigades, Divisions and Commands.

Two members of the Executive.

All members of the Army Council.

The Chief of Staff, the Adjutant-General and the Quartermaster-General.

8 Only Volunteers on the Active List shall be eligible as delegates to the General Army Convention.

9 A majority of the General Army Convention may invite anyone whom they wish to attend to speak.

10 The Chairperson of the General Army Convention shall be chosen by the General Convention.

7. Duties and Powers of the Executive:

1 The Chairperson of the General Army Convention or his/her representative shall, within forty-eight hours of the termination of the

Conventions, summon a meeting of the Army Executive over which he/she shall preside during the election of a Chairperson and Secretary. The Army Executive shall then proceed with the election of an Army Council of seven members.

2 The Army Executive shall meet at least once every six months. The Secretary of the Executive shall be responsible for the summoning of the members.

3 It shall be the duty of the Executive to advise the Army Council on all matters concerning the Army.

4 The Executive shall have powers, by a majority vote, to summon an Extraordinary General Army Convention.

5 A member of the Executive who, for any reason, ceases to be an active member of Oglaigh na hEireann shall cease to be a member of the Executive.

6 Casual vacancies on the Executive shall be filled by cooperation after any substitutes that may be elected by the General Army Convention have been exhausted. Vacancies shall be filled within a period of one month.

7 The Executive shall hold office until the following General Army Convention shall elect a new Executive.

8 An extraordinary meeting of the Executive shall be summoned by the secretary of the Executive when a majority of the Army Council or a majority of the Executive so decide.

9 Two-thirds of the available members shall constitute a quorum of the Executive, for co-option purposes only. Full Executive powers shall not be vested in less than five members.

8. Duties and Powers of the Army Council:

1 The Chairperson of the Army Executive or his/her representative shall, as soon as possible after the election of the Army Council, summon a meeting of the Army Council, over which he/she shall preside, until a Chairperson and Secretary have been elected.

2 The Army Council shall meet at least once a month.

3 Vacancies occurring in the Army Council shall be filtered from substitutes elected by the Executive or co-opted by the Army Council in advance. Co-options by the Army Council must be ratified by the Executive at its next meeting.

4 Any active Volunteer shall be eligible for membership of the Army Council. The Army Council shall have the power to:

1 Conclude peace or declare war when a majority of the Council so decide. The conclusion of peace must be ratified by a Convention.

2 Appoint a Chief of Staff and ratify all appointments to the Commissioned ranks.

3 Make regulations regarding organisation, training, discipline, equipment and operations, such as will ensure that the Army will be as efficient as possible.

4 Take all necessary steps to secure co-ordination with other republican organisations.

5 Keep in touch with all foreign organisations and countries which may help the Army in any way.

6 Arrange for the care of wounded Volunteers and their dependants and the dependants of Volunteers killed, imprisoned or on active-service.

The Chief of Staff, Adjutant-General and Quartermaster-General shall be entitled to attend and speak at all meetings of the Army Council but not be entitled to vote unless they are members of the Army Council.

Four members shall constitute a quorum of the Army Council.

A member of the Army Council who, for any reason, ceases to be an active Volunteer, shall cease to be a member of the Army Council.

9. Selection of Delegates:

Delegates to the Command Conventions shall be elected by ballot as follows:

1 At each parade called for the purpose, each unit in Command Area shall elect a delegate to attend the Command Convention.

2 One member of the Command Staff, elected by the Staff at a special meeting called for the purpose.

3 The Command OC sall be entitled to attend and vote at the Command Convention.

4 Each Command Convention shall meet when instructed by the Army Authority and elect one delegate when the total number of Volunteers who parade for Unit Conventions do not exceed twenty, and two when the number of Volunteers do not exceed fifty, and one delegate for each twenty additional Volunteers on parade at Unit Conventions.

Brigade Conventions:

Where the Independent Unit is a Brigade, a Brigade Convention may be held consisting of the delegates elected by the Units, Battalion Staffs and the Brigade Staff, with the power to pass or reject any resolution brought forward by these delegates. The delegates from each Battalion shall each elect their own delegates to the Army Convention.

Election of Brigade, Divisional and Command Staff delegates to the General army Convention.

Two delegates shall be elected at a meeting of General Headquarters Staff officers, with the exception of the Chief of Staff, Adjutant-General and Quartermaster-General.

Resolutions to General Army Convention:

Command Conventions and the meetings of GHQ for the election of delegates to General Army Convention shall have the power to discuss any matter relating to the Army or to the Nation and to pass resolutions regarding such matters. These resolutions shall be forwarded to GHQ within the time specified by the Army Authority and shall appear on the agenda for the General Army Convention.

10. Changes to the Constitution:
It shall require a two-thirds majority of a General Army Convention to change articles in this Constitution.

OGLAIG NA hEIREANN (IRISH REPUBLICAN ARMY)
GENERAL HEADQUARTERS GENERAL ARMY ORDERS
(REVISED 1987)

General Order No. 1
1 Membership of the Army is only possible through being an active member of any army Unit or directly attached to General Headquarters. Any person who ceases to be an active member of a Unit, or working directly with General Headquarters, automatically ceases to be a member of the Army. There is no reserve in the Army. All volunteers must be active.
2 The duties of a Volunteer shall be at the discretion of the Unit Commander. If for a good and genuine reason a Volunteer is unable to carry out the normal duties and routine which obtains in the Unit, the OC may allot him/her some special duties. So long as he/she performs these duties satisfactorily and makes regular reports he/she shall be considered as an active Volunteer.
3 Leave of absence may be granted to a Volunteer in the case of illness or for other valid reason.
4 A Volunteer who, for any reason, ceases to maintain contact with his/her Unit or with General Headquarters for a period of three months shall automatically cease to be a member of the Army.
5 The provision of this General Order does not apply to Volunteers in prison.

General Order No. 2
Volunteers when making the Army Declaration promise '. . . to obey all orders and regulations issued by the Army Authority and any superior officers'.
1 Where an order issued by a duly accredited officer has been disobeyed, the Volunteer in question must be suspended immediately, pending investigation of the case.

2 Any Volunteer carrying out an unofficial operation is automatically dismissed from the Army and is liable to immediate repudiation.

Minimum penalty for breach of this order: Dismissal.

General Order No. 3

1 All applications for re-admission by those who were dismissed, or who resigned from the Army, must be submitted to the Army Council or delegated authority, who alone have the power to sanction reinstatement.

2 Where a Volunteer is summarily dismissed from the Army he/she may apply to his/her Unit OC to have his/her case tried by Court-martial. Such application must be made within seven days from the date of receipt of notification of dismissal.

3 Once a Court-mrtial has confirmed such a dismissal, then as in all other cases, any further appeal or application for reinstatement must be forwarded to the Army Council through the Unit Commander.

General Order No. 4

Any member of Oglaigh na hEireann may be a member of a political party which recognises the partition institutions of government as sovereign authorities for the Irish people.

General Order No. 5

PART 1

A Volunteer shall not:

Swear or pledge allegiance or recognition to the partition institutions of Government of the Six or Twenty-six County states.

Swear or pledge recognition of their legitimacy as sovereign governing bodies of the Irish people.

Swear or pledge himself/herself in any way to refrain from using arms or other methods of struggle to overthrow British rule in Ireland.

Minimum penalty for breaches: Dismissal.

PART 2

When arrested a Volunteer shall:

Remain silent.

Refuse to give any account of his/her movements, activities or associates, when any of these have any relation to the organisation or personnel of Oglaigh na hEireann.

Refuse to make or sign any statements.

PART 3

A Volunteer shall:

Refuse to obey any order issued by the partitionist authorities requiring him/her to leave Ireland or reside inside or outside a specified area in Ireland.

Refuse to give any undertakings about his/her future behaviour. Volunteers released from prison on ticket-of-leave are bound by this.

Minimum penalty for breaches: Dismissal.

PART 4

Any Volunteer committed to prison forfeits all previous rank and shall report into the Oglaigh na hEireann structure for debriefing and further instructions.

A Volunteer's attitude in court shall be at the discretion of the Army Authority.

Maximum penalty for breaches which are not also a breach of orders in Part 1: Dismissal with ignominy.

PART 5

No Volunteer should succumb to approaches or overtures, blackmail or bribery attempts, made by the enemy and should report such approaches as soon as possible.

Volunteers who engage in loose talk shall be dismissed.

Volunteers found guilty of treason face the death penalty.

General Order No. 6

Committees under Army control will have their terms of references clearly laid out for them. They will adhere strictly to these terms of reference. In case of departure from these the individual or individuals responsible will be removed from the Committee. The Army Auhtority has the right to remove any member of such Committees from the Committee at any time.

General Order No. 7

Volunteers are forbidden to undertake hunger-strikes without the express sanction of General Headquarters.

Maximum penalty for breach: Dismissal.

General Order No. 8

1 Volunteers are strictly forbidden to take any military action against 26 County forces under any circumstances whatsoever. The importance of this order in present circumstances especially in the border areas cannot be over-emphasised.

2 Minimum arms shall be used in training in the 26 County area. In the event of a raid, every effort shall be made to get the arms away safely. If this fails, the arms shall be rendered useless and abandoned.

3 Maximum security precautions must be taken when training. Scouts must always be posted to warn of emergency. Volunteers arrested during the training or in possession of arms will point out that the arms were for use against the British forces of occupation only. This statement should be repeated at all subsequent Court proceedings.

4 At all times Volunteers must make it clear that the policy of the Army is to drive the British forces of occupation out of Ireland.

General Order No. 9

Firing parties at funerals are only allowed in the case of volunteers who die on active service or as a direct result of enemy action. General Headquarters permission must be obtained.

General Order No. 10

No member of Oglaigh na hEireann shall make any statement either verbally or in writing to the Press or Mass Media without General Headquarters permission.

Volunteers are forbidden to advocate anything inconsistent with Army policy.

Minimum penalty for breaches: Dismissal with ignominy.

General Order No. 11

Any Volunteer who seizes or is party in the seizure of arms, ammunition or explosives which are being held under Army control, shall be deemed guilty of treachery. A duly constituted Court-martial shall try all cases. Penalty for breach of this order; Death.

NOTE: As in all other cases of death penalty, sentence must be ratified by the Army Council.

General Order No. 12

A Volunteer with knowledge of the whereabouts of Army property which is not under Army control shall report such information immediately to his/her OC.

Minimum penalty for failure to do this: Dismissal.

General Order No. 13

1 Any Volunteer who attempts to lower the morals or undermine the confidence of other Volunteers in Army leadership or in any individual in

the Army control shall be deemed guilty of treachery.

2 Any Volunteer taking part in a campaign of slander and denigration against another Volunteer thereby weakening authority and descipline, and bringing the Army into disrepute, shall likewise be deemed guilty of treachery.

Minimum penalty: Dismissal.

3 All Volunteers are expected to act in an honourable way so as the struggle is not harmed or undermined.

Any Volunteer who brings the Army into disrepute by his/her behaviour may be guilty of a breach of his/her duties and responsibilities as a Volunteer in Oglaigh na hEireann and may be dismissed.

General Order No. 14

Oglaigh na hEireann is a voluntary organisation and Volunteers resign membership by giving notice to the relevant Army Authority. However, no Volunteer or former Volunteer may join any other military organisation where his/her training, experience and knowledge gained in Oglaigh na hEireann could be used by that organisation.

General Order No. 15

No Volunteer convicted by a Court-martial on a capital offence can be executed if that Volunteer can show that he did not receive instructions in the Green Book. The officer(s) responsible for recruiting this Volunteer and clearing his/her application shall be held responsible for neglect and being in breach of this order.

COURTS OF INQUIRY

1 A Court of Inquiry may be set up to investigate allegations against any member of the Army, any alleged irregularity, or any other matter affecting the Army.

2 The Court may be convened by the OC or any Unit or by the CS. The Convening Authority should supply the Court with specific terms of reference in writing, setting out the precise nature of the matters to be investigated.

3 The Court shall consist of three members, one of whom will be appointed President by the Convening Officer of his/her representative. Any active Volunteer may be appoined to sit on a Court of Inquiry.

4 The powers and duties of a Court of Inquiry are to examine all witnesses who appear before it and, having considered all the evidence, to make specific recommendations to the Convening Authority. It has no power to bring in any verdict or to pass any sentence. It may recommend Court-martial proceedings, but decision on this point rests with the Convening Authority.

NOTE: The powers and duties of the Court of Inquiry should be made clear to the members of the Court and to all witnesses appearing before it, by the convening Authority or his/her representative.

5 The members of the Court, should be supplied with copies of all General Army Orders, as they may be required for the drawing up of recommendations.

6 Witnesses summoned to appear before the Court should be accommodated in a separate room to that in which the Court is held. They should be cautioned beforehand that they are not to discuss the matters being investigated, among themselves. An officer should be detailed to remain in the room with the witnesses. The witnesses will be called singly before the Court to testify.

7 Evidence should be taken on oath which will be administered to each witness by the President. Should a witness object to testifying on oath, he/she must state the objections to the Court. Unsworn testimony may be taken, but will not carry the same weight as sworn testimony. Once a witness has been examined, he/she may be recalled as often as the Court requires, to answer any further questions the Court wishes to put. For this reason, witnesses will not be allowed to leave the precincts of the Court except with express permission of the Court.

8 If the Court so decided, it may call for additional witnesses to those summoned by the Convening Authority.

9 The recommendations of the Court shall be made in writing and signed by the three members of the Court. These recommendations, together with a record of the proceedings and all documents connected with the inquiry, shall be forwarded to the Competent Authority by the President. NOTE: The President appoints one member of the Court to record the proceedings unless a note-take or other means of recording is specially provided by the Competent Authority.

OATHS FOR COURTS OF INQUIRY

To be taken by each member of the court.

I — swear by the Almighty God that I will conduct this Inquiry without fear, favour or affection.

And I swear that I will not disclose the vote or opinion of any member of the Court unless required to do so by the Competent Authroity. And I swear not to disclose the recommendations of the Court until they have been disclosed by the Competent Authority.

To be taken by each withness:

I — swear by Almighty God that my evidence to the Court shall be the truth, the whole truth and nothing but the truth.

To be taken by the official note-taker:

I — swear by Almighty God that I will maintain inviolate the proceedings of this Court, and that I will not disclose its proceedings unless required to do so by the Competent Authority.

COURT-MARTIAL

1 A Court-martial is set up by the OC of any Unit, or by the CS, to try any Volunteer on a specific charge or charges.

2 The Court shall consist of three members of equal rank or higher than the accused.

3 The Convening Officer will appoint one member of the Court as President.

4 When a Court-martial is set up by a Unit OC, the Adjutant of the Unit, or some members of the Unit delegated by the Adjutant to do so, will act as Prosecuting Council. When the Convening Authority is the CS, he/she may appoint any officer other than the Adjutant-General to act as Prosecuting Counsel.

5 The accused may call on any Volunteer to act as his/her Defence Counsel or, if he/she desires, may defend the case himself/herself.

6 A copy of the charge shall be supplied to the accused in reasonable time before the case is heard to enable him/her to prepare defence. The Convening Authority may either supply the accused with a summary of the evidence it is proposed to place before the Court, or arrange for a preliminary hearing at which witnesses for the prosecution will give on oath, a summary of their testimony. At such preliminary hearings, neither defence nor prosecution counsel will be present, but the accused may cross-examine the witnesses. The evidence shall be taken down in writing from each witness, shall be read over to the accused and shall be signed by him/her. If the accused wishes to make a statement or give evidence on oath, he/she must be cautioned that anything he/she says may be taken down and used in evidence at any subsequent hearing of the case.

7 If the accused objects to any of the three officers comprising the Court, the objection will be examined by the remaining two members and, if upheld, the member objected to will be replaced.

8 The Convening Authority will supply the Court with a copy of the charges and with copies of General Army Orders.

9 The Convening Authority will ensure that the Prosecuting Counsel is in possession of all the facts relevant to the case and that all prosecution witnesses are present at the Court.

10 During the hearing of the case, all witnesses wll be kept in separate rooms as in the case of a Court of Inquiry. The only persons present in

the Court shall be the members of the Court, the accused, the Defence Counsel (if any), Prosecuting Counsel and note-taker (if any) and the witness under examination.

11 Evidence should be taken on oath which will be administered to each witness by the President. Should a witness object to testifying on oath, he/she must state the objections, to the Court. Unsworn testimony may be taken, but will not carry the same weight as sworn testimony. Once a witness has been examined, he/she may be recalled as often as the Court requires to answer any further questions the Court wishes to put. For this reason, witnesses will not be allowed to leave the precincts of the Court except with the express permisison of the Court.

12 At the start of the case, the President will read each charge to the accused and ask the accused if he/she pleads guilty to the charge.

13 Witnesses when called to testify will be cross-examined first by the Prosecuting Counsel and then by the Defence Counsel, or by the accused if conducting his/her own defence. Witnesses may be questioned by any member of the Court. Should either Counsel wish to recall a witness who has already testified, permission of the Court must first be obtained. The Court may recall any witness. Witnesses may not leave the precincts of the Court without permission from the Court.

14 At any time it so desires, the Court may go into private session to decide on points which may arise, such as the admissibility of evidence.

15 When all witnesses have testified, Defence Counsel will sum up and make closing address to Court. This will be followed by summing up and closing address of the Prosecuting Counsel. The Court then goes into private session to consider its verdict and sentence.

16 For a breach of any General Army Order, the Court shall have power to impose a lesser penalty than that laid down in such order.

17 The verdict and sentence of the Court shall be set down in writing and signed by three members. This, together with a summary of the evidence, must be forwarded by the President of the Convening Authority. Sentnece is subject to the ratification of the Convening Authority.

NOTE: In the case of the death penalty sentence must be ratified by the A/C. (Army Council)

18 The accused may forward an appeal against the verdict or sentence or both to the Adjutant-General who will place it before the Competent Authority. The appeal should be forwarded by accused through his/her OC who, in turn will forward it to the Adjutant-General with a signed copy of verdict and sentence and a summary of the avidence. The Competent Authority may order a new trial or reduce the penalty, but may not increase the penalty imposed by the Court.

NOTE: The President appoints one member of the Court as recorder, unless a note-taker or other means of recording the proceedings is specially provided by the Convening Authority.

OATHS FOR COURT-MARTIAL

To be taken by each member of the court:

I — swear by the Almighty God that I will try the accused on the issues presented to the Court without fear, favour or affection.

And I swear that I will not disclose the vote or opinion of any member of the Court or any proceedings of the Court unless required to do so by the Competent Authroity.

And I swear not to disclose the verdict or sentence of the Court until they have been disclosed by the Competent Authority.

To be taken by each withness:

I — swear by Almighty God that my evidence to the Court shall be the truth, the whole truth and nothing but the truth.

To be taken by the official note-taker:

I — swear by Almighty God that I will maintain inviolate the proceedings of this Court, and that I will not disclose its proceedings unless required to do so by the Competent Authority.

NOTES FOR COURT-MARTIAL

1 On the Court assembling, the Convening Authority or his/her representative reads the order convening the Court.

2 The President asks the accused if he/she has any objection to any member of the Court. Members of the Court retire and consider any objections, and decide whether objection is to be upheld or rejected.

3 If any objection is upheld, the Convening Authority or his/her representative nominates another member.

4 The President appoints one member of the Court to record the proceedings, unless a note-taker is epcially appointed by the Convening Authority.

5 The President then reads the charge or charges to the accused and asks him/her to plead to each separate charge.

6 The Prosecutor presents his/her authority to the Court and makes the opening statement for the prosecution, outlining the charges.

7 The Prosecutor then calls witnesses to substantiate case for the prosecution.

8 Accused or his/her Counsel cross-examine witness for the prosecution.

9 When evidence for the prosecution is closed, the accused or his/her Counsel makes opening statement for the defence.

10 Witnesses for the defence are then called.

11 Accused or his/her Counsel makes closing statement for the defence.

12 Prosecutor makes clsoing statement for the prosecution.

13 Court may ask for records as to the character and record of the accused.

14 The Court retires to consider the findings on each charge and to award the sentence.

The Court may award a separate sentence or punishment on each charge on which the accused is found guilty of, or one sentence or punishment, to cover more than one charge.

15 Where different sentences are proposed, the Court shall vote first on the lesser sentence proposed.

16 Members of the Court shall vote on sentence according to their seniority, the junior members voting first.

17 The President of the Court shall be responsible for forwarding to the Competent Authority.

(a) The written records or other records of the proceedings of the Court and all documents connected with the trial.

(b) The findings and sentence of the Court.

18 The oath to witnesses shall be administered by the President of the Court.

CODE OF CONDUCT
(Issued 1987)

No serious guerrilla organisation can exist or hope to achieve victory without a number of prerequisites.

One one side of the coin these include comradeship, an internal structure (or infrastructure), rules and regulations, an ability to recruit, and a brief in achieving objectives. On the other side there has to be public support and the commanding of the admiration and respect of the public.

Where comradeship is lacking and where there are no rules and regulations one can see from past INLA feuds how disagreements can degenerate into anarchy and demoralise one's base of support.

The Irish Republican Army is one of the oldest surviving guerilla armies in the world. It has a long tradition of struggle but at certain times in its history a number of the prerequisites for success were absent – conditions were not right, but most importantly nationalist opinion in the North was not ripe for a sustained armed struggle. All this changed in the 1960s with the attempted repression of the Civil Rights Movement and from then until now the struggle as taken on a steady momentum of its own.

The IRA's objectives are set down in a written constitution (which can only be amended by General Army Convention: the last IRA Convention was in 1986). The IRA however, is regulated by a set of General Army Orders (which can be amended at any time by an Army Council). Volunteers have always been expected to be familiar with the Constitution and General Army Orders, but in recent years familiar also with the Green Book which is a further breakdown of the aims and objectives of the organisation, the tactics of how to conduct oneself during interrogation.

Enemy

The British government has attempted to undermine the struggle, deter people from fighting and sap the morale of Volunteers and supporters through a number of measures.

It kills people, it jails people, it consistently repeats that it will not give way to the IRA, it ridicules one's objectives as being unrealistic and unachievable. It attacks the methods such as the commandeering of cars, the taking over of houses, fighting a war in the streets in which people live, the execution of informers, etc. All of this is so much hypocrisy compared to the commandeering of a country and British insitutionalised violence and sectarianism. Most objective people – and not necessarily sympathetic people – can see through the hypocrisy, and only ongoing politicisation and publicity can really counter it.

It is IRA successess that demoralise the British and undermine their case. Ongoing IRA successes reinforce the belief in victory which in turn will lead to icreased support.

Behaviour

No organisation and no organisation's members are above reproach. The behaviour of Volunteers on operations and how republicans conduct themselves in their private lives will, where exploitable, be used by the British, the media, and the SDLP, and the Movement's other detractors to undermine the Movement in the minds of the general public.

When Mao's Red Army was fighting the revolution in China its Code of Conduct was summed up succinctly, (if idealistically) as follows:

Three General Rules of Discipline
1 Obey orders in all actions.
2 Do not take a single needle or piece of thread from the people.
3 Hand all booty over to headquarters.

And the Eight Reminders

1 Talk to people politely.
2 Be fair in all business dealings.
3 Return everything you have borrowed.
4 Pay for anything you have damaged.
5 Don't beat or bully people.
6 Don't damage crops.
7 Don't flirt with women.
8 Don't illtreat prisoners of war.

This is somewhat idealistic but one gets the drift about striving for the optimum in good behaviour and the necessity of avoiding scandal. Given the pervasiveness of the media in everyone's lives nowadays it is therefore even more essential for republicans to consider the effect of their attitudes and behaviour of supporters. To be conscious of how their behaviour could be used to ridicule the Movement and thus unjustifiably bring the struggle into disrepute.

The Republican Movement relies on a voluntary code of conduct (through Volunteers can still be dismissed under General Army Orders for blatant actions which bring the Movement into disrepute) and below are some of the guidelines expected of members:

1 Republican Volunteers are expected to be truthful in their dealings with other comrades and other sections of the Movement.

2 They are expected to be honest in all matters relating to the public, both in terms of official and private business. Whilst the majority of members are from working-class backgrounds, a business-person (who is also a known republican activist) who provides a poor service to the public or who exploits the public in business dealings is no asset to the republican cause.

3 Republicanism stands for equality and an end to sexism. Male Volunteers who mistreat or exploit their partners are flying in the face of this principle. Volunteers must practice domestically what the Movement preaches publicly.

4 Anyone promoting sectarianism or displaying sectarian attitudes should immediately be disciplined.

Republicanism has an international dimension which means respecting as equals other nationalities and races. Anyone who pays lip service to international solidarity and then slips into mimicking the racist attitudes which are typical of an imperialist mentality should be immediately upbraided. All people are equal and everyone has an international duty to oppose racism and oppression from wherever it emanates.

6 Our culture is something of which we should be proud, it is part of our

identity and it can also be used, not in a chauvinistic sense, but against the British to show the separateness of our identity as an individual nation. Republicans who do not subscribe, to Irish culture, or who have no interest in promoting the Irish language, should respect those who are making progress on this front against considerable odds. It is simply laziness which prevents people from attempting to learn their native language: no-one is that busy!

6 The Green Book makes reference to people who take alcohol urging them to be extremely careful. Under excessive drinking people's tongues loosen, people whom one wouldn't normally trust become 'great friends', and one is vulnerable to the temptation of engaging in 'loose talk'.

7 Apart from the security risk, a drunken republican is hardly the best example of a freedom fighter, he or she is open to ridicule from the Movement's detractors.

The activities of republicans even engaged in innocent celebations would be used by the enemy, so vulnerable are ambassadors of freedom struggle on this issue! So be moderate and be careful and rememer what you represent. If you need to 'let off steam' then be discreet.

8 Alcohol affects different people in different ways, turning some aggressive people into affectionate doves, and making some normally pleasant people nasty and unbearable!

Under alcohol people's attitudes can also undergo unpleasant changes: respect towards others, one's partner, the Movement, can temporarily diminish leaving one with a lot of apologising and more than a hangover the following day. Dependency on alcohol is also a major weakness which the Special Branch will be quick to exploit.

The code set out here represents mere commonsense and is a reminder to all activists of their responsibilities. No-one has been press-ganged into republicanism. If you cannot to the struggle the honour of your service, then do not do it the dishonour of a disservice. It is as simple as that.

Volunteer' Rights
(issued 1988)

Volunteers should be well versed in General Army Orders and Court of Inquiry and Court Martial procedures. They should understand that they are aimed not only at ensuring the IRA runs smoothly within these agreed disciplinary codes, but also at protecting the rights of Volunteers. While everyone is accountabled to disciplinary process under General Army Orders, this is not their only function. They are there to protect the Army and as the Army is its Volunteers, they must serve to protect the Volunteers as well.

Communications within the Army are of vital importance. Thus all Volunteers should: be aware of how the Army structure works and of how a Volunteer can and should pass grievances or observations upwards. The onus is on the Volunteer to do this in a non-disruptive way, working through and using the proper channels all the time. All Volunteers should have access to their immediate superiors. This is through normal Army channels to GHQ. If this is unsatisfactory then there is access through GHQ to Army Council. The onus is on each tier, if requested, to pass requests upwards.

Security permitting, a Volunteer should always get an answer. Whether the Volunteer agrees with the answer is irrelevant: once Volunteers exhaust the channels, Army disicpline demands that the answer be accepted. Final redress can be sought through the Army Council. Issues which are not important enough to warrant this should not be permitted to cause disruption or harmful dissensions. The onus is on the Volunteers to behave at all times in a correct, positive and responsible manner avoiding personal conflict or diversions from our main task.

Suspension of Volunteers should be conducted sparingly. Where suspensions are necessary they should not be of lengthy duration. Except in special circumstances Volunteers should not normally be suspended, unless facing charges, eg a Volunteer facing a court of inquiry should not normally be suspended. However, when a court of inquiry decided to press charges, this would normally involve suspension until the charges are adjudicated on. Special circumstances where a Volunteer could be suspended by a competent senior authority could for example, include a refusal to obey an Army order.

The above deals with suspension of membership of the Army. Suspension of a Volunteer from specific duties or a position in the Army is permissible at the discretion of a competent senior authority. Again the normal right to appeal applies. Summary dismissal of a Volunteer should be avoided except in the most extreme circumstances. Every Volunteer has the right to a court of inquiry. It should be noted that such a court, arising out of a summary dismissal, is a court, where those responsible for the dismissal will have to stand over their actions. They are not permitted to introduce new evidence other than that on which the dismissal was based. Volunteers summarily dismissed have seven days in which to appeal against the dismissal.

Courts are established by the Army Authority. Thus recommendations by courts must be agreed on by the Army Authority before they are acted on, or made known to other volunteers.

All of the above places a heavy responsibility on those holding positions within the Army. The Adjutant General is responsible for discipline. The Adjutant General or those to whom he/she has delegated responsibility should be consulted in all cases involving the possible dismissal of Volunteers.

An organisation like ours which seeks political objectives based upon the principles of justice and freedom, must ensure that these principles are applied internally and in our dealing with one and other.

Volunteers, and this includes everyone from the CS to the Unit Volunteer, must be treated in a fair and overhand way.

APPENDIX 2

THE BLOODY SUNDAY TRIBUNAL

THE LAW OFFICES OF
SMITH DORNAN & SHEA PC

WWW.SDS-LAW.COM
E-MAIL: RSMITH@SDS-LAW.COM

355 LEXINGTON AVENUE	P.O. BOX 5089
SEVENTEENTH FLOOR	17 SOUTH DUBOIS PLACE
NEW YORK, NEW YORK 10017	MONTAUK, NEW YORK 11954
(212) 460-5518	(631) 668-0818
TELEFACSIMILE (212) 529-3449	TELEFACSIMILE (631) 668-0819

--x
THE BLOODY SUNDAY TRIBUNAL
The Rt Hon Lord Saville of Newdigate (Chairman)
The Hon Mr William L. Hoyt
The Hon Mr John L. Toohey
--x

SECOND WITNESS STATEMENT OF MARTIN DILLON

I, MARTIN DILLON, residing at Sunnyside, New York 11104, will testify as follows:

1. I have been a journalist reporting on current affairs in Northern Ireland for over three decades. From 1968 to 1973, I was a newspaper reporter, first for the *Irish News*, and then for the *Belfast Telegraph*. I then worked full-time for the BBC in Northern Ireland and London for 19 years, from 1973 to 1992, as a senior producer, news reporter, and program editor. After I left my full-time BBC position in 1992 to become a free-lance journalist,

I produced documentaries for several media entities, including Channel Four Television, RTE, and again, the BBC. I am also the author of a dozen published books, most of which are non-fictional, journalistic works on the subject of the conflict in Northern Ireland. My books include, but are not limited to, the following titles:

The Dirty War (Century Hutchinson, Random House, and Routledge, New York)

Political Murder in Northern Ireland (Penguin)

25 Years of Terror: The IRA's War Against the British (Doubleday/Transworld)

The Shankill Butchers: A Case Study in Mass Murder (Century Hutchinson and Random House)

The Enemy Within: A History of the IRA in Britain (Doubleday and Transworld)

God and the Gun: The Church and Irish Terrorism (Orion Books and Routledge)

Rogue Warrior of the SAS (John Murray and Random House)

Stone Cold: The True Story of Michael Stone and the Milltown Massacre (Century Hutchinson and Random House)

Killer in Clowntown: The IRA and The Special Relationship (Century Hutchinson and Random House)

2. I submit this second witness statement on the limited subject of (a) my conversations with Field Marshall Sir Michael Carver ("Lord Carver"), who at the time of Bloody Sunday was Chief of the General Staff of the British Army, and (b) a conversation that I had with British

Prime Minister Edward Heath ("Mr. Heath") on the subject of my conversations with Lord Carver.

3. I interviewed Lord Carver on camera in late 1993 or early 1994, for a 1994 Channel Four Television documentary of which I was the writer and presenter, namely, "The Last Colony" (the "Documentary"). The Documentary, which also was broadcast by RTE, addressed the outbreak of "The Troubles" and the mistakes made by the British Government during the early years of that conflict. My interview with Lord Carver was conducted in his home and witnessed by Mr. Ian Kennedy, who was the Executive Producer of the Documentary, as well as the camera crew and director.

4. During my interview with Lord Carver, with reference to Bloody Sunday in particular, he told me that he received a telephone call on the afternoon of the tragedy. His comment to me on the subject of that telephone call remains fixed in my memory. He said: "It seemed fewer casualties than I had been expecting." The following is a portion of his on-air comments that were included in the Documentary, in which he gave me this account and further stated that "the military action on Bloody Sunday was supposed to be to arrest ringleaders":

> My first reaction when told about it on the telephone [He had confirmed off camera that he received the call on the afternoon of Bloody Sunday] was that it seemed fewer casualties than I had been expecting. Remember, what ran up to this was that William Street in Londonderry was being gradually reduced to ruins by gangs of thugs who beat the whole place up and it was strongly felt this couldn't go on, and the military action on Bloody Sunday was supposed to be to arrest ringleaders of this in order that something could be done about them.

5. I found Lord Carver to be a very reliable and forthright witness concerning the historical period in which Bloody Sunday occurred. Indeed, he was central to an investigation that I was conducting for Channel Four into a conflict between the British Army and the Heath government. In that connection, during the same interview discussed above (but placed later in the Documentary, so as not to confuse two issues in terms of time scale), Lord Carver told me about discussions within the Heath government's secret Cabinet Committee dealing with Northern Ireland affairs, known as the GEN 42.

6. In particular, Lord Carver told me about discussions among that

Committee not long after Bloody Sunday, in the Spring of 1972. According to Lord Carver, Mr. Heath told him during these discussions that British soldiers had the right to shoot protesters because "they were enemies of the Crown." Lord Carver told me that he responded to Mr. Heath by saying that such a directive from Mr. Heath would be unlawful, and by asking Mr. Heath if he was prepared to appear in court to defend soldiers who undertook such an action. Lord Carver was clearly appalled at what Mr. Heath reportedly had told him. The following on-camera exchange between Lord Carver and myself was included in the Documentary:

> LORD CARVER:
> It was being suggested that it was perfectly legal for the Army to shoot somebody whether or not they were being shot at, because anybody who obstructed the Armed Forces of the Queen was, by that very act, the Queen's enemy. This was being put forward by a legal luminary in the Cabinet. I said to the Prime Minister I could not, under any circumstances, permit or allow a soldier to do that because it wouldn't be lawful.

> MYSELF:
> Was the Prime Minister's view that the Attorney General was agreeing that this was lawful?

> LORD CARVER:
> I think he did say that his legal advisers suggested to him that it was all right and I said, you are not bound by what they say. What I am bound by is my own judgment of whether the act of the soldier would be legal, because it is the courts that decide in the end – not the Attorney General or the Lord Chancellor.

7. Lord Carver further told me that according to Mr. Heath, whom Lord Carver said he had questioned to determine the identity of the above-referenced "legal luminary in the Cabinet," this person was the then-Lord Chancellor Hailsham ("Lord Hailsham"). Lord Carver told me specifically that according to Mr. Heath, it was Lord Hailsham's advice, given outside of the above-referenced GEN 42 meeting, upon which Mr. Heath had relied for the proposition that it was legal for British soldiers to shoot unarmed protesters in Northern Ireland.

8. For legal reasons, Channel Four declined to include in the Documentary Lord Carver's statement about Mr. Heath's reference to

Lord Hailsham, and my subsequent question to Mr. Heath himself about whether Lord Hailsham had advised so (see Paragraph 9 below). Channel Four's lawyers said they were unsure if Lord Carver would support me, should Lord Hailsham challenge the Documentary in Court.

9. I tried to confirm Lord Carver's report in an interview that I conducted with Mr. Heath in his home in Salisbury. Mr. Heath denied that he would have authorized anything unlawful, after I pressed him about the matter and revealed to him that the allegation had come from Lord Carver. After the interview, Mr. Heath warned me that I allegedly was in possession of classified information, and he ordered me to quickly leave his home.

10. As I was leaving, Mr. Heath said that Lord Carver was arriving for lunch that day, and that he would ask him about the issues I had raised. Several days later, I asked Lord Carver if he had been invited to Mr. Heath's home on the day in question. He replied that he had certainly not received such an invitation.

11. I further understand that Mr. Heath telephoned the Chairman of Channel Four to complain about my interview. I suggested to Channel Four's legal adviser and its editor, David Lloyd, that I was prepared to re-interview Mr. Heath and, in advance, submit to him a list of perhaps 30 questions. I understand that the offer was put to Mr. Heath, but that he declined.

12. I believe that the conversation within the Cabinet Committee, as reported by Lord Carver, was significant, even though it occurred a few weeks or months after Bloody Sunday. Most importantly, it typified the mindset in place within Number 10 during that period, in which officials at the highest levels of the British Government took the view that civilian protesters from the Catholic community in Northern Ireland were "enemies of the Crown" (or "the Queen's enemy"), who justifiably could be shot, even if they did not shoot at soldiers.

Subscribed this 18th Day of November, 2002

_____

MARTIN DILLON

SELECT BIBLIOGRAPHY

Anderson, Brendan, *Joe Cahill: A Life in the IRA*; The O'Brien Press, Dublin, 2002

Anderson, Chris, *The Billy Boy*; Mainstream Publishing, Edinburgh, 2002

Bardon, Jonathan, *A History of Ulster*; Blackstaff Press, Belfast, 1992

Bishop, Patrick and Maillie, Eamon, *The Provisional IRA*; Corgi, London, 1998

Coogan, Tim Pat, *The Troubles*; Hutchinson, London, 1995

Cusack, Jim and McDonald, Henry, *UVF*; Poolbeg, Dublin, 1997

De Baroid, Cairan, *Ballymurphy and the Irish War*; Pluto Press, London, 1990

Harenden, Tony, *Bandit Country*; Coronet Books, London, 1999

Holland, Jack and McDonald, Henry, *INLA: Deadly Divisions*; Poolbeg, Dublin, 1994

Jordan, Hugh, *Milestones in Murder*; Mainstream Publishing, Edinburgh, 2002

Kitson, Frank, *Low Intensity Operations: Insurgency, Subversion and Peacekeeping*; Faber, London, 1971

McArdle, Patsy, *The Secret War*; Mercier Press, Dublin, 1984

Moore, Chris, *The Kincora Scandal*; Marino Books, Dublin, 1996

Stewart, A.T.Q., *The Narrow Ground: Aspects of Ulster 1609–1969*; Faber & Faber, London, 1977

Urban, Mark, *Big Boys' Rules*; Faber, London, 1992

Televisions Programmes:

Channel Four, *The Last Colony*; Documentary by Fast Forward Productions, Holywood, N. Ireland, 1994

Ware, John, BBC *Panorama* Documentary, 23 June 2002

SELECT BIBLIOGRAPHY

INDEX